Culinary Culture in Colonial India
A Cosmopolitan Platter and the Middle-Class

Utsa Ray

CAMBRIDGE
UNIVERSITY PRESS

Cambridge House, 4381/4 Ansari Road, Daryaganj, Delhi 110002, India

Cambridge University Press is part of the University of Cambridge.

It furthers the University's mission by disseminating knowledge in the pursuit of education, learning and research at the highest international levels of excellence.

www.cambridge.org
Information on this title: www.cambridge.org/9781107042810

© Utsa Ray 2015

This publication is in copyright. Subject to statutory exception and to the provisions of relevant collective licensing agreements, no reproduction of any part may take place without the written permission of Cambridge University Press.

First published 2015

Digitally Printed at Replika Press Pvt. Ltd.

A catalogue record for this publication is available from the British Library

Library of Congress Cataloging-in-Publication Data
Ray, Utsa.
Culinary culture in colonial India : a cosmopolitan platter and the middle class / Utsa Ray.
pages cm
Includes bibliographical references and index.
Summary: "Discusses the cuisine to understand the construction of colonial middle-class in Bengal"-- Provided by publisher.
ISBN 978-1-107-04281-0 (hardback)
1. Food habits--India--Bengal--History. 2. Food habits--Social aspects--India--Bengal--History. 3. Middle class--India--Bengal--History. 4. Bengal (India)--Social life and customs. I. Title.
GT2853.I5R39 2014
394.1'2095414--dc23
2014003925

ISBN 978-1-107-04281-0 Hardback

Cambridge University Press has no responsibility for the persistence or accuracy of URLs for external or third-party internet websites referred to in this publication, and does not guarantee that any content on such websites is, or will remain, accurate or appropriate.

Contents

List of Images, Maps and Tables	v
Preface	vii
Introduction	1
1. Introducing 'Foreign' Food: Changes in the Gastronomic Culture of Colonial Bengal	23
2. The Cosmopolitan and the Regional: Understanding Bengali Cuisine	62
3. Aestheticizing Labor? An Affective Discourse of Cooking in Colonial Bengal	106
4. Constructing 'Bengali' Cuisine: Caste, Class and Communal Negotiations	149
5. Fashioning the 'Bengali' Middle-Class: Dilemma of the Regional and the Subregional	192
Conclusion	229
Select Bibliography	239
Index	265

List of Images, Maps and Tables

Images

1. *Bhim Nager Rasogolla*. Advertisement in *Anandabazar Patrika* (Kolkata, 1940). — 25
2. "Basanta Cabin College Street". Advertisement in *Anandabazar Patrika* (Kolkata, 1937). — 57
3. 'Sabai pete pare' "Anyone can have Indian tea which is the pride and pleasure of India." Advertisement by ITMEB in *Jugantar* (Kolkata, 05.02.1939). — 60
4. Advertisement of 'Dalda' vegetable oil during its launching period. Advertisement in *Jugantar* (Kolkata, 08.07.1939) — 166
5. 'For vitality, Energy, and Health Bengal Milk Bread Machine Made untouched by Hand'. — 175
6. A paisely motif of *gahana bori*. — 227
7. A tiara motif of *gahana bori*. — 227

Maps

1. Early Medieval Eastern India — 197
2. Early twentieth century Eastern India — 206

Tables

1. Husked and unhusked rice — 31
2. Gardeners rewarded for growing exotic crops — 46
3. Comparison of recipes — 70

Preface

The research for this work was begun when I was writing my dissertation at Pennsylvania State University between 2003 and 2009. Generous support from the Department of History, Pennsylvania State University and the Research and Graduate Studies Organization at the same institution enabled me to pursue my field work. In India, the research for this work was conducted chiefly in Calcutta. I take this opportunity to thank the staffs of the CSSS, Calcutta archive, the National Library, the Bangiya Sahitya Parishad, the West Bengal State Archives, the Agri-Horticultural Society, and the West Bengal State Secretariat Library. In addition, I would also like to thank the staff of the India Office Library in London. Kamalika Mukherjee at the Centre for Studies in Social Sciences made my research there exceedingly smooth. I would also like to thank Manaswita Sanyal for letting me use images from the Hiteshranjan Sanyal Memorial Collection at CSSS, Calcutta archive for my book.

Comments and suggestions made by fellow South Asianists as well as other social scientists at the University of Central Lancashire, Conference on South Asia at Madison, South Asia Graduate Student Conference at the University of Chicago, Annual meeting for Association for Asian Studies, Association for Social Anthropologists of UK and Commonwealth and at Department of History, Jadavpur University have benefitted this project immensely. I will never forget that this work was blessed in its infancy by none other than Stephen Mennell. Parts of this work have been published in *South Asian History and Culture*, *Aitihasik*, *Modern Asian Studies* and *Indian Economic and Social History Review*. I want to take this opportunity to thank the editors of these journals.

Mrinalini Sinha's knowledge of the field and her supervision sustained me when I was writing this dissertation. I remain indebted to her because she still remains my biggest support in converting this dissertation into book. I deeply regret that Kumkum Chatterjee left this world before she could see my dissertation turning in to a book. It was she who inspired me to write my fifth chapter on subregional influences on food. Professors Joan Landes and Nancy Love have enlightened me with ideas and suggestions that transcend the field of South Asia. I remember with gratitude my teacher Rajatkanta Ray and Subhash Chakrabarty at Presidency College and my teachers at University of Calcutta.

This project could not have been conceived without Gautam Bhadra's help who has not only provided fantastic references but also helped me think beyond a simple narrative of food history. Opportunities to discuss my work, at various stages, with Dipesh Chakravarty, Muzaffar Alam, Tanika Sarkar, and Sumit Sarkar were very rewarding. I am also indebted to Rochona Majumdar for her comments. Enormous support that I gained from Institute of Development Studies, Kolkata, especially from Amiya Bagchi and Achin Chakrabarty made this book possible. I would also like to thank all my colleagues in the Department of History at Jadavpur University.

Sanjeet Chowdhury has lent me his personal collection for which I am grateful. Without his help this project could never be complete. Shymal Bera has not only lent me his invaluable collection of *mangalkabyas*, but his invaluable insights have enabled me to think about the project in new light. Prabir Mukhopadhyay and Rajatkanti Sur have gone out of their way to help me find materials for my book. Ishita and Ishani, my compatriots in the history of food enlivened this work through their numerous suggestions. As always Rajarshi Ghose helped me to conceptualize the structure of many of my chapters. His immense knowledge about a range of subjects which transcends his own interests enriched this manuscript. I also thank Cambridge University Press and specifically Suvadip Bhattacharjee for their constant support.

My in-laws have been extremely supportive and encouraging. I thank them for their love. My father who strongly motivated my interest in academics has been most enthusiastic about my project. My mother has always taught me that the primary purpose in life is pursuit of independence. Her tremendous capacity for hard work has encouraged me to pursue this dissertation with zeal. My sister, the best imaginable has been a constant support. My in-laws have been extremely supportive and encouraging. I thank them for their love. Kaka, Kaki and Pishimoni have filled my life with their love and their confidence in me. I would also like to thank Dada, Borda, Chhorda, Soumyada, Rima, Bitopidi, and Swapna for all their support. Ahona, Auritro, Irabati and Abhilasha have provided tremendous joy. In Calcutta friends like Srabasti and Srijita, and in Chicago Arnab, Mridu, Wafi, Qudsia, Mona and Vaidyanatha have offered their help whenever I needed them. Kamalika kept encouraging me with her pep talks whenever I lost my confidence. Bahar came to me when I was writing this book and needless to say that she makes the world seem like a wonderful place in which to live. Finally, this book would never be able to see the light of the day had it not been for Rajarshi. At every stage of this work as in every stage of life he remains my greatest pillar of support. I can never thank him enough for being there.

Introduction

In a short story written in early twentieth century, Charan Ghosh, a middle-class Bengali arrives at a restaurant named Anglo-Mughlai Café in Calcutta with his friend Mr Chatterjee, looking for his lost son, Bnatul.[1] As he enters the restaurant, Charan is aghast at the smell of meat that greets him. He is rather shocked, but he finds the restaurant to be full of young customers like Bnatul, who seem to be relishing exotic items like the *'Murgir French malpoa'* (a confection similar to pancake), made from chicken, with delight.[2]

This short passage is taken from Ratarati (Over the Night), a short story written by Rajshekhar Basu (who wrote under the nom de plume Parashuram), perhaps the best known Bengali satirist in early twentieth century. Though much exaggerated by Parashuram's characteristic humour, 'Ratarati' in a sense encapsulates the change in middle-class taste in colonial Bengal. Charan Ghosh, like his friend Mr Chatterjee, is appalled by the drastic transformation in gastronomic habits of a sizable portion of the Bengali middle-class population. However, that the restaurant was pretty crowded is a pointer to the fact that many of these changes had come to stay. The story epitomises such changes as it ends with the possibility of Bnatul's marriage with Neri, a young girl who is also a connoisseur of European literature. Neri is a quintessential child of colonial modernity, who is equally adept at making cutlets as well as cooking *shaker ghonto* (green leaves finely chopped and cooked with or without vegetables, generally with some gravy.).[3] This hybridity of taste tells us the story of the construction of the colonial middle-class. The *Murgir French Malpoa*

---

[1] Parashuram,'Ratarati' (1929–1930). Reprinted in *Parashuram Galpasamagra*, ed. Dipankar Basu (Kolikata: M.C. Sarkar & Sons Pvt. Ltd., 1992), 226–242.

[2] Ibid., 228–229.

[3] Ibid., 240–242.

evidences not just the fecundity of Parashuram's humour, but also demonstrates the changing culinary culture of the Bengali middle-class. In its symbolism of the use of an *indigenous* template to forge a *cosmopolitan* commodity the *Murgir French Malpoa* represents the larger story of the self-fashioning of the middle-class in colonial India.

This book utilises cuisine to understand the formation of the colonial middle-class. It demonstrates that the evolution of Bengali cuisine as a brand was central to the self-fashioning of the middle-class in colonial Bengal. Without doubt culinary practices underwent a sea change under the impact of colonialism. However, the colonial transformation quickened the emergence of a plethora of food practices that went on to constitute Bengali cuisine as a brand. In effect, Bengal as a cultural and special signifier crucially arbitrated the articulation of the colonial discourse of taste. However, unlike food cultures in other parts of the world, Bengali cuisine not only refused to become national and remained emphatically regional, it also kept its domestic identity intact. The Bengali cuisine that emerged in colonial Bengal never assumed the public character that *haute cuisine* did in France. Those who frequented the fancy restaurants set up by the British in Bengal were few in number. The middle-class was more likely to visit small eateries and hotels. Although many a times these hotels were given apparently "European names" like Café-de-Monico, they were more likely to be owned by local people. The quintessential Bengali cuisine constituted food consumed by the middle-class in these small eateries, and the food they ate at home. This lack of commercialisation of the Bengali cuisine actually became a marker of its aesthetic superiority, a cultural capital that went into the making of the Bengali middle-class. This middle-class was much more than a class of people who were made by turning over capital for profit.[4] Rather, the accumulation of different forms of capital, which are described in Bourdieu's seminal work as social and cultural capital, had an overriding influence on the every day practices of the colonial middle-class.[5] As Tithi Bhattacharya rightly argues in her book on class, education, and culture during the colonial period, prioritizing education and pedantry over money defined the shaping of the Bengali middle-class.[6]

---

[4] Peter Earle, *The Making of the English Middle-Class: Business, Society and Family Life in London, 1660–1730* (Berkeley and Los Angeles: University of California Press, 1989).
[5] Pierre Bourdieu, *Distinction: A Social Critique of the Judgment of Taste* (London: Routledge, 1984).
[6] Tithi Bhattacharya, *The Sentinels of Culture: Class, education, and the Colonial Intellectual in Bengal (1848–85)* (New Delhi: Oxford University Press, 2005).

SELF-FASHIONING THE MIDDLE-CLASS

Assumption of power by the British Crown in 1857 entailed a systematic imperial intervention in political and socio-economic structure of the colony. Though the British State feigned distance from its subjects, it set up rigorous imperial intervention through bureaucratic modes of power. It was through dialogues and resistance to this new imperial intervention that the colonial middle-class formulated a new discourse of politics. The particular socio-economic context of colonial Bengal and the peculiar position of the Bengali middle-class within it produced this discourse.

In eastern India, racially discriminating administrative policies encouraged an exclusively European dominated economy of Calcutta and its hinterlands at least till the outbreak of the First World War. The result was a check to the growth of Indian enterprise. There was, however, no dearth of professionals and service groups, whose numbers continued to rise thanks to the needs of British commerce and the British administration.[7] Rajat Kanta Ray has described this process of the decline of Bengali entrepreneurship and the rise of the professional Bengali elites as a two-tiered formation of the middle-class. The first stage in the formation of social groups in Calcutta contained the making of compradors attached to the officers of the East India Company, or private British traders. There were a few entrepreneurs who emerged from their ranks and made huge fortunes by speculative and commercial activities in the first half of the nineteenth century. However, as the industrial capitalism of Britain made further inroads into the economy of Bengal, the European business houses, which acquired local expertise themselves, no longer needed Bengali partnership. Bengalis were not taken in as partners in the new export-oriented manufacturing enterprises that developed in the second half of the nineteenth century. This led to a collapse of the Bengali industrial enterprise and an increasing dependence of these families on income from land. Growing dependence on land, and adoption of the life style of the older landlords of Bengal turned the new rich families of Calcutta into landed notables within two or three generations. The second stage in the formation of the middle-class involved the making of an intermediate layer that populated the new apparatus of the colonial government after the rebellion of 1857. They were the products of Western education, which in its turn had transformed traditional groups of salaried literati into a set of English-educated professional class. However, soon

---

[7] Rajat Kanta Ray, *Social Conflict* and *Political Unrest in Bengal, 1875–1927* (Delhi: Oxford University Press, 1984).

this group of people discovered that despite their qualifications, they would always remain marginalised in the administrative structure of the colonial state.

The grievances of both these groups constituted middle-class politics in colonial Bengal. According to Ray, British economic interest did not allow an overall development of the economy by Bengali entrepreneurs. Instead, the British capital twisted the economy into a colonial mold that impaired the organic connections between the literate and the rustic levels of the Bengali society.[8] The urban professional Bengalis had no independent position in the economy, nor did they control the new productive forces that could be invested in their struggle for political power. This lack of a productive role, Ray argues, failed to connect the middle-class society of Calcutta with the working population of Bengal.[9] Higher education in the English language, solely as a means of entry into a profession, remained confined to Bengali middle-class men. Their concentration in urban professions created the enormous distance of this group from the sphere of social production.[10] The distortion of the economy of Bengal shaped the cultural refashioning of the middle-class. Thus their critique of colonial rule took a strange form that appropriated the colonial state's critique of them as their vantage point.

Scholars have long debated about the origins of the middle-class in colonial India. While traditional scholarship focused on the economic origins of this class, in recent years scholars have become increasingly interested in knowing how this class fashioned itself. Earlier scholars often treated the middle-class as a sociological category. One of the first major works in this field was B.B. Misra's classic book on the Indian middle-class.[11] Misra defined the Indian middle-class as a product of colonial education and the administrative structure introduced by the British colonial state in India. This middle-class has been described as mere 'compradors' by the Cambridge School historians.[12] The

---

[8] Ibid., 11.

[9] Ibid., 29–35.

[10] Partha Chatterjee, *Bengal 1920–1947: The Land Question*(Calcutta: K.P. Bagchi & Company,1984)12–13.

[11] B.B. Misra, *The Indian Middle-Classes: Their Growth in Modern Times* (London: Royal Institute of International Affairs, 1961).Reprint, Delhi: Oxford University Press, 1983.

[12] John Gallagher, Gordon Johnson, and Anil Seal, eds., *Locality, Province and Nation: Essays on Indian Politics 1870 to 1940* (Cambridge: Cambridge University Press, 1973); Anil Seal, *The Emergence of Indian Nationalism: Competition and Collaboration in the Later Nineteenth Century* (London: Cambridge University Press, 1968).

attempt to label the middle-class as a status group[13] has been critiqued by those who have seen the middle-class as a de facto social group.[14] These approaches have been critiqued sharply for their tendency to treat the middle-class as a fully formed sociological category chiefly determined by economic factors. While acknowledging the role of colonial education in the creation of the colonial middle-class, scholars such as Partha Chattrejee and Dipesh Chakrabarty have focused on the creativity of indigenous responses to British rule. While they agree that several ideas related to bourgeois domesticity, privacy, and individuality, which created modern educated Indians, came from European modernity, they also argue that the colonial Indian middle-class had their own versions of modernity that made them different from the European middle-class and made them what they were.[15]

Recent scholars acknowledge that the politics of the Indian middle-class revolved around contesting colonial categories. However, drawing on Pierre Bourdieu's concept of the 'cultural capital,' these scholars try to delve into the contradictory forces that mark the self-fashioning of the middle-class. Sanjay Joshi, for instance, asks us to look away from traditional sociological indicators of income and occupation in order to understand the middle-class.[16] In his book on the colonial middle-class in North India, Joshi argues that being middle-class was a project of self-fashioning, which was accomplished through their public sphere politics and cultural entrepreneurship in colonial north India.[17] In many ways, this form of self-fashioning of the middle-class was not necessarily peculiar to colonial conditions, as several scholars now tend

---

[13] J.H. Broomfield, *Elite Conflict in a Plural Society: Twentieth-Century Bengal* (Berkeley & L.A.: University of California Press, 1968).
[14] S. N. Mukherjee, *Calcutta: Essays in Urban History* (Calcutta: Subarnarekha, 1993).
[15] Partha Chatterjee, *Nationalist Thought and the Colonial World: A Derivative Discourse?* (Delhi: Oxford University Press, 1986); Partha Chatterjee, *The Nation and its Fragments: Colonial and Postcolonial Histories* (Princeton, NJ: Princeton University Press, 1993); Dipesh Chakrabarty, "Postcoloniality and the Artifice of History: Who Speaks for 'Indian' Pasts?" *Representations 37*, Special Issue: Imperial Fantasies and Postcolonial Histories (Winter 1992): 1–26; Dipesh Chakrabarty, *Provincializing Europe: Postcolonial Thought and Historical Difference* (Princeton and Oxford: Princeton University Press, 2000).
[16] Sanjay Joshi, *Fractured Modernity: Making of a Middle-Class in Colonial North India* (New Delhi: Oxford University Press, 2001).
[17] Ibid., 2.

to talk about the middle-class in a comparative and connective framework.[18] These scholars contest ideas about alternative modernities claiming that an overt emphasis on local historical processes ultimately end up making the Western modernity appear global.[19] They also critique such assumptions that the middle-class in the West originated in a local context completely severed from any transnational influence.[20]

Colonial transformation of the relations of production contextualized the cultural articulation of a new set of values, prejudices, and tastes for the colonial middle-class, reflecting both regional and cosmopolitan flavours. This regional as well as cosmopolitan nature of Bengali cuisine emerged from myriad caste-based, communal, and gendered negotiations. In this sense, the making of a Bengali taste can be compared to Kajri Jain's theorization of Indian calendar art as an instance of 'vernacularizing capitalism' by which she implies adapting certain postulates of capitalist modernity to local circumstances.[21] This book explores local contexts to analyse what I call the 'hierarchical cosmopolitanism' of middle-class taste. However, my book neither claims that the project of the self-fashioning of the middle-class was an instance of alternative modernity, nor does it argue that the locality of the Bengali middle-class helped in producing some sort of indigenism. The middle-class in colonial Bengal borrowed, adapted, and appropriated the pleasures of modernity and tweaked and subverted it to suit their project of self-fashioning. In this sense, the colonial Bengali middle-class is much similar to the modern Malay consumer who can easily retain their Malay and Islamic identity at the same time, responding positively to the expanding markets and modern demands of fashion.[22]

---

[18] A. Ricardo Lopez and Barbara Weinstein, eds., *The Making of the Middle-Class: Toward a Transnational History* with an afterword by Mrinalini Sinha (Durham and London: Duke University Press, 2012).

[19] A. Ricardo Lopez and Barbara Weinstein, introduction to *The Making of the Middle-Class: Toward a Transnational History*. Edited by Lopez and Weinstein (Durham and London: Duke University Press, 2012): 10-11.

[20] John Smail, *The Origins of Middle-Class Culture: Halifax, Yorkshire 1660–1780* (Ithaca & London: Cornell University Press, 1994). For a critique of such self-contained emergence of the middle-class in the West, see Simon Gunn, "Between Modernity and Backwardness: The Case of the English Middle-Class," in Lopez and Weinstein eds. Op cit, 58–74.

[21] Kajri Jain, *Gods in the Bazaar: The Economics of Indian Calendar Art* (Durham and London: Duke University Press, 2007).

[22] Johan Fischer, *Proper Islamic Consumption: Shopping among the Malays in Modern Malaysia* (Copenhagen, Denmark: NIAS Press, 2008).

Encouraged by a growing trend in the history of consumption and the middle-class, a number of scholars have come together to delve deeper into what they consider the defining characteristic of a middle-class in present day India – consumption.[23] These scholars believe that even though there was an absence of a mass consumer society, consumption practices have played a strong role in the constitution of South Asian society, culture, and economy since the eighteenth century. The other category that these scholars purport to problematize is the category of the middle-class itself. They argue that there was not a single Indian middle-class, but 'a varied set of actors characterised by anxieties that reflected often-straitened material circumstances, ambivalences steeped in their own contradictory strivings for new identities, and ethical conceptions that frowned upon the embrace of material goods.'[24] These scholars find that economic positions could never be a single analytical tool for defining the middle-class. Some people who described themselves as middle-class were quite wealthy, while others had limited access to resources making them resemble the upper ranks of the working class. Being middle-class implied embracing such patterns of consumption that would distinguish them from Indian princes and rural magnates on the one hand, and from workers, artisans, and villagers on the other. As Sumit Sarkar rightly observed, this middle-class distanced itself from what it considered luxury and corruption of the aristocracy as well as from the ways of those who soiled their hands with manual labour.[25]

While agreeing that the middle-class is heterogeneous, this scholarship to link consumption with the construction of the middle-class has been taken to task by those who argue that middle-classness is manifested through every day practices and not consumption. Consumption of commodities juxtaposed with everyday practices of life is called upon in order to understand the hierarchical nature of the middle-class.[26] This work emphasises consumption of a new

---

[23] Douglas Haynes, Abigail McGowan, Tirthankar Roy, and Haruka Yanagisawa eds., *Towards a History of Consumption in South Asia* (New Delhi: Oxford University Press, 2010).

[24] Douglas E. Haynes and Abigail McGowan "Introduction", in Haynes, Mcgowan, Ray, and Yanagisawa eds., *Towards a History of Consumption in South Asia* (New Delhi: Oxford University Press, 2010): 1-25.

[25] Sumit Sarkar, "The City Imagined: Calcutta of the Nineteenth and Early Twentieth Centuries," in *Writing Social History* (Delhi: Oxford University Press, 1997): 159–185

[26] Henrike Donner and Geert De Neve, *Introduction to Being Middle-class in India: A way of life*, ed. Henrike Donner (London and New York: Routledge, 2011): 1–22.

culture of food by the middle-class in colonial Bengal, which was intertwined with their everyday gastronomic practice and which, in doing so, qualifies attempts to understand the middle-class simply as a discursive formation.[27] While I argue that rhetoric of taste became a cornerstone in the discursive formation of a middle-class Bengali cuisine, this discourse was embedded in the material culture of Bengal.

SITUATING BENGALI CUISINE

In order to understand how an alimentary culture became central to the self-fashioning of the Bengali middleclass, the history of the colonial middle-class in Bengal needs to be mapped out. One might ask the question why am I calling this cuisine a 'Bengali' cuisine? Was there not a 'Bengali' cuisine in ancient or medieval Bengal? In his *Bangalir Itihas (History of the Bengali people)* Niharranjan Ray has described the social structure of ancient Bengal as the history of the Bengali people.[28] His book draws our attention to the social and the material history of the Bengali people in ancient Bengal. However, people in ancient Bengal did not conceptualize themselves as part of a 'Bengali' nation. It was not until much later in the colonial period, that a certain consciousness of one's association specifically with the region of Bengal emerged. The Bengali Hindu middle-class who constituted their own ideas of identity, taste, and aesthetics through new forms of social institutions constructed this idea of the 'Bengali' nation.

A visible transformation in the material culture aided the self-fashioning of the middle-class. Refinement in food, education, music, literature, and deportment defined this middleclass. These everyday practices also embodied the essence of 'Bengaliness' for this middle-class. The rhetoric of cuisine is one of the fulcrums on which this idea of a regional nationalism rests. The colonial Bengali middle-class, however, did not try to find a place in the larger geography of the nation through this rhetoric of cuisine. In fact, the 'Bengali' cuisine had very specific contours. It assimilated different elements but never purported to become a national cuisine.

---

[27] Dror Wahrman, *Imagining the Middle-Class: The Political Representation of Class in Britain, c.1780–1840* (Cambridge: Cambridge University Press, 1995); and Sarah Maza, *The Myth of the French Bourgeoisie* (Cambridge: Harvard University Press, 2003).

[28] Niharranjan Ray, *Bangalir Itihas: Adi Parba* (Kolkata: Dey's Publishing, 1993 [1400 BS]): 696–697, first published in 1949 (1356 BS).

The endeavors of the middle-class in colonial Bengal entailed not only their critique and appropriation of a new gastronomic culture, but also celebration of their regional history and culture, and not necessarily that of the nation. However, Bengal itself became an eponym of the nation.[29] This book shows that even within the idea of Bengal, we find a subregional consciousness of history. There was not necessarily a contradiction between the exploration of the history of a smaller region within Bengal and the exploration of a broader history of Bengal. This history writing as a middle-class project aimed at infusing a sense of belonging in the region. One of the cookbooks examined here, Kiranlekha Ray's *Barendra-randhan*, exemplifies how a region's history was imagined to have existed in everyday life.[30] *Barendra-Randhan*, which is an account of the history of food in *Barendrabhumi* (northern Bengal) was a small part of a bigger project, promotion of the regional history of *Barendrabhumi*. Indeed in other parts of India, for instance in contemporary Maharashtra, there was a keen interest in subregional specialisations.[31]

This book is confined to colonial Bengal, specifically urban Bengal where major colonial institutions flourished. The reason for restricting this study to colonial Bengal is to understand why despite considerable incorporation of other elements into its fold, what we know today as Bengali cuisine is definitely not the national cuisine of India. Certain dishes clubbed together as North Indian food becomes the signifier for Indian food. Of course, it would be banal to argue that some sort of conspiracy was in place that promoted the culinary culture of one region and suppressed that of another. French *haute cuisine* as we know emerged from distancing itself from local cuisines, whereas in China and Italy certain regional cuisines became high cuisine.[32] However, until almost the beginning of this millennium there was no effort on part of the Bengali entrepreneurs to project Bengali food as *haute cuisine*. Although now several gourmet restaurants boast of 'authentic' Bengali cuisine, this public face of Bengali cuisine was conspicuously absent even about thirty years back. This

---

[29] For a wonderful analysis of the relationship between regional cuisine and national cuisine see Raymond Grew, "Food and Global History," in *Food in Global History*, ed. Raymond Grew (Boulder, Colorado: Westview Press, 1999).

[30] Kiranlekha Ray, *Barendra-randhan* (Kolkata: Subarnarekha, 1999 [1328 BS]), first published in 1928 BS [c.1921].

[31] Prachi Deshpande, *Creative Pasts: Historical Memory and Identity in Western India, 1700–1960* (New York: Columbia University Press, 2007).

[32] Arjun Appadurai, "How to Make a National Cuisine: Cookbooks in Contemporary India," *Comparative Studies in Society and History* 30, no. 1 (January 1988): 3–24.

regional focus, however, does not limit the scope of this study. Instead, the book's description of the project of self-fashioning of a middle-class through the lens of food holds true not only of other regions in India, but also in other settings where such self-fashioning of the middle-class is visible.

Arjun Appadurai observes rightly when he asserts that it was only after independence in a new urban India that a national cuisine emerged, fuelled by cookbooks.[33] These men of the middle-class, and especially their wives, who traveled all over India and culled the idea of different regional cuisines, helped to form a national cuisine. This middle-class was nationally linked by their tastes in magazines, clothing, film, and music, and by their interpersonal networks in many cities. The exchange of recipes by the middle-class women blended in to produce a national cuisine.[34] While it is true that a national cuisine emerged only in post-independence India, I find it doubtful that regional cuisines were blended together in order to produce this national cuisine. It was the cuisine of a particular region that came to be labeled 'Indian' cuisine.[35]

Practices of food and imagination of the kitchen as the epicenter of domestic space have been described as central to a discourse of nationalism.[36] The discourse and debates on these practices and social spaces supposedly aided in conceptualizing an idealized Indian nation. More specifically, Bengali and Indian have been overlapped to argue that Bengali nationalism was just the flip side of Indian nationalism. I argue in this book that focusing extensively on nationalist ideals of middle-class rhetoric on cuisine tends to rob it of other factors that this cuisine entailed. Of course, there were anxieties about health or even intrusion into sacred space like kitchen, but simply slapping the label of nationalism on middle-class cuisine oversimplifies a broader discourse of taste. The middle-class' capacity to assimilate is beyond doubt. This assimilation also brought about a harsh critique of the new changes in gastronomic culture

---

[33] Ibid.

[34] Ibid.

[35] For a discussion on how national cuisines are constructed by politicians, food marketers, and other food professionals, see Warren Belasco and Philip Scranton, "Introduction", *Food Nations: Selling Taste in Consumer Societies*, ed. Warren Belascoand Philip Scranton (New York, London: Routledge, 2002).

[36] Jayanta Sengupta, "Nation on a Platter: The Culture and Politics of Food and Cuisine in Colonial Bengal,"*Modern Asian Studies* 44, no. 1 (2010): 81–98; Rachel Berger, "Between Digestion and Desire: Genealogies of Food in Nationalist North India,"*Modern Asian Studies*, First View Article, (May 2013): 1–22.

in its wake. The complexities of colonial modernity produced a discourse of taste highly refined in its content. The middle-class strived for this refinement, which in its turn would provide its scaffolding. The class that would emerge through this process of material change and the subsequent discourse of taste will search for its identity as a class in the region where it was ensconced.

Colonial Calcutta became the habitat of this new Bengali middle-class. Calcutta was expanding from the last few years of the eighteenth century. Much before the takeover of India by the Crown, Calcutta began to attract European institutions, communities of merchants, and indigenous professional classes. It also became a locus for migratory labour.[37] Vast majority of the population began to settle down in Calcutta from the latter half of the eighteenth century and the early nineteenth century, when Calcutta was being transformed from a small European settlement into a prosperous commercial city.[38] By 1850, Calcutta's population reached the number of 400,000. The indigenous middle-class who settled down in Calcutta had ties with the rural areas of Bengal for a long period, where they still had their permanent abode compared to their temporary residence in Calcutta. Even when some families chose to settle permanently in Calcutta, they still often retained their rural ties. Social relationships of this group tended to be determined by the villages they were native of, rather than the city itself.[39]

Historians such as Sinha, Mukherjee and McGuire have argued that the middle-class' politics was crucially determined by the fact that even though its habitus was the colonial city its ties with the countryside especially through traditional kinship networks remained robust. According to them, their politics was thus defined by a juxtaposition of two factors- 'tradition' and 'modernity'. Even though my argument draws a lot on the works of these scholars, it differs in one crucial respect. I argue that the cultural idiom that the Bengali Hindu middle-class articulated cannot be understood in terms of a conflation with tradition and modernity. In fact, the factors that Sinha, Mukherjee and McGuire recognise as traditional were products of the contorted socio-

---

[37] P.J. Marshall, "General Economic Conditions under the East India Company," in *History of Bangladesh (1704–1971)*, vol. 2 *Economic History*, ed. Sirajul Islam (Dhaka: Asiatic Society of Bangladesh, 1992): 79–80.

[38] S.N. Mukherjee, *Calcutta: Myths and History* (Calcutta: Subarnarekha, 1977): 16.

[39] John McGuire, *The Making of a Colonial Mind: A Quantitative Study of the Bhadralok in Calcutta, 1857–1885* (Canberra: South Asian History Section, Australian National University, 1983): 10.

economic context produced by colonial rule. The broader conditions of colonial capitalism ensured that the Bengali middle-class had much in common with its Victorian counterpart. However, creative maneuvers on part of the colonised middle-class critically reconstituted the criterion and the mores that defined it as a class. Through the innovation of new expressive mediums that facilitated the modern articulation of a blissful 'tradition' the middle-class Hindus constructed a new "Bengali' cuisine which is best described as hybrid.

The printmedia enabled the Bengali Hindu middle-class to voice their opinion through various forms of literature such as journals, memoirs, and autobiographies. While these literary works evidence a sense of loss that the middle-class experienced under the oppressive working conditions in Calcutta, such moments of desolation are more often than not framed together with snapshots of an imagined idyllic life in the villages. The modern colonial situation necessitated the construction of a 'traditional' precolonial village life. However, along with these works, print also made available a number of other texts. These were the cookbooks and the recipe columns published in periodicals as well as domestic manuals. These recipes evince that the new life in colonial Calcutta was bringing in certain forms of pleasure. Undoubtedly, the colonial Bengali middle-class reeled under economic want. Nevertheless, in everyday life they created a 'cultural idiom' they could call their own.

HIERARCHICAL COSMOPOLITANISM

If one important purpose of my book is to assess the significance of the regional in the self-fashioning of the colonial middle-class, then another is to tie up the notion of the regional with the notion of the global. Making of a 'Bengali' cuisine was a part of the making of a project of regional history undertaken by a group of people who did not see their being rooted in a region to be contradictory to a sense of cosmopolitanism among them. Cosmopolitanism is a very loaded term and I am aware of its dangers. In case of cuisines, cosmopolitanism alludes to openness to culinary cultures from anywhere. For instance, Humanist cuisine in Italy has been described as cosmopolitan cuisine in the sense of its being receptive to new modes of taste.[40] Scholars have pushed us to go beyond such conventional locus of cosmopolitanism. Any practice

---

[40] Brian Cowan, "New World, New Tastes: Food Fashions after the Renaissance," *Food: The History of Taste*, ed. Paul Freedman (Berkeley/LA: University of California Press, 2007): 199–200.

anywhere in the world that might think beyond the perimeters of the local can be explored as cosmopolitan or 'ways of inhabiting multiple places at once'.[41] Examples of such translocal and transregional practices of cosmopolitanism are manifold. In fact, culinary traditions in almost all countries are results of radical change, of additions of exotic ingredients, and importations of ideas from all over the world. Thus Mexican food bears little resemblance to the almost meatless food of the Aztecs.[42] However, colonisation was not the only process through which colonies adapted or changed their culinary habits. Even what we now know as French cuisine was not recognizable as distinctly French before the time of the Napoleonic period. It is only after Georges Auguste Escoffier (1846–1935) the famous French restaurateur and culinary writer codified *haute* cuisine, that the modern French cuisine became apparent.[43] I argue that as a result of constant interactions of different cuisines, a hybrid cuisine was produced in colonial Bengal that emanated partly from a sense of pleasure in capitalist modernity.

This book makes the claim that although it never became widely commercialised and never came under the rubric of a standardized Indian cuisine, Bengali cuisine cannot be labeled as indigenist and was cosmopolitan in its own way.[44] That neither the cosmopolitan, nor the vernacular is a given artifact has been convincingly argued.[45] The point was to cosmopolitanize the domestic and yet keep its tag of 'Bengaliness.' The resultant cuisine was hybrid,

---

[41] Sheldon Pollock, Homi K. Bhabha, Carol A. Breckenridge, and Dipesh Chakrabarty, "Cosmopolitanisms,", *Public Culture* 12, no.3 (Fall 2000): 577–589.

[42] Raymond Sokolov, *Why We Eat What We Eat: How the Encounter Between the New World and the Old Changed the Way Everyone on the Planet Eats* (New York: Summit Books, 1991).

[43] Ibid.

[44] For a discussion on how women of royal households acted as gastronomic entrepreneurs and created a kind of culinary cosmopolitanism in the Indian courtly kitchens during the height of British empire, see Angma D. Jhala, "Cosmopolitan Kitchens: Cooking for Princely Zenanas in Late Colonial India," in *Curried Cultures: Globalization, Food, and South Asia*, ed. Krishnendu Ray and Tulasi Srinivas (Berkeley/Los Angeles/ London: University of California Press, 2012): 49–72.

[45] Sheldon Pollock, "The Cosmopolitan Vernacular," *The Journal of Asian Studies*, 57, no. 1 (February 1998): 6–37. In case of vernacular history writing, scholars have shown how these histories retained an ancient tradition of cultural memory albeit staying within the bounds of rational scientific knowledge. For a discussion of vernacular history writing see Raziuddin Aquil and Partha Chatterjee, eds., *History in the Vernacular* (Ranikhet: Permanent Black, 2008).

in many senses like its makers. In arguing for the openness of Bengali cuisine, I intend to go beyond such simplistic arguments that have made a simple connection between consumption of Western food and modernisation.[46] The hybridity of Bengali cuisine was quite a complex affair. While stew became a part of the Bengali diet, it was made palatable to the local taste by addition of ghee or clarified butter and spices like ground turmeric or cumin.[47] Such reconstruction of the modern was an attempt at reconstructing the Bengali identity itself. The Bengaliness here encompasses much more than an essence of a region. This attribute is also closely imbricated in the self-fashioning of the middle-class. In order to be distinct, this middle-class did not simply forego all the pleasures emanating from a capitalist modernity. However, often new pleasures were imagined to have ancient roots in the Vedic traditions. Pastry thus becomes a derivative of the Bengali word *pishtak*.[48] Domesticating what came from outside thus made the self essentially hybrid. The instance of Japanese rice is a case in point. Californian or 'foreign' rice comes to stand for chemicals and thus impurities to the Japanese self, whereas Japanese rice is considered to be a product of the land and hence pure. What this discourse on the Japanese rice and the Japanese self conceals is that Japan domesticated imported rice and thus Japanese self is always hybrid.[49]

By showing that hybridity was a part of the cosmopolitanism of the colonial middle-class, I also contest such arguments that so-called 'foreign' foods are cooked at home only after liberalisation happened in the 1990s in India.[50] So-called '*Mughal*-inspired' dishes were not the only traits of Bengali cosmopolitanism. To argue that it was only after globalisation that the middle-class was able to appropriate some kind of cosmopolitanism is to ignore

---

[46] Katarzyna J. Cariertka, "Western Food and the Making of the Japanese Nation-State,", in *The Politics of Food* eds. Marianne Elisabeth Lien and Brigitte Nerlich (Oxford, New York: Oxford University Press, 2004): 121–139.

[47] Bipradas Mukhopadhyay, *Pak-pranali*, vols.1-5 (Kolikata, 1928 [1335 BS]):, first published in 1897 (1304 BS): 406–407.

[48] Rwitendranath Thakur, *Mudir dokan* (Kolikata, 1919 [1316 BS]): 91.

[49] Emiko Ohnuki-Tierney, "We Eat Each Other's Food to Nourish Our Body: The Global and the Local as Mutually Constituent Forces," in *Food in Global History* ed. Raymond Grew (Westview Press, 1999): 249–251.

[50] Henrike Donner, "Gendered Bodies, Domestic Work and Perfect Families: New Regimes of Gender and Food in Bengali Middle-Class Lifestyles," in *Being Middle-Class in India* ed. Henrike Donner (London and New York: Routledge, 2011): 47–72.

different layers of hybridity of Bengali cuisine.[51] This hybridity of food is a product of capitalist modernity, which would not have been possible without the 'Columbian Exchange.' In colonial Bengal the emergent cuisine generally utilised Bengali ingredients and British modes of cooking, but sometimes these basic elements were reversed or rendered more complex by addition of others. Whatever the degree of heterogeneity, the resulting dishes were presented as the products of an 'authentic' cuisine. Bengali cookbooks and recipe columns discussed even such dishes like guava jelly in these terms. In fact, majority of the British cookbooks written for the British residents in India included recipes from all over Europe. And Indian *soojee* could easily be used in place of semolina. Although there was often an endeavor on the part of the middle-class to search for reference points in ancient traditions, it should not be mistaken for indigenism. It was rather a device to make colonial modernity comfortable for one's self. Taking delight in gorging on cutlets in the new emerging eating places did not fail to affect the middle-class. However, just like there are limits to any cosmopolitanism, open-endedness of the cosmopolitanism of the Bengali middle-class was also fenced off by several negotiations.

Pierre Bourdieu's theorisation of taste in the formation of the bourgeoisie and the bourgeois ethos is immensely insightful in the study of any self-fashioning of the middle-class. However, Bourdieu does make it clear that he was writing in the context of a French society. Thus a contextualisation is warranted before we apply Bourdieu's conceptualisation of the habitus to understand the formation of the colonial middle-class. Bourdieu's classic conjecture that the conditions of a class are defined by the relation that this class has with other classes is also true when we talk about the colonial middle-class. The habitus of one class that differentiates it from another is what made the colonial middle-class. However, the situation for the colonial middle-class becomes even murkier when the notions of class and taste also get entangled with the question of caste and community.

Bourdieu writes that the taste for the bourgeoisie implied a self-imposed austerity, restraint, and reserve. Hence the bourgeois art often called for the denial of the social world as well as the refusal of the ostentation.[52] The French bourgeoisie expressed a penchant for 'modesty' in food preferences as this was opposed to what Bourdieu called the spontaneous materialism of the working classes. In other words, in order to become suitable for the bourgeoisie, food

---

[51] Ibid.
[52] Bourdieu, *Distinction*.

had to be severed from its material context and presented in a form that would enhance its distance from the organic world. In the case of colonial Bengal, the middle-class did aim for a refinement of taste, which was found in their inclination for simple food. However, they craved simplicity in cooking because they thought it was withering away rapidly. For this middle-class, in fact, it was the food that the lower classes supposedly ate in the villages that symbolized restraint and charm. Whether the food that the working class ate expressed Bourdieu's 'spontaneous materialism' was not a concern of the colonial middle-class. It was how the latter perceived the eating practices of the former that became significant in the self-fashioning of the middle-class. Issues of caste and communal negotiations made these perceptions even more complex. When it came to defining the contours of the community, taste became not just visceral but often took violent undertone.[53]

Undoubtedly, the much idealized modernity of the Western middle-class was also full of contradictions and there are many similarities between the European middle-class and that of the colonial middle-class in their deployment of social hierarchies. Thus in many senses this form of self-fashioning of the middle-class was not necessarily peculiar to colonial conditions. This becomes evident from a number of works on the relationship between taste and formation of the middle-class in other parts of the world.

Looking at the self-fashioning of the middle-class in the West, scholars have focused on the material practices of the middle-class to understand how a specifically culturally defined class-based discourse was formed that marked the middle-class off from other classes. Three primary issues are common in all these works: a concern about the definition of taste, the notion that often taste that enables the self-fashioning of the middle-class is gendered, and the place that pleasure and luxury items generally hold in the making of a

---

[53] For a discussion of significant distinctions between Bourdieu's middle-class and the middle-class in countries like India, see Leela Fernandes, *India's New Middle-class: Democratic Politics in an Era of Economic Reform* (Minneapolis, MN, USA: University of Minnesota Press, 2006). Fernandes has argued that the middle-class that Bourdieu wrote on was shaped by internal processes within the French national context, whereas in India the middle-class had to constantly negotiate with external forces like 'Westernisation' or 'globalisation'. Linguistic dexterity in the English language in modern India and the acquisition of English education in colonial India put the Indian middle-class in a role of national leadership. However, this same hold in English language also created the distance of this English-speaking middle-class from the vernacular elites as well as the subaltern groups.

particular palate for the middle-class. For the nineteenth century middle-class in the Western world, two strategies became essential for their self-fashioning. An appraisal of work became a marker of bourgeois gentility and the source of respectable identity.[54] The second strategy that the middle-class adopted for carving out their identity was by bringing in a perceptible change in their lifestyle. The leisured life that the middle-class had to forego in order to work was restored at middle-class homes. It became the responsibility of middle-class women to display restraint and gentility while redesigning middle-class homes.[55] In fact, bourgeois women's role as taste makers and consumers for the family often enabled them to move out of the private space of home into the public space of the marketplace, as in the case of France.[56] Genteel taste was not a style of individual choice, it was rather 'an expression of adherence to middle-class values,' characterised by restraint and self-control.[57] Taste was definitely associated with pleasure and luxury, but the luxury objects the middle-class pined for were very different from those cherished by the aristocracy. The definition of luxury was changing. Luxury no longer simply meant opulence or excess. Instead, luxury or pleasure was also a manifestation of enlightenment and bourgeois modernity, of fashion and global commerce far removed from the display of courtly splendour of earlier times.[58]

The role of taste and consumption in the construction of the middle-class is undeniable. While a certain set of value encompasses middle-class culture all over the world and there are certain traits that are common to the formation of a global middle-class, contextualisation of the history of the middle-class is necessary. Undoubtedly, the idea of a refined taste that is so integrally associated with the formation of a middle-class always becomes a marker of standards of good and bad, acceptance of certain things, rejection of some others, and in Pierre Bourdieu's apt phrase 'disgust for other tastes.' However, in situations like in colonial or post-colonial India, the modern middle-class had a double-edged task; it had to define itself as modern while keeping a distance from

---

[54] Linda Young, *Middle-Class Culture in the Nineteenth Century America, Australia, and Britain* (Basingstoke, Hampshire, New York: Palgrave Macmillan, 2003): 71–73.

[55] Ibid.

[56] Whitney Walton, *France at the Crystal Palace: Bourgeois Taste and Artisan Manufacture in the Nineteenth Century* (Berkeley/Los Angeles/London: University of California Press, 1992): 49–69.

[57] Ibid., 155.

[58] Maxine Berg, *Luxury and Pleasure in Eighteenth-Century Britain* (Oxford: Oxford University Press, 2005).

the so-called Western modern. Second, the acts of consumption that defined this middle-class had to draw boundaries with other classes.[59] Thus the colonial elite would either devise a national art that would be different from the so-called European practice by incorporating folk art forms but thoroughly sanitising it in the process,[60] or by trying to improve literary standards and sanitise tastes by drawing a boundary with the innumerable popular tracts and literature that were written in an everyday language.[61] Recent works on the Indian middle-class focus on taste and consumption in order to figure out how exactly the Indian middle-class tried to 'become' modern, while keeping a certain distance from 'Western modernity.'[62] While this could mean appropriating a new beverage like coffee as a marker of middle-class identity in Tamilnadu, the middle-class culture of drinking coffee was defined in relation to what/who the middle-class considered their 'other'. New institutions known as 'coffee hotels' emerged in Tamilnadu, which were usually run by the Brahmins.[63] Tea, associated by the middle-class with urban working class culture, became the 'other' of coffee.[64] The middle-class body became a site that would set boundaries for communities or classes. Thus, what the body

---

[59] Mark Liechty has shown how in modern Nepal, middle-class life in Kathmandu is mediated by local caste logic and other religion-based notions of propriety and suitability that in turn shape middle-class notions of honor and prestige. The Nepali middle-class fashion themselves in relation to their other through commodities and consumer practices. See Mark Liechty, *Suitably Modern: Making Middle-Class Culture in a New Consumer Society* (Princeton, New Jersey: Princeton University Press, 2003).

[60] Tapati Guha-Thakurta, *The Making of a New 'Indian' art: Artists, Aesthetics and Nationalism in Bengal, c.1850–1920* (Cambridge: Cambridge University Press, 1992).

[61] Anindita Ghosh, *Power in Print: Popular Publishing and the Politics of Language and Culture in a Colonial Society, 1778–1905* (New Delhi: Oxford University Press, 2006).

[62] Certain acts of consumption become modes of constructing identity. These acts enable the middle-class to fashion themselves as a 'modern' middle-class. However, in the process of self-fashioning, the Indian middle-class mould these acts in a manner that would not make them 'western'; for instance, see Emma Tarlo, *Clothing Matters: Dress and Identity in India* (Chicago: The University of Chicago Press, 1996); Abigail McGowan, 'An All-Consuming Subject? Women and Consumption in Late-Nineteenth- and Early-Twentieth Century Western India,'*Journal of Women's History* 18, no. 4 (2006): 31–54; A.R. Venkatachalapathy, *In Those Days There Was No Coffee: Writings in Cultural History* (New Delhi: Yoda Press, 2006); Markus Daechsel, *The Politics of Self-Expression: The Urdu Middle-Class Milieu in mid-twentieth century India and Pakistan* (London and New York: Routledge, 2006).

[63] Venkatachalapathy, *In Those Days*, 16–25.

[64] Ibid.

would consume also became relevant for the middle-class to be different from other communities or to choose select components of colonial modernity.[65] The way the middle-class would fashion themselves would imply not just creating a distinct taste for themselves, but also fashioning it in a manner that would set them apart from all other classes.[66]

Food or culinary practices are a crucial indicator of the differences that the middle-class had with other classes, castes, and communities. The changes in dietary patterns led directly to the issue of a healthy body. The middle-class considered gustatory pleasure as one of the chief sources behind the debilitation of the Bengali body. The first and foremost concern was with the formulation of an ideal type of diet. This discourse of an ideal diet was also conflated with discourse on 'pure' food. Although couched in a scientific language, purity often had a double meaning. Apart from denoting clean and hygienic food, 'pure' also implied ritual purity. 'Pure' food was something intrinsically Hindu and elite, uncontaminated by the lower classes. These concerns acted as the guiding principle behind the construction of a healthy body of the colonial modern. However, this construction of the body was more rhetorical than actual. The body was fractured; it was torn between the attempts to create a 'pure' somatic conception and the intake of the pleasures of capitalism that irked those who looked to a 'tradition' in order to construct a healthy body.

Scholars have demonstrated the political nature of diet, basically identifying dietary politics as a marker of colonial difference and of scientific authority coexisting with that of Indian deprivation and loss. This book reaches beyond the much-debated discourse of colonial difference by conceptualising the body at a more basic level, that is, its sustainability. The body, in this case a Hindu middle-class Bengali body, was discursively constituted through debates around the culture of food as an organic entity that was capable of sensory enjoyment. However, I also show that the self-fashioning of the middle-class was not simply a discursive project. This fashioning was made possible because of actual changes in material culture in colonial Bengal affecting the middle-class palpably. Thus the narrative of Bengali cuisine is as much about the celebration of domesticity and regional cosmopolitanism as about the fissures that helped in the self-fashioning of the Bengali middle-class. The more 'refined' the cuisine became, the more its distances from 'other' cuisines grew.

---

[65] Markus Daechsel, *The Politics of Self-Expression: The Urdu Middle-Class Milieu in mid-twentieth century India and Pakistan* (London and New York: Routledge, 2006).

[66] Tarlo, *Clothing Matters: Dress and Identity in India*.

A Bengali quest for culinary modernity was composed of myriad quibbles. A 'refined Bengali' cuisine could only be produced through the construction of its internal and external others. This book describes the ways through which the colonial Bengali middle-class negotiated their gastro-cultural politics. These negotiations were accomplished by simultaneous critique and appropriation of foreign goods and a celebration and idealization of 'peasant' food in the middle-class discourse of taste. However, the middle-class kept the definition of peasant deliberately ambiguous. Muslims who could count as the majority of the cultivators did not fall within the ambit of the 'peasant' as perceived by the middle-class. On some rare occasions, they were employed as cooks in upper class households but they never gained an entry to the sacred space of women's kitchen.

One of the chief arguments in this book is that the middle-class in colonial Bengal indigenised new culinary experiences that they experienced as a result of colonial modernity. This process of indigenisation was an aesthetic choice that was imbricated in the upper caste and patriarchal agenda of the middle-class social reforms. While enabling the middle-class to soak in new culinary pleasures, this process of indigenisation also made possible certain social practices, including the imagination of the act of cooking as a classic feminine act and the domestic kitchen as a sacred space. In these acts of imagination, there were important elements of continuity from the precolonial times, especially evidenced in the reinstitution of caste-based norms of gastronomy. The process of indigenising new gastronomic practices was at the same time anti-colonial yet capitalist, cosmopolitan yet gendered and caste-based. Like any other middle-class, the life of the colonial middle-class was a happy blend of customs of the so-called modernization as well as the traditional social hierarchies. Being a middle-class was a project whereby the colonial middle-class tweaked both the earlier norms and the newly earned privileges to their own advantage.[67]

---

[67] Sanjay Joshi, *Fractured Modernity: Making of a Middle-Class in Colonial North India* (New Delhi: Oxford University Press, 2001); Sanjay Joshi, "Thinking about Modernity from the Margins: The Making of a Middle-Class in Colonial India," in *The Making of the Middle-Class: Toward a Transnational History* ed. A. Ricardo Lopez and Barbara Weinstein(Durham and London: Duke University Press, 2012): 29–44.

SOURCES AND STRUCTURE

This work draws extensively upon autobiographies, memoirs, and articles written in the newspapers and Bengali language tracts in journals. These were written by the middle-class and are significant pointers to new discourse emerging on the middle-class taste of restraint and elegance. In order to understand what a regional cosmopolitanism meant, I have explored cookbooks and recipe columns published in journals such as *Punya*, *Paricharika*, and *Antahpur*, early twentieth century wedding menus and advertisements on new restaurants, and on food and beverages like tea.

Any study on any aspect of food in colonial Bengal should begin with revenue proceedings of the lieutenant-governor of undivided Bengal. These documents are useful in understanding the colonial state's interpretation of a 'rational' agriculture. These documents, along with other official documents on scarcity and famine, are also evidences of the staple diet of the general population in colonial Bengal. Among the non-official records, proceedings of the Agri-Horticultural Society of India corroborate my thesis about the colonial state's attempts to introduce British fruits and vegetables in the Indian soil and their failures. Advisory tracts on gardening written by the middle-class, published tracts on agriculture of the colonial state as well as the proceedings and reports of the Municipal Department on new restaurants and eateries that I have used are all instances of changes in the gastronomic culture of the colonial middle-class.

There was a sea change in the material culture of the colonial Bengali middle-class from mid-nineteenth century onwards, which defined their habitus. Chapter 1 describes the changes in the gastronomic culture of colonial Bengal, focusing primarily on the changes introduced by the colonial state in the realm of agriculture followed by the introduction of different provisions like biscuits and essences generally manufactured and sold by European companies. Several such provisions made 'new' food a possibility for at least the middle and the upper-middle-classes as they frequented new restaurants and hotels that begun springing up in Calcutta from the 1830s.

Chapter 2 delves deeper into analysing the nature of cosmopolitanism in Bengali cuisine. Through a focus on naming in the first section, this chapter argues that Bengali cuisine was hybridised as a result of appropriation and incorporation of British elements. However, in the discourse of taste, the 'foreign,' which was a primary reason behind the hybridity of Bengali food, was understood to have emerged from a composite of Indo-Aryan traditions. Thus, the cosmopolitan in a sense contributed to the making of what one might label the regional, in this case, the 'Bengaliness' of the middle-class and their taste. In the second section, this chapter demonstrates how the cosmopolitanism of Bengali cuisine is different from French *haute* cuisine and how the Bengali middle-class is significantly different from Bourdieu's bourgeoisie. The Bengali cuisine that emerged in colonial Bengal never assumed a public character comparable to that of *haute* cuisine in France.

Chapter 3 examines the notion of aesthetic as deployed by the middle-class in their self-fashioning. The colonial middle-class believed that a refined cuisine could only be produced by women and thus a distinct image of women was created and linked to the creation of a refined taste. This chapter argues that this idealization of women's cooking was couched in a language of gender and class. If chapter 3 investigates how the cosmopolitan nature of Bengali taste emerged from gendered negotiations, then chapter 4 provides further entry into the fissures that marked this cosmopolitanism, especially the negation of other tastes. This chapter examines how the issues of caste and class played into the self-fashioning of the middle-class. It also seeks to understand how the Bengali middle-class taste played with tropes that can be described as 'Hindu,' at best.

Chapter 5 shows that even within the idea of Bengal, there was a subregional consciousness of history. This chapter examines certain subregional cookbooks as well as histories, which exemplify how a region's history was imagined to have existed in everyday life. The chapter thus concludes by looking at the ambiguity of 'Bengaliness' of the middle-class as well as their cuisine.

1

Introducing 'Foreign' Food
Changes in the Gastronomic Culture of Colonial Bengal

Bengal witnessed a sea change in its material culture with the advent of British rule. Despite the critique against many of these changes as being 'foreign,' there was no denying the fact that Yardley lavender soaps, pince-nezes, silk curtains, and gramophones had become an integral part of Bengali middle-class homes by early twentieth century. Generally speaking, while vases of Chinese design, rugs, carpets, mahogany tables, gilt Louis Quinze furniture often resembling furniture of the Buckingham Palace, console tables with marble tops, chandeliers, wall brackets, Venetian mirrors, over mantels without mantelpieces and an upright piano adorned the drawing-rooms of the great mansions of Calcutta, middle-class homes had to be satisfied with calendars and photographs hung from the wall. Sometimes the upper rung of the middle-class could afford Venetian blinds and mosaic floors. Middle-class women took delight in purchasing new dress fabrics like chintzes, organdies, and Japanese silks.[1] Many English-educated women also learnt stitching designs with wool on carpets. This practice of making designs on carpets even reached women

---

[1] Nirad C Chaudhuri, *The Autobiography of an Unknown Indian* (Mumbai: Jaico Publishing House, 2000): 439–442, 451; Dinendrakumar Ray, *Pallichitra* (Kolikata: Ananda, 1983 [1390 BS]): 104, first published in 1904 (1311 BS). For a detailed discussion of the changes in social space within the domestic space, see Rosinka Chaudhuri, *Freedom and Beef Steaks: Colonial Calcutta Culture* (New Delhi: Orient Blackswan, 2012). Chaudhuri has convincingly shown how the Indian drawing room emerged through the course of 1920s and 30s from an 'exercise in colonial mimicry to an attempt at self-definition and national identity,' 121.

in the villages from the towns.² Even *Chandimandaps* (family shrine where people often got together for evening soirees) were decorated with colorful hanging lamps.³ One of the largest transformations took place in the realm of gastronomy. Gastronomic pleasures reached their heights, both because of the slowly increasing number of hotels and restaurants and because of the new recipe books that made it easier to have 'exotic' cuisine at home. This newness came under critique. However, for those who partook of this new experience and also for those who critiqued it, there was no denying the fact that the practice of modernity had become a quotidian affair.

By the late nineteenth century, different provisions that made cooking European food in India an easy affair became readily available. These provisions, like biscuits or essences were generally manufactured and sold by European companies like Huntley & Palmer. By the beginning of the twentieth century such foodstuff were being manufactured and marketed by Indian companies from Delhi, Lucknow, Dumdum, and Calcutta.⁴ In the Indian Industrial and Agricultural Exhibition at Calcutta in 1906–07, chocolates made by Indian companies such as Soyaji Chocolate Manufacturing Company Ltd. from Baroda were exhibited. A variety of condensed milk and milk powder from Calcutta, Baidyabati, Munshiganj, Rajshahi, and Bombay were also displayed at the exhibition.⁵ What is even more interesting was the fact that Messrs. Meyer Soetbeer & Co. of London displayed a kind of patent food that was prepared partly from Indian cereals.⁶ Indian ingredients in British food were also becoming a reality with the enormous changes in the material culture ushered in by colonialism.

The Indian Industrial and Agricultural Exhibition demonstrated the undisputable fact that products never heard of before in India not only became available in the market, but had also started being manufactured in the country itself. But what is most significant is the fact that this exhibition highlighted changes in the dietary practices of the Indians. The number of Indian companies producing tea, coffee, and cocoa would not have risen to such a scale, had there not been a sufficient demand for these products within the country itself. However, one needs to remember that demands are not

---

² Niradchandra Chaudhuri, *Atmaghati Bangali: Aji hote shatabarsha age*, vol. 1 (Kolkata: Mitra o Ghosh Publishers Ltd., 1991 [1399 BS]): 54–55, first published in 1988.
³ Ray, *Pallichitra*.
⁴ *A Report of the Indian Industrial and Agricultural Exhibition* (Calcutta, 1906–07).
⁵ Ibid., 24–26.
⁶ Ibid.

Introducing 'Foreign' Food 25

IMAGE 1: *Bhim Nager Rasogolla*: Advertisement in *Anandabazar Patrika*, (Kolkata, 1940 [1347 BS]) (*Courtesy*: Visual archive of CSSSC)

Note: Image 1 is an advertisement for *rasogolla* [cottage cheese balls soaked in sugar syrup] made by the Bhim Nag confectioners of Bhawanipore, Calcutta. By the 1940s even Bengali entrepreneurs were investing in canned food and importing them. The advertisement clearly stated that canned *rasogolla* was kept in an airtight container and would not get spoiled even if they were to be stored for a prolonged period. While *rasogolla* was being marketed primarily for its taste, the advertisement also mentions that it was good for health. Labeling *rasogolla* as healthy was a way of appeasing those who objected to the consumption of sweetmeats sold in the market. This advertisement demonstrated how Bengali entrepreneurs were making use of the modern techniques of canning to market something they called intrinsically 'Bengali.'

necessarily inevitable. Often, demands for consumption of 'new' food were created by the colonial state. The line of reason that worked behind the creation of such demands often had cultural intonations, but was mired in the politics of the colonial state. Such constructions of demands for 'new' food can best be understood by the changes that the British colonial state tried to introduce in the realm of agriculture.

EXPERIMENTS WITH FOOD: 'COLUMBIAN EXCHANGE'?

Bengal was the first colonial settlement of the British in India where the British initiated most of the experiments of their rule. It served as a laboratory where the British colonial state was reordering the scene of agrarian production with an express intention to introduce 'scientific' and 'rational' agriculture in the colony. This reordering of existing structures was based on a cultural stereotyping of the colonised subject as backward and inept at agricultural practices. This definition of rationalisation and development, of course, was driven by needs of global capital. However, a crude desire for profit making was whitewashed by what the colonial state propounded as ideals of improvement in the colony.

The introduction of new food crops by the colonial state was bound to affect the gastronomic culture of the middle-class. Although many of this new food often remained restricted to the palette of the Anglo-Indian population,[7] they did affect the lifeworld of the colonised in certain ways. Hence it is necessary to explore responses of the Bengali colonial middle-class to these so-called attempts of rationalisation and improvement of agriculture. While some welcomed these changes in agriculture, others provided a strong critique of the profiteering motives of the colonial political economy. A thoroughgoing analysis of these agricultural practices and their critique is needed in order to understand the discourse of taste articulated in the material culture of food in colonial Bengal.

Adaptation of new food crops or what is more popularly known as the 'Columbian Exchange' has been an issue of constant investigation for many scholars. In the early 1970s, Alfred Crosby proposed that imperialism shaped the world by bolstering the exchange of commodities.[8] Crosby argues that most

---

[7] In this context, the term 'Anglo-Indian' refers to Britishers who resided in India.
[8] Alfred W. Crosby, *The Columbian Exchange: Biological and Cultural Consequences of 1492* (Westport, Connecticut: Greenwood Publishing Company, 1972).

of the cuisines in the old world are a consequence of 'Columbian Exchange.' Crosby's failure to talk about the ruthlessness of colonial rule has been much qualified by the classic work on sugar by Sidney Mintz.[9] By analysing the class structure of the British society as well as the colonial economy, Mintz draws a valuable connection between the working class in Britain and the slaves whose labour kept the sugar plantations functioning. It is in this historical context, that the meaning of sugar as a commodity is formed and is dovetailed neatly with the narrative of power. Other scholars have also argued that the British Empire almost forced on its colonies an urge to possess items available only from Europe. These included, for example, French brandy and wines for African consumption, and goods grown and manufactured by the slaves in America for the use of those slaves from Africa onboard the slave ships.[10] These scholars' contention is that the imperial and economic power transformed hitherto insignificant local products into commodities for profit and global exploitation.

While agreeing with Mintz and other scholars on the point of coercion by the imperial powers to create or cultivate taste of the colonized, I argue that an overt focus on a narrative of coercion tends to underplay various layers of responses to these policies. When the Bengali middle-class carved out a discourse on taste, this discourse had uneven contours. The various strands in this discourse could range from a sharp critique of the policies of the colonial state to adaptation and internalisation. Both the critique and the adaptation led to the construction of the 'Bengali' cuisine.

AGRICULTURAL POLICIES OF THE COLONIAL STATE

The impact of the introduction of new food on the material culture of the Bengali middle-class cannot be explained without thoroughbred analyses of the agricultural policies of the colonial state. Several scholars have discussed the impact that the colonial state's agricultural policies had on production in Bengal. Binay Bhushan Chaudhuri's 'Commercialization of Agriculture' is

---

[9] Sidney W. Mintz, *Sweetness and Power: The Place of Sugar in Modern History* (New York: Viking Penguin Inc., 1985); *Tasting Food, Tasting Freedom* (Boston: Beacon Press, 1996).

[10] James Walvin, *Fruits of Empire: Exotic Produce and British Taste, 1660–1800* (New York: New York University Press, 1997), 174–176.

definitely one of the pioneering researches on the impact of the colonial state's agricultural policies on food production and peasant indebtedness.[11]

Chaudhuri points out that in Bengal the *zamindars* (landlords) leased out, in perpetuity or for short periods, portions of their own estates to peasants at a rent that was much higher than the revenue *zamindars* paid to the government. The result was peasant indebtedness. This indebtedness necessitated distress sale of the peasant's food crops. The consequent depletion of his food stock obliged him to buy food from the market in those months when there was not enough food grown at his fields. Chaudhuri calls it an example of distorted commercialisation as it blurred the usual distinction between a subsistence crop and a commercial crop.[12] In fact, it is in this context that rice becomes significant as a commodity. Rice increasingly began to play the role of a cash crop, moving away from being a subsistence crop.

Chaudhuri explains the process of commercialisation by showing the relation between cash crops like jute and rice, and subsistence crops.[13] The growth of commercial crops such as jute resulted in the reduction of the aggregate acreage of rice cultivation. Under the stimulus of rising prices of jute, peasants cultivated a larger portion than usual of their holdings with jute, relying for the purchase of food on the money derived from the sale of jute.[14] While this had a definite impact on the production of local rice, a growing urban and industrial population necessitated an expansion of the rice trade. According to an official estimate of 1874, out of the twenty million *maunds* (1 *maund* = 82.3 pounds = 37.4 kilograms) that was imported into Calcutta for the sole purpose of export, seven million *maunds* of rice were consumed by the population in Calcutta.[15] Commercialisation of rice, which began in the late nineteenth

---

[11] Binay Bhushan Chaudhuri, "Commercialization of Agriculture," in *History of Bangladesh 1704–1971*, vol. 1 of *Political History*, ed. Sirajul Islam (Dhaka: Asiatic Society of Bangladesh, 1992).

[12] "Commercialization of Agriculture," in *History of Bangladesh 1704–1971*, vol. 2, *Economic History*, ed. Sirajul Islam (Dhaka: Asiatic Society of Bangladesh, 1997), first published in 1992, 293–348.

[13] Chaudhuri, "Growth of Commercial Agriculture in Bengal 1859–1885," in *Agricultural Production and South Asian History*, ed. David Ludden (New Delhi: Oxford University Press, 2005), first published in 1994, 145–181.

[14] Ibid., 153.

[15] Ibid.

century continued into the 1940s. Total exports of paddy and rice from Bengal to other provinces of India and abroad comprised between 4.5 percent and 7.5 percent of Bengal's annual production.[16] Gradually, rice became more of a cash crop than a subsistence food crop. But even then, rise in the price of rice resulting from the exports of rice was subject to fluctuations in the world market. Saugata Mukherjee, for example, argues that in the 1920s one could see large increase in the exports of rice from all the important rice growing countries of Southeast Asia, like Siam, Indo-China, as well as from Burma. Import of the Burma rice was one of the chief reasons behind a substantial fall in the price of rice after 1930s.[17]

For the British, rice experimentations in Bengal had a strategic value; it opened up markets in Europe. These experimentations slowly petered out as the commercial significance of rice dwindled in comparison to cash crops like jute, and rice began to be exported from Southeast Asia to feed the population of Bengal. This is corroborated by the *Report of the Bengal Paddy & Rice Enquiry Committee* in 1940.

> Although paddy is by far the most important food crop grown in Bengal and accounts for the bulk of agricultural production in this province, its economic predominance in its social life is masked by the peculiar position of jute as the cash crop of Bengal.[18]

This report further stated that dealings in marketable surplus of paddy hardly exerted as much influence on the monetary transactions of the cultivator as those in jute.[19] The reason behind this is stated to be the declining demand for Indian rice in Europe and consequent loss of markets. The report prescribed

---

[16] *Report of Bengal Paddy and Rice Enquiry Committee*, 2 vols, 1940. Cited in Partha Chatterjee, "Agrarian Structure in pre-partition Bengal," in *Perspectives in Social Sciences. Three Studies on the Agrarian Structure in Bengal 1850-1947*, ed. Asok Sen, Partha Chatterjee, Saugata Mukherjee (Calcutta: Oxford University Press, 1982), 185.

[17] Saugata Mukherjee, "Some Aspects of Commercialization of Agriculture in Eastern India 1891–1938," in *Perspectives in Social Sciences 2: Three Studies on the Agrarian Structure in Bengal 1850-1947*, ed. Asok Sen, Partha Chatterjee, Saugata Mukherjee (Calcutta: Oxford University Press, 1982), 256–257.

[18] Government of Bengal Department of Agriculture and Industries., Report of the Bengal Paddy and Rice Enquiry Committee, vol. II (Calcutta, 1940)

[19] Ibid.

import of high quality seeds. Colonial methods and practices were also offered as solutions for securing a high yield of the paddy crop and the defects and drawbacks in the system of cultivating paddy in India was blamed for the low yield. These solutions, however, failed to explain why Bengal, which produced innumerable varieties of rice, needed to fall back on colonial modes of production to increase its yield. This information can be obtained from W.W. Hunter. In the twenty-four *pargannahs*, for example, one could find two principal varieties of rice, *aus* or spring rice and *aman* or winter rice. At least thirty varieties of *aus* were produced in this district alone. These were: *Kalia jamira, Surja Mani, Tupua Khali, Kersai, Kali payanji, Hariheba, Begunbichi, Sitahar, Khubui, Banshphul, Gangajali, Parang, Beni bachal, Phepari, Here Kalia, Sultan jeta, Pana jhure, Ais bere, Ais Mani, Ghisal, Dulsal, Piprasal, Karimsal, Benaphuli, Kalandi, Matisal, Lakshmiparijat, Bhatna, Maliagur, Maslot*.[20] This list is a clear indicator of the capability of indigenous cultivators to grow at least thirty varieties of rice from a single type, a fact often ignored by the colonial state. Santoshnath Seth who wrote an extensive text on rice in Bengal, also provided an elaborate discussion of varieties of rice produced in Bengal.[21]

Seth mentions that the world produced 12 million tons of rice in 1923. India produced half the quantity of this rice. Burma and Siam (Thailand) produced half of what India produced. However, it was still Burma that supplied rice to Bengal, especially during famines.[22] Seth identifies two reasons behind this. First, India exported one third of what it produced to Europe and America. Second, the British, and the Marwaris, the trading group from Rajasthan, had started speculating on Burma rice. Seth explained that these groups kept receiving information about the rice from the wholesalers in Burma through telegraph and immediately raised the price and sold it in Calcutta. It was in their interest that Burma rice continued to be imported into Bengal. Thus gradually Bengal was sucked into the cobweb of global capital. Even her exports to the world underwent constant fluctuations. Table 1 shows the enormous fluctuations in the export trade in husked and unhusked rice.

---

[20] W.W. Hunter, *A Statistical Account of Bengal: Districts of the Twenty-four Parganas and Sunderbans, vol. 1* (London, 1875), 134–143.
[21] Mahajan Shree Santoshnath Seth, "Sahitharatna," in *Bange Chaltatwa* (Kolikata 1925 [1332 BS]).
[22] Ibid., 365–366.

TABLE 1: Husked and unhusked rice[23]

	1878–79		1879–80		1880–81		1882–83	
	Cwt. (cwt=50.80 kilograms)	Rs.	Cwt.	Rs.	Cwt.	Rs.	Cwt.	Rs. ($1=Rs.49)
Paddy								
• To Ceylon	9,616	26,475	1,437	2,670	6,527	10,220	10,795	14,920
• To other countries	263	879	70	226	181	320	726	1,065
Total	9,879	27,354	1,507	2,896	6,708	10,540	11,521	15,935
Husked Rice								
• To UK	456,153	25,89,490	705,056	36,08,568	1,311,825	45,08,571	1,406,572	42,50,706
• To Cape of Good Hope	96,842	6,79,220	53,763	3,64,642	105,283	5,37,923	68,250	3,05,477
• To Mauritius	1,069,230	55,06,828	604,176	30,64,047	742,432	29,27,104	558,812	16,76,204
• To Reunion	259,089	13,49,134	186,535	9,71,886	107,128	1,85,332	430,007	13,71,369
• To S. America	380,281	21,19,694	339,126	16,96,814	378,874	13,25,172	375,077	11,17,264
• To W. Indies	237,240	13,02,127	220,431	11,24,278	216,709	7,76,198	299,584	9,60,447
• To Aden	50,585	2,69,332	97,824	4,67,434	244,424	7,87,803	115,276	3,36,455
• To Arabia	451,154	23,41,128	547,540	24,25,261	744,307	23,70,517	503,255	14,06,689

[23] Collector of Sea-Customs, Calcutta. *Introduction to the Annual Accounts of the Sea-Borne Trade And Navigation of the Bengal Presidency and of its Chief Port and each of its Subordinate ports for the Official Year 1882–83*, Bengal Revenue Proceedings, Miscellaneous(Calcutta,1884), xxxi.

	1878–79		1879–80		1880–81		1882–83		
	Cwt. (cwt=50.80 kilograms)	Rs.	Cwt.	Rs.	Cwt.	Rs.	Rs.	Cwt.	Rs. ($1=Rs.49)
• To Persia	26,514	1,36,326	56,838	2,45,325	53,607	1,26,377	21,064	57,537
• To Ceylon	2,345,364	1,22,68,254	886,327	45,80,748	1,289,735	43,88,822	1,527,414	41,15,444
• To China	3,432	22,230	913	5,798	1,298	5,880	51,295	1,76,387
• To Java	------	------	------	------	1,033	2,820	------	------
• To Maldives	47,534	2,03,258	26,951	1,00,465	62,502	1,69,168	42,015	1,17,083
• To Straits Settlements	46,017	2,55,138	23,025	1,18,247	130,642	3,73,941	126,234	3,77,045
• To Australia	89,144	6,97,274	39,705	2,63,609	83,133	4,79,042	70,036	3,47,855
• To Other Countries	142,465	7,88,769	42,873	2,18,648	175,876	6,89,757	1,012,666	25,95,174
Total	5,701,035	3,05,28,202	3,831,083	1,92,55,170	5,948,208	2,09,54,427	6,601,497	1,92,11,136

Source: see n.93

As can be seen from the data in table 1, export of paddy increased by 1,642 cwt between 1878 and 1883. However, there was a decline in terms of price almost by Rs. 11,419. We also see constant fluctuations in the quantity of rice exported. While 9,879 cwt rice was exported in 1878–79, it was reduced to 1,507 cwt the next year. In terms of husked rice, 5,701,035 cwt rice was exported in total in the year 1878–79. This quantity increased by 900, 462 cwt by the year 1883. Price of rice also increased from Rs. 1,92,55,170 to Rs. 2,09,54,427. But then again the price of rice dropped to Rs. 1,92, 11,136, despite an increase in export.

This elaborate discussion on the colonial experimentations with rice and fluctuations in the international rice market is necessary in order to fully grasp the changes in the gastronomic culture of the middle-class in colonial Bengal. In middle-class imagination, the significance of rice as a commodity was enormous. Rice was not merely a staple in Bengal, it was also a potent cultural symbol of 'Bengaliness' and thus many debates and discourses of the literati in Bengal revolved around rice. It is in this context of 'indigenous' versus 'foreign' that the colonial state's experimentations with Carolina rice in Bengal start making sense.

CAROLINA RICE EXPERIMENTATIONS IN COLONIAL BENGAL: 'RATIONAL' AND 'MODERN?'

Rice was introduced in south Carolina in the 1690s and by the 1720s it became the region's dominant export.[24] Between 1690 and 1720, south Carolina rice became established in the world market because exogenous factors caused serious shortfalls in the supply of basic foodstuffs to western Europe.[95] The export of Carolina rice to Europe increased over a hundredfold between c.1700s to the 1770s.[25] Between 1740 and 1760, Carolina rice became a major supplier in the European rice market[26]. Thus Carolina rice was integrated into the Atlantic economy through colonialism.

In an article published in the *American Historical Review*, Peter Cocklanis argues that by the first half of the nineteenth century, the American Revolution and the Napoleonic Wars impeded the flow of American rice to Europe. At around the same time, regional harvest failures as well as industrialisation, urbanisation, commercialisation, and population growth resulted in an increase

---

[24] R.C. Nash, "South Carolina and the Atlantic economy in the late seventeenth and eighteenth centuries," *Economic History Review* xlv, vol 4 (1992), 677–702, 679.
[25] Ibid., 680.
[26] Ibid., 688.

in European demand for foodstuffs and industrial crops, including rice.[27] South Carolina no longer remained the principal supplier for the Western markets, because it faced intense competition from Bengal, Java, Lower Burma, Siam and Indo-China.[28] Cocklanis' argument is of course more about the decline of the American rice in relation to the rise in supply of rice from Bengal. When he talks about rice from Bengal, what he has in mind is the innumerable variety of local rice grown in Bengal, which started occupying major Western markets in the first half of the nineteenth century. However, he does not take into account the fact that the Carolina rice experiments in Bengal began from the 1860s with the intention of importing Carolina rice from India to Europe. Import of Carolina rice by the British from India to Europe can also mean the supremacy of the British as colonisers who could bring in 'rational' agriculture to its colony in order to 'improve' its material culture. The cultivation of Carolina rice was a symbol of that 'rational' agriculture. It was in fact, colonialism that connected this rice to colonial India as a way of inaugurating a 'modern' mode of agriculture.

The success of colonialism lay in the power of the colonial capital that could interweave the material culture of Africa with America and then with India. However, within this grand narrative, there are little histories that fracture the narrative of the grand history of the empire. The colonial state did not implant 'rational' and 'modern' agriculture in the soils of the colony. It was in fact, the experience of the coloniser in the colony that helped in a discursive formulation of a 'rational' and 'modern' agriculture by the imperialists. Judith Carney, for instance, challenges the conventional interpretation of rice history in the Americas that assigns Europeans the role of adapting a crop of Asian origin to New World conditions. According to Carney, it was the transfer of an entire cultural system from Africa to the Americas, as a result of the trans-Atlantic slave trade, that assisted the development of rice culture in the Americas, especially Carolina.[29] Rice figured crucially among the seeds that accompanied the African slaves to the Americas, and the slaves planted the crop wherever there was a congenial social and environmental condition. In facilitating the adaptation of this staple, slaves drew upon a sophisticated

---

[27] Peter A. Cocklanis, "Distant Thunder: The Creation of a World Market in Rice and the Transformations It Wrought," *The American Historical Review*. 98, no. 4 (October 1993): 1050–1078.

[28] Ibid.

[29] Judith A. Carney, *Black Rice: The African Origins of Rice Cultivation in the Americas* (Cambridge, Massachusetts, London, England: Harvard University Press, 2001).

knowledge system that informed cultivating and processing methods. Carney argues that contrary to the conventional knowledge, rice cultivation was known in west Africa long before the arrival of the European traders.[30] This indigenous African expertise mediated the diffusion of rice cultivation to the Americas, and offered a means to negotiate the terms of labour in conditions of slavery.[31] In a way, then, the Africans who were shipped from Africa to south Carolina in order to work as slaves in the rice plantations made possible the cultivation of Carolina rice that fed Europe.

In case of Carolina rice experimentations in Bengal, we have to keep in mind these narratives that make the story of modernity complex and demonstrate its connections with colonialism. The Director of Agriculture, Bengal, summed up in a note that although Carolina rice was supposed to have originated in Madagascar, the origin of this paddy could be traced to Bengal, from where a cargo ship carrying paddy to America was wrecked in the Indian Ocean. The Director stated that a consignment of a bag full of paddy was saved from the wreck and then carried to Madagascar. Carolina rice had its origins in this bag of paddy.[32] In other words, this rice already grew in Bengal. The validity of this story is debatable. However, this narrative turns the story of the origins of modernity on its head. The entire story of the Carolina rice cultivation in Bengal problematises colonial notions of a 'modern' and 'rational' system of agriculture. Apparently based on notions of modern technology, 'rational' agriculture was more about a supremacist agenda. Thus the British became the carrier of a 'rational' agriculture while the colonised 'lagged' behind.

In 1866, the Government of India recommended Carolina rice cultivation in Bengal arguing that it was immune from being affected by bad weather. In July 1868, the Agricultural & Horticultural Society printed and forwarded copies of a pamphlet on the experimental cultivation of Carolina paddy in Bengal to the Board of Revenue. This pamphlet was distributed to the district commissioners. The cantonment magistrate of DumDum reported that he had put about two and half seers of each kind of acclimatised and Carolina paddy into seed-beds, and when about a foot high, the young plants were transplanted five or six in a bunch. Although all germinated freely, a small quantity of seeds were carried away by birds. In Hooghly, the collector attributed failures in

---

[30] Ibid., 27–36.
[31] Ibid.
[32] Government of Bengal, Department of Agriculture and Industries, *Report of the Bengal Paddy and Rice Enquiry Committee, vol. II* (Calcutta, 1940), 50–54.

experiments to the quality of the seed itself and to the lateness of the season. In Howrah too the seeds were received too late to be cultivated.[33]

On the basis of observation of these experiments, the lieutenant governor stated that the failure of the experiment in several cases was due to 'the lateness of the supply of seed.' He, along with the Board of Revenue, advised that these experiments had to be repeated and requested a fresh stock of seed to be supplied early.[34] However, even four years after the experiments began, the colonial state failed to make it successful. One can grasp better the causes of the failures in the experimentation from the analyses of the colonial officials themselves in 1874.

Persistent failures in Carolina rice experiments in India necessitated an inquiry by the colonial officials. They communicated with the commissioner of agriculture at Washington, who forwarded samples of rice seed sent from India to two gentlemen, Robert Habershams and James R. Sparkman in the southern states of the United States of America.[35] These two men opined that the seeds of Carolina rice sent from India were of inferior quality than the rice produced in the United States. The reason behind its degeneration was deterioration of grain under what they called a 'foreign culture.' What they implied by this statement was that even grains of the best quality deteriorated under a change of climate.[36]

By 1874, it was clear that the experiments were failures. However, the colonial discourse could not remain confined to explaining failures of the experiments in terms of natural decline. A mere explanation of the failures in terms of the lateness of seed or inclement weather conditions implied that the colonial officials were inadequately informed about the colony, and thus their control of the colony could never be complete. What was required was

---

[33] Letter from T.B. Lane, Esq., Officiating Secretary to the Board of Revenue, Lower Provinces, to the Government of Bengal, in the General Department, 10th April, 1869, File no. 1602c, Proceedings of Lieutenant Governor Of Bengal, General Department,, Fort William, West Bengal, 18–80.

[34] Letter from H.S. Beadon, Esq., Officiating Under-Secretary to the Government of Bengal, to the Secretary to the Government of India, Home Department, 28th April, 1869, File no. 1664, Proceedings of Lieutenant Governor of Bengal, General Department, Fort William, West Bengal.

[35] From Her Majesty's Secretary of State for India, to the Government of India, 23rd December, 1875, File no. 63(Revenue), Proceedings of Branch II-Agriculture, Financial Department, India Office London.

[36] Ibid.

a discourse of a so-called 'rational' agriculture. Scapegoats were found right away. The colonial state blamed the colonised subject because he had neither a theoretical nor a practical knowledge to make such an experiment successful.[37] This attitude summarises what may be termed the theoretical background of the introduction of Carolina rice in India. Eugene Schrotthy, a British journalist stated succinctly, agriculture as practiced in Europe had always been considered a noble art. Consequently, the improvements effected in Europe in the mode of cultivation had been great, and in keeping with the general advance of education and civilisation.[38] According to Scrotthy, in eastern countries, agriculture did not progress from what it had been two or even three thousand years ago. The Carolina rice-plant was essentially the same as that cultivated in India, but European energy subjected it to such a careful cultivation in the rich soil of America, that the result was the production of a grain that surpassed in its nutritive and other qualities the best Patna rice.[39] He attributed the failures to the ignorance of Indian officials and recommended American methods of cultivation to make it successful.[40] Scrotthy's statements epitomised the colonial state's perception of the colonised subject. While Scrotthy championed European agriculture on the basis of reason and progress, the twin pillars of enlightenment, his arguments showed that he was not prepared to admit that the colony possessed these two qualities. The colonial state tried to introduce modern agriculture in the colony on the ground that the colony still used a backward agricultural system. The discourse on the backwardness of the colony served to endorse the idea of a better form of agriculture that was a product of European brilliance.

Arguments on backward agriculture of the colony, however, could not hide the fact that Carolina paddy could hardly be called the best quality rice. Everywhere, seeds contained a huge quantity of husk and rubbish. While in Hooghly the amount was small, in Howrah it amounted to 20 percent of the seed, in Mymensingh one-third of the seed and in Fureedpore, in eastern Bengal, a substantial portion of the seed was mere husk. In all, 25 percent

---

[37] Memorandum by Offg. Collector of 24 Pargunnahs, 16th April, 1875, Colln 6–14; No. 346, Proceedings of Branch II-Agriculture, Head. No. 2- Produce and Cultivation, Financial Department, Calcutta, May 1875.

[38] Eugene S. Schrotthy, O.C.U.G, *The Principles of Rational Agriculture Applied to India and its Staple Products* (Bombay, 1876), 3.

[39] Ibid., 190–192.

[40] Ibid.

of the entire quantity consisted of husk and trash.[41] However, the colonial government decided not to pay any heed to the reasons behind the failures in Carolina rice experimentations in Bengal. Attention now was fully turned to Madras Presidency. The experiment was not worth a sacrifice altogether because Carolina rice commanded almost three times the price of Patna rice in the European markets. Even the Madras experiments, it seems, did not succeed for very long. Analysts found the reason behind its failure in grain processing. A certain Robertson observed in his report, 'It is – possible that the very high price that Carolina rice imported from America commands in England is due chiefly to the very superior way in which it is prepared for the market.'[42] In Madras, the husk was hardly removed and there was no attempt to remove the dark-colored surface that was found beneath it. This was because grain processing was performed by means of a pestle, a mortar, and a bamboo sieve in Madras instead of the elaborate steam machinery employed in America.[43]

Evidently, the Carolina rice experimentation in Bengal in particular, and in India in general, was largely a failure. This failure provokes several questions. One can never identify a sole over arching factor behind the failures in these experimentation. There are several interconnected ones. These experiments are significant because they lay bare the crux of colonial state's agricultural policies. Colonial discourse of a 'rational' agriculture was based on cultural stereotyping. The operation of the colonial state within a specific power structure defined the nature of the proposed 'modern' agriculture in the colony. The crude logic of colonial capital lay behind the so-called philanthropic interests. It was definitely not for feeding the colonised subjects, but for feeding the metropole that the Carolina rice was introduced in India. India served as a laboratory for colonial experimentations with diet.

INTRODUCTION OF 'NEW' FOOD: IMPROVEMENT AND AESTHETICS

Since many of the experiments with 'new' food crops often failed, scholars tend to understate their history. However, we need to look beyond these failures.

---

[41] From R. Knight. Esq., Asst. Secretary to the Government of Bengal, Financial Department, to the Secretary to the Government of India, Department of Revenure, Agriculture & Commerce, 9th December, 1874, File no. 3540, Colln. 6–141, Proceedings of Financial Department, Calcutta. [WBSA].

[42] L. Liotard, *Memorrandum Regarding Introduction of Carolina Rice into India* (Calcutta, 1880), 73.

[43] Ibid.

Why did the experiments take place at all? Was it simply for the purpose of making profits? I argue that behind these new experiments with agricultural production there lay a much broader discourse of colonial understanding of agriculture. An urge for improvement and rationalisation accompanied the drive for profit. Since so-called methods of improved cultivation could not increase the productivity of land, agricultural policies were couched in a cultural language. However, these experiments did leave a mark on the diet of the population, even if not to a great extent. To understand how exactly a modern cuisine was being conceived, we need to look at the materialist history of food crops along with their cultural significance.

The question of a rational agriculture and improvement was conjoined with the question of aesthetics. How to bring the European gardening system to India? Many of the new food crops introduced in India were a direct result of the Columbian Exchange and some of them came from Europe itself. These crops were chiefly introduced by the Portuguese traders in the seventeenth century. They brought in a number of crops with them, amongst which the most extraordinary was the introduction of potato, introduced rather late.[44] Tomato, okra, and the ubiquitous chili pepper also came around this time.[45] Amongst the fruits from the new world, most notable example is that of the pineapple. Grown originally in the Portuguese possessions on the western coast, by the end of the sixteenth century, it became common enough in areas in the eastern parts of India like in Bengal. Papaya and cashew nut were also introduced by the Portuguese in India, but these took time to spread.[46] This was in fact true about potatoes, tomatoes, and okra. Although introduced by the sixteenth century, these vegetables never became a common item of diet until the nineteenth century when the British colonial state took the initiative to spread them on a much larger scale. The introduction of exotic vegetables by the colonial state had two purposes. One was to bring new (modern) food to the subject population as a symbol of progress. The other was to recreate a sense of belonging for the coloniser in the colony.

Colonial experiments in Bengal obviously did not remain confined to rice. Transforming the palette of the colonised was also an agenda of the

---

[44] Irfan Habib, "Mughal India", in *The Cambridge Economic History of India, vol. 1: c.1200–c.1750* eds. Tapan Raychaudhury and Irfan Habib (Cambridge: Cambridge University Press, 1982), 218.

[45] Irfan Habib, *The Agrarian System of Mughal India 1556–1707*, rev. ed. (1963; repr., New Delhi: Oxford University Press, 1999), 53.

[46] Ibid., 54–55.

colonial state. Thus the 'emasculated rice-eating' Bengali population needed substitution in alternative food items for rice. Of course, the chief emphasis was laid on the cultivation of wheat in Bengal, which was a rare practise until then. But introduction of wheat was also accompanied by the desires of the colonial state to bring about radical changes in the food habits of the subject population by bringing in what might be called 'foreign' food. Wheat was grown in other parts of India, especially in the northern and western parts. However, it was generally not consumed in Bengal. The colonial state argued that wheat would be advantageous in situations of scarcity. No explanation was given as to why the state would not take more initiative to ensure a steady supply of rice. The British colonial state considered the 'rice-eating' Bengalis to be weak and emasculated compared to the 'wheat-eating' population of northern India and consequently encouraged them to consume wheat. Along with wheat, manioc was also suggested as a substitute for rice.

One official broached the option of manioc as an alternative for rice in the year 1874. He argues that it did not make sense to cultivate rice in Bengal since it was dependent on rain.[47] In case of drought, rice could not be relied on. He suggested the introduction of manioc or cassava, 'the root of which is of same nature as rice, as delicious as the potato and keeps fresh underground for years, indifferent to great changes of heat or cold.'[48] After this, the advantages of manioc were explained in great details.

> It is got easily, sealing it is a large branchy shrub, and numerous knots, or leafy marks on the branches are each a new plant. In calling the branches to plant, slips are made about three inches long, and include two or three of these knots, and yet each plant will form say twenty to sixty September slips, and therefore as many new plants.

The explanation goes further:

> Planting is very simple and may be done in any soil, but a soft or sandy soil suits best, the tuberous root developing easier where there is little bind in the soil. Once surface cleaned with a broad hoe, slight matches, two or three inches deep, to be made a yard or two apart, and cuttings laid in and lightly

---

[47] Letter From R.M. Gunning, Esq., to the Right Hon'ble the Earl of Derry, & c.,&c., &c. Palmaras Estaco da Estrada Pedro II, 13 September, 1874, File no. 17-2-12. Proceedings of Branch II- Agriculture. Head No. 2- Produce and Cultivation, Financial Department, March, 1875, Calcutta.
[48] Ibid., 37.

covered. If the soil is deep or sandy, it may be raised into little heaps or ridges, and the slips are then placed in the same way. Planting can be done during the whole year; but the best time is when the cold season is ending, when leaves have fallen and when it is ripe. Soon the pretty, fine, partite leaves show above ground, and all the further cultivation needed is to weed or hoe mound it (pulling the earth against the plant) twice or thrice a month when plants will have flowered, and roots will be ready to eat. But they are larger and more mealy when two months old, and keep growing for two years longer. ---The great object should be to have it spread rapidly over different districts as a good root to be used as potato, but afterwards its other uses may be availed of. The peeled root is grated on a common grater by a hand-wheel, or by one driven by machinery, into a soft pulp, and this, after the water is pressed out, heated in copper pans, is the farina of universal use. From this can be made tapioca and a nice starch known here as "palvilho," and in England as "Brazilian arrowroot." Farina is dry and used alone, or with many dishes. The rationale in it necessitates and stimulates saliva, and thus assists digestion. Made into a paste with boiling water, it is used with fish or fried in little cakes. It keeps in bags for a long time without souring, and so can be carried from one district to another in the usual way of commerce.[49]

This lengthy description served two purposes. First, the colonial language of command could not be just constricted within a disciplinary regime. It was not that easy to simply order an experiment to be done. This difficulty in introducing an experiment often resulted from the reluctance of the cultivators to cooperate with colonial experimentations. The cultivators were often persuaded by the native landlords who explained the benefits of a particular cultivation to them. Hence, advantages of manioc needed such a lengthy explanation. Second, this passage demonstrated the desire to extend the scope of the colonial capital. The colonial state's intent to introduce manioc in Bengal was much inspired by the enormous success of manioc in Brazil. But what is most striking in the passage is the mention of manioc in the form of arrowroot in Britain. Arrowroot, a modern food in the metropole traveled from Brazil to Britain and had the potential to be introduced in India. However, herein lay a mistake. This mistake was the lapse in colonial knowledge-system to grasp the entire information about the colony. It was soon figured out that manioc or cassava could not be grown in the soils of Bengal and rice proved to be a much more potent crop, at least in Gangetic Bengal.

---

[49] Ibid.

A letter from an official of the Royal Botanical Garden began thus: '---manioc is not much appreciated in India by natives.'[50] It was also stated in the same letter that like rice, manioc also relied on a good supply of water.[51] Hence, it could not be a good substitute for rice. But what was more interesting was another letter that stated that manioc was already grown in some parts of India and hence did not have to be imported from Brazil.[52] A similarity can be found in this context with British experimentation with cinchona in the Nilgiri Hills in southern India. Kavita Philip demonstrates that the transplantation of cinchona saplings from Andean mountains to the Nilgiri Hills brought the local knowledge of a subsistence economy into the global arena of free enterprise.[53] The cinchona plant was brought from Peru, nurtured in the Kew Garden in Britain and then planted in the Nilgiri Hills. According to Philip, cinchona experimentations had a symbolic success because the British made it look like a sign of 'progress.' They turned a commodity that was not being used in the jungles of South America to a commodity of great use.[54] Manioc experiments tell us a similar narrative whereby a locally grown crop was given a different interpretation by the colonial state.

Like manioc, the British colonial state tried to introduce potato on a much larger scale than the Portuguese had done in India. Potato had retained its lower class label in England throughout the eighteenth and nineteenth centuries because it was cheap and easy to prepare.[55] Potato, a sturdy vegetable, was accepted by the Irish in the seventeenth century as a safeguard against famine. The English were much responsible for making the Irish accept this food, which was detested in England itself as a 'food of the poor.'[56] This

---

[50] Letter From Surgeon G. King, M.B., Superintendent, Royal Botanical Gardens, to R. Knight, Esq., Asst. Secretary to Government of Bengal, 4th March 1875, Howrah, File no. 17-1-2, Proceeding No. 146, Proceedings of Branch II–Agriculture, Head No. 2–Produce and Cultivation, Financial Department, Calcutta, March, 1875, 38–39.

[51] Ibid.

[52] Letter from G. Hamilton, Esq., Under-Secretary of State for India, to Under-Secretary of State for Foreign Affairs. 11th November, 1874, File no. 17-1-2, Proceedings of Branch II–Agriculture. Head No. 2–Produce and Cultivation, Financial Department, India Office, London, Calcutta, March 1875, 38.

[53] Kavita Philip, *Civilizing Natures: Race, Resources, and Modernity in Colonial South India* (New Brunswick, New Jersey: Rutgers University Press, 2004).

[54] Ibid., 171–195.

[55] Larry Zuckerman, *The Potato: How the Humble Spud Rescued the Western World* (Boston & London: Faber & Faber, 1998), 260.

[56] Ibid.

Introducing 'Foreign' Food

attitude motivated the English to bring this experiment to India as well. A constant search for substitutes for rice led the colonial state to concentrate on the cultivation of potatoes and peas.[57] Those who already sowed potato were asked to instruct others to sow it too.[58] In general, potatoes were grown by the British in the hills from where they came to Calcutta. The colonial state then sent these potatoes to various other districts in Bengal. Soon, however, a debate formed around whether potato should be cultivated in the form of a seed or as a crop. Whereas one official, J. Stalkkart argued that it was much easier to send the seed to districts instead of the crop[59], G. King, superintendent of the Botanical Gardens, called the sowing of seeds 'nonsense.'[60] He, in fact, argued that potato was not a very reliable crop and a great area of land needed to be covered with seeds. Hence, instead of sowing the seeds, potatoes needed to be planted out.[61]

Similar suggestions were put forward for the introduction of carrots, barley, and peas.[62] However, not much was done to figure out a way to make the local palate accustomed to these new crops. Finally, it was found out that crops like cucumbers and pumpkins, which were already being sown in Bengal, were the most beneficial in times of scarcity. It was a gross underestimation of what grew in the colony that led the colonial state to introduce new food-crops. These new crops, which were not too useful in times of scarcity, however, could not hide the fact that new vegetables and fruits were pouring into the markets

---

[57] Letter from J. Stalkartt, Esq., to His Excellency Lord Northbrook, Viceroy and Governor-General of India, 31 October, 1873, Hope Town, File no. 15–1, Proceedings of the Hon'Ble The Lieutenant-Governor of Bengal, Scarcity and Relief, General Department, Calcutta, 1873.

[58] Ibid., 647.

[59] Ibid.

[60] Letter from G. King, Esq., Superintendent, Botanical Gardens, to the Offg. Secretary to the Government of Bengal. 20th November, 1873, Botanical Gardens, File no. 15–2, Proceedings of the Hon'ble Lieutenant-Governor of Bengal, Scarcity and Relief, General Department, Calcutta, 1873, 649.

[61] Ibid.

[62] Letter from J. Stalkartt, Esq., to His Excellency Lord Northbrook, Viceroy and Governor-General of India, 31st October, 1873, Hope Town, File no. 15–1, Proceedings of the Hon'ble Lieutenant-Governor of Bengal, Scarcity and Relief, General Department, Calcutta, 1873, 647; Letter from Col. E.T. Dacton, C.S.I., Commissioner of Chota Nagpore, to Col. E.A. Rowlatt, Dy Commissioner, Maunbhoom, March 1874, Calcutta, File no. 15-4/5, Proceeding No. 2487, Proceedings of General Department, Calcutta, March, 1874.

of Bengal. The British colonial state in India went on trying to convince the masses to cultivate these new vegetables. Way back in 1831, missionaries in Srirampur apprised the government of the need to alleviate the lot of the cultivators. In their view, these people had hardly any knowledge of cultivation and they needed to be encouraged to grow new food crops. These missionaries suggested that the government bring in new food crops from abroad to India.[63] Alan Octavian Hume, the founder of the Indian National Congress, also argued several years later, that more initiative should have been taken by the government to improve agricultural production in India.[64] The definition of improvement remained vague and undefined.

Improvement also brought with it the question of aesthetics. It was not enough to grow radishes, pumpkins, eggplants, arums, and cucumbers. They needed to be accompanied by what would look colorful and beautiful like strawberries and peaches. In the 1840s, Colesworthy Grant scoffed at the inferiority of Indian vegetables, which he argued, arose partly due to the ignorance of native gardeners.[65] Hume's view was echoed in an argument by another author in *Calcutta Review* in 1869. It began thus:

> Considering the length of time that the English have been masters of India, they can hardly be congratulated on the extent or success of their efforts, either in making themselves acquainted with the vegetable productions of so noble a possession, or in utilizing and adding to them.[66]

The author put an emphasis on 'rational and scientific' modes of agriculture and gardening as a form of art. He also advised on how to turn agriculture into pure botany. Scientific discourse thus became conflated with cultural stereotyping. Modern agriculture was seen as the marker that made the British colonial state superior to the colonised subject. The author accused the Indian gardener of ignorance of practices such as rotation of crops and change of seeds. The concern of the author, it seems, was more with what the British had to endure on their breakfasttable like 'flavour-less melons and half-swelled grapes' and 'odoriferous mangoes and guavas,' than with what could actually improve

---

[63] *Hindusthaner khetra o Baganer Krishisamajer Kritakarmer Bibaran Pustak* (Sreerampore, 1831), 10.

[64] A.O. Hume, *Agricultural Reform in India* (London, 1879): 20–25.

[65] Colesworthy Grant, *An Anglo-Indian Domestic Sketch: A letter From an Artist in India to His Mother in England* (Calcutta, 1849): 100–123.

[66] "Indian Economic Botany and Gardening," *The Calcutta Review*, vol. 49 (Calcutta, 1869): 187–205.

Introducing 'Foreign' Food 45

the diet of the masses. The way fruits were produced was also criticised by the author as unscientific. The area that fruits were grown in was described by him as 'deep, damp, four sided spaces,' in which emaciated country vegetables were grown in an irregular pattern rather than what the author considered to be a proper space, that is in squares. That the author was more concerned about the diet of the British in India and not the masses can be figured out from his frequent mention of the '*mali*' or the gardener who worked in the garden and not the peasant or the cultivator who worked in the fields.[67] These endeavors to plant gardens in colonies that would provide both a steady supply of food to the colonists as well as crops suitable for export were of course not unique to colonial India. In colonial Burkina Faso, French officials forced villagers to cultivate potatoes and green beans, forbidding the latter to sell their harvests. This forced cultivation was mainly pursued in order to bring the European garden to colonies.[68] European vegetable gardening became a mandatory subject of study at all local schools, intended to teach the local peasantry 'improved' farming techniques by the 1930s. As a result, a market developed for cultivated garden vegetables in place of gathered varieties.[69]

This desire to recreate a home-like situation in the colony made 'difference' the crux of colonial discourse–'beautiful' versus 'mundane.' This attitude was also nurtured by the Srirampur missionaries who otherwise took genuine interest in such matters like printing and publication. Way back in 1822, they encouraged people to grow plums, cherries, apricots, nectarines, strawberries, raspberries, and gooseberries in the Bengal Presidency. In return, the cultivators were promised a gold coin or hundred rupees, which was valued high in those days.[70] It was decided that individual British officials would distribute seeds to the gardeners who would then sow them. The missionaries began motivating cultivators by promising an award of fifty rupees for growing good peas, cauliflowers, potatoes, artichokes, and strawberries.[71] But even in 1827, members of Agricultural Society were thoroughly dissatisfied with the strawberries produced and no rewards were given.[72] However, within a year a

---

[67] Ibid.
[68] Susanne Friedberg, "French Beans for the Masses: A Modern Historical Geography of Food in Burkina Faso," in *The Cultural Politics of Food and Eating: A Reader* eds. James L. Watson and Melissa L. Caldwell (Malden, MA, Oxford, Victoria: Blackwell, 2005), 21–41.
[69] Ibid., 27–30.
[70] *Hindusthaner khetra* (Sreerampore, 1822), 225.
[71] Hindusthaner khetra, Sreerampore, 9 June, 1826, 236.
[72] Hindusthaner khetra, Sreerampore, 16 April, 1827, 244.

number of native gardeners succeeded in growing several 'exotic' vegetables. Lord Amherst, the Governor-General of India, gave out awards to those men in an award ceremony in Townhall.[73] Table 2 lists the names of the gardeners awarded and the crops they grew.

TABLE 2: Gardeners rewarded for growing exotic crops

Names of gardeners	Locality	Area of land	Vegetables grown
Nabakishore	Khidirpur	6/ bigha	cauliflower
Judhisthir	Khidirpur	4/ bigha	cauliflower, spinach, and carrot
Tinkari	Muchikhola	4/bigha	turnip, spinach, and peas
Joseph	Muchikhola	14/bigha	cauliflower and potato
Gangaram	Sonai	3/ bigha	cauliflower and turnip
Ramchandra	Sonai	3/bigha	potato
Kunchil	Muchikhola	2/bigha	potato and cauliflower
Iswar	Madhuli	3/bigha	potato and Chinese potato
Jaynarayan	Kedup	2/bigha	broccoli and cauliflower
Ramchand	Josli	3/bigha	potato
Biswanath	Shyambajar	2/bigha	capsicum
Lakshminarayan	Jaruli	3/bigha	potato and spinach
Ramchand	Nimta	3/bigha	peas and potato
Chidam	Gannia	1/bigha	turnip
Kalachand	Rampur	4/bigha	cauliflower and broccoli
Gour	Rampur	2/bigha	broccoli and cauliflower
Badar	Chandannagar	2/bigha	potato
Gopidhar	Akra	1/bigha	French bean
Shree	Muchikhola	4/bigha	turnip and bean
Ramchand	Gobra	3/bigha	peas and potato
Kalu	Alipur	2/bigha	peas and turnip
Kartik	--------	-----------	carrots and peas
Banamali	Akhra	1/bigha	French bean
Chhidam	Jarulia	3/bigha	carrots
Neelu	Sonai	4/bigha	French bean and spinach
Madan	Bardhitola	3/bigha	potato
Kunchil	Alipur	2/bigha	peas and broccoli
Swarup	Tengra	-----------	potato
Tanu	Alipur	3/bigha	turnip and French bean

[74]*Source:* see note 145

---

[73] *Hindusthaner khetra*, (Sreerampore, 16 June, 1828), 262.
[74] *Hindusthaner khetra* (Sreerampore, 16 January, 1828), 265–66.

Introducing 'Foreign' Food 47

This lengthy list of gardeners suggests the extent to which the colonial state was interested in introducing new food crops in the colony. The list shows how these experiments were carried out not just in Calcutta, but in several other places in Gangetic Bengal. These experiments were given a 'scientific and rational' basis by the Agri-Horticultural Society of India around the 1860s. The experiments that were carried out by peasants and cultivators themselves began to be institutionalised in a much more systematic manner. The nurseries of the Horticultural Gardens connected the rest of the world with the colony. In July 1859, the Society received a small assortment of seeds from North America and West Indies for experimental cultivation in its nursery garden.[75] These seeds included the 'finest Jamaican gynep,' which was considered to be much tastier than the leechee, upon which it was grafted; sapodilla, a fruit already well-known in West Indian fruit; Devereux grapes from Alabama; and American wild fruit Persimmon amongst others.[76] The results of these experiments were mixed. It was reported for instance, in the Horti-Floricultural exhibition held in the Town Hall on 31st March, 1859, that the asparagus and the artichokes that were cultivated were not up to the standard required.[77] The new variety of American long pod beans, on the other hand, grew in large quantities and was of excellent quality. Celery too had fine specimens, although it was grown in small quantity.

A similar experiment was also carried out with cocoa. The tropical climate of Latin America was thought to be similar to the tropical climate of India and different from the climate of the metropole. It was described thus:

> The cheap common beverage of the people in Central America, called "chocolate," is obtained from the seed of the cocoa plant, "Theobroma Cacao," which grows freely in the hottest climate of the country, between the tropics, at an elevation ranging from 50 to 3,000 feet above the sea level, and one kind found even at the higher altitude in favorable situations.[78]

It was recommended that cocoa should be grown in hilly places in India.[79] But contrary to the advice, the experiment was eventually carried out in

---

[75] Proceedings of 13th July, 1859, *Journal of the Agricultural & Horticultural Society of India*. Vol. xi; part II, ed. The Committee of Papers, Calcutta, July 1859–December 1860.
[76] Ibid., Lii-Liv.
[77] Ibid., xxx-xxxii.
[78] Letter from Capt. BeBourbel, R.E. to the Under Secretary of State for India, 11th August, 1869, Proceeding no. 1, Proceeding of Government of Bengal, Land Revenue Branch, Revenue Department, Calcutta, WBSA, February, 1870, 1-5.
[79] Ibid.

Botanical Gardens, situated on the Gangetic plains, close to Calcutta, thus a far cry from the hilly area recommendation. Naturally, the plants died.[80] These recurrent failures of new experiments in the colony were thus indicative of the loopholes in colonial knowledge-system and their mode of 'rational' agriculture.

RESPONSES TO COLONIAL POLITICAL ECONOMY: CRITIQUE AND APPROPRIATION

The responses of the middle-class to colonial experiments with the new food crops were multilayered. Their responses can neither be described as an unconditional acceptance nor as a total rejection. The Bengali middle-class adapted these new foodcrops in accordance with their own interests. In their reception of new fruits and vegetables they were often unorthodox. But when these experiments directly interfered with their staple diet, they resorted to a cultural critique of the colonial political economy.

The cultural perception of the Bengali middle-class revolved around rice. Paul Greenough rightly observes that in the cultural perception of the Bengali population, prosperity refers to the possession of stocks of paddy or paddy-wealth that enables one to feed another person.[81] Rice formed the staple of a Bengali diet and other food like vegetables, pulses, or fish were accompaniments rather than a main dish. Hence, any interference with rice meant the disruption of a lifeworld. Some, of course, made a critique of the administrative policies of the government for this disruption. However, this often melted into a romanticisation of the past, the pre-colonial, and what was imagined as a pure and unadulterated village life that nursed subsistence agriculture. What this romanticisation camouflaged was the murky side of this mythical past as well as the present. This critique also needs to be situated contextually. Objections to cultivate *Tetka* and *Chali* rice are pointers to this argument.

In the year 1875, British administration in Bengal tried to expand the cultivation of *Tetka* and *Chali* rice in Bengal. This rice was grown only in portions of Midnapore district. However even there this rice was not much

---

[80] Sub. Report from the Superintendent of the Botanical Gardens regarding the failure of the experimental cultivation of cocoa plant, Proceeding no. 23; Letter from Superintendent of Botanical Gardens to the Secretary of the Government of Bengal, 24th February, 1870, Proceedings of Government of Bengal, Land Revenue Branch, Revenue Department, Calcutta, March, 1870.

[81] Paul R. Greenough, *Prosperity and Misery in Modern Bengal: The Famine of 1943–44* (New York: Oxford University Press, 1982), 25.

valued on account of its small outturn and costs of cultivation.[82] The motive behind the introduction of these varieties of rice was the substitution of *Tetka* and *Chali* for *aman* paddy which grew in hundreds of variety. The colonial government tried to justify their motives by arguing that this substitution would ultimately benefit the cultivators.[83] However, inhabitants of those villages where these new forms of rice were to be introduced objected to this because they were already content with the *aman* crop they cultivated. The colonial government interpreted this attitude as ignorance, consequently rebuking the villagers as short-sighted.[84]

Nevertheless, experimental cultivation of *Tetka* and *Chali* rice began in *pargannah Mahesarah* in Bankura district in western Bengal.[85] The work of distribution was entrusted to the deputy collector, Jagatbandhu Khan. Khan's responsibility included explaining to people the advantages of *Tetka* and *Chali* rice, mode of cultivation to be adopted, and the nature of the soil on which this crop was to be grown. Two ninety-nine *maunds* and thirty-eight *seers* (32 ounces) of seed were advanced to two hundred and thirty-seven persons of sixty-three villages. The area to be sown with seed was one thousand one ninety-nine *beegahs* (1 *beegah*=0.33 acres=0.13 hectares) and ten *cottahs* (1 *beegah* = 20 *cottahs*). Apart from this, eight *maunds* of seed were given to Joykrishna Mukherjee of Uttarpara in Hooghly.[86] Even though satisfactory in the beginning, by the end of the year 1875, the experiment proved to be a failure. Hardly twenty-one *maunds* were produced from two *maunds* of seed grown on eight *beegahs* of land.[87]

---

[82] Letter from Baboo Joykishen Mookerjee, to Assistant Secretary to the Government of Bengal, Ooterpara, 11th February, 1875, Ooterpara, Colln. 6–12, Proceeding of the Government of Bengal, Branch II- Agriculture, Head No. 2- Produce and Cultivation, Financial Department, Calcutta, February 1875, 31.

[83] Letter from W.R. Larmince, Esq., Off. Collector of Bankoora, to the Commissioner of Burdwan Division, 3rd February, 1857, Burdwan, Proceeding No. 1623, Proceedings of Branch II- Agriculture. Head No. 2-Produce and Cultivation, Financial Department, Calcutta, March 1875, 36.

[84] Ibid.

[85] Letter from Sir W.J. Herschell, Bart, Off. Commissioner of Burdwan Division, to the Off. Secretary to the Government of Bengal, Financial Department, 30th July 1875, Proceeding no. 132, Proceedings of, Branch II, Agriculture. Head No. 2- Produce and Cultivation, Financial Department, Calcutta, August 1875, 53.

[86] Ibid.

[87] Letter from C.T. Buckland, Esq., Commissioner of Burdwan Division, to Secretary to the Government of Bengal, 16th December 1875, Proceeding no. 249, Proceedings of

It was not that *Tetka* and *Chali* were not grown in Bengal at all. However, the quantity cultivated was really small. It could by no means surpass the volume of rice already cultivated in Bengal. Objections of the cultivators to grow a form of rice that could hardly compare to the rice they already grew needs to be juxtaposed with the imaginary world of the Bengali middle-class. The latter took recourse to romanticising this lost world of the peasants. Peasants came to represent subsistence agriculture for the middle-class. However, soon cultivators themselves took a backseat and an 'imaginary' peasant world of abundance was created.

The steady decline of rice as a subsistence food crop in competition with jute was embedded in this imaginary world of abundance. Here, it becomes very difficult to separate the cultural critique from the political and economic one. Radhakamal Mukhopadhyay, who wrote a number of tracts on agricultural production under colonial rule in Bengal, categorically stated in around 1915 that only those crops were being cultivated that had the potential of being exported and sold at a high price in the foreign markets. This was the reason why the cultivators were forced to grow jute instead of rice.[88] Mukhopadhyay further wrote that since jute was not a foodcrop, jute cultivation inevitably resulted in a decline in the production of rice. He was extremely critical of the cultivation of jute on the soils that were used for rice production.[89] Mukhopadhyay's critique was definitely from a political-economic angle. But he was also aware of the emotive angle. He narrated a brief account to explain how the phenomenon of commercialisation of rice affected the lifeworld of ordinary people. A landlord, Mukhopadhyay wrote, once invited his subjects for lunch and offered them pieces of jute to eat. He told his subjects, 'How can I offer you anything other than what you grow in my land to eat? Since you have abandoned rice for jute, you cannot expect to eat anything other than jute.' The subjects apologised and began cultivating rice again.[90] The commercialisation of rice thus implied an intrusion into the lifeworld of the colonised.

A tract summarising the causes of famine and poverty in Bengal put it thus: 'A Bengali's life revolves around rice. Therefore rice is the staple food of the

---

Branch II-Agriculture, Head No. 2- Produce and Cultivation, Financial Department, Calcutta, WBSA, December 1875, 154–155.

[88] Radhakamal Mukhopadhyay, *Daridrer krandan* (Baharampur, 1915 [1322 BS]), 133–139.

[89] Ibid.

[90] Ibid.

Bengali race.'[91] For this author, famine in essence implied the scarcity of rice. This mourning for rice was also evident in journalist Panchkari Bandopadhyay's writings in 1915 (1322 BS). Bandopadhyay blamed the decline of subsistence agriculture for the scarcity of rice in colonial Bengal.[92] What needs to be observed here is that rice became a generic name for food; not just food, rice also began to signify a whole imagined life-style that was lost under the British rule. The names of *Annapurna* and *Lakshmi*, the bounty-providing deities were mentioned again and again in this context. *Annapurna* became a synonym for plenty and the present colonial rule became a synonym for dearth. Paul Greenough demonstrates that in the mythology of Bengal, *Lakshmi* has always been portrayed as a compassionate mother who took pity upon the poor and the suffering by blessing them with enough for subsistence.[93]

Greenough also maintains that according to the Bengalis, cooked rice is the best form of nourishment.[94] He endorses Ronald Inden and Ralph Nicholas' view that cooked rice is a symbol of the bodily substance that a family, as the co-sharers of the body of the living 'master' of the family, has in common.[95] Although the master does not cook rice, Greenough argues, he is the dispenser of rice, the giver of subsistence. It is by possessing the paddy, a symbol of abundance that a man becomes a master.[96]

While Greenough's argument about the cultural world of the Bengalis is partly true, it has to be contextualised. Greenough often assumes that this cultural perception made the famine (in this case he is discussing the famine of 1943–44) complicated for there was a contradiction between the imagination and the inherent reality of the Bengalis. However, it was the politico-economic situation under colonial governance that shaped this cultural world of the Bengalis. The Bengali middle-class constructed a discourse of abundance that had its basis in the economic context of colonial Bengal. Increasing

---

[91] Radhikanath Bandopadhyay, *Durbhikkha o daridrata: Karon anusandhan ebong nibaraner upay* (Calcutta, 1896/1897).

[92] Panchkari Bandopadhyay, *Panchkari Bandopadhyayer rachanabali*, Vol 2., eds. Brajendranath Bandopadhyay and Sajanikanta Das (Kolkata: Bangiya Sahitya Parishat, 1951 [1358 BS].

[93] Paul R. Greenough, *Prosperity and Misery in Modern Bengal: The Famine of 1943–44* (New York: Oxford University Press, 1982), 23.

[94] Ibid., 19.

[95] Ronald B. Inden and Ralph W. Nicholas, *Kinship in Bengali Culture* (Chicago: University of Chicago Press, 1977), cited in Greenough, *Prosperity*, 18–19.

[96] Ibid., 19–25

commercialisation of rice, which was a subsistence crop, and loss of rice fields due to the cultivation of cash crops, dealt a huge blow to the images of self-sustenance that the middle-class drew. This was evident in a lecture published in the newspaper *Mashik Basumati* around 1922.

> Bengalis were quite happy before the advent of British rule. Barn full of paddy, cows in the cowsheds, fish in one's own pond, and spinning wheels in every house– Bengalis never suffered from scarcity of rice and clothes. After that one could see a dearth of rice in the country of *Annapurna* (the rice-giving deity).[97]

Although this quote did not make a direct critique of the colonial rule, it is quite apparent that the author drew a sharp distinction between the pre-colonial and colonial times. Pre-British times were symbolised by abundance while the colonial period was held responsible for scarcity. It is in this context that political economy became intertwined with cultural perceptions. An onslaught on food crops affected the palette; colonial rule represented a disruption of the most basic aspect of life: diet.

An analysis of the middle-class romanticisation of rice, however, warrants a much more nuanced reading of the affective critique of the middle-class. There is no one strand that can give a shape to this critique. Romanticisation was also accompanied by a desire to stay away from a discourse that could perpetually bind them to subjection. A desire to move away from the label of 'rice-eater' led people like Baneswar Singha to urge Bengali peasants to grow crops like pulses and potatoes instead of rice, like the peasants in northern India.[98] It can be easily understood that Singha's arguments followed from the colonial distinction between the 'rice-eating' Bengalis and the 'wheat-eating' Punjabis. However, the line of argument that Singha drew can hardly be called affective. He made a critique of the cultivation of rice in Bengal on the ground that rice had lesser chances of survival than wheat and pulses in cases of scarcity.[99]

The middle-class discourse of taste cannot be explained only with a narrative of the romanticisation of a so-called past of abundance. At least some of the middle-class welcomed the change in their diet that followed the introduction of new fruits and vegetables in Bengal. Sometimes, of course, these new fruits

---

[97] Ratanmani Chattopadhyay, "Anna-samasya o Bangalir nischestata," a summary of the lecture delivered on the occasion of Bhabanipur Brahmo Samaj Bhadrotsav, *Mashik Basumati*, 2, no. 5 (February/March 1922 [Falgun 1329 BS]): 550–559.

[98] Baneswar Singha, *Durbhikkha nibaraner upay* (Srihatta, 1919 [1326 BS]).

[99] Ibid., 1–7.

and vegetables were not received because they were perceived to be 'foreign' food. But more often than not they seemed to be a welcome change to the diet of at least the middle-class–who can imagine a winter meal in contemporary Calcutta without cauliflowers and cabbages? Middle-class men began to take an initiative in growing these fruits and vegetables. Ibne Majuddin Ahmad, a devoted Muslim preacher, purchased seeds for cultivating cauliflowers and cabbages as well as imported manure in his village garden from the Gardening Association of Calcutta.[100] He also inspired students in his *madrasa* (Islamic educational institution) to grow British and American vegetables in the agricultural field.[101] Umesh Chandra Sen, for instance, wrote:

> One needs to sow 'foreign' seeds in order to produce admirable fruits and vegetables.--- W. Chu grew a watermelon in the gardens of Toms Lane in Calcutta, the size of this watermelon was much bigger than the watermelons of this country. Many rich people in Calcutta have grown gigantic sugarcanes. Therefore, these plants are not produced from seeds of this country.[102]

Sen's book had a detailed instruction for growing turnip, beet, broccoli, arrowroot, artichoke, celery, lettuce, leek, and squash.[103]

It might seem that Sen was all too elated by the introduction of new fruits and vegetables by the British colonial state in India. But actually Sen gave it a different twist. Of course, seeds for the new vegetables came from abroad and were sold by different nurseries in and around Calcutta. But the novelty lay not with the seeds, but with the climate of the colony. As Sen wrote, 'Our water and soil are so good that it can grow any plants whatsoever.'[104] It was the climate that made new vegetables and fruits taste so good. Sen and many others like him contradicted the view of the colonial state that tropical climate was not suitable for the production of new crops like Carolina rice. It should also be mentioned in this context that apart from forty varieties of 'fresh American seeds,' like cabbages and cauliflowers, nurseries like N.G. Chatterjee's Pikeparrah Nursery (established in 1869) or the Dum-dum nursery institutionalised and promoted sowing of vegetables that already existed in pre-colonial Bengal. These were vegetables like *chichinga* (snake gourd), *sags* (green leafy vegetables), *palla shasha* (an indigenous form of cucumber), *lao*(gourd), *jhinga* (ridge gourd)

---

[100] Ibne Majuddin Ahmad, *Amar sangsar-jiban* (Kolikata, 1914 [1321 BS]), 23.
[101] Ibid., 374–75.
[102] Umeshchandra Sen, *Krishi-chandrika*, Ist & 2nd part (Serampore, 1875), 63.
[103] Ibid., 69–118.
[104] Ibid., 63.

and the like.[105] Thus it was neither an involuntary acceptance nor a complete disregard for existing fruits and vegetables, but a synthesis of both that defined the Bengali middle-class cuisine. This adaptation took place at many levels.

It was stated in the *First Annual Report of the Agricultural Department of Bengal* in 1886 that bone meal produced excellent results when used as manure on rice and other crops, and this was being used even by the upper castes.

> Bone-meal was distributed among selected *talookdars* in *Burdwan*, and was used as manure on rice, and other crops, with beneficial results. Brahmins are now glad to take it in their clothes, with their own hands, though perfectly aware of what it is they are taking. The pundits have declared that there is no harm in their doing so. [106]

The use of animal bones or skins in food would have been considered a taboo by the upper caste Hindu Bengalis even thirty years back. In the year 1918, Baneswar Singha, who wrote quite a few tracts on agricultural production, also made a case for the use of bone-dust as manure.[107] This was a radical change in the mode of production. Bone-meal was used not only for new vegetables, like mangold, sugar-beet, turnip, and wheat, which were not native to Bengal,[108] but also for rice, which marked a physical barrier between the upper caste Bengalis and the lower castes. Boiled rice could be accepted only from someone who belonged to the same *jati* or caste[109]. One would not touch or eat rice cooked by a person belonging to the lower castes. However, it will be too simplistic to argue that social hierarchies withered away. Using bone-meal for rice cultivation was definitely a radical change. However, social stratifications remained.

Peasants, who mostly belonged to the lower castes, now bore the brunt of the middle-class. They were rebuked for ignoring the cultivation of 'exotic' vegetables. In fact, cultivators were now blamed for conservatism. Haladhar Guha, who wrote several tracts on agriculture, called the cultivators lazy and orthodox as they did not try out new food crops.[110] However, Irfan Habib

---

[105] Advertisement in *The Indian Mirror*, 12th May, 1897; 18th May, 1897, Calcutta edition.
[106] *First Annual Report of the Director of the Agricultural Department, Bengal* (Calcutta, 1886), 23.
[107] Baneswar Singha, *Krishi-prabandha* (Srihatta, 1918), 119.
[108] Ibid.
[109] Ronald B. Inden and Ralph W. Nicholas, *Kinship in Bengali Culture* (Chicago: University of Chicago Press, 1977), 50.
[110] Haladhar Guha, *Krishiniyamabali o jamidari mahajani hisheb* (Dhaka, 1875),3.

maintains in his essay on Mughal India that not only did Indian peasants grew innumerable crops, India was prepared to accept new crops as well. The rapid spread of crops introduced first by the Portuguese and later by the British was made possible by the peasants.[111] Subsistence agriculture became a theme of the pre-colonial world, which was romanticised by the middle-class. Subodhkinkar Nanda Majumdar was astonished that the responsibility for a sacred work like agriculture could be taken up by the 'trivial, illiterate peasants.'[112] Social hierarchies were being defined differently. This new rhetoric was part of a hegemonic project of the middle-class by which they portrayed themselves as the true modern, willing to try out new things. Jaminiranjan Majumdar, who gave detailed instruction on potato cultivation, blamed the peasants for insufficient cultivation of potato.[113]

Although several people wrote instruction manuals on the cultivation of 'exotic' crops, it has to be acknowledged, that until very recently, these fruits and vegetables were unavailable in the markets of Calcutta. Even when such fruits and vegetables were sold in the Calcutta market, it obviously meant that these foodstuffs were brought over from the hilly tracts of northern Bengal. In these hilly tracts, like Darjeeling and Kalimpong (often the summer residence of the British), peasants who were described as 'illiterate and lazy' by people like Haladhar Guha and Subodhkinkar Nanda Majumdar grew those fruits that were being adopted gradually by the Bengali middle-class. Amongst the fruit trees grown by the cultivators in places like Kalimpong, Siliguri, and Kurseong, one could find oranges, Washington navel oranges, pears, pineapples, raspberries, pomegranates, plums, strawberries, and peaches. Amongst these fruit trees, the cultivation of oranges and pineapples on these hills expanded on a tremendous scale. Every year at least thousands of such trees were planted all over the district.[114] Even in Gangetic Bengal, like in Nadia and Murshidabad, *goalas* (milkmen) regularly sowed Japanese millet.[115]

---

[111] Irfan Habib, 'Mughal India', 217–218.

[112] Subodh Kinkar Nanda Majumdar, "Krishi o sar 'kopir chash'," *Grihasthamangal* 3rd year, no. 9 (Kolikata, Poush 1336 BS [c.December/January 1930]): 290–294.

[113] Jaminiranjan Majumdar, *Alur chash* (Kolikata, 1335BS[c.1929]).

[114] Report on the Agricultural Demonstration Works undertaken in the Government Estates of Kalimpong, Siliguri, Kurseong, and Sadar Subdivisions for the year 1929-30; *Annual Report of the Department of Agriculture, Bengal for the year 1929-30*; Agriculture and Industries Department, Agriculture Branch(Calcutta, 1930), 158-163.

[115] Appendix III, Annual Report of the Second Economic Botanist, Bengal, for the year 1929-30, *Agricultural and Industries Department, Agriculture Branch for the year ending 1929-30* (Calcutta, 1930), 52-54.

CONSUMING PASSION: NEW EATING PLACES AND THE SEDUCTION OF BISCUITS

For many Indians, consuming 'new' food was not always possible within the domestic space. For them, the new hotels and the restaurants that sprang up in Calcutta from the nineteenth century held such temptations. These hotels formed a convenient locus for those who could easily gorge into a chicken cutlet without being concerned about polluting their home. At the same time, the pleasures of eating out could be realised in these new public eateries. All over India, these eateries at first served as meeting places for the Anglo Indians. Coffee houses were set up for them, serving ices and sherry-cobblers.[116] However, such beverages as well as the coffee houses were chiefly for the benefit of the British residing in India. The Spences' hotel was one of the first hotels established in Calcutta in the 1830s. It later transformed into a limited company owned by both the British and the Indians in the 1860s. In 1841, a second hotel emerged, named the Auckland Hotel, which later became the famous Great Eastern Hotel. It was here that Bipin Chandra Pal the nationalist, and his friends often visited. By the 1870s and 1880s, Bengalis had started taking an active interest in the hotel business in European quarters. Sen Brothers, for instance, started the hotel Esplanade in 1874 and another the next year.[117] By the 1940s, several small eating places cropped up in Calcutta. These were tiny eateries like 'Basanta Cabin' serving toast and boiled egg, and 'Chachar Hotel,' all ran by Bengalis. Two other small Bengali hotels called 'Café-de-Monico,' and 'Bengal Restaurant' were established around 1936. Some other eateries called '*pice* hotel' (where a full meal was supposedly served for 1/16th of a rupee) or '*bhater* hotel' (rice hotels where daily meals were served) catering to people with small budgets, chiefly students, also emerged by the 1940s. These places served meals consisting of rice at a cheap price.[118] In Bibhutibhshan Bandopadhyay's (1894–1950) accredited novel, *Adarsha Hindu Hotel* (Ideal Hindu Hotel), the hotel was primarily like a rice hotel, where daily meals were served for daily wage earners and other office-goers.[119] This hotel

---

[116] William Knighton, *Tropical Sketches – or Reminiscences of an Indian Journalist*, Vol. 1 (London, 1855), 150-151.

[117] B.V. Roy, "Calcutta, Old and New: Taverns and Hotels," *The Calcutta Municipal Gazette xlv, No. 3* (Calcutta, 14 December 1946): 45–46.

[118] Pratulchandra Gupta, *Alekhya darshan* (Kolkata, 1990), 30–43.

[119] Bibhutibhshan Bandopadhyay, "Adarsha Hindu Hotel," in *Upanayas Samagra*. Vol. 1 (Kolkata: Mitra o Ghosh, 2005), first published in 1940, 292–408.

Introducing 'Foreign' Food   57

was situated near the railway station so that commuters could easily avail of the facility. Although not one of the high-end hotels, this hotel was divided hierarchically into the first class and the second class.[120] While those who ate at the first class could get better quality food like split green gram, those who ate at the second class could only aim for a combination of red gram and split black gram.[121] Often the latter's lentil soup would be mixed with rice starch to make up for the diminishing quantity if it became less than the number of heads who ate.[122] Mukhopadhyay's novel portrayed how these rice hotels functioned and held up the image of an ideal rice hotel where everyone would get to eat similar meals.

IMAGE 2: "Basanta Cabin College Street". Advertisement in *Anandabazar Patrika* (Kolkata, 1937 [1343 BS]).

Notes: Image 2 shows an image of *Basanta Cabin*, a small eatery in Calcutta. Even such small eateries as this became distributors of tea, which was becoming a craze almost cutting across classes.
(*Courtesy*: Visual Archive of the CSSSC)

---

[120] Ibid., 321.
[121] Ibid., 381.
[122] Ibid., 321.

Definition of food changed in relation to the public and the private. Pal also wrote about how the public/private divide dominated the consumption scenario in Calcutta. Pal stayed in a hostel when he first came to Calcutta from Sylhet in eastern Bengal. Residents in such hostels were not allowed to bring in food that could hurt Hindu sentiments. However, loaves and biscuits had become quite common in Calcutta and these were not forbidden in the hostel. Residents could of course consume whatever they wished, outside the hostel.[123] Pal and his friends found new pleasures of gastronomy in these newly emerging hotels. Later, Pal, forced to be on a vegetarian diet after his mother's death, followed it only at home. But as he told us, his evening meals always consisted of boiled eggs and crabs that he relished in the public eateries.[124] There was thus a sharp distinction between what one consumed at home and what one ate in the public eateries. However, notions of the public and the private also need to be problematised in this context. A hostel, which was considered a 'public' place as opposed to home, had rigid rules for food, whereas at least some like the Tagores and other upper middle-class Hindus had started enjoying 'new' food at their home. But generally speaking, newly emerging hotels served as abodes of gastronomic pleasure. These eateries not only introduced new food, they also changed eating habits.

Bholanath Mukhopadhyay's satirical text *Apnar mukh apuni dekho* sums up the pleasures of eating in a public eatery. In an imaginary conversation between two friends it is brought out that eating in a restaurant was a learning experience for a Bengali who has recently learned to take pleasure from new gastronomic practices. Even if one did not know the name for a particular item of food they could find it out from the display list at a restaurant.[125] Mukhopadhyay was extremely critical of what he described as 'worm-infested ham' served in the restaurants, but did admit that eating at a public eatery raised the social status of the colonial middle-class.[126]

New pleasures had a much broader social spread even if to a limited extent. Since many of these foodstuffs were produced on a large scale their price was naturally quite low. As a result new food like tea could be consumed even by those at the lower rung of the social ladder. That even the poorest took delight

---

[123] Ibid.
[124] Ibid.
[125] Bholanath Mukhopadhyay, *Apnar mukh apuni dekho* (Kolkata: Prajnabharati, 1982 [1389 BS]), 62, first published in 1863.
[126] Ibid.

in having tea can be found in a number of Bengali novels of the period. Thus the pleasures in a sense cut across class and caste boundaries, which were loathed by a number of indigenous elites. Biscuits became immensely significant on its account of being labeled a forbidden food and hence heavily tempting.

Bipin Pal describes in his autobiography this introduction of new food like loaves and biscuits. Sylhet, where Pal lived when he was a child, had only two bakeries, unlike Calcutta.[127] Pal narrates an incident that proves how seductive the dance of new food was.

> It was just before the Pujas. I had an attack of fever; and had been put on a liquid diet for about a week. Though I was then free from fever, my father would not let me have solid food yet. And I was ravenously hungry. I appealed to my nephew from Calcutta to get something from the baker's. At night-fall he went out quietly and brought some hot and crisp biscuits, the very smell and touch of which made my mouth water profusely. But I dared not to take these immediately, lest I should be discovered in the act by my father who was very inquisitive about what we took, especially when we were unwell. So I put these away on the top of the mosquito-curtain over my bed, and waited for the time when my father would retire to bed and I would find the coast clear for my dinner. Now, my bed was set by a door facing the pond in our outer yard. It was rather a close evening; and my father after taking his meals, took up his huble-buble and sat on my bed, and gradually moved up to its very centre, and reclining on my pillow, commenced to enjoy his after-dinner smoke. At the sight of my father in this position, all my wits seemed to leave me. I was in a terrible funk. What would be my fate, if when he had finished his smoking and wanted to go to bed, he should stand up and discover my stock of hot biscuits over his head! I was not hopelessly lacking in mental resources; and taking off my shirt and throwing it on the top of the mosquito-curtain from the other side of the partition that separated my bed from my father's *farash*, I commenced to complain of a feeling of chill and called out to the servants to fetch my shirt. But where could those poor people find it? So I commenced to search for it myself; and after looking a bit here and there, at last went up to my bed at the back of my father, and saying that I had found it on the top of the mosquito-net, rolled up the incriminating things in it and ran out with the bundle to another room, and lay low there until my father had retired, when we had our own little forbidden feast.[128]

---

[127] Bipin Chandra pal, *Memories of My Life and Times: In the Days of My Youth (1857–1884)*, vol. 1 (Calcutta: Modern Book Agency, 1932), 135.
[128] Ibid., 135–136.

This apparently facetious anecdote reveals a fundamental fact about the changes in gastronomic culture in colonial India. That Pal did not throw away the biscuits and ultimately relished them in spite of the potential threat of being caught by his father proves that new food had carved its niche in society. What really captured the imagination of the people was tea. In this context, endeavors of The Indian Tea Association to popularise tea were successful indeed.[129] In fact, as Lizzy Collingham argues, tea often improved intercommunal relations. It was considered to be free from the burden of purity associations and hence easier to share with members of other castes.[130]

IMAGE 3: 'Sabai pete pare' "Anyone can have Indian tea which is the pride and pleasure of India." Advertisement by ITMEB in *Jugantar* (Kolkata, 05.02.1939).

Notes: Image 3 illustrates how the advertisements tried to capture the attention of the mass. This advertisement kept harping on the fact that five cups of Indian tea could be consumed for only one *paisa* (penny), thus making it possible for a large number of people to consume it. In its appeal to such a broad spectrum of population, capitalism created a new social bonding through consumption of new food like tea.
(*Courtesy*: Subodh Bose and the Visual Archive of the CSSSC)

---

[129] Gautam Bhadra, *From an Imperial Product to a National Drink: The Culture of Tea Consumption in Modern India* (Calcutta: Centre for Studies in Social Sciences, Calcutta, in association with Tea Board India, 2005).

[130] Lizzy Collingham, *Curry: A Biography* (London: Chatto and Winders, 2005),201.

Evidently, at least a large segment of the middle-class took delight in the 'new' food that came with colonialism. However, this new food was appropriated within the fold of domestic cuisine in Bengali homes. Bengali cuisine as such never took up a public character even though the gastronomic culture in Bengal underwent a radical transformation for all time to come.

2

The Cosmopolitan and the Regional
Understanding Bengali Cuisine

Changing eating patterns in colonial Bengal revolved around the issues of hybridity and authenticity. These issues operated at two levels. On one level British food was appropriated within the fold of 'traditional' cuisine to create a modern cuisine. In this context, some of the indigenous elites clamoured for retaining the 'authenticity' of food, while some of them welcomed new food. However, both these positions need to be problematised. Curry powder was accepted only as a new ingredient for cooking and was regarded by the Bengali cookbook writers to be a figment of the British imagination. On the other hand, both British and Bengali ingredients were combined to create a 'hybrid' recipe; but proving the 'hybrid' to be 'authentic' became a primary concern. Thus hybridity and authenticity were merely flip sides of the same coin. At another level, the middle-class imagined a romantic past of plenitude for themselves. This imagery created an organic history for the middle-class wherefrom the question of 'authentic' cuisine emerged. At the same time, this middle-class also succumbed to pleasures of modernity and the hybrid cuisine that emanated from it. All these issues played out at the level of rhetoric as well as the material culture of the middle-class. This gastronomic culture was definitely cosmopolitan if by cosmopolitan we imply the proclivity to embrace the global. However, cosmopolitanism itself is a loaded term and it can have as much implications for the global as for the regional. This chapter will show that the cosmopolitan in a sense contributed to the making of what one might label the regional, in this case, 'Bengaliness' of the middle-class and their taste.

WHAT'S IN A NAME? MAKING OF A 'NEW' CUISINE

A thoroughbred analysis of cookbooks is necessary in order to understand the nature of cosmopolitanism of Bengali cuisine. The first Bengali cookbook *Pakrajeswar* came out in 1831. The next book that followed was *Byanjan-ratnakar* in 1858. In 1879 another book called *Pakprabandha* was published, which was written by an anonymous Bengali woman. However, the book that first became significant as a Bengali cookbook was written by Bipradas Mukhopadhyay (1842–1914). This was *Soukhin khadya–pak* published in 1889. Later the two volumes of *Soukhin khadya-pak* were combined and published as *Pakpranali*. Before this, Mukhopadhyay published a monthly periodical of recipes called *Pak pranali* in 1883. The next significant Bengali cookbook that came out around 1900 was Prajna Sundari Devi's (1870–1950) *Amish o Niramish Ahar*, volume 1. The second volume of *Amish* was also published around the same time and the third volume, which was mostly a discussion of non-vegetarian recipes, came out in the year 1907.

Although they wrote in Bengali, the authors of *Pakrajeswar* and *Byanjan-ratnakar* were not writing for the general Bengali population. These cookbooks were written under the patronage of the king of Burdwan (a district of Bengal).[1] Sripantha, who compiled and edited these two texts, wrote in the introduction to the texts that the authors of these two recipe books drew heavily on recipes from the Mughal period; they were definitely not writing a book of everyday Bengali recipes. The recipes had a heavy overtone of Farsi influence and were mostly oriented towards non-vegetarian dishes, especially fowl and mutton.[2] In Sripantha's opinion, this absence of what he considers 'Bengali influence' is hardly unusual given the fact that the king of Burdwan, the patron of these cookbook writers, hailed from Lahore and not from Bengal. Hence, there was a distinct 'Mughal' influence on the cookbooks.[3] While there is no denying the fact that there was an overt influence of *Mughlai* cuisine on the writers of *Pakrajeswar* and *Byanjan-ratnakar*, it is debatable if there is at all any form of Bengali cuisine that can be deemed devoid of any other influence. Even

---

[1] Bisweshar Tarkalankar, *Pakrajeswar*, 2nd ed. (Kolikata, 1879 [1286 BS]) in *Pakrajeswar o byanjan- ratnakar*, ed. Sripantha (Kolkata, 2004), first published in 1831; Anon., *Byanjan-ratnakar*, 1st ed. (Kolikata, 1858), in Sripantha *ed., Pakrajeswar o byanjan-ratnakar* (Kolkata, 2004).

[2] Sripantha, introduction to *Pakrajeswar o byanjan- ratnakar* (Kolkata, 2004).

[3] Ibid.

the 'Mughal' or 'Persian' component in *Pakrajeswar* and *Byanjan-ratnakar* is often given a local flavour. Mutton recipes described there hardly prescribed the use of onion or garlic, something frequently used in *Mughlai* cuisine. The author of *Pakrajeswar* clearly stated that since people in the region hardly consumed onion, he had refrained from listing it as an essential ingredient in the recipes.[4] *Byanjan-ratnakar* also did not include onion and garlic in its repertoire of recipes. It can be understood that the readers of *Pakrajeswar* were mostly Hindus who were not very accustomed to having garlic and onion in their food as yet. Another section contained recipes of wheat products, which were absent in recipe books published later. *Pakprabandha*, which came out in 1879 and was later edited by Pyarimohan Kabibhushan, was quite different from the two earlier books in the sense it incorporated garlic and onion in its recipes. It was, in all probability, written by a woman who did not want her name to be published.[5] Increase in the uses of onion and garlic for recipes supposedly written for the Bengali middle-class Hindus already began to show changes in diet patterns among the middle-class in colonial Bengal.

The first most popular Bengali recipe book was Bipradas Mukhopadhyay's *Soukhin Khadya-Pak,* which was published in 1889. As already stated, Mukhopadhyay had published a monthly periodical of recipes called *Pakpranali* in 1883. Later, Mukhopadhyay compiled them into a single volume by the same name in 1887/88 (1304 BS).[6] A thorough discussion of both Mukhopadhyay's and Prajnasundari Devi's cookbooks is needed in order to understand how hybridity defines the cosmopolitanism of Bengali cuisine. Both Mukhopadhyay's and Prajnasundari's cookbooks are classic examples of the changing diet of the Bengalis. The vegetable recipes that Mukhpadhyay described were mostly made from vegetables already available in India. However, he did have recipes on cabbage and cauliflower, which were new vegetables. Since cabbage was a new vegetable, Mukhopadhyay deemed it necessary to first introduce cabbage to his readers.

---

[4] *Pakrajeswar,* 11

[5] Pyarimohan Kabibhushan, ed. , *Pakprabandha* (Kolikata, 1934).

[6] Bipradas Mukhopadhyay, *Pak pranali* (Kolikata, 1928 [1335 BS]), first published in 1887 [1304 BS]). Shibram Chakrabarty, the satirist, in a fictional account narrated the protagonist's total lack of culinary skills and eventual failure in attempting to cook an onion soup according to a recipe from *Pak pranali*. For further reference, see Shibram Chakrabarty, "Pakpranalir bipak", in *Shibram Rachana Samagra*, complete edition, vol. 2 (Kolikata: Annapurna Prakashani, 1991[1398 BS]), 208-212, first published in 1985 [1392 BS].

Mukhopadhyay tried to make his readers aware of different categories of cabbage, like drumhead and sugar loop. One can also know from *Pak pranali* that cabbage seeds were brought into India every year from abroad. A detailed discussion of how to choose and clean a cabbage precedes the recipes in the first volume of *Pak pranali*, the periodical: this discussion became imperative since cabbage was a new vegetable.[7] In the periodical, as well as the cookbook, so-called Bengali recipes happily co-existed with 'new' recipes, which ranged from British to Italian to French cuisines. Recipes included Jewish fried fish, Italian mutton, French mutton cutlet, English chop, plum pudding, ginger pudding, hasty pudding, orange jelly, Irish stew, orange custard, French toast and the like. What has to be noted in this context is that the nomenclature itself was becoming hybrid. For example, Mukhopadhyay had recipes for English *bhuni khichuri* (*Khichuri* was a dish made of rice, lentil, and spices consumed commonly by people all over India) and English shik kebab (shik kebab, again, was a form of skewered mutton generally eaten by the Muslims in India).[8] When the British came to India they came to thoroughly enjoy *Khichri/Khichuri*.[9] Mukhopadhyay went one step further and gave an English flavor to an Indian dish. It was thus a constant process of hybridisation where both the British elements as well as the 'Indian' elements were retained.

This play of nomenclature is perhaps most evident in both Mukhopadhyay's and Prajnasundari's use of the term 'curry.' The authenticity and meanings of the term curry have been debated upon by scholars. In her discussion of the Indian diaspora, Uma Narayan traces the question of authenticity to colonial India where curry was basically constructed as a hodge-podge of Indian spices.[10] This imagined 'Indian cuisine' traveled to Britain and gained popularity among the British there who claimed that the curry powder sold in Britain was much more authentic than the Indian version of curry powder.[11] However, for the colonial residents in India, a love for curry was not that easy, since they were preoccupied with keeping their racial purity intact within the colony. Narayan

---

[7] Bipradas Mukhopadhyay, *Pak Pranali*, vol. 1 (Kolikata, 1883), 98–100.

[8] Bipradas Mukhopadhyay, *Pak Pranali*, 175, 357.

[9] David Burton, *The Raj at Table: A Culinary History of the British in India* (London, Boston: Faber and Faber, 1993), 83-85; Lizzy Collingham, *Curry: A Biography* (London: Chatto and Winders, 2005), 119.

[10] Uma Narayan, "Eating Cultures: Incorporation, Identity, and Indian Food," in *Dislocating Cultures/ Identities, Traditions, and Third-World Feminism* (New York and London: Routledge, 1997), 161–219.

[11] Ibid., 166.

here is concerned with the hybridity of curry. In her opinion, the curry that is called authentic in Britain was after all a product of British imagination. This construction of authenticity, as Narayan argues, lingers into the post-colonial era, through the imaginings of the diasporic population as to what constitutes authenticity. At the same time non-diasporic population imagines certain types of food as stereotypically Indian and therefore 'authentic.'[12]

Parama Roy is also concerned with the hybridity of food, but in a slightly different manner. In her work on the Indian diaspora, and particularly Madhur Jaffrey, the popular Indian-born British food writer, Roy dwells upon the question of authenticity of food.[13] Jaffrey, Roy argues, is most critical of the so-called Indianness of 'curry.' In one of her books, Jaffrey ridiculed curry powder as a random mixture of spices that was made by an Indian chef for his colonial master when he left for England.[14] While sneering at the curry powder as inauthentic, Jaffrey herself referred to some of the curry powders sold in Britain. In many of her recipes, she herself recommends curry powder for what she considered to be authentic Indian recipes. This staying power of curry, according to Roy, unsettles its authenticity. Authenticity thus needs to be contextualised. It is a particular situation that leads to a demand for authenticity. Just the way a random curry powder became a metaphor for authentic Indian food in the colonial period, Roy argues, for many Indian restaurants in the West in recent times, so-called curry powder became an easy way to toss up authentic Indian food. The concept of authentic India holds some archetypal images for the west. This image was constructed by the diasporic Indians for the West. The Indianness of curry powder in Roy's opinion was what the Indian chef wanted the British to believe.[15] While Narayan and Roy have definitely explored the fluidity of both British and Indian identity through an analyses of curry, a further dissection of the term actually tends to problematise identity politics even further.

The term curry' found place in *Pakpranali*. We get to know about recipes such as lamb curry, egg curry, prawn curry, and English rohu fish curry in Mukhopadhyay's cookbook. He liberally uses onion and garlic in these

---

[12] Ibid.

[13] Parama Roy, "Reading Communities and Culinary Communities: The Gastropoetics of the South Asian Diaspora," *Positions: East Asia Cultures Critique 10, No.2* (2002): 471–502.

[14] Madhur Jaffrey, *An Invitation to Indian Cooking* (New York: Vintage Books, 1973; Reprint New York, 1975), 6, cited in Roy, Op cit.

[15] Roy, "Reading Communities and Culinary Communities".

recipes.[16] However, for Mukhopadhyay curry had an entirely different definition, quite different from what the British recipe writers suggested. Mukhopadhyay defined curry thus: 'Europeans learnt to cook "curry" from the Jews and the Jews learnt it from the Muslims.'[17] When Mukhopadhyay wrote recipes for curry, he was quite emphatic that he was either following the Muslims or the English. He did not consider curry to be a Hindu dish and hence put it within quotes. He wrote that the English did not use ground spices in their curry and invented something called the 'Calcutta-curry-powder.' The Calcutta-curry-powder was composed of a mixture of one tablespoon of poppy seeds, one tablespoon of turmeric powder, half teaspoon red chili powder, half tea spoon cumin, and one tea spoon salt.[18]

Lizzy Collingham argued that curry was created for the British in India.[19] Her interpretation of curry is of course drawn from her readings of Anglo-Indian memoirs and cookbooks. However, it seems from Mukhopadhyay's account that the colonised were eager to erase all connections with curry. Hence Mukhopadhyay connected curry to a different trajectory. Although Prajnasundari was not so emphatic about severing ties with curry, she hardly used the English formulaic recipe for curry, which was generally made out of a hodge-podge of spices called curry powder.[20] Prajnasundari used different recipes for curry and these recipes were applied to quintessentially Bengali vegetables like *enchor* (raw jackfruit) and *mocha* (banana flower) and fishes like *hilsa* and *parshe*.[21] She used different spices for each recipe of curry. Her play with name in this context again is noteworthy. She named one dish '*firingi* [Anglo-Indian] *curry*' even though she uses *patol* [wax gourd], a vegetable native to Bengal in this item.[22] Neither *firingi*, nor curry can be called either British or Bengali, but hybrid. This hybridity was a product of colonial modernity and the reason for cosmopolitanism of the colonial middle-class.

Although Mukhopadhyay claimed that curry did not originate in India and hence cannot exactly be called an Indian dish (here Mukhpadhyay equated

---

[16] Mukhopadhyay, *Pak-Pranali*, 276-279.
[17] Ibid., 272.
[18] Ibid., 273.
[19] Lizzie Collingham, *Curry: A Biography* (London: Chatto and Winders, 2005), 118.
[20] Prajnasundari Debi, *Amish o niramish ahar*, vols 1 & 2 (Kolkata: Ananda Publishers, 2000), first published in 1907.
[21] Prajnasundari Debi, *Amish o niramish ahar*, vol. 1, 336, vol. 2, 236, 245.
[22] Prajnasundari Debi, *Amish o niramish ahar*, vol. 2, 235.

India with Hindus), he was not necessarily writing under the pretense of making a so-called authentic and indigenous cuisine. Apart from a large number of Mughlai recipes (still without onion and garlic), Mukhopadhyay's book had a number of recipes from other regions of India. He stated that yellow lentils grew better in northern India rather than in Bengal. Hence it tasted better, if cooked in a Hindustani (non-Bengali, specifically north Indian) way. In its recipe, Mukhopadhyay incorporated asaphoetida, which was not used frequently in Bengali cuisine as yet.[23] Similarly he included recipes for Kashmiri lentils and Gujarati dishes in his cookbook. Nowhere in the book did Mukhopadhyay have any pretense that he was venturing to construct a national cuisine. He never tried to find a connection between different categories of cuisine he had in his recipe book. His reading public was definitely the Bengali middle-class and Mukhopadhyay here was making possible various avenues for creating a Bengali cuisine that would ultimately be a gastronomic delight.

Kiranlekha Ray, whose book *Jalkhabar* came out in c.1924, demonstrated similar trends in writing recipes.[24] Her recipes were very much like Mukhopadhyay's and Prajnasundari's, including recipes from other regions of India. A significant feature of her recipe book was that whenever she described a recipe that did not have an Indian name, she put the word in English script next to the Bengali script. If she wrote omelet in Bengali, it was always followed by the word omelet in English within parenthesis. These included a number of words: ice-cream, ice-cream custard, cake cream, apple charlotte, apple jelly, apple mincemeat, potato mince pie, Worcestershire sauce, egg snow, cottage pie, marmalade, pudding, trifle, cutlet, custard, Christmas cake, Christmas pudding, croquette, chocolate éclairs, grilled chicken, chicken hotpot, cheese fritters, jam tart, tapioca cream, fricassee, and the like. Similarly when Ray used highly technical terms such as crystallisation, amorphous, and fermentation, she preferred to write it in English. Ray made a distinction between what was foreign and what was not by her emphasis on the use of language. However, she showed considerable courage in making so-called traditional recipes foreign. Although Saratchandra Ray, Kiranlekha's husband, professed in the introduction to her cookbook that the recipes for yogurt and *sandesh* given by Kiranlekha were authentic recipes from *Varendrabhumi* (northern Bengal), Kiranleka put vanilla and strawberry essences in these preparations.[25] What

---

[23] Mukhopadhyay, Op cit., 118–119.
[24] Kiranlekha Ray, *Jalkhabar*, ed. Aruna Chattopadhyay (1924; repr., Kolikata, 2000).
[25] Ray, *Jalkhabar*, 65.

needs to be mentioned in this context is that *sandesh*, something claimed to be authentic Bengali by Ray, was made from *chhana* or cottage cheese that the Portuguese brought into Bengal.[26]

Binapani Mitra's book *Randhansanket* was published much later, in 1955. In her introduction to the book, she claimed that she had written these recipes much earlier, and her children persuaded her to publish them in the form of a cookbook.[27] Even though, unlike Mukhopadhyay, she did not have a lengthy discussion on curry, it seems that Mitra did not consider curry itself to be authentically Indian. It needs to be mentioned that Mitra had curry recipes for fish like *koi*, which was only found in Bengal.[28] However, Mitra's *koi* curry did not contain the curry powder that was used in Anglo-Indian cuisine. She simply used ground onion, ginger, turmeric, and *ghee* or clarified butter for the *koi* curry. But she, like Kiranlekha Ray, is quite indifferent to the supposed purity of food. Mitra's book had recipes for such hybrid food like *khirer* toffee (thickened-milk toffee).[29]

A comparison of so-called English recipes given by the Bengali middle-class such as Prajnasundari Devi, along with those given by British residents in India will help us ascertain how much innovation the colonial middle-class indulged in while cooking non-indigenous food. Table 1.3 compares recipes for custard sauce, plum pudding, arrowroot pudding, and tipsy pudding given by an Englishwoman residing in India in the mid-nineteenth century with the same recipes given by Prajnasundari Devi.

The comparison shows emphatically that the latter contains more detailed and elaborate instructions on how to make specific food items. The addition of more spices, especially spices such as nutmeg or cloves is more clearly noticeable in the recipes given by Prajnasundari Devi. Even while she stuck to the basic recipe, the addition of *ghee* to her puddings makes her ingenuity and creativity worthy of mention. However, she was not unique in this respect. Such playing around with ingredients can be noticed in most recipes published by the middle-class from late nineteenth century. In fact, this hybridity of gastronomy was also clearly visible in the gastronomic culture of the British residents in India as we will see in the final section of this chapter.

---

[26] K.T. Achaya, *Indian Food: A Historical Companion* (Delhi: Oxford University Press, 1994), 132.
[27] Binapani Mitra, *Randhansanket* (Kokata, 1955).
[28] Ibid., 126–127.
[29] Ibid., 246.

TABLE 3: Comparison of recipes

Recipes by Englishwoman in India[30]	Recipes by Prajnasundari Devi[31]
CUSTARD SAUCE	CUSTARD SAUCE
Ingredients: • ½ pint new milk, boiled with two ounces of sugar • A bit of cinnamon *Method:* Flavour with vanilla essence, or almond if preferred; add the well-beaten yolks of 5 eggs, and a little salt, with a tablespoon of cold milk, and stir over the fire till thick; whisk to a froth.[32]	*Ingredients:* • 3 white onions • two eggs • a spoonful of clarified butter (*ghee*) • ½ a teaspoon of salt • six tablespoon milk • one lime or one tablespoon vinegar • 1½grams cinnamon • 3 cloves, one small cardamom, • 8-10 celery leaves • one tablespoon flour *Method:* Slice the onions into four, steam them and mince them. Pour ghee into the saucepan. Put in onions and whole spices. After stirring for a while add some milk. Add celery and salt. After it comes to a boil add some flour mixed with water. When the mixture thickens add vinegar.[33]
PLUM PUDDING	PLUM PUDDING
Ingredients: • 6 ounces chopped beef suet • 6 ounces raisins • 8 ounces currants • 3 ounces flour • 3 ounces bread-crumbs • 5 eggs • Little nutmeg, ginger, mace, and cinnamon	*Ingredients:* • One or two stale bread of about 250 grams • 250 grams flour • 125 grams of lard • 90 grams candied peel • 30 nuts • 3 eggs • 60 grams currants • 60 grams raisins

---

[30] A Lady Resident, *The Englishwoman in India: Containing Information for the Use of Ladies Proceeding to, or Residing in, The East Indies, Or the Subjects of Their Outfit, Furniture, Housekeeping, The Rearing of Children, Duties and Wages of Servants, Management of the Stables, And Arrangements for Travelling. To which are added Receipts for Indian Cookery*, 2nd ed. (London: Smith, Elder And Co., 65, Cornhill, 1865).

[31] Prajnasundari Debi, *Amish o niramish*, vol. 2.

[32] A Lady Resident, *The Englishwoman*, 162.

[33] Prajnasundari, *Amish o niramish*, vol. 2, 118.

The Cosmopolitan and the Regional

Contd.

Recipes by Englishwoman in India	*Recipes by Prajnasundari Devi*
- ½ teaspoon salt - 4 ounces sugar - 3 ounces candied peel - ½ pint milk - 1 wineglass brandy *Method:* Beat the whites and yolks of the eggs separately, and put the brandy in last: boil for six hours.[34]	- 250 grams of sugar - one tablespoon ghee - a little water *Method:* The bread needs to be made into crumb by rubbing them between both palms. Lard needs to be finely chopped and mixed with finely chopped candied peel. Then slivered nuts, currants, raisins, lard, and candied peel are to be mixed with the bread crumbs. Add sugar. Mix in three eggs. This mixture is then spooned onto a flesh towel. Ghee is to be added. Then this towel is tied together and dropped into a vessel of boiling water. This mixture will be steamed.[35]
ARROWROOT PUDDING *Method:* Make a small basin of very thick milk arrowroot; stir into it five eggs well beaten, three ounces of butter, a tablespoon of wine or brandy, the juice of a lime, two tablespoons of sugar, and a few drops of any essence. Bake with sifted sugar on top.[36]	**ARROWROOT PUDDING** Ingredients: - 60 grams of arrowroot - 4 and a ½ cups of milk - 4 eggs - half a nutmeg - 125 grams of sugar - one table spoon of butter *Method:* First mix arrowroot with one cup of milk and then stir in slowly the rest of milk. Put it on fire and keep on stirring. After this mixture thickens, remove it from fire and let it cool. In another utensil mix egg yolk and sugar together. Keeping one teaspoon of butter aside, mix the rest of the butter with the egg yolk and sugar mixture. Now mix this with the arrowroot. Pour in this mixture into a buttered pie-dish. Sprinkle some ground nutmeg over the top and let it bake for twenty minutes.[37]

---

[34] A Lady Resident, *The Englishwoman*, 165–166.
[35] Prajnasundari, *Amish o niramish*, vol. 2, 358–359.
[36] A Lady Resident, *The Englishwoman*, 167.
[37] Prajnasundari, *Amish o niramish*, vol. 2, 356.

Contd.

Recipes by Englishwoman in India	Recipes by Prajnasundari Devi
TIPSY CAKE *Method:* Take a small round sponge cake and soak it with wine, a little brandy, or milk punch. When it has been soaked well through, pour over it a very good custard; place some jam, marmalade, or guava jelly over the top, and whip the whites of six eggs to a hard snow and pile over it; the yolks can be used for the custard.[38]	TIPSY CAKE PUDDING *Ingredients:* • One three-four days old sponge cake • three cups of sweet wine • 2 wineglass brandy • one lime *Method:* Keep the cake in a glass pudding-dish. Soak it with wine, brandy and lime juice mixed together so that the cake is well soaked. Arrange slivers of nuts around the cake. Now pour over it some milk custard. Tipsy pudding cannot be made much before the meal. It should be prepared two hours before a meal is ready.[39]

Source: See the respective footnotes.

Hybridity became a frequent occurrence in the recipes we find in most of the Bengali periodicals that appeared around this time. Often, a mutton chop recipe or a potato stew recipe contained ingredients like *ghee* or clarified butter, which was mostly used for Hindu ritual practices[40]. The periodical *Paricharika* came with a recipe for muffin made of potato and *patol* (a very locally-grown and locally consumed vegetable).[41] Mitra often used items such as canned fruits, several types of essence, and gelatin for her recipes. Kiranlekha Ray, however, taught techniques of preserving or canning fruits such as strawberries, apples, and peaches at home.[42] But she also used new utensils like cake mould, pie dish, and patty pan.[43] The availability of different foreign food had become so enormous that it was easily possible for an upper middle-class family to afford them. But the consumption of the 'foreign' also had the danger of adapting something that was alien, at least for some. This alien had to be localised by indigenising the 'foreign.' The 'foreign' and the 'indigenous' were put together through the creation of a particular Vedic tradition.

---

[38] A Lady Resident, *The Englishwoman*, 173.
[39] Prajnasundari, *Amish o niramish*, vol. 2, 373–374.
[40] Prajnasundari Debi ed., *Punya* 8 (3rd year, April 1902): 49–51.
[41] Sucharu Debi ed., *Paricharika* (Kolikata, April 1905): 268–269.
[42] Ray, *Varendra*, 31.
[43] Ibid., 137–138.

Both Prajnasundari and Rwitendranath Tagore contributed to the making of this Vedic tradition. Prajnasundari's cookbook never showed any concern for preserving the so-called authenticity of food. Similarly, Rwitendranth Tagore also made several interesting observations about the hybridity of nomenclature in his text, *Mudir dokan*.[44] Rwitendranth Tagore refers to social interaction between the East and the West, which he claims, existed from ancient times. According to Tagore, 'Just like the Europeans are adopting our rice these days, European food like chop, cutlets have become "*gharoa*" (quotidian) amongst us.'[45]

Both Tagore and Pragyasundari were of the opinion that several European foods derived their names from Indian ones. Tagore, in fact, had an elaborate argument on such nomenclature. For instance, Tagore argued that most European food like pies and pancakes derived their names from Sanskrit. *Pup* and pie belonged to the same genre of food. Since the Vedic *pup* had been converted into *pua* in Bengali, it is not totally improbable that *pup* was distorted to become pie in English. Tagore also considered omelet 'our food' which the West had taken and has now come back to the East. He writes that the Vedic word *ambarish* (a pan for frying bread) is the etymological origin for omelet.[46] For Tagore, the English always 'fed on Indians.' He argued that even bread, which constituted one of the staples of the English, was not their own.[47]

> The word bread came from "*bhrastra*" which means a pan for frying bread. *Bhrath* came from *bhrastra* just like Maratha is derived from Maharastra. "*Bhrat*h" became "*brot*" in German and consequently bread in English. Something which is "*bhrastra*", that is something that can be fried in a pan is bread. At first Europeans were satisfied with the bread. --- These days they are fattened with our rice and lentils, but even this seems trivial when I see that they have always enriched their country since ancient times by borrowing terminology and knowledge from the gigantic store of knowledge in India.[48]

Prajnasundari also stated that both the Bengali word *bhaji* and the English word 'fry' originated from the Sanskrit etymon *bhrij* which meant cooking.[49]

---

[44] Rwitendranath Tagore, *Mudir dokan* (Kolikata, 1919 [1316 BS]).
[45] Ibid., 66.
[46] Ibid., 91.
[47] Ibid., 89-93.
[48] Ibid., 92-93.
[49] Prajnasundari Debi, *Amish o Niramish*, vol. 1, 32.

Thus according to Tagore and Prajnasundari, whatever was new had its origins in the Aryan tradition. They argued that whatever modern India consumed as a concoction of 'the East and the West' was actually a product of a Vedic tradition. In that sense European cuisine had always been hybrid. Aryan languages were transformed into Sanskrit during the Vedic period and had enormous influence on several modern civilisations.[50] Tagore's work was indebted in many senses to the works of British Orientalists like Sir William Jones. Jones had grouped Sanskrit, Greek, Latin, Gothic, Celtic, and Old Persian together calling them the descendant languages from proto Indo-European language.[51] Jones further added the idea that Sanskrit literature was a repository of the most ancient written records of Indo-European languages.[52] Tagore's arguments were of course conjectural and often verged on romanticising Indian 'tradition.' His world view was nothing unique, but part of a middle-class cosmos whose cosmopolitanism demanded a universalism quite akin to those claimed for by any other middle-class in any other parts of the world. The gastronomic culture of this middle-class cannot simply be labeled a hybrid culture. Hybridity here implies seeking purity of origins to understand the nature of Bengali food is to misunderstand the culinary culture that engendered this cuisine. This culinary culture was a creative response to new possibilities thrown open by colonial modernity wherein food became a locus for the construction of a refined middle-class self.

SITUATING THE BENGALI COSMOPOLITAN

Abanindranath Tagore, the scion of the Tagore family of Jorasanko and himself a renowned painter and litterateur cherished the new culture of food that was fast becoming a regular feature at least in the upper-middle or upper class families in Bengal. He was much fond of the pudding and chicken stew cooked by his *bawarchi* (Muslim cook) Taleb Ali. There was a separate kitchen

---

[50] Ibid., 43–44. It needs to mentioned that this reference to 'Aryan' tradition has been an issue of constant fixation of cultural nationalism. Thus, the middle-class claimed on many occasions that whatever was labeled 'modern' or even 'Western,' such as women's education, women's volition in marriage and so on, had existed in ancient India.

[51] William Jones, *The Works of Sir William Jones*. 6 vols (1807), Anna Maria Jones ed., cited in Thomas R. Trautmann, *Aryans and British India* (Berkeley/Los Angeles/London: University of California Press, 1997), 38.

[52] Ibid.

where Brahmin cooks prepared *shukto* (a light broth of vegetables), fish curry or lentil. But Tagore could not appreciate such 'Brahminical' dishes twice a day.[53] Tagore in fact had an interesting take on such new culture of food. He told his grandsons that Taleb Ali's cooking could not compare anywhere near to the culinary skills of Navin, someone who cooked for the Tagores when he was young. However, Navin's forte was in cooking for gigantic parties where tables were set in an elaborate manner with forks, spoons, knives, and plates arraigned in proper ways. But with time such culture had become much more domesticated. Hence Taleb Ali's cooking was perfect for a time when someone could cherish such new food within the comfortable zone of one's inner space.[54] This domestication of the cosmopolitan was the crux of middle-class taste in colonial Bengal. Thus, Abanindranath himself took an intense interest in learning dishes like corn-flour pudding from Mrs Beeton's cookbook. However, his interest was not confined to learning so-called exotic dishes. He also read up recipes in Bengali books like *Hajar Jinish* and appreciated them equally.[55]

This cosmopolitanism of Tagore was something that defined middle-class taste. This section tries to ascertain the precise meanings of cosmopolitanism in relation to taste. An analysis of two texts on gastronomy shows that colonialism lent a distinct flavour to cosmopolitanism whereby the vernacular or the regional itself becomes cosmopolitan. In *Bhojan shilpi Bangali* (Bengalee, the connoisseur of food), Buddhadeb Bose (1908–1974) wrote that the element that set apart Bengali cuisine from all other cuisines was its distinctive nature of domesticity.[56] Although this characteristic disbarred Bengali cuisine from being a part of the world cuisine, according to Bose, this nature of the Bengali cuisine saved it from the vulgarity of commercialisation. Bengali cuisine had originated at home and from familial affection.[57] Bose's account was replete

---

[53] Mohanlal Gangopadhyay, *Dakshiner baranda* (Kolkata; Biswabharati, 1907 [1414 BS]), 120–121, first published in 1981 [1388 BS].

[54] Ibid., 120. In fact, this comfort was becoming so usual that often men would publicly repent traveling to foreign land and eating food cooked by a foreign cook. This repentance was more like a charade because the same men would immediately go back home and enjoy a hearty meal of chicken curry cooked by a Muslim cook. See Sudha Mazumdar, *Memoirs of an Indian Woman*, edited with an introduction by Geraldine Forbes (Armonk, New York, London, England: An East Gate Book M.E. Sharpe, Inc., 1989), 120.

[55] Ibid., 121–122.

[56] Buddhadeb Bose, *Bhojan shilpi Bangali* (Kolkata: Bikalpa Prakashani, 2004), 18.

[57] Ibid.

with his aestheticisation of Bengal cuisine. Bose, for instance, praised 'Bengali cuisine in its uniqueness of naming simple dishes in diverse ways.

Bose took delight in explaining that even subtle differences in the techniques of cooking made Bengalis name their dishes in different ways. He ridiculed the word curry saying that delicate Bengali dishes could not be clubbed together under this monochromic umbrella called curry.[58] However, Bose opined that this distinctiveness did not confine Bengali culinary skills. Instead, it indicated that Bengali cuisine had synthesised several other cuisines in its fold.[59] Bose urged that on one hand, fruits and vegetables that the foreigners brought in were indigenised. On the other hand, the Bengali cuisine, unlike cuisines in other parts of India, wove Aryan and non-Aryan traditions of eating together. The result was the production of a liberal and well-planned cuisine.[60]

In his appraisal of Bengali cuisine, Bose compared it with European and Chinese cuisines. He argued that Chinese cuisine, which was so renowned for its variety, was devoid of dairy products as well as bitter dishes. European cuisine too did not include bitter dishes in their items for delicacies.[61] According to Bose, a Bengali kitchen assembled all the six flavors mentioned in ancient Indian treatise: bitter, hot, acidic, sweet, sour, and pungent, along with non-vegetarian food items. Bose compared Bengali sweetmeat makers with those of Switzerland and the techniques adopted by Bengalis to cook fish with that of the Fins.[62]

What is at stake in Bose's romanticisation of the Bengali cuisine? Bose's essays on food expressed a kind of nostalgia for a lost world and a desire to capture that world. As Damayanti Basu Singh, Buddhadeb Bose's daughter, stated succinctly in the preface to his book, Bose was driven by a nostalgic urge to document a history of Bengali cuisine.[63] This nostalgia for the past arose when Bose's lifeworld was shaken by the Second World War and the partition of Bengal in 1947. Bose wrote that the ram-shackled world of the Bengali middle-class could not gather itself after it was partitioned in 1947.[64]

---

[58] Ibid., 10.
[59] Ibid., 13.
[60] Ibid.
[61] Ibid.
[62] Ibid., 13–14.
[63] Damayanti Basu Singh, Preface to *Bhojan shilpi Bangali* by Buddhadeb Bose (Kolkata: Bikalpa Prakashani, 2004), i–iii.
[64] Ibid., 24.

Lamentation for this lost world is best reflected in Bose's novel, *Golap Keno Kalo* (Why is the rose black) written around 1967.[65] Bose himself was from the eastern parts of Bengal. Many of the refugees, who came to Calcutta after the partition of Bengal and inhabited refugee colonies, were mostly from well-to-do middle-class families in Dhaka. The protagonist of *Golap Keno Kalo* remembered the world that was left behind by the refugees. These refugees had to stay in squalor in Calcutta, sometimes two or three families huddled together. They could not afford to spend money on anything more than two courses of meal a day. The protagonist of *Golap* adumbrated what these refugees ate in their halcyon days in eastern Bengal before the partition of India in 1947. A description of the consumption of food in pre-partition eastern Bengal did not just restrict itself to mere eating; it led one to the level of a gourmet:

> The feast started with bitter gourd and crispy small fish with pulses, then appeared the jet black *koi* (a fish belonging to the genre of cat fish) who slept on a cauliflower pillow laid on a bed of oil that was a color of reddy red-so big that a large bowl could not contain it. Some other day a meal began and ended with *hilsa* (perhaps the most popular fish of the Bengalis)---Some day it could be the large *pabda* fragrant with cilantro, some other day it could be *magur* cooked with potato, garlic and onion.---Another day, one could have Kolu Miyan-r *Bakharkhani* (a type of bread consumed in eastern Bengal) which was of a well-rounded shape and it was light, crispy, and layered.---And last but not the least was the vegetarian fare cooked by my grandmother –that was another world, inhabitants of that world were modest, they had strange names, and gourd skins and pumpkin seeds were also respected in that world. But what came out of these unadvertised sources is unimaginable even by the best chefs of Paris. My mother and grandmothers could make a huge range of dishes with three or four ingredients and with hardly any paraphernalia; in this, they resembled those painters who conjured innumerable colors from just seven shades of rainbow.[66]

Such a vivid description was an indicator of the ram-shackled and dilapidated world of Bengal after 1947. The lamentation for what was lost continued in post-colonial Bengal. But what was apparent was this definition of taste, the claim to a refined palette in which the Bengali food connoisseur was no different from the French gourmet. It is by keeping this sense of refined taste

---

[65] Buddhadeb Bose, *Golap keno kalo* (1967), excerpt in Buddhadeb Basu, *Bhojan*, 34–35.
[66] Buddhadeb Bose, *Golap keno kalo* (1967), excerpt in Buddhadeb Basu, *Bhojan*, 34–35.

in mind that Bose drew a picture of a kaleidoscopic world of food that did not merely represent a hearty meal, but also provided an aesthetic flavour. Thus the meal was simple and yet refined. For Bose, the Bengali middle-class who inhabited this world was not a glutton but a gourmet. Since the Hindu Bengali middle-class was deprived of this pleasure after the partition in 1947, Bose mourned the death of a fine art that was Bengali cuisine, which in his opinion constituted a major contribution of the Bengalis to the world.[67] Bose's text makes it amply clear that Bengali cuisine epitomises Bengaliness. The idea of Bengal as a liberal, cosmopolitan, and yet familial was born from this discourse on taste. Perceived this way, Bengal stood quite distinctive, complete in itself.

Taste was therefore translated into a lifeworld and cuisine was the representation of this lifeworld. Unlike Bose, who was more of a centrist in his class politics, Gopal Haldar's (1902–1993) approach to literature was from a leftist point of view. Haldar, in fact, spent considerable years of his life in prison for his political beliefs. Thus it does not come as a surprise when we see that Gopal Haldar's *Adda* (social gathering of friends) is a little different from Bose's text.[68] Haldar did not consider Bengali cuisine to be classic like Bose did. However, Haldar made a distinction between what was classic and what was original or the root of everything. This root spread itself into literature, fine art, and the art of cuisine.[69] Although denying the role of classic in the development of Bengali cuisine, Haldar did believe that the Bengali cuisine had not been able to completely internalise the colonial cuisine into its fold.[70] Haldar, like Bose, attributed this lack of internalisation to the rationing policies of the state and the consequent black marketeering following the Second World War, which continued even after India became independent. Here, it seems that by internalisation Halder implied incapacity to digest. However, Haldar admitted that this semi-internalisation of food, like cakes and ice creams, along with what Bengalis ate since ancient times constructed the 'Bengali' cuisine. This reception of the 'new' contributed to the cosmopolitan character of the Bengali cuisine.[71] At a much earlier period, the poet Nabindchandra Sen (1847–1939), proudly claimed that on his first visit to his native village near Chittagong as a deputy magistrate in early twentieth century, he first introduced what he calls 'Anglo-Vernacular' culinary skills of his wife to the

---

[67] Ibid., 35.
[68] Gopal Haldar, *Adda* (Kolkata: Punthipatra, 2004).
[69] Ibid., 49.
[70] Ibid., 50–51.
[71] Ibid., 56.

prevalent social feasts. Sen's wife prepared a blend of Hindustani, *Mughlai*, and Christian dishes where the quintessential Bengali *luchi* (fried flour bread) could easily replace bread as a 'side dish'.[72]

Both Basu and Haldar wrote at a time when food habits of the Bengalis were affected by what may be called post-colonial economic complexities. On the one hand, the rationing policy of the imperial state continued from the colonial era. On the other hand, the black marketeering of food stocks made buying food at a soaring price prohibitive for the middle-class. The result was a curtailment of refineries in taste, a compromise with aesthetics. Basu and Haldar had precisely this imagery in mind when they wrote about taste. Although they wrote from different perspectives, their writing had one point in common. They were defining Bengali cuisine as a liberal and cosmopolitan cuisine, which had the potential of incorporating all other flavors and indigenising them. And it was the Bengali middle-class (read Hindus) who reframed this cuisine within a gastronomic paradigm.

Haldar chose a few people to demonstrate who a Bengali gastronome was. One of them was Rangin Haldar, a teacher who specialised in training cooks in the fine art of cuisine. Whether Rangin Haldar had lentil soup or pudding, it had to be served in a proper manner, which Haldar consumed with immense patience and appreciation. Haldar considered gastronomy to be an ethos of life and its decline to be a decline of art.[73] Hirankumar Sanyal, a literary critic and a cultural activist was another example that Gopal Haldar chose to reassert his point of a Bengali gourmet. To understand art, Hirankumar Sanyal urged one to look back at rural Bengal, at the fresh *hilsa* from the village rivers, at the vegetables grown in the fields of these villages, at juice squeezed from dates and jaggery, and sweets made from jaggery. However, Sanyal added to it by stating that the sense of art and aesthetics that a Bengali nurtured was not restricted to rural Bengal. He claimed that they were equally enthusiastic about Firpo, Fluries, and Trinka (confectionaries and restaurants in Calcutta).[74] Buddhadeb Bose's naming of the text itself was an indicator of the position of the gastronome. A gastronome, for Bose, was one who developed his taste with care, an attitude reflected abundantly in his book.

---

[72] Nabinchandra Sen, *Amar jiban*, vol. 2, ed. Sajanikanta Das (Kolikata: Bangiya Sahitya Parishat, 1959, 1366 BS]), 319.
[73] Ibid., 64–67.
[74] Ibid., 68.

These discussions of aesthetics and taste by two well-known writers whose writings continued in the post-colonial era can be compared to Kant's concept of an aesthetic judgment. For Kant, aesthetic judgment is a judgment of taste. The ground determining taste is subjective; that is, it is dependent on individual feelings of pleasure and pain. That is why a judgment of taste can never be based on logical reasoning.[75] However, Kant also argues that aesthetic judgment tries to make an appeal to universality. Although its basis is individual feelings, a judgment of taste asserts the existence of a correct answer on the availability of an object.[76] Bose and Haldar wrote from this angle of individual feelings, with perspectives of pleasure and pain emanating from cuisine. However, in their documentation and description of this cuisine they went beyond a mere culinary discussion. Their interest focused on the refinement of taste and had a universal claim for refined and cosmopolitan Bengali cuisine. These gastronomes were trying to carve a niche for the Bengali cuisine in the larger discourse of nationalism, keeping its distance from all other cuisines that had been commoditised. In doing so, these gastronomes also made it clear that the construction of a refined taste was after all a handiwork of the middle-class.

Claim for a refined and cosmopolitan Bengali cuisine arose from the complexities that the middle-class Bengali Hindus experienced because of colonialism. This aestheticisation was not merely one of a gastronome, who was a connoisseur of French *haute* cuisine. This aestheticisation was also a struggle for homing, or what Dipesh Chakrabarty has described as 'at home in capitalist modernity.' Chakrabarty argues that an attempt to make capitalist modernity comfortable for oneself is an eternal process.[77] Chakrabarty focuses on the specific practice of *adda* (a form of social gathering where friends get together for long and informal conversations) in Calcutta to understand how one struggles to be at home in modernity. *Adda,* as prevalent in the early twentieth century, was gendered; it was a form of predominantly male social bonding. Chakrabarty argues that the *adda* that defined the urban space of Calcutta in

---

[75] Immanuel Kant, *Critique of Judgment*, trans. with and introduction by J.H. Bernard (New York: Hafner Press, London: Collier Macmillan Publishers, 1951); Douglas Burnham, *An Introduction to Kant's Critique of Judgment* (Edinburgh: Edinburgh University Press, 2004).

[76] Immanuel Kant, *Critique of Judgment*, trans. with and introduction by J.H. Bernard (New York: Hafner Press, London: Collier Macmillan Publishers, 1951).

[77] Dipesh Chakrabarty, *Provincializing Europe: Postcolonial Thought and Historical Difference* (Princeton and Oxford: Princeton University Press, 2000), 180.

the first half of the twentieth century gradually petered out in its last three decades. This *adda* played a significant role in defining Bengali modernity and specifically came to be labeled as 'Bengali.' Bengalis invested *adda* with ideals of life, vitality, essence, and youth.[78] *Adda* is a site where debates of modernity are carried out and yet it is a world that makes the middle-class feel at home; it is the locus of the familiar. Therefore, the idea of *adda* evokes a sense of yearning in Bengali writings.[79]

Similarly, the sentiments that emerged in the writings of people like Bose and Haldar, or even in the thoughts of Rangin Haldar and Hiran Sanyal, who were mentioned by Gopal Halder in his *Adda*, constantly remembered a world of delectables that was conspicuous by its absence. But then they reconstructed this world through an aestheticisation of what they had lost and what they continued to cherish. Buddhadeb Bose and Gopal Haldar treated gastronomy as an art where each and every component that created this art was reflected: the end product was judged and appreciated from a perspective of refined taste. Practices surrounding food were one of those quotidian and integral aspects of life that changed because of colonial modernity and yet retained its tag of Bengaliness.

REGIONAL COSMOPOLITANISM: DOMESTICITY OF BENGALI CUISINE

Gopal Haldar states categorically in *Adda*, that 'in India the Bengali community has at least one quality– s/he knows how to savour. S/He is a connoisseur of taste and palette.'[80] Haldar considers Bengali sweetmeats to be a unique creation that cannot simply be described as an art or as a craft. This creation was an integral part of the lifeworld of Bengali middle-class nested in the village communities.[81] It was from this domestic life in the small villages, that the Bengali cuisine emerged. Thus Hirankumar Sanyal, the self-proclaimed cosmopolitan gastronome opined:

> We will definitely take pleasure in new food, in the new restaurants. But a Bengali's talent lies in his domesticity and not in his commercial ventures.

---

[78] Ibid., 213.
[79] Ibid., 212.
[80] Haldar, *Adda*, 47.
[81] Ibid.

Hence, there is not a single restaurant for Bengali cuisine in Calcutta. Each Bengali household carries a unique characteristic as far as culinary practice is concerned. Our country excels in the art of gastronomy which flourishes in home. Thus, we need the goddess of this art and your fate will be decided by the proper selection of the mistress of the house.[82]

This celebration of domesticity then becomes the crux of middle-class taste. An affinity to incorporate and indigenise new elements coexisted with a love for the traditional. While new food was often celebrated, the middle-class abhorred the new locus for consuming them. Modernity had its seduction. There was no denying the fact that this new gastronomic culture had become a part and parcel of life. However, the response that this new culinary culture received was complex. It was neither a complete disavowal, nor a wholehearted reception. The ambivalence of the discourse on middle-class taste nurtured this culture and the way Bengali cosmopolitanism turned out to be can be attributed to a large extent to this complexity.

The notion of a self-sustaining village life where money did not have an overriding precedence over simplicity became all important. The life in the village reflected the world of an eternal tradition where rituals were celebrated in their most intimate forms. Festivals or *vratas*(ritual observance ceremony) that were celebrated often had connections with gastronomy. Often times, food was the nucleus around which many of these festivals and *vratas* revolved. Romanticisation of the rural life became an obsession with authors like Dinendrakumar Ray, otherwise known for his penchant for writing mystery series. Ray wrote a number of texts on village life named *Pallichitra* (Images of a village) and *Pallibaichitra* (Wonders of a village). Ray's accounts are replete with references to festivals that are celebrations of food, harvest or bounty. For instance, he refers to *Bhagabati Yatra* (cow worship), which included a ritual involving milk-boiling of milk. The mistress of the household was supposed to mix milk with rice and jaggery and boil them together. The resultant rice pudding was then distributed among the children of the house.[83] Ray observes that 'the intimate connection of the rice pudding with this auspicious day enhanced the flavor of this simple rice pudding.'[84]

---

[82] Ibid., 69.
[83] Dinendrakumar Ray, *Pallichitra* (Kolikata: Ananda Publishers, 1983 [1390BS]), first published in 1904 [1311 BS]).
[84] Ibid., 25.

These festivals became significant on account of their links with the rural life. What made this life notable was its total absence from the colonial urban space. Most of the middle-class who reminisced about this life had left their rural homes and migrated to cities and towns in search of jobs. The grueling life of the city made this middle-class look back to the villages, which became a utopian world of the uncorrupted, unpolluted, and pristine precolonial past. Thus English education was blamed for a disinterest in festivals, but mostly it was the physical distance of the cities from the villages that made celebrating these festivals and rituals almost impossible.[85]

Navanna or rice harvest was one of the most celebrated festivals because of its relation to rice, the staple of the Bengalis. Hence, the middle-class wrote about rice harvest with a great deal of adoration and reverence. *Navanna* was much talked about because it was integrally connected with the cultivation of new rice and thus to the life of the peasants. The colonial middle-class considered this peasant life to be invaluable for being untarnished by colonial modernity. Rev. Lal Behari Day wrote a fictitious account of a peasant's life in Bengal, as he was keen to preserve those traits of simplicity that the middle-class thought were fast disappearing. Day's book had two chapters extensively devoted to *Navanna* and another similar festival, *Sankranti*. Authors like Day took it upon themselves to bring back these memories of pristine delights for the middle-class. Day described *Navanna* thus:

> It was on a bright, sunny morning of the pleasant month of November–that the joyous festival of the *Navanna*, or the new rice took place. This festival, in which the first fruits of the paddy-field are offered to the Gods before they are used by human beings, must not be confounded with the general harvest, which does not take place till a month after. ---after one *prahara* and half (that is about half past 10 o' clock in the morning) is the most auspicious moment for offering and eating the new rice and no one may eat that rice unbathed. There is in that basket in the corner of the big room a large quantity of the new rice, untasted yet by man or beast; that large *handi* is filled with milk; in another basket are contained all the fruits and esculent roots of the season, cut into small pieces. --- the family priest mixes the new rice (unboiled) with the milk and the fruit and the edible roots, repeats a lot of Sanskrit prayers, blows the conch-shell with his mouth–which means–a proclamation to the Gods to the effect that the feast is ready and that they would come and partake of it.[86]

---

[85] Dinendrakumar Ray, *Pallibaichitra* (Kolikata: Ananda Publishers, 1982 [1389BS]), first published in 1905 [1312 BS]).

[86] Rev. Lal Behari Day, *Bengal Peasant Life*, new ed., (Calcutta: Macmillan And Co. Ltd, 1928), 204–209.

Such minute details of the festival that Day elaborated on were necessary because he was not merely writing for the middle-class, but for the wide world to see what an untainted village life looked like. Although the moot point of Day's account was to show the essence of a region named Bengal, he also needed for the outside world to see it and prove it was in no way any inferior than the life in the West. Thus he compares the dinner of a Bengali villager to that of an Englishman:

> That day the dinner is required to be unusually grand.--- Animal food being prohibited to the class of Hindus to which Badan (protagonist's father) belonged, and wines being out of the question, the reader may easily imagine in what the magnificence of the dinner consists. There was in the first place, boiled rice, without which no Bengali can exist; in the second place, *dal*, or boiled pulse; in the third place, two or three kinds of greens fried in mustard oil; in the fourth place, about half a dozen sorts of vegetables like the potato, brinjal, *potol* (striped gourd), *ucche* (bitter gourd), *paniphal* (water cress), and others, fried in the same fragrant oil; in the fifth place, a hodge-podge, called *tarkari* (vegetable curry), of three or four sorts of vegetables; in the sixth place, fish fried in the eternal mustard oil; in the seventh place fish cooked in tamarind; and in the eighth or last place, *paramanna*, that is, rice par excellence, a pudding made up of rice, milk, and sugar or molasses. Such are the delicacies which seem to make up a first-rate dinner for a Bengali *raiyat*; and though the English sybarite may laugh at the concoction till his sides burst, it must be acknowledged by every right-thinking person that the materials of the *raiyats*' dinner, though perhaps less nutritive are more innocuous than the highly-seasoned dishes and intoxicating beverage of the lucculuses of Europe.[87]

The simplicity of this rural meal held Day's attention, which he flaunted to the world. In his opinion, like those of his ilk, this simplicity of a peasant's meal, which was cradled in domestic surroundings, made it worthy of remembrance. Festivals like *Navanna* became desirable for the urban dweller and his melancholic life. Taking new rice together with one's family was filled with such delight and significance that the urban dweller could then be content to return to the city armed with these happy memories.[88]

This culinary culture was definitely very different from any *haute* cuisine because for the middle-class, this gastronomic culture was also spiritual. The association of food with the festivals and especially with the gods dissociated it

---

[87] Ibid.
[88] Ray, *Pallibaichitra*, 35.

from gourmandising.[89] However, the fact that food itself was not insignificant at all to a middle-class discourse on taste can be fathomed from the way it became central to any Bengali festival, whether celebrated by the Hindus or the Muslims. *Sankranti*, a celebration that followed the harvest, is a case in point.

> The harvest is followed by a festival, greatly enjoyed by the peasantry, and called *pita sankranti*, or the feast of cakes. It is so called from pita, cake and *sankranti*, the last day of the month, as it always takes place at the end of the month *Pausha*, which comprises half of December and half of January. The festival lasts three days. Early in the morning of the first day of the feast, Alanga, Sundari, and Aduri (women of the house) bathed, and boiled different kinds of pulse-like grain, *kalai, barbati, mug*, which they formed into a sort of thick paste. They next extracted the kernel of the cocoa-nut, mixed it with treacle, and fried it. They then took out a large quantity of rice, which they filled with either various kinds of the prepared pulse, or the prepared kernel of the cocoa-nut, or cream, and covered them up. These rice balls were then put in a *handi* of boiling water; and in a few minutes the pita was fit to be eaten. These cakes are usually eaten with treacle. A larger sort of cakes is usually prepared, called *askes*, which are of two kinds, the dry and the wet; the former being eaten along with treacle, and the latter soaked in milk. A thinner species, called s*aruchaklis*, is very much esteemed.--- On one of the festival days Alanga made a *pita* of a monstrous size in the shape of a cat, which was offered to *Shasthi*, the protectress of children. These rude and somewhat unwholesome cakes may not suit the taste of refined palates, but they are vastly enjoyed by the peasantry, who get no harm by them.[90]

This village life, a symbol of the pristine in the musings of the middle-class, was also the last repository of the residues of a precolonial past, an undying tradition. The past indeed became a site of gastronomic pleasure. In this context, subsistence became associated with an imaginary past.

For the Bengali middle-class, the past symbolised an abundance of milk and fish along with rice. They argued that these foods had made the Bengalis a valorous race in the past.[91] They further believed that the colonial presence

---

[89] For a detailed discussion of food being the link between men and Gods and how it ensures their mutual cooperation, see R.S. Khare, *The Hindu Hearth and Home* (Durham: Carolina Academic Press, 1976); Khare, *Culture and Reality: Essays on the Hindu System of Managing Foods* (Simla: Indian Institute of Advanced Study, 1976).

[90] Ibid., 210–214.

[91] Rajnarayan Bose, *Se kal aar ekal*, ed. Brajendranath Bandopadhyay and Sajanikanta Das (Kolikata: Bangiya Sahitya Parishat, 1874), 42–48.

destroyed this abundance by systematically undermining the subsistence agriculture. A romantic landscape was etched as the cradle for food that had nurtured the people of the soil. Fish, for instance came to be connected to the landscape of Bengal, its riverine tracts, and amphibious life. Nibaranchandra Chaudhuri, an official working at the Bihar Agricultural Department, wrote in his tract of 1913: 'All Bengalis, irrespective of being rich or poor could easily avail fish because of the abundance of rivers, ponds, canals, and various other water bodies.'[92] Chaudhuri associated fish with courage and wisdom.[93] Nikunjabehari Datta, who wrote another tract in 1925 on fish in a journal edited by the Gandhian nationalist Satishchandra Mukhopadhyay, advocated the consumption of fish with rice. He argued that fish was a staple of the Bengalis, which had to accompany rice with every meal. He therefore lamented the steady decline of fish cultivation in colonial Bengal.[94] The general saying was that fish and rice constituted the Bengali 'body' and nourished it. What inevitably followed from this argument was the general contention that the abundance of nutritious food that the middle-class described had become scarce as well as expensive in colonial Bengal.

Eating nutritious food was tied to another streak in the middle-class discourse on taste– making a spectacle of food and thus of the 'Bengali' body. Rajnarayan Basu (1826–99) lamented the inability of the Bengalis in his days to digest nutritious food. He said that students could easily eat rice thrice a day in those ancient days when learning took place in the village schools. Men could digest even hard shells of coconut.[95] Everyone knew the stories of *'Adhmoni Kailas'* and *'Munke Raghu'* who could consume tons of food. Jatindramohan Datta(1895–1975), who wrote with the pseudonym Jamdatta, and contributed to several Bengali newspapers and journals such as *Jugantar, Shanibarer Chithi, Prabasi, Kathasahitya, Modern Review* and many others, published a couple of articles in 1951 on the legends of *'Adhmoni Kailas'* and *'Munke Raghu.'* Jamdatta wrote that *'Munke Raghu'* consumed a *mon/maund* (1 maund=82.3pounds=37.4 kilograms) of food after fasting for one day. *'Adhmoni Kailash'* supposedly ate

---

[92] Nibaranchandra Chaudhuri, *Khadya tattva–A Treatise on Food* (Kolkata: The Indian Gardening Association, 1913), 58.
[93] Ibid.
[94] Nikunjabehari Datta, "Banglay matsyabhab" (Bhadra), *Mashik Basumati Sahitya Mandir, 1* (Kolikata, 3rd year, 1925 April/May–June/July [1331 Baisakh-Asharh BS]): 660–666.
[95] Bose, *Se kal*, 42–48.

half a *mon/maund* of sweets, vegetables and *luchi* anytime and anywhere.[96] So being able to eat vast quantities of food was a sign of a robust constitution free from ailments like indigestion. Jamdatta also wrote about a few other men from the late nineteenth century Bengal who could consume huge amounts, to people's awe and delight. One such person was one '*Banrujye Mashai*' (Mr. Banerjee) who could eat sixty-four mangoes after a full meal of *luchi*, fried eggplants, vegetables, lentil soup, yogurt, and sweetmeat. This was a sign of heroism, almost untainted by modern disciplinary regimes of the body. Another instance was that of Ramchandra Chattopadhyay, who could consume an entire jackfruit or an entire *Hilsa* fish.[97] Jamdatta believed that the enormous rise in prices since the Second World War was responsible for the lack of appetite in food. This enormous capacity of the 'Bengali' body to consume food was often marveled at even when the middle-class urged for restraint and moderation in consumption.[98]

The diet of a villager became an object of romanticism for the urban middle-class. Apart from signifying a simple meal, this diet also came to stand for homegrown and homemade nutritious food. The home also carried nostalgia of the rural as opposed to the 'new' food served in the public eateries of urban Calcutta. The 'pure' food of the domestic space was juxtaposed with the 'impure' and 'new' food served in hotels and restaurants. The middle-class stated that the new food engendered all kinds of diseases not perceived earlier. The old and the new food became divided through a line of division drawn by science. Chunilal Basu wrote:

> It was a universal practice at one time, with the old and the young in every Bengali household, to take, as the first thing in the morning, a handful of wetted and softened grams, either with salt and ginger or with brown sugar (*goor*).--- The practice should be revived, and sprouting grams should be our

---

[96] Jamdatta, "Sekele Katha," *Jugantar Samayiki* (Kolikata), May 20, 1951, 9–10.

[97] Ibid.

[98] Often, the colonial Bengali 'middle-class' perceptions of a robust body emerged in response to the construction of an image of an effeminate Bengali race by the colonial power structure. For a detailed discussion of gendered body as a site of politics, see John Rosselli, "The Self-Image of Effeteness: Physical Education and Nationalism in Nineteenth-Century Bengal," *Past and Present* 86, vol. no. 1 (February 1980): 121–148; Mrinalini Sinha, *Colonial Masculinity: The "Manly Englishman" and the "Effeminate Bengali" in Late 19th Century* (Manchester: Manchester University Press, 1995); Indira Chowdhury, *The Frail Hero and Virile History: Gender and the Politics of Culture in Colonial Bengal* (Delhi, New York: Oxford University Press, 1998).

daily food in the morning, prefereably with brown sugar, which contains vitamin, whereas white sugar contains none. The re-establishment of this practice will, to some extent, make up the deficiency in protein and vitamin in our present-day Bengali diet.[99]

The language that Basu used here was one that he borrowed from the medical terminology he had acquired through his colonial education. But he gave it a different twist when he championed 'traditional' food consumed in the villages with the 'new' food consumed in colonial Calcutta. Srishchandra Goswami, who wrote a tract on the health of the Bengali students in 1930, found the reason for the emasculation of the Bengali youth in the 'new' food, which he argued lacked protein.[100] He quotes extensively from Vivekananda to prove his point:

> We have begun to consume tea and biscuits in place of milk and yogurt- we are eating fried food and fruits—we have learnt to eat *luchi* and *kachuri* (deep fried round shaped flour bread) fried in lard instead of puffed rice and sweets made from coconut. As a result people are suffering from diabetes and dyspepsia. Swami Vivekananda (eminent religious preacher and reformer) has quite justifiably argued that bread is poison. Do not touch it. Yogurt is really good. Throw away fried food and sweetmeats sold in the shops. Fried food is poison. There is nothing in flour. Wheat flour is more nutritious. One should not consume too much spice. Elites of Calcutta wear glasses, eat sweetmeats, ride cars, and die from diabetes.---Imitating Calcutta, places like Dhaka, Bikrampur, Birbhum, and Bankura have banished whole black lentil, poppy seed paste, and puffed rice from their diet to become civilised. They have started consuming fried food and sweetmeats sold in the shops. This is the result of being urban.[101]

Apparently, this angst for the decay of middle-class body due to consumption of new food and a championing of an imagined peasant's diet was nothing unique to Bengal. Even in colonial north India, the Urdu middle-class discourse constantly worried about the decline of middle-class health due to consumption of novelty foods such as cakes, biscuits, machine made bread and chocolates. The peasants on the other hand were praised in this diet because

---

[99] Chunilal Basu, *Food* (Calcutta, 1930), 107.
[100] Srishchandra Goswami, "Bangali chhatroder swasthya gelo je," *Grihasthamangal*, No. 1 (4th Year, April/May 1930 [Baisakh 1337BS]): 1–5.
[101] Ibid.

of their consumption of the so-called traditional food like fruits, vegetables, and course bread.[102]

A number of authors took the responsibility for apprising the Bengali middle-class of what constituted nutritious food and of the means to escape diseases like acidity and dyspepsia. Dr Sundarimohan Das (1857–1950), who had joined the medical department of the Calcutta Corporation in 1890 and was one of the founder members of the National Medical College, drew up a long list of such food. These included food such as lentils, broad beans, eggplant, turnip, cabbage, onion, leafy vegetables, puffed rice with coconut, beaten rice, yogurt, cucumber, papaya, guava, blackberry, and homemade food.[103] In 1931, another contributor to the same journal observed that 'earlier when one ate puffed rice, beaten rice, jaggery made from cane for snack, no one had heard of "dyspepsia." Even today many villagers who eat such food instead of food sold in the market are healthy and strong; they have not heard of "dyspepsia".'[104] Food became pure on its account of being of the past, an imaginary 'golden age,' produce of a subsistence economy. But above all, this utopian rural life offered those who had migrated from the villages to the cities and the towns an image of comfort to cling on to.

> Where have gone those days! Where are those responsibilities, din and bustle, sincerity? Picking leafy vegetables, bitter gourd, fruits; Bathing in the morning and making sandalwood paste, decorating the idol and the temple, weaving garlands; cooking vegetables, grinding spices, arranging ingredients for day's cooking; kids would eat boiled rice with vegetables in the morning, sometimes this might be *khichuri* (a hodge-podge of rice and pulses) or rice mixed with clarified butter; this meal could be wheat bread or stale rice and vegetables in the winter which could again become rice soaked in water or desserts made from semolina in the months of summer.--- so much work to do--- leafy vegetables, boiled vegetables, fried vegetables, *chenchki, charchari, sharshari, ghanta* (different kinds of cooking for vegetables), batter fries, curry, sweet, bitter and spicy *shukto* (a light broth of different vegetables), *labra* (a hodge-podge of vegetables), labra for festivals (where one puts dry roasted

---

[102] Markus Daechsel, *The Politics of Self-Expression: The Urdu middle-class milieu in mid-twentieth century India and Pakistan* (London and New York: Routledge, 2006), 101–103.

[103] Dr. Sundarimohan Das, "Sulabh khadya," *Bangalakshmi*, 6th year, No. 4 (February/March 1931 [Phalgun 1337 BS]): 283–86, reprinted in Aswinikumar Chattopadhyay ed. *Grihasthamangal*, 4th year, No. 12 (March/April 1931 [Chaitra 1337BS]): 326–329.

[104] Basantakumar Chaudhuri, "Baje kharach," *Grihasthamangal* 5th year, No. 12 (May/June, June/July 1931 [Jaistya, Asharh 1338BS]): 30–35.

and ground coriander seeds), dry roasted and ground seeds of green leafs (mixed with ground ginger), mushy vegetables mixed with fried balls made from pulses, soaked chickpeas, ground coconut, ground sesame/poppy seeds/ mustard seeds or fennel, milk, yogurt, or a batter of wheat. --- sweetmeats made from cottage cheese, fruits, rice pudding, so much. Bathing, setting a table[105], pouring water in one's glass, laying out salt, lime, chilies, ginger, *kasundi* (mustard sauce), pickle, serving rice.[106]

The world that Hemantabala Debi (b. 1894 [1301BS]) created from her memories of her childhood cannot be just labeled simple. In fact, if her account is to be trusted, it becomes evident that preparations related to food or the entire gastronomic culture in general was quite elaborate and painstaking affair. However, as Hemantabala and her ilk want us to believe, the elegance of this culinary culture lay in its restraint. This culture, unlike its Western counterpart, flourished in unassuming, homely surroundings and in common households, and not in public eating places. For many amongst the middle-class, one of the greatest fears was that this world was falling apart with colonial modernity. Hemantabala Debi's comments reflected similar sentiments:

> I do not like this tea-drinking life. What did we eat in those days? Bitter leaves soaked water, soaked chickpeas with ginger and salt, molasses. Then someone would have fruits, puffed rice or flattened rice. Some might eat leftover fried flour bread. Others might have eaten puffed rice with cucumber, puffed rice with radish, puffed rice with coconut, puffed rice with boiled or fried vegetables.--- Having "foreign" food like bread, eggs and cake insult Indian culture.--- We have so many types of sweets in our country. But whenever we forget our God and cheat ourselves that is the end of it all.
>
> Who is God? He is the symbol of memories of our ancestors, of the loved ones. He is an object of affection. Offer him food and then eat. This is a sign of proper culture.---
>
> We should sit properly on the floor and eat rather than sit at the table. Why do we need to imitate another culture, sacrificing Indian culture altogether.---

---

[105] It needs to be remembered that Hemantabala Debi's 'setting a table' was very different from what we mean by setting a table now. The process she describes involves cleaning the floor and arranging food platters on it before a person takes their seat on a mat on the floor to eat from the elaborate platter laid out before them.

[106] Hemantabala Debi, *Hemantabala Debi rachanasankalan*, ed. Jasodhara Bagchi and Abhijit Sen (Kolkata: Dey's Publishing, 1992), 239–244.

You can have "foreign" food in the hospital, but at home you should have what you can offer your God.---Let us bring back that *andarmahal* (inner domain of the house), that kitchen, rice-husking machine, store room, cowshed, granary, fruit orchard, kitchen garden. Let us bring back that gigantic household. Let *grihalakshmi* (deity of household) settle in her home. After all householders look after the renunciates![107]

Food was the nucleus of the world etched by Hemantabala Debi and others, but the role of gastronomy was perceived differently. Food was an object of love and affection and the spiritual tenor encompassing it. Food was offered to the deities and then consumed by men and women. Thus, whatever were to be offered to the gods had to be painstakingly crafted. Amritalal Basu wrote in his description of the festival for the worship of the goddess Durga how decorations were made from fruits and sweets. 'Fruits such as coconut, banana, bottle gourd, pumpkin, wood apple, sugarcane, lime and pomegranates were hung from the roof. And then two platters were laid out in the front of the deity and sweets were arranged on those platters according to their size.'[108] The aesthetics of presentation of food was deeply related to spirituality whereby a man's homage to a higher being was paid through everyday practice of food. Thus women made

> — red globulets prepared with shredded coconut and molasses, snowy white, feathery chips, crescent-shaped affairs strewn with almonds, pistachios, raisins and flavoured with cardamom seeds. Fragile cream wafers stamped in delicate designs, sugar cakes, plates of atap rice, and brown sugar piled up high and crowned with a banana, bowls of milk and honey and yogurt for the Goddess. In wicker trays and tiny baskets displayed delicious balls of parched rice, fried and rolled in golden syrup, crisp popcorn coated with molasses, and fresh crunchy puffed rice, together with roasted graham treated with treacle.[109]

It was after all a culinary culture deeply ensconced in the essence of Bengal where the gods were as much a part of the domestic space as were men.

---

[107] Ibid.

[108] Amritalal Bose, "Puratan Panjika," in *Amritalal Basur smriti o atmasmriti*, ed. Arunkumar Mitra (Kolkata:Sahityalok, 1982), 106–107, first published in *Mashik Basumati* between 1923–1924 [1330–31 BS].

[109] Sudha Mazumdar, *Memoirs of an Indian Woman*, edited with an introduction by Geraldine Forbes (Armonk, New York, London, England: An East Gate Book M.E. Sharpe, Inc., 1989), 25.

MAKING 'BENGALI' CUISINE: REGIONAL VERSUS COSMOPOLITAN

The middle-class considered certain gastronomic practices as reflecting Bengali domesticity and hence essential components of a Bengali cuisine. Discussions on new social feasts bring out these points quite emphatically. One unifying theme ran through these discussions of feasts. This unifying theme was that of a simple pristine village life where money did not surpass simplicity in primacy. New social feasts epitomised the dominance of a money economy ushered in by capitalist modernity. It was possible for people from even the lowest rung of the social structure to spend money on organising feasts that irked many middle-class literati.[110] In his memoir, Bipin Pal observes the limited circulation of money in the villages during his childhood. Social honor was defined by caste.[111] Pal narrates an incident to elucidate his point:

> A very significant story in elucidation of this fact was current in our neighborhood during my young days. We had a very rich zemindar or landlord in a neighbouring village who came of a lower caste. Once he had invited his caste-people to a feast in his house. He made great preparations for the dinner and brought out all his bell-metal platters and cups and glasses, such as are usually used in the house of Brahmins, Kayesthas and Vaidyas, or the so-called Bhadraloks, for his guests. His idea was, of course, to honour them in this way. But when his guests saw all these things, they refused to sit down to their meals. The host was very perplexed by their attitude.--- After repeated questions, the oldest among them, who had led his fellows, said in ill-concealed anger: "have you invited us to your house to insult us?" Host--- wanted to know what his offence was. "Your offence" cried the old man,- "Don't you know that we cannot entertain you in this way when we ask you to our house. We are poor, we have neither plates nor glasses nor carpets in our house. Have you invited us to insult us by this display of your riches? We won't touch food in your house unless you can serve us exactly in the same way as we are able to entertain you when you come to us." At this all the plates and glasses and

---

[110] The middle-class made a sharp critique of such excess and material wealth by delinking money from wealth. Wealth for the middle-class came to signify politeness and respectability, which money as a material substance could not buy. For a discussion of a middle-class critique of money and a discourse of wealth as a whole world of culture, see Tithi Bhattacharya, *The Sentinels of Culture: Class, Education, and the Colonial Intellectual in Bengal (1848–1885)* (New Delhi, Oxford University Press, 2005).

[111] Bipin Chandra Pal, *Memories of My Life and Times*, vol. 1 (Calcutta: Modern Book Agency,1932), 116–118.

cushions had to be removed, plain banana leaves had to be brought and set, and it was then that these poor people would agree to accept the hospitality of their rich caste-man.[112]

New feasts were blamed because many felt that these feasts were an excuse for squandering money. Also, these feasts encouraged food bought from the market whereas earlier, women of the house used to cook for such feasts. According to some texts, westernisation led to the degeneration of indigenous culture and a decline of principles.[113] Rochona Majumdar convincingly demonstrates in her work that every aspect of the Bengali marriage ceremony assumed a strictly ritualised, standard form with their attendant feasts and trousseaux since the late nineteenth century.[114] Giving of lavish gifts was also accompanied by printing menu cards, not just for weddings, but also for other occasions such as engagement ceremonies. Writing a menu card was a significant new feature. These menu cards provided the upper and the upper-middle-classes an opportunity to exhibit their wealth through new modes of display. These menu cards were symptomatic not just of changes that were taking place in the realm of social feasts but also of changes in the nature of food that was to be consumed.

A comparison of two menus can demonstrate the changes that came about in the feasts. In the middle-class discourse, feasts in the villages generally did not contain non-vegetarian dishes. Use of refined flour in the social feasts was a much later affair.[115] Rice was served in most of the feasts and in funerals *chivra* (rice flaked) with yogurt were commonly served.[116] *Luchi* or fried flour bread was more of a luxury.[117] Even when *luchi* was introduced at the weddings they

---

[112] Ibid.
[113] Basantakumar Chaudhuri, "Baje kharach," *Grihasthamangal*, 5th year, nos. 2 & 3 (May, June 1931 [Jaistha, Asharh 1338 BS]): 30–35; Kaviraj Indubhushan Sen, *Bangalir khadya* (Calcutta, 1928), 69.
[114] Rochona Majumdar, *Marriage and Modernity: Family Values in Colonial Bengal* (Durham: Duke University Press, 2009).
[115] Panchkari Bandopadhyay, "SeKal aar Ekal," in *Panchkari Bandopadhyayer rachanabali*, ed. Brajendranath Bandopadhyay and Sajanikanta Das, vol. 2 (Kolikata: Bangiya Sahitya Parishat, 1951 [1358 BS]),313, first published in *Prabahini*, June/July 1915 [27 Ashar 1322 BS]; Shree Mahendranath Datta, *Kolikatar puratan kahini o pratha* (1973; repr., Kolkata: Mahendra Publishing Committee, 1978), 90–92.
[116] Ibid.
[117] Bandopadhyay, "Sekal aar Ekaal ," 313.

were large in size and thick in diameter.[118] A rural feast in the late nineteenth century would generally consist of *luchi*, and a couple of vegetables like one made with pumpkin (without salt).[119] Along with these, four types of sweets made from cottage cheese (made from cow's milk) were served on an earthen platter.[120] These sweets were generally made at home or by a sweetmeatmaker specifically appointed to make sweets for the feasts. Curd, thickened milk, and sweets made from thickened milk like *gulabjamoon* were served from around the 1870s.[121] Leafy vegetables and fried *patol* (striped gourds) also began to be served around this time in communal feasts.[122]

Marks of westernisation were also seen in buying food like sweets and *singaras* (a conical fried patty stuffed with vegetables). Vivekananda, the famous preacher and reformist, lashed out against such food bought from the market.[123] Although Vivekananda argued that these fried food like *singara* and *luchi* were the source of dyspepsia among the Bengalis, his chief concern was that these foodstuff were not unique to the region. These food were 'new' and increasingly incorporated into the diet of the Bengalis and were therefore considered with apprehension.[124] Journalists like Panchkari Bandopadhyay also argued that the Bengalis were happy eating puffed rice, rice, fish, vegetables produced in the kitchen garden, *ghee*, and milk. Wastage of food was strictly looked down upon. Instead of discarding the starch obtained from rice, people consumed it with milk and sugar. Women became furious if members in the family wasted rice. It could even be given to the cow but never discarded.[125] Bandopadhyay wrote, 'Frugality and restraint saved a Bengali from hunger. --- And today

---

[118] Amritalal Basu, Op cit., 168.
[119] Jogendrakumar Chattopadhay, "Sekaler bhoj," in *Smritite sekal*, ed. Prabir Mukhopadhyay (Kolkata: Charchapad,2009), 99–109, first published in *Bangashree* (May/June 1934 [Jaisthya 1341 BS]); Datta, *Kolikatar puratan kahini*, 70–72; Basu, *"Puratan panjika,"*168; Datta, *Kolikatar puratan kahini*, 90–92.
[120] Bandopadhyay, "SeKal aar Ekal," 313; Basu. *"Puratan Panjika"* 168; Datta, *Kolikatar puratan kahini*, 90–92.
[121] Basu, *"Puratan panjika,"* 168.
[122] Basu, *"Puratan panjika"* 168; Datta, *Kolikatar puratan kahini*, 90–92.
[123] Swami Vivekananda, *Prachya o paschatya* (Kolikata: Udbodhan Karyalay, 1954 [1361 BS]), 18th reprint, 39–64.
[124] *Luchi* in fact came to be defined as something essentially Bengali soon after.
[125] Panchkari Bandopadhyay, "SeKal aar Ekal,"in *Panchkari Bandopadhyayer Rachanabali*, ed. Brajendranath Bandopadhyay and Sajanikanta Das, vol. 2 (Kolikata: Bangiya Sahitya Parishat, 1951 [1358 BS]), 313.

Bengalis are crying for rice'.[126] The implication of Bandopadhyay and many like him was definitely that a money-based economy was taking the place of subsistence economy and new feasts typically represented that economy of splendor. Jogendrakumar Chattopadhyay(b.1867), a regular contributor to journals like *Tattvabodhini, Bangadarshan, Bharati, Sahitya,* and *Prabasi* as well as Sunitikumar Chattopadhay, a reknowned scholar of linguistics, noted with grief-laden wonder the increasing expenditure of wedding ceremonies. They also observed that the number of ceremonies surrounding a wedding also increased simply to display pomp. They referred to the ceremony of *paka-dekha* (fixing the match) and the consequent squandering of money for the occasion, which was absent in olden days. Traditional weddings, they wrote, were simply preceded by an *ashirvad* (blessing the bride and groom) and a sharing of sweets. But the modern *paka-dekha* ceremonies could never be complete without forty to fifty dishes for a single ceremony.[127] Sunitikumar Chattopadhyay was also appalled at the introduction of fish in the new feasts. He narrates an incident from probably the beginning of twentieth century, when men were scandalised to find fish curry being served at a wedding feast. However, within twenty years of this incident, the groom's family refused to eat in feasts where fish was not served. Chattopadhyay considered this a rude jolt to Indian and Hindu traditions and cultural sensibilities and was vehemently opposed to new customs like eating at a table.[128]

There were definitely some perceptible changes in the feasts. A wedding menu card from urban Calcutta in 1925 showed an enormous array of food. The card was divided into different sections, like vegetarian items, non-vegetarian dishes (separate lists for both fish and meat) finger food, pickles, fresh fruits, dried fruits, dessert, and juices.[129] The list was a long one. Vegetarian items included *luchi,* fried eggplant, fried pointed gourd, sweet rice, green jackfruit curry, cabbage ball curry, mango chutney, ginger chutney, dried apricot chutney, and papaya chutney. Non-vegetarian items included rice made with fish, a vegetable made with fish head, a hodgepodge of fish, *bekti* [a type of

---

[126] Ibid.
[127] Jogendrakumar Chattopadhay, "Sekaler bibaha," in *Smritite*, 142–153, 146–148, first published in *Prabasi*(1938 [1345BS]), 25–33; Sunitikumar Chattopadhyay, "Amader samajik pragati," in *Bharat-sanskriti* (1957 [1364 BS]; repr., Kolikata: Mitra o Ghosh, 1963[1370 BS]), 204–209.
[128] Sunitikumar Chattopadhyay, "Amader samajik pragati", 204–209
[129] Wedding menu from the wedding of Pratima Debi and Kanailal Gangopadhyay. (From Indubala Debi's album.)

fish] fry, shrimp with bottle gourd, fish balls, prawn kebab, two other prawn preparations, roasted carp, *hilsa* made with yogurt, and four forms of meat preparations. Amongst fruits, there were oranges, apples, pineapples, mangoes, pears, guavas, papayas, Indian plums, cucumbers, and bananas.[130]

One engagement-ceremony menu surpassed even this wedding menu in splendor and variety. In 1927, the feast for the engagement ceremony for Indira Devi consisted of *luchi*, fried leafy vegetables, fried pointed gourd, Bengal gram, vegetables made from banana blossom, cauliflower and peas curry, cottage cheese curry, rice made with cottage cheese, cucumber *raita* (an yogurt dish), ground raisin chutney and a chutney made from dried apricots and dates amongst the vegetarian items. Non-vegetarian food also had a long list, and surpassing even the elaborate presentation of the wedding menu mentioned earlier, this menu had the dessert section divided into three subsections, according to different categories of sweets. Even beverages had two sections: one for juice and the other was called the 'fancy water' section, which incorporated new beverages like soda water, lemonade, lime juice soda, and icecream soda.[131] Another engagement ceremony two years later, in 1929, incorporated peach pudding, pear pudding, pineapple pudding, and ice cream in its menu.[132]

What became apparent from such description of menus was the huge expenditure on food. Of course, such expenditure occurred only amongst a few upper and upper-middle-class Bengalis, which incurred the wrath of those who were living in an imagined tradition. But the inescapability of a new culture of money dominated these feasts, not only in their liberal acceptance of new food items, but also in the new customs and features that became associated with it. Menu cards also implied that even if the classes lower in rank to upper-middle classes were not always able to organise such elaborate feasts, at least they were partaking of pleasures of consumption in these new feasts. The regional and the cosmopolitan coexisted in a 'Bengali' self and contributed to the making of the Bengali cuisine.

Comparison of menus in feasts of the older rural community and the new social feasts were constantly fraught with tension. A custom that became obsolete with the coming of new and much more elaborate feasts was that of *sora bandha* (carrying home left-over food). In fact, *sora bandha* was a major

---

[130] Ibid.

[131] Engagement menu from the engagement ceremony of Indira Debi. (From Indubala Debi's album.)

[132] Ibid.

issue of discussion in many texts on the new feasts. *Sora bandha* implied that guests could take whatever they could not eat and even more food back home with them. Generally, one could take home sixteen *luchis* and a dozen pieces of *sandesh*. Often small children accompanied the invited person simply to help carry food back home with them.[133] For those who idealised an imagined village life, the obliteration of this custom signified an erosion of affective memories. According to Jogendrakumar Chattopadhyay, there were two reasons for the disappearance of this custom. First of all, he blamed imitation of the western civilisation and consequent disaffection for one's family. Second, he argued that the new feasts had become so elaborate and expensive that it was no longer possible to sustain such a ritual.[134] Chattopadhyay narrates an incident to elaborate his point:

> Once a landlord saw a young man leaving without taking his leftover food. He became upset and said, 'These days men have become really selfish. Is your own consumption in the feast going to fill the stomach of your family? How could you forget your mother and siblings who are waiting for you?'[135]

It would be a mistake to assume that most of the middle-class were lamenting the disappearance of *sora bandha* like Chattopadhyay. In fact, there were many like Saratkumari Chattopadhyay who absolutely abhorred this practice and considered it to be a detriment to the progress of civilisation. They were only too happy to see this practice of taking leftover food home obliterated from the memory of a Bengali gastronomic culture. Saratkumari Chaudhurani welcomed the disappearance of *sora bandha* from new feasts as she described it as a vulgar ritual.[136] This practice incurred much expenditure and Chaudhurani writes that even if only fifty people were invited to a feast, food had to be prepared for almost two hundred people. Chaudhurani was glad that modern women did not indulge in taking *luchi* from the plate and

---

[133] Chattopadhyay. "Sekaler bhoj," 99–109, 103.
[134] Ibid., 103–104.
[135] Ibid., 102.
[136] Saratkumari Chaudhurani, "Meye joggir bishreenkhala," in *Saratkumari Chaudhuranir Rachanabali*, ed. Brajendranath Bandopadhyay and Sajanikanta Das (Kolikata, 1950 [1357 BS]), 215–222, first published in *Bharati* (Kolikata, December 1908 [Poush, 1316 BS]); Saratkumari Chaudhurani, "Ekal o ekaler meye," in *Saratkumari Chaudhuranir Rachanabali*, ed. Brajendranath Bandopadhyay and Sajanikanta Das (Kolikata, 1950 [1357 BS]), first published in *Bharati o Balak* (Kolikata, 1891 [Aswin-Kartik, Magh, 1298 BS]).

keeping it aside for taking home with them, as did women in earlier times.[137] However, according to Chaudhurani, the practice of expenditure remained the same even in modern day feasts.[138] Mahendranath Datta was also quite critical of this custom and ridiculed by saying that even when the sugar syrup spilled from the sweets onto a woman's sari she would insist on carrying the *sora* home with her.[139]

THE COSMOPOLITAN/REGIONAL: THE COLONSER AND THE COLONISED

As the discussions until now show, the line between cosmopolitanism and regionalism cannot be drawn clearly in respect to the gastronomic culture in colonial India. The same person who was adaptive of new gastronomic culture could also cling to what they considered to be the essence of Bengal in other respects. However, the onus of being a cosmopolitan certainly did not rest on the shoulders of the colonised alone. In fact, the British residing in India could actually be pretty regional in the sense that they often clung to their type of cuisine and steered clear of the native variety. However, such was the magic of colonial modernity that ultimately this middle rung of the Empire had to adopt what they found in the colonies. The recipe of mango marmalade given by Steel and Gardiner could not have been possible had the British not encountered mango in India. The role mango played in the life of the British in India can be understood from the advertisement preceding Mrs. John Gilpin's text in her cookbook *Pakwan-ki-kitab: Memsahib's Guide to Cookery in India*:

> FOR COUNTLESS AND TASTY DISHES
> USE
> ORIENTAL CANNERY Co'S
> **MANGO PULP**
> A delicious Indian Fruit Pulp of great food value and highest purity.
> The only perfect substitute for the fresh ripe Graft Mango
> to enjoy at any time or place.
> If your grocer hasn't it ask him to get it for you.[140]

---

[137] Chaudhurani, "Ekal o ekaler meye."
[138] Chaudhurani, "Meye joggirbishreenkhala,"215–222.
[139] Shree Mahendranath Datta, *Kolikatar puratan kahini*, 13–18.
[140] Advertisement by the Oriental Cannery Co. in Mrs. John Gilpin. *Pakwan-ki-kitab: Memsahib's Guide to Cookery in India* (Bombay: A.J. Combridge & Co., 1914).

Bengali cookbooks need to be read alongside the English cookbooks written for the British in colonial India. There was a definite change visible in the cookbooks that appeared after 1857. Scholars such as Collingham, Narayan, Susan Zlotnick, and David Burton have noted that the British became more conscious about preserving their British identity after 1857.[141] The cookbooks consequently began urging for a simpler British diet. Colonel Kinney-Herbert emphatically wrote under the pseudonym Wyvern:

> Our dreams of to-day would indeed astonish our Anglo-Indian forefathers. With a taste for light wines, and a far more moderate indulgence in stimulating drinks, has been germinated a desire for delicate and artistic cookery. The molten curries and florid Oriental compositions of the olden time- so fearfully and wonderfully made –have been gradually banished from our dinner tables.[142]

The revolt of 1857 led to the abolition of the rule of the East India Company and direct rule by the crown in India. Consequently what followed was an unprecedented degree of racialization of colonial politics. The British residents in India were now expected to keep their distance from the natives. Based on this phenomenon, most scholars have almost taken for granted that it was to avoid the earlier Indian ensemble of food (which the British began to consider too native and rich and spicy to be included on their table) that the British changed their diet after 1857. Nowhere is this change more visible than in Wyvern's *Culinary Jottings*. Wyvern asked his readers to concentrate on simple meals. He argued for a reformist cookery by which he implied a reformation of Anglo-Indian cooking. This reformist cookery meant to do away with even the use of curry powder in Anglo-Indian cooking. However, what was prescribed could not be called a typically English cuisine. In most of the menus suggested by Wyvern majority of the recipes were of French origin. Here are some samples:

Menu No. VII
For a party of six

---

[141] Collingham, *Curry*; Narayan, "Eating Cultures"; David Burton, *The Raj at Table*, Susan Zlotnick, "Domesticating Imperialism: Curry and Cookbooks in Victorian England," *Frontiers: A Journal of Women's Studies* vol. 16, no. 2/3; Gender, Nation, and Nationalisms, (1996): 51–68.

[142] Wyvern, *Culinary Jottings for Madras* (Madras, 1878; first ed. 1879), 1–2.

Consomme a la Royale.
Pomfret a la maitre d'hotel.
Filets de pigeon a la Bordelaise.
Cotelettes de mouton a la Mainteon.
Fillet de bouef aux haricots verts.
Canapes de becassines.
Œufs aux topinambours.
Tourte de cerises.
Boudin glace aux confitures.
Fromage, hors d'ouevres.
Dessert.[143]

Menu No. VIII
For a party of six
Pot au feu.
Filets de pomfret sauce aux capres.
Pegeon en aspic, sauce ravigotte.
Cotelettes de mouton, sauce soubise.
Poularse braise a la jardinière.
Aubergines a l'Espagnole.
Beignets d'abricots.
Puree de fraises glace.
Fromage, hors d'eouvres.
Dessert.[144]

Menu No.XVII
For a little home dinner
Potage au pauvre home.
Darne de seer en papillote.
Cotelettes de mouton au macedoine de legumes. Moringakai au gratin.
Tartelettes d'amandes.
Fromage, hors d'oeuvres.
Café noir.[145]

Thus reform had a very specific racial implication for Wyvern. The 'spicy' native was being marked as an outcast. French cuisine which had already become the haute cuisine of Europe was also becoming the cuisine of the British Empire. Steel and Gardiner were quite critical of the ordinary Indian

---

[143] Ibid., 220.
[144] Ibid., 225.
[145] Ibid., 257.

cook who they argued, did not know how to cook anything other than steaks, chops, fried fish, and quails for breakfast. They complained:

> Tea made and poured out by a *Khidmatgar* at a side table, toast and butter coming in when the meal is half-finished, and the laying of the table for lunch while the breakfast eaters are still seated, combine to make new-comers open their eyes at Indian barbarities.[146]

Evidently, it was the union of the British food and the so-called Indian style of entertainment that the authors were worried about. Distaste for their former enemies in India, however, did not keep the recipe book purely British. It included recipes from all over Europe such as Italian salads, German salads, Spanish salads, and Russian salads. Indian food was in fact, contrasted not so much to the British food but to what has been rightly regarded as 'continental' food in Indian English. A small section on Indian dishes was included but the authors point out rather disapprovingly that most of the Indian dishes were extremely greasy and sweet and not suitable for the British palate. However, the focus on preserving identity needs to be problematised. Even those in favour of a more respectful English cuisine after 1857 could not do away with Indian food altogether.

From *The Indian Cookery Book*, published in 1869, it seems that so-called reformist endeavours of those who tried to erase whatever Indianness was left in British cuisine, were in vain. The author of this book who had stayed in India for thirty five years was not eager to do away with the kind of hybrid meals that prevailed before 1857.[147] In fact, as the name suggests, *The Indian Cookery Book* was basically a compilation of Indian recipes beginning from rice dishes like *khichri* and *pulao* to preserves like *kasundi*. There were in fact very few 'pure' British recipes and hardly anything French.[148] If this book had recipes for Indian dishes, then Mrs John Gilpin's book had recipes that could actually be called 'hybrid.' Gilpin, for instance, gave recipes like curried

---

[146] F.A. Steel and G. Gardiner, *The Complete Indian Housekeeper & Cook: Giving the duties of mistress and servants the general management of the house and practical recipes for cooking in all its branches* (1898; repr., London: William Heinemann, 1902), 45.

[147] A Thirty-Five Years Resident, *The Indian Cookery Book: A Practical Handbook to the Kitchen in India Containing Original and Approved Recipes in Every Department for Summer Beverages and Home-made Liqueurs: Medicinal and Other Recipes Together With a Variety of Things Worth Knowing* (1869; repr., Calcutta: Thacker, Spink & Co. 1931)

[148] Ibid.

beef slices with Italian *pulao*. Curried beef basically entailed a liberal use of curry powder.[149] In fact, Gilpin's recipe book was full of recipes that mixed an indigenous ingredient with a non-indigenous one. Such items included curried macaroni, vegetable curry, and American *bhoota* (corn).[150]

Thus while the Indians began receiving new fruits and vegetables, the British also began to incorporate Indian ingredients in their cooking, even though they avoided Indian styles of cooking. Steel and Gardiner wrote:

> Indian flour from many local mills, notably at Delhi and Bombay will be found quite equal to Snowflake American, and more than half as cheap again. Indian vermicelli or *semai* is no bad substitute for Italian, and *soojee* will take the place in all recipes of semolina. It is, in fact, the 'florador' of English shops. Wheaten groats or *dulliya* make excellent porridge.[151]

Names of the ingredients changed but the use remained the same. Collingham argues that the new cookbooks were specifically written for the British women in India who wanted to create a home environ in the colony. Thus the focus was more on cheese crumb croquettes, thick kidney soup, and Yorkshire pudding rather than on curries and Indian *pulaos*.[152] However, Collingham admits that even after the takeover of India by the British crown and consequent attempts by the British in India to retain their identity by restraining themselves to a more on sober English food, hybridity of cuisine could not be avoided. English women often did not know how to cook. Moreover Indian kitchens were not equipped for British cooking. As a result they often had to depend on the *bawarchis* (Indian Muslim cooks) who incorporated their own knowledge of cooking while making English food.[153] The preservation of identity need not necessarily forego the pleasurable experience of curry. Making macaroni with curry powder could easily preserve a British identity while retaining pleasures of consumption. What also needs to be taken into account is that it was often not the case that the *bawarchis* were responsible for the hybridisation of Anglo-Indian cuisine. Collingham in this case argues that *bawarchis* often had a problem in understanding what

---

[149] Mrs. John Gilpin, *Pakwan-Ki-Kitab. Memsahib's Guide to Cookery in India* (Bombay, 1914), 52.
[150] Ibid, 56, 131,168.
[151] Ibid., 12.
[152] Collingham, *Curry: a Biography*, 161.
[153] Ibid., 160–161.

was asked of them. Hence they Indianised British cuisine.[154] However, what needs to be noted here is that cookbooks written by Anglo-Indian writers often had an Urdu edition. Steele and Gardiner's book, *The Indian Cookery Book* and *Dainty Dishes for Indian Table* both had Urdu editions specifically written for the *bawarchis*. Although *Bawarchis* were not always literate, it was expected that someone in the family who could speak Urdu would be able to explain recipes in Urdu to the *bawarchis*. Thus the *bawarchis* did not necessarily have a problem in understanding what was asked of them. When the Anglo-Indian writers wrote the recipes they were reliving their experiences as citizens of the empire, the experiences of pleasures they could not totally erase from their memory.

Jennifer Brennan's memoir of India makes it clear that hybridity was a part of the British cuisine even in the twentieth century.[155] In fact, it is the hybridity of the British cuisine in colonial India that Brennan takes delight in. Brennan was born in India in the year 1935. Her maternal great-grandfather had sailed from Britain to India where Brennan's father met her mother. Brennan admits that the lunch or 'tiffin' that the British had in the twentieth century was much lighter than in the previous century. This tiffin, for example, included spiced tomato soup with saffron cream, cool green almond and water cress soup and the like.[156] But, Brennan says that they continued having cucumber *raita* (yogurt dish), *tamatar bhujia* (a vegetarian dish made out of tomatoes), *machi kebab* (fish kebab), *saag ghosh* (mutton with spinach), *aam murghi* (chicken with mangoes), *pathan* chicken pilaf, *dhal charchari* (a lentil dish), and *jhalfraizie* (an essentially Anglo-Indian dish) for lunch.[157] If on the one hand, Brennan had cooked ham and Scottish whisky marmalade on her plate, her breakfast platter also included *nimboo* curd (lemon yogurt) and *sooji* (semolina) on the other.[158] And her favourite memory was that of her grandmother churning butter from buffaloes, which she would spread on *chapatis* (Indian wheat bread) and eat with marmalade for breakfast.[159]

The cosmopolitan nature of gastronomic practices was perhaps most visible when it came to the matter of medicinal use of new food. Doctors like Chunilal Bose, who otherwise advocated strengths and nutritional values of traditional home-cooked food championed newly found baby food such as

---

[154] Ibid.

[155] Jennifer Brennan, *Curries and Bugles: A Memoir and a Cookbook of the British Raj* (New York: Harper Collins Publisher, 1935).

[156] Ibid., 80–85.

[157] Ibid., 85–117.

[158] Ibid., 72–75.

[159] Ibid., 16.

Allenbury's food and Mellin's food. He also meticulously noted down recipes for arrowroot pudding, chicken broth, and meat tea, which he prescribed for his patients along with more commonly known food for the ailing made with boiled rice or rice flakes.[160] Thus, the line between what was British and what was Bengali was becoming quite blurred. For many in the middle-class thus being a Bengali could mean several things at a time.

This adaptation and incorporation of food thus happened at all levels, but at least till late twentieth century it did not take up a public character. Especially, the Bengali cuisine that emerged in colonial Bengal never assumed a public character as *haute* cuisine assumed in France. This lack of commercialisation of Bengali cuisine actually became a marker of its aesthetic superiority in the Bengali Hindu middle-class discourse of taste. Although it never became widely commercialised and never came under the rubric of a standardised Indian cuisine, Bengali cuisine cannot be labeled as indigenist. Although some middle-class men craved for rice even while traveling in other parts of India,[161] at least some of them who ventured as tourists to Europe happily cherished French cuisine and croissant and were happy to forego fish curry for a while.[162] The point was to cosmopolitanise the domestic and yet keep its tag of Bengaliness. The resultant cuisine was hybrid, in many senses like its makers. Thus, Dwijendranath Tagore, the eldest brother of Rabindranath Tagore compared *amritee*, an essentially Bengali sweet to cake in a poem.

> As I have no other
> O Charlie, brother,
> Friend in need
> In will and deed,
> Send I to thee
> Sweet Amritee
> Do not refuse
> To make good use
> Of eleventh Magh cake[163]
> For Bordada's Sake. (26-9-25)[164]

---

[160] Chunilal Bose, *Khadya*, 6th ed (1910; Repr., Kolikata, 1936), 381–404.
[161] Baradakanta Sengupta, *Bharat bhraman*, vol. 1 (Kolkata, 1877 [1284 BS]), 58–60.
[162] Pratap Chandra Ghosh, *Bangalir Europe darshan* (Kolkata, 1888), 34–36.
[163] Eleventh *Magh* is the foundation day of Brahmo Samaj, the monotheistic faith conceptualised first by Rammohun Ray.
[164] Banarasidas Chaturvedi, "Bordada Srijukta Dwijendranath Thakur," *Biswabharati Patrika*, Nabaparjay 8, (1903 [Sraban 1410 BS]), 66–72, 71, first published in *Bharatiya Gyanpith* (Kashi, 1988).

Inspector Sundar *babu*, one of the chief characters in Hemendra Kumar Ray's (1888–1963) detective fictions, would often assert emphatically that he adored the British because they had brought chicken cutlet to Bengal, but he also celebrated the invention of *sandesh* and *rasogolla* by the Bengalis.[165] In Ray's fictions, Bengali domestic servants could cook excellent potato salads and tea cakes.[166] The narrative of Bengali cuisine is thus as much about the celebration of domesticity and regional cosmopolitanism as about the fissures that helped in the self-fashioning of the Bengali middle-class. The more 'refined' the cuisine became, the more its distance from the cuisines of the lower orders grew. Also, while some aspects of what could be labeled as 'Mughlai cuisine' was appropriated within the folds of this Bengali cuisine, it was scoured and rinsed so well as to make it look like a Hindu cuisine, thus erasing elements of its 'other.'

---

[165] Hemendrakumar Ray, "Sajahaner mayur," in *Hemendrakumar Ray rachanabali*, vol. 9, ed. Geeta Datta and Sukhamay Mukhopadhyay (Kolkata: Asia Publishing Company, 1986), 11–12.

[166] Hemendrakumar Ray, "Sonar paharer jatri," in *Hemendrakumar Ray rachanabali*, vol. 5 ed. Geeta Datta & Sukhamay Mukhopadhyay (Kolkata: Asia Publishing Company, 1983), 71.

3

Aestheticizing Labor?
An Affective Discourse of Cooking in Colonial Bengal

In colonial Bengal the nature of cooking transformed in a significant way: it became gendered like never before. Though even in pre-colonial India women were largely responsible for cooking, this act was never defined within the specific parameters of gender roles. In several texts written in medieval Bengal, cooking was done by women but they were not specifically seen as inhabiting the domestic space. In other texts, specifically in *Vaishnava* (a particular religious sect that was inspired by Chaitanya, a religious preacher)literature, even if men did not directly cook for Chaitanya, the way they served him food symbolised acts of devotion to the preacher.[1] In nineteenth century Bengal, however, a discursive space was constructed wherein women were situated as passionate cooks solely responsible for cooking. The business of cooking was caught up in a new rhetoric: a new façade of cooking became visible, the façade of an aesthetic act. Cooking came to be defined in affective terms, in terms of art and educative principles.

The notion of affect became so significant in the act of cooking because this culinary performance was elevated to a higher plane of everyday existence in the lives of the middle-class. The aesthetics of cooking has been reflected to some extent in the *Vaishnava* texts as a form of devotional exercise. However,

---

[1] For a detailed account of what Adwaitacharya and Sarbabhouma Bhattacharya, two well-known disciples of Chaitnya fed him, see Bijanbihari Bhattacharya, "Adwaitacharya ebong Sarbabhouma Bhattacharyer Grihe Mahaprabhur Bhojanbilas," in *Bangabhasha o bangasanskriti* ed. Bijanbihari Bhattacharya (1985; Repr., Kolikata: Ananda Publishers, 1994), 190–201.

for the colonial middle-class, cooking was also an integral part of 'becoming.' The way the middle-class constructed themselves revolved around making cooking a gendered act. Cooking, which in a middle-class utopian world was presented in a colorful mould by middle-class women somehow lent this act of labor a different flavour when compared to the act of cooking done by newly employed servants in middle-class homes. At the same time, the notion of discipline was also incorporated in this gendered discourse of cooking which was the crux of the modernity of the middle-class in colonial Bengal. Everyday food needed to be cooked and presented in a manner that would evince restraint, beauty, and elegance– traits that create middle-class taste– not to be left in the hands of hired cooks.

In the middle-class discourse, tastefulness, restraint and cleanliness was tied with the notion of the pleasure of eating, which was to be marked off from 'mass cooking' or 'mass eating'. Thus, in order to be separated from excess, and the 'mass' element of cooking, middle-class gastronomic culture had to be cradled within the domestic space. However, this domestic space was not untrammeled by the new changes, a very significant one being the introduction of hired male cooks within one's home. The colonial middle-class who was also ensconced in new professions in their 'public' life, like their nineteenth century counterparts in the Western world was quite keen on not letting professionalism intrude their private space. Home not only became the space where the middle-class could live a life of leisure, it was also the place where women played an active role as taste makers that constructed the middleness of the middle-class, a phenomenon perceived in almost all industrialised nations in the nineteenth century.[2] Bourgeois women now infused home, the site of consumption, with an essence of domestic culture.[3] In the middle-class discourse of taste, women created the sensibilities for men in order to escape the tyrannies of the outside world, and providing escape routes for fulfillment in familial love and cultural life.[4] Thus, a different form of labour had to be constructed, which could enhance the middleness of middle-class culture.[5]

---

[2] Linda Young, *Middle-Class Culture in Nineteenth Century America, Australia and Britain* (Palgrave Macmillan, 2003).

[3] Karin Wurst, *Fabricating Pleasure: Fashion, Entertainment and Cultural Consumption in Germany, 1780–1830* (Detroit: Wayne State University Press, 2005).

[4] Ibid.

[5] Joane Hollows, "Science and Spells: Cooking, Lifestyle and Domestic Femininities in British *Good Housekeeping* in the Inter-War Period," in *Historicizing Lifestyle: Mediating Taste, Consumption and Identity from the 1900s to 1970s* ed. David Bell and Joanne Hallows(Hampshire, England, Burlington, VT, USA: Ashgate, 2006).

This middleness could only be enhanced if in the middle-class discourse of taste, women's cooking could be situated vis-à-vis the labour of paid male cooks. The affective politics of the respectable Bengali middle-class revolved around their scorn for manual labour which was perceived in the practices of the hired cooks and their constant aestheticisation of women's cooking. The rhetoric on cooking, aestheticised women's cooking by comparing it with love and affection. But the process in which the act of cooking was aestheticised needs to be situated in its socio-economic context, especially with the changing economic scenario in Bengal. Two changes especially warrant our attention. Sharatchandra Pandit's (better known as *Dadathakur*) satirical poems capture these changing tides of the time, as in this one:

> Jadu was well fed by his mother and aunts
> Jadu comes to the city in search of jobs
> His newlywed wife too comes with him
> She then assumes the supervisory role of Jadu's household
> Oriya Brahmin comes and becomes the mistress of the house
> He has now become Jadu's own in places like the kitchen and the market---
> One day Jadu found pieces of soil and stone inside the rice
> He literally swallows the hodge-podge of eggplant, potato and radish.[6]

Thus by the 1930s, Oriya Brahmins were taking over the kitchen with their rice and lentil.[7]

In the course of the nineteenth century, Calcutta emerged as the economic base of the British Empire. The new factories and industries that were emerging needed a large labouring population to work in it. This attracted a large number of population from Bihar and upper India to Calcutta in search of jobs in these new places. At the same time there was also a large floating population of servants, cooks, gardeners, sweepers, washer men, and similar groups among whom Bengalis and Oriyas figured most prominently.[8] The

---

[6] Sharatchandra Pandit, "Aahar madhuri," in *Dadathakur rachana samagra* ed. Jangipur-Sangbadgosthi with an introduction by Hiren Chattopadhyay (1983; Repr., Kolkata: Biswabani Prakashani, 2006 [1403BS]), 181, first published in *Jangipur Sangbad*, Year 16, no. 18, 1929 [1336 BS].

[7] Sharatchandra Pandit, "Sabhyer sahadharmini," in *Dadathakurrachana samagra*, ed. Jangipur-Sangbadgosthi, (1983; Repr., Kolkata: Biswabani Prakashani, 2006 [1403BS], 181, first published in *Jangipur Sangbad*, year 16, no. 19, 1929 [1336 BS]).

[8] Rajat Kanta Ray, *Social Conflict and Political Unrest in Bengal 1875–1927* (Delhi: Oxford University Press, 1984), 38.

bulk of this working population in Calcutta had no natural link with the respectable Bengali society in Calcutta. As Rajat Kanta Ray argues, this so-called respectable society came to be divided into two groups of people, the propertied magnates who looked down upon the service class and the professional men who scorned manual labour and valued education as a source of earned income.[9] Cultural politics of these two groups, especially the latter, was defined by their imagination of the public and the private space.

While the industrial working class was outside the boundaries of the everyday life of the Bengali middle-class society, the other labouring population who worked within the middle-class homes could not be avoided. Domestic labour of people who formed the myriad categories of gardener, door keeper, sweeper, or washer men is beyond the scope of this book. Here the focus is on professional male cooks vis-à-vis middle-class women who cooked for their family as the former was the only group of people who had direct access to one of the most 'private' spaces in home –the kitchen– which was imagined to be a domain of the women of the household. Middle-class assumptions of who should cook revolved around the formation of a spatial discourse, which in its turn had broader implications for class and gender.

The other big change was in the lives of middle-class Bengali women. It was almost considered natural that Western-educated Bengali middle-class men would need to converse with a wife, who would also be educated to some extent. Thus the middle-class advocated female education with the thought that education would make women better mothers and better wives and equip them better for housework. At first a few Bengali Hindu men objected to female education on the ground that many of the early schools were started by missionaries. But by the 1850s, Indian men themselves started organising institutions for female education. While in 1863, there were 95 girls' schools with a total attendance of 2,500, by the year 1890 this number increased to 2,238 schools with more than 80,000 students.[10] For Muslim women, the first significant institution was the Faizunessa Girls High School in Comilla.[11] In 1882, a group of young Muslim progressives in Dhaka led by Abdul Aziz,

---

[9] Ibid., 39.
[10] Ghulam Murshid, *Reluctant Debutante: Response of Bengali Women to Modernization, 1849–1905* (Rajshahi: Rajshahi University Press, 1983), 43.
[11] Sonia Nishat Amin, "The Orthodox Discourse and the Emergence of the Muslim Bhadramohila in Early Twentieth Century Bengal," in *Mind Body and Society: Life and Mentality in Colonial Bengal*, ed. Rajat Kanta Ray (Calcutta: Oxford University Press, 1995), 391–392.

Bazlul Karim, Fazlur Rahim and Hemayetuddin, founded the Anjuman-e-Ahbabe-Islamiya. The primary purpose of this institution was fostering socio-cultural regeneration among Muslims in the field of female education. There were other liberal reformers like Kazi Motahar Hossain and Abul Fazal who made significant contribution to the cause of female education in the early decades of the twentieth century.[12] Partha Chatterjee argues that formal education became a requirement for the 'new' woman and nationalist ideology called for women to achieve cultural refinement through modern education. However, it was also demanded that the new woman be different from the Western woman.[13] The question of a proper curriculum for women stirred the Bengali middle-class.

THE PEDAGOGY OF COOKING: THE CHANGING CURRICULUM OF THE 'NEW' WOMAN

In her work on the changing role of women in colonial Bengal, Meredith Borthwick has shown how new techniques of education, culinary skills, and hygienic trainings were created to hone the traditionally used skills of new woman.[14] Since Borthwick's work is on the overall change in women's lives in colonial Bengal, she naturally does not delve into details about what the specific social requirements were that actually made cooking an exacting act. For this, the discourse that emerged on cooking needs to be read more carefully. Through introducing new curriculum on cooking in educational institutions, Bengali middle-class valorised women's cooking as an act of love. To make this idealisation concrete, each and every act of cooking as well as the kitchen space was glorified by the Bengali middle-class.

Schools like the *Utterparah Hitakari Sabha* included cooking in its list of subjects for study, and a cooking prize was awarded by the *Madhya Bangla Sammilani* in 1889.[15] The *Mahakali Pathshala*, established on conservative Hindu principles in the year 1893 placed great emphasis on the learning of

---

[12] Ibid., 409–410.

[13] Partha Chatterjee, *The Nation and its Fragments: Colonial and Postcolonial Histories* (1993; repr., New Delhi: Oxford University Press, 1995), 128–129.

[14] Meredith Borthwick, *The Changing Role of Women in Bengal 1849–1905* (Princeton, N.J.: Princeton University Press, 1984).

[15] *Indian Mirror*, Sunday Edition, 7th July, 1878; *Bamabodhini Patrika*, 4:3, 296 (September 1889), described in Meredith Borthwick, *The Changing Role of Women in Bengal*, 211–212.

Aestheticizing Labor? 111

culinary skills. Even in the so-called modern educational institutions like the Victoria College, cookery was included in the curriculum.[16] Apart from the inclusion of culinary skills in schools and colleges, various domestic manuals and women's journals began publishing recipes for the benefit of modern women.

Jadunath Mukhopadhyay, a well-known practitioner of Western medicine wrote an instruction manual addressed to his daughter.[17] This manual was a classic example of what the middle-class wanted women to appropriate from the new education. Mukhopadhyay, in this manual, brushed aside what could earlier be called women's obligations to her household, such as worshipping the family deity or observance of certain rituals. According to Mukhopadhyay, education needed to be devised in a way that would teach women how to take care of their husbands.[18] Of course, a husband could never stay well eating semi-boiled pulses, unsalted fish curry or oversalted vegetables.[19] Thus, the chief purpose of women's education was to teach women how to take good care of her household and family.[20] Instruction manuals written for Muslim women also gave such advice.[21] Cookbooks, giving women detailed instruction for cooking, began to be published since the late nineteenth century. However, as Meredith Borthwick argues, this extant literature was created more for widening the culinary skills of women rather than teaching them to cook from scratch.[22] Borthwick further maintains that culinary skills never decreased. In fact, they became more exacting to suit different social requirements.[23]

While Borthwick analyses how culinary skills became an issue for discussions on educational curriculum, what needs to be mentioned here is that apart from being considered part of a discipline, cooking was being defined as educational in another way too. Education was given a cultural definition in the context of culinary skills. Instructions for cooking went beyond cookbooks and domestic manuals. It became an integral part of the overall education for

---

[16] Ibid., 98–100.
[17] Jadunath Mukhopadhyay, *Bangalir meyer niti-siksha (putrir prati pitar upadesh)* [(Ranaghat, 1889 [1296 BS]).
[18] Ibid., 312–313.
[19] Ibid., 313.
[20] Ibid., 312.
[21] Lutfur Rahman, "Preeti-upahar," in *Lutfur Rahman Rachanabali*, vol. 2 ed. Ashraf Siddiki (1927; repr., Dhaka: Ahmad Publishing House, 1987).
[22] Borthwick, *The Changing Role*, 215–216.
[23] Ibid.

women. Bipradas Mukhopadhyay, who wrote a number of immensely popular cookbooks as well as cookery columns, lamented that the culinary education that was consistently celebrated in ancient India was on its deathbed. He blamed women's lack of interest in cooking for this degeneration of culinary education. In fact, through his cookbook he intended to provide instructions on cooking for 'new' women.[24] Priyanath Basu drew up the following list of what women were supposed to know by way of their work in and around the kitchen:

> What women are supposed to learn--- where to store rice and lentils, storing pickles efficiently, how to prepare pickles, chutney and fruit preserves according to season, how to begin cooking, how to make good food in jiffy at a low cost, what should be cooked first and what later, how to cook *pulao* (a fancy rice dish), curry, *korma* (a meat dish made with yogurt), chop, cutlet, lentils, vegetables, leafy vegetables, chutney, varieties of sweets for different festivals, how to prepare mango juice, papaya juice and the like, how to make food look good, how to serve food aesthetically, how to make barley, arrowroot to cure patients, how to make varieties of soup, etcetera.[25]

Another detailed set of instructions was given in an article named "Ramanir Kartabbya," (Women's Responsibilities) published in the monthly periodical *Bamabodhini* over a period of four months. Here the anonymous writer laid down how each room of a house was to be managed. Instructions were chiefly meant for the bedroom, storeroom, the kitchen and a study room for children. The last room was definitely a new phenomenon in nineteenth century Bengal, especially in middle-class homes. The primary focus was definitely on cleanliness: 'Potatoes should be stored at one corner of the storeroom. --- These potatoes should be kept on a thin layer of sand bordered by a line of bricks so that the sand does not get scattered through the kitchen.'[26]

Such instructions almost reminds us of the way a child is first introduced to letters or grammar. Priyanath Basu assumes a narrative voice appropriate for instructing someone totally inept or novice in the art of cooking. One could find a number of proverbs on the *pash-kora-mag*, that is, the western-educated woman. One such proverb ridiculed educated women for their

---

[24] Bipradas Mukhopadhyay, *Pak-pranali* (Kolikata, 1906 [1313]).
[25] Priyanath Basu, *Grihadharma* (Kolikata, 1936), 161–163.
[26] "Ramanir Kartabbya,"*Bamabodhini* (February/March 1886 [Phalgun 1293BS]), republished in *Nari o paribar: Bamabodhini Patrika (1270-1329 Bangabda)*, comp. and ed. Bharati Ray (Kolkata, Ananda Publishers, 2002), 115–116

inability to cook: 'When women wear shoes, rice and vegetables get burnt'.[27] Here, shoes indicated the new changes in colonial Bengal. The implication of the proverb was that Western/modern changes had wreaked havoc in Bengali women's lives making her forget her responsibilities towards her family. One award winning essay in *Bamabodhini* mentioned the enormous significance of cooking amongst women of older generations from traditional families who had to feed a large number of relatives every day. The new women were blamed for their dependence on hired cooks.[28] The new woman supposedly idled away her time making fancy embroideries or listening to gramophone. But it was also written for little girls so that they were not influenced by these new women. It was hoped that when these little girls became wives following these advices, they will not be too Westernized; however, they were also not supposed to be like the quarrelsome traditional women. One might remember Bankimchandra Chattopadhyay's diatribe against modern women in his essay "Prachina o Nabina."[29] He chastised modern women for their idleness in household chores. He argues that traditional women were adept at running a household and their ethics in life was magnificent, by which he meant their respect for their husbands. However, he also admits that women in the bygone days had no aesthetic sense and spent time picking up fights on trifle matters with the world.[30] The general argument was for the construction of women who would be ideal taste-makers. Their education, which was not to be limited to culinary skills, was supposed to make them exercise restraint not just in their appearance but also in the way they presented their culinary skills.

Chandranath Basu (1844–1910), a Hindu revivalist, instructed women on the need for a large and clean kitchen, well-lit and airy.[31] A clean kitchen became important as a result of a new focus on hygiene. Reformist Muslims such as Rokeya Sakhawat Hossain considered cooking to be another form of

---

[27] Sushilkumar De, ed., *Bangla prabad chhara o chalti katha* [1945[1352 BS]; repr., Kolikata: A. Mukherjee & Co. Ltd., 1952[1359 BS]), 626.

[28] Kumudini Ray, "Hindu narir garhyastha dharma: Bamaganer rachana," *Bamabodhini* (October/November,1894 [Kartik 1301BS]), republished in *Nari o paribar: Bamabodhini Patrika (1270-1329 Bangabda)* comp. and ed. Bharati Ray (Kolkata: Ananda Publishers, 2002), 176–179.

[29] Bankimchandra Chattopadhyay, "Prachina o nabina," Bibidha Prabandha, 2nd part, *Bankim rachanabali*, vol 2 (Kolikata: Sahitya Samsad, 1973 [1380 BS]), 249–254, first published in 1879.

[30] Ibid.

[31] Chandranath Basu, *Garhyasthapath*, 2nd ed. (Kolikata: 1887 [1294 BS]), 20–22.

rational science. She emphatically maintained the need for culinary education for women.

> ---Cobwebs decorate the storeroom frequently. Spices like coriander and fennel are mixed together. It takes an hour to figure out where one has stored sugar. There is a musty smell hanging in the air. --- A teapot is used as a serving bowl for fish and vegetables like gourd and pumpkin are chopped and kept in a flour strainer. Tamarind chutney is kept in a brass pot! ---Who will ever deny the need for culinary education for the mistress of the house? --- Family members' well being depends on the food cooked by the mistress of the house. Uneducated cooks often cook *korma* with yogurt in copper vessels without an enamel base, which almost equals to poison; Muslims often suffer from dyspepsia, this is because of unhealthy food habits.---
>
> Mistress of the house needs to learn about medicine and chemistry along with cookery. What are the qualities of specific food, how long does it take to cook different ingredients, who needs to eat what, all these subjects encompass the knowledge that the mistress of the house must acquire. --- It is not enough to keep the dining place clean, the mistress of the house must ensure that even the air around the dining place is pure.[32]

Aestheticisation of women's cooking thus was extremely complex. While several traits of the middle-class discourse on refined cuisine was tied to concepts of devotion and spirituality, the notion of a rational and scientific mode of learning was also a part and parcel of such discourse. Chunilal Basu, the noted chemist had an entire section in his book on food, on how to cook hygienically and keep a kitchen clean.[33] Addressing women, he gave clear instruction on cooking rice in a way that would retain all its nutrients. He also had clear instructions for use of clay pots, cleaning utensils and keeping the kitchen spic and span.[34] In a nutshell, there was not much contradiction between a spiritual understanding of hygiene and a rational inclination towards aesthetic culinary performance. For Dineshchandra Sen (1866–1939), a historian of Bengali literature, cleanliness was a matter of concern. He emphatically stated that a clean kitchen was essential for cooking.[35] He

---

[32] Rokeya Sakhawat Hossain, "Sugrihini," in *Rokeya rachana samgraha* ed. Miratun Nahar (1904; repr., Kolkata: Biswakosh Parishad, 2001), 38–40.
[33] Chunilal Bose, *Khadya* 6th ed (1910; repr., Kolikata,1936), 213–214.
[34] Ibid.
[35] Dinesh Chandra Sen, *Grihasree* (Kolkata, Gurudas Chattopadhyay and Sons, 1915 [1322 BS]), 84–85.

reprimanded women who had the habit of wiping their hands on their clothes after cooking. He instructed women to be aware of the needs of her family members. Women were asked to use proper spoons and ladles while serving food. Sen also urged women to see to it that rice and lentil were thoroughly cleaned before being cooked.[36] This attitude to cleanliness, hygiene, and organisation in the kitchen, all associated with Victorian ideas of domesticity were also reflected in periodicals like *Bamabodhini* and even in cookbooks like Bipradas Mukhopadhyay's *Pak-Pranali*.[37] Many praised British women for their proclivity to neatness. In these periodicals it was stated quite emphatically that there was an integral relationship between neatness and beauty (often referred to as *shree*) which turned a house into home. A dirty kitchen was an eyesore according to many.[38] In fact, those who wrote in periodicals like *Bamabodhini* advised women to read books on English housekeeping in order to enhance the beauty of their households.[39] This emphasis on new aspects of cleanliness, hygiene, and order, however, did not necessarily focus on new techniques that had the potential of making one's life easy. For instance, except for Chunilal Basu's *Khadya*, these advisory tracts hardly mentioned the use of Icmic cooker, invented by Indumadhab Mullick in the early twentieth century. Icmic cooker was a special type of cooker in which rice, pulses, and vegetables could all be cooked together and fast. This extremely convenient invention was not deemed necessary for women, since the middle-class considered women to have ample time for cooking for her loved ones. Hence rice needed to be cooked on slow fire for a long time and vegetables needed to be boiled thoroughly before it was cooked.[40] Icmic cooker could at best be used by bachelors. Women were considered natural cooks. In his introductory section to his cookbook, Bipradas

---

[36] Ibid.

[37] "Grihasree sampadan," *Bamabodhini* (Kolkata:September/October 1883 [Aswin, 1290BS]), republished in *Nari o paribar: Bamabodhini Patrika (1270-1329 Bangabda)* comp. and ed. Bharati Ray (Kolkata, Ananda Publishers, 2002), 89–93; "Ramanir kartabya," *Bamabodhini* (January/February 1886 [Magh 1293])republished in *Nari o paribar*, 112-115; "Ramanir kartabya," *Bamabodhini* (February/March 1886 [Phalgun 1293BS] republished in *Nari o paribar*, 115–116; "Ramanir kartabya," *Bamabodhini* (March/April 1886 [Chaitra 1293BS], republished in *Nari o Paribar*, 117–119; Bipradas Mukhopadhyay, *Pak-pranali* (Kolikata, Gurudas Chattopdhyay & Sons., 1933 [1340 BS]), cited in Pradip Kumar Basu "Adarsha paribare adarsha randhanpranali," *Anushtup*, 32(1) (Kolkata, 1997): 14–40.

[38] "Grihasree sampadan,"89–93.

[39] Ibid., 91.

[40] Dineshchandra Sen, *Grihasree*, 84–85.

Mukhopadhyay endorsed the stereotype of little girls who took delight in creating their own world of kitchen with dust or soil.[41]

Although women were seen to be adept at cooking naturally, modernity and Western education were often blamed for the growing decline in women's interest in cooking. The middle-class literati imagined and constructed a 'Golden Age' of Bengal, when they argued all women knew how to cook. In the nineteenth century men tried to construct a Hindu-Aryan identity for them in order to contend with the loss of self-esteem with colonial conquest.[42] The Aryan identity and the search for a glorious history were relevant for all Hindus and especially for the Bengali men because of its association with vigor, conquest, and expansion. Since the latter group was often ridiculed by the colonial state as emasculate, hence the need arose for forging a new identity.[43] Although in Bengal the 'Aryan' theme was often localized, glossing over the racial connotations and inducting so-called non-Aryan elements into the Aryan fold,[44] what cannot be denied is that this construction of a Hindu identity almost always involved the constitution of a powerful image of womanhood, which as Uma Chakravarti has argued, dynamised the image of a companion of the past into a force for the present and the future.[45] This imagined Aryan woman could also fight the colonial state along with the men folk in the public domain as long as she retained her feminine virtues. But these feminine virtues flourished in the domestic sphere, which was marked out for distinct gendered performances like cooking.

One needs to keep in mind that the discourse about an imaginary past is very complex. Even in the supposed 'golden age', it seems men were as adept at cooking as were the women. This is apparent from Panchkari Bandopadhyay's essay entitled 'SeKal aar Ekal,' (Those Days and These Days) in 1915.[46]

---

[41] Bipradas Mukhopadhyay, *Pak pranali*, 3.

[42] Uma Chakravarti,"Whatever Happened to the Vedic Dasi: Orientalism, Nationalism, and a Script for the Past," in *Recasting Women: Essays in Colonial History* ed. Kumkum Sangari and Sudesh Vaid (New Delhi: Kali for Women, 1989); Swarupa Gupta, *Notions of Nationhood in Bengal: Perspectives on Samaj, c.1867–1905* (Leiden, Boston: Brill, 2009).

[43] Ibid.

[44] Swarupa Gupta, *Notions of Nationhood in Bengal: Perspectives on Samaj, c. 1867-1905* (Leiden: Brill, 2009), 28–29.

[45] Chakravarti, "Whatever happened to the Vedic dasi," 53.

[46] Panchkari Bandopadhyay, "SeKal aar Ekal,"*Prabahini* (1922 [1322 BS]) reprinted in *Panckari Bandopadhyayer racanabali*, vol. 2, ed. Brajendranath Bandopadhyay and Sajanikanta Das, (Calcutta: Bangiya Sahitya Parishat, 1951[1358 BS]).

Bandopadhyay, who praises women of the bygone era, also mentions the fact, that in 'those days', all men knew how to cook. Many Brahmin scholars were great cooks as well.[47] It is not clear as to which period Bandopadhyay refers to as 'those days.' But what is apparent, even from this not-so-clear text about the bygone, is the fact that the skill for cooking was not restricted to women as a group. Hasan Butler, a well-known and sufficiently educated chef wrote a cookbook named *Pak-Pranali Siksha* sometime around the 1940s. Butler mentions in the preface to his book that since all girls' schools had cooking in their curriculum he decided to write this cookbook. He also anticipated that all women would have to cook in the future. Hence, such a cookbook will be useful for them.[48] Butler was an exceptional chef and had cooked extensively for aristocratic Muslim families and British residents in Dhaka.[49] But his case was definitely not the norm. In another instance, Jyotirindranath Tagore, who was Chaudhurani's maternal uncle, mentions a French chef, called Cathrin, employed in their home. Cathrin was responsible for preparing the dinner for guests, and the food for home was cooked by an upper caste hired cook.[50] However, Cathrin also cooked for family members when they craved Western food.[51] The fact that the food was cooked by a *mlechcha* (foreign and impure) did not bar the Tagore family members from relishing Cathrin's cooking. However, one should mention that the Tagores were an exceptional family and the instance of a French cook cooking for the family members was more an exception than a norm. While it is true that male members of some of the middle-class families were acquiring a taste for what would be considered 'impure' foods by the upper caste Hindus, how far that taste extended to women is debatable.

When middle-class Bengalis insisted upon the inclusion of cookery in the curriculum at schools, they often argued that this was because cookery was a part of the curriculum in Britain too. However, one cannot simply call this a derivative modernity. Unlike in Victorian England, where cookery was clearly a subject of women's education, in colonial Bengal the discourse of cooking was gendered in a more complex way. Judith Walsh argues that the nineteenth

---

[47] Ibid.
[48] Hasan Butler, *Pak pranali siksha* (ND).
[49] Ibid., Butler provides certificates of Muslim Zamindars and British officials of Dhaka in his book as a proof of his excellence in culinary art.
[50] Basantakumar Chattopadhyay, *Jyotirindranather jibansmriti* (Kolkata: Pragyabharati, First Print, 1919 [1326 BS], 51–52.
[51] Ibid.

century reformation of Hindu domestic ideas grew out of the interactions of a hegemonic, transnational, nineteenth century domestic discourse and indigenous domestic concerns and practices.[52]

Walsh juxtaposes Bengali domestic manuals along with Euro-American domestic manuals written in the nineteenth century. Unlike the Euro-American manuals which were written overwhelmingly by women, Bengali domestic manuals were written chiefly by men. Walsh still sees Bengali domestic manuals in the same light as Euro-American domestic manuals because she sees domestic space as a site that reveals women's agency.[53] In her review of Walsh' book, Mrinalini Sinha argues that there is a difference between Bengali manuals and Euro-American manuals in the sense that Bengali men used the domestic space as a site to construct their own identity unlike Euro-American women who used domestic space to forge their identity.

Unlike Victorian England, where a clear cut demarcation was visible between the public and the private sphere, in colonial Bengal the demarcation was much more complex. Although women were situated in space of the family kitchen and had the responsibility of preparing food, the knowledge of cooking came primarily from men. In this sense, colonial Bengal's experience resonated with that of nineteenth century France where one form of culinary journal was specifically addressed to women instructing them on basic domestic cooking. However, the other set of journals catered to the needs of the culinary profession, which became increasingly organized between 1870 and 1900 in France.[54] In colonial Bengal, of course, great chefs like Escoffier or culinary schools of equivalent fame never existed. The male cooks who cooked within one's home never found the place that a woman had in the middle-class discourse as an author of refined taste. Hence, the need arose to instruct and remind women of their expertise in culinary skills. While women were not considered lesser beings so far as the art of cuisine was concerned, it was often lamented that they had abandoned their natural knack in the matter, and hence needed the guidance of men–the principal architects of the project for the cultivation of 'good taste.' Cooking became an object of reification. It

---

[52] Judith E. Walsh, *Domesticity in Colonial India: What Women Learned When Men Gave them Advice* (Lanham, Boulder, New York: Rowman and Littlefield Publishers, Inc., 2004).

[53] Ibid.

[54] Amy B. Trubek, *The Empire of the Senses: French Haute Cuisine and the Rise of the Modern Culinary Profession, 1870–1910* (Unpublished Dissertation: University of Pennsylvania,1995), 171–173.

was defined as the most important of all household activities since it produced food. Everything around cooking had to be sacrosanct and clean as it came to be prepared with *yagna* (a Hindu worshipping ritual involving fire) and the kitchen was considered a sacred place where one could read scriptures.[55] Bhudeb Mukhopadhyay, the famous journalist went on to write that a home which did not promote good cooking was not a good home as it neglected a part of sacred rites.[56] Middle-class men who began to take a keen interest in the subject of cookery now traversed what was considered to be a woman's domain.

While both Walsh and Sinha are right in their analysis of nineteenth century domestic manuals, a subtle change had nevertheless taken place by the 1940s. Late nineteenth to early twentieth century domestic manuals as well as debates on cooking as a subject in school for women were still struggling with the new changes and the specific nature of English education ushered in by the British colonial state. Hence, the discourse constantly critiqued the influence of modern (read Western) practices on women in particular and on the society at large. But after straining the Western influences like playing piano or reading a novella, a perfect culinary curricular could be formed, which exercised restraint, elegance, and very significantly, a distinct cosmopolitanism. Priyanath Basu, for instance, instructed on the need to make pickles, but he did not end his list without some advice on the necessity of preparing a variety of soups. Another writer, Prasannamayi Devi (1857–1939) described how her mother and aunt resembled none other than Annapurna (the bounty deity) herself when they prepared culinary delights for a literary meeting that assembled at their place. But this Annapurna was adept at preparing mutton chops served with Worcester sauce too, apart from Bengali sweets.[57] While the nineteenth century middle-class was torn between these contrary pulls, by the 1940s, appropriation of colonial influence on cuisine had become an integral part of the perceptions of the middle-class. What did not change was the glorification of women's cooking. A woman writing a cookbook in post-colonial India boasted that her daughter-in-law, who had a bachelor's degree, could cook for ten people at ease.[58] Even her granddaughter, who had a

---

[55] Bhudeb Mukhopadhyay, *Paribarik prabandha* (Hooghly, 1895 [1302 BS]), 138–141; Pratapchandra Majumdar, *Streecharitra*. 3rd ed (Kolikata, 1936), 138–141.
[56] Ibid., 189–197.
[57] Prasannamayi Devi, "Purba-katha," in *Phire dekha*, vol. 1 (Kolkata: Subarnarekha, 2011), 55, first published in 2010.
[58] Nripendrakumar Bose, *Pakshalar panchali*, with an introduction by Sudakshina Debi (Kolikata: Nath Bothers, 1977 [1384 BS]), 1–2.

degree in political science from Cambridge University, cooked something every day.[59]

Randhan-siksha (Learning to Cook), a text book written by Snehalata Das, principal of Barishal Girls' High School, formed a part of the curriculum for women's education.[60] This text was specifically incorporated in the syllabus for girls of seventh, eighth, and tenth standards. This text was written and predicated on the belief that cookery was a form of science having both practical and theoretical implications. By now, the middle-class had come to perceive gastronomy in general and the practice of cooking in particular to be an art. Here, in Snehalata Das' textbook we see an exception. For Das, culinary skills required rational, objective perceptions that needed to be exercised in a systematic and uniform manner, so that it could be taught in schools to young girls.[61]

By the time Das was setting up a cookery curriculum for girls, the Bengali middle-class diet changed for all times to come. It was almost taken for granted that a girl needed to know how to make custard or mutton stew just like she also had to be steeped in the art of making immensely complex Bengali sweets. When a girl reached the tenth standard she was introduced to what Das called 'simple English cookery,' which basically meant making beverages like tea, coffee, cocoa, mashed potato, potato chips, or toasting bread.[62]

Girls who were in the seventh standard only required to learn to make what was considered essentially Bengali food like Bengali sweets. Slightly older ones were introduced to more complex culinary skills. While some of the recipes in the text book were on complicated Bengali dishes chiefly made from fish, most of the recipes were on food incorporated and appropriated into Bengali cuisine. These could be anything from *korma* to *dorma*. It was only in the syllabus for tenth standard that Das discussed recipes for food that she identified as specifically English, like puddings or cakes.[63] Perhaps the rationale behind such arrangement was consideration of a girl's maturity and her level of education. As the girl grew up and became more familiar with the outside world, she was introduced to cuisine other than what she could learn within the domestic space. The debate was not any longer on whether to have a mutton breast cutlet or a *shukto*. The middle-class now wondered whether to

---

[59] Ibid.
[60] Snehalata Das, *Randhan-siksha*, vol. 3, 3rd ed. (Kolikata, 1948).
[61] Ibid.
[62] Ibid., 131–143.
[63] Ibid.

have stewed gooseberry or stewed rhubarb.[64] What remained constant was the image of women as passionate and devoted cooks. There also emerged a more specific distinction between the male and female acts of cooking, and this in turn was also linked to the role that food came to occupy in late nineteenth century in the construction of a refined middle-class culture.

THE MALE COOK VERSUS THE LADY OF THE HOUSE: PAID LABOUR CONTRA LABOUR OF LOVE

In making a detailed survey of the nature of jobs in the different districts in Bengal for *A Statistical Account of Bengal*, W. W. Hunter found that in the area around Calcutta, the number of cooks was as high as 5152, and the number of *masalchis* or assistant cooks was 14.[65] In Nadia, the number of male cooks hired was 876 and in Jessore a somewhat smaller number of 77.[66] Overall, the number of female cooks was much smaller than the number of male cooks and in Jessore no women were hired as cooks. In a short story 'Dine Dakati' written in the early twentieth century, Sarachchandra Das, the author, mentions that women domestic workers in a house were not allowed to enter the kitchen, which was totally controlled by Brahmin cooks.[67]

The actual number of cooks being hired in Bengali middle-class homes is perhaps not much big until much later, that is, in the early twentieth century. What is significant here is the symbolic weight that hired cooks carried within the home. The hiring of cooks was a new phenomenon in Bengali middle-class homes in the second half of the nineteenth century. These cooks would generally be male. Women were definitely employed in domestic service but more as aides in the kitchen rather than as cooks. Even in public eating places like in boarding-houses and some restaurants that were emerging at this period, cooking was a male profession. A large number of men who migrated from the villages to the city in search of work often took up cooking as a profession. The commercialisation of agriculture resulted in a decline of peasant subsistence production, which necessitated a migration to the towns.

---

[64] Ibid., 181.
[65] W.W.Hunter, *A Statistical Account of Bengal. Districts of the 24 Parganas and Sunderbans*, vol. 1 (London, 1875), 49.
[66] W.W.Hunter, *A Statistical Account of Bengal. Nadiya and Jessor*, vol. 2 (London, 1875), 39, 186–191.
[67] Sarachchandra Das, "Dine dakati," in *Goenda aar goenda* ed. Ranjit Chattopadhyay and Siddhartha Ghosh (1931 [1338 BS]; repr., Kolkata:Ananda Publishers, 1992[1399BS]).

While at home cooking was considered a feminine task, when translated into being a profession, it became a male job, marking a distinct demarcation in the realm of culinary practice.

Such gendering of culinary practices has long been a topic of curiosity and study among scholars. Scholars like Jack Goody and Stephen Mennell have associated it with a hierarchisation of cuisine. In his comparative study of Europe and Asia with Africa, Goody has shown how the development of *haute* cuisine in the former and simple cuisine in the latter can be associated with the gendered spaces of cooking in each of these cases.[68] In the case of Europe and Asia, Goody has argued that a difference between high and low gets interpreted in terms of a difference between male and female. While everyday cooking was mostly done by women, in the royal courts, men who cooked turned this daily cooking into the high cuisine of the court.[69] In Africa, on the other hand, women normally cooked at the court of kings and the dishes they prepared were no different from the ones they were cooking at home.[70]

Stephen Mennell conjectures a theory that the employment of male cooks in cooking as a public profession has a legacy in courtly cuisine and court as a social institution originated from military establishment.[71] He speculates that men always served as cooks with modern armies, and their function in the courtly kitchens began as an extension of that role. After these men established a stronghold over courtly kitchens, they also became responsible for the refinement of culinary art. This is more so because the court itself developed as the locus for the arts of consumption.[72] Subsequently as the courtly cuisine developed into *haute* cuisine, social differences also emerged surrounding *haute* cuisine. The result is a social differentiation from the everyday food of the lower orders and from the women who cooked it.[73]

Goody's analysis of the development from simple cuisine in Africa and *haute* cuisine in Asia and Europe follows a unilinear trajectory. When placed in the context of colonial Bengal, the demarcation of culinary practice, and

---

[68] Jack Goody, *Cooking, Cuisine, and Class: A Study in Comparative Sociology* (Cambridge: Cambridge University Press, 1982).
[69] Ibid., 193.
[70] Ibid.
[71] Stephen Mennell, *All Manners of Food: Eating and Taste in England and France from the Middle Ages to the Present* (Oxford, UK; New York, U.S.A.: Basil Blackwell, 1985), 201.
[72] Ibid.
[73] Ibid.

the construction of high and low assumes a rather distinctive character. Both Goody's and Mennell's arguments on a gendered development of *haute* cuisine cannot be applied in this context. The Bengali middle-class believed that a refined cuisine could only be produced by women. A distinct image of women was created and linked to the creation of a 'good' Hindu Bengali middle-class cuisine—and here the male cook took a back seat. The superiority of women's cooking was not simply predicated on their ability to maintain a ritual purity in the space of the kitchen, as Goody would argue, but more so upon their ability to infuse the act of cooking with love and affection, which the hired male cook never could. The lady who cooked in her own kitchen came to be seen as the exact opposite of the male cook, who essentially exchanged his labour for money.

In her work on the gendered character of French culinary art, Jennifer Davis has stressed on the significance of affect in women's culinary labour by arguing that in early nineteenth century France, sentiment emerged as the central feature of the discourse on women's cooking. When women cooked well, it reflected their love for the diners rather than culinary skill or experience.[74] On the other hand, Davis argues, for men to cook well, it required literacy and a broad education on their part.[75] In the realm of cuisine, a distinct demarcation of 'public' and 'private' therefore emerged in eighteenth and nineteenth century France. While Davis' conjecture about the development of *haute* cuisine in France can be applied to some extent in the case of colonial Bengal, again it can be said to be only partially true. In colonial Bengal, in the domain of the 'private,' women's culinary practice symbolised love and affection, but when men cooked in similar situations it reflected nothing but manual labour. The men who cooked in middle-class homes could hardly be compared to those that were the creators of *haute* cuisine. The history of taste takes its own form in specific situations and how a specific cuisine is constructed is integrally tied with historical contexts. While *haute* cuisine flourished in the public sphere, the refinement of Bengali cuisine had to be engraved in the domestic space of home. However, these spaces were never really clearly defined.

Scholars like Partha Chatterjee and Tanika Sarkar have explored the issue of the public and the private spheres in the context of colonial Bengal. While Tanika Sarkar has argued that for the middle-class Bengali men who were

---

[74] Jennifer J. Davis, *Men of Taste: Gender and Authority in the French Culinary Trades, 1730–1830* (Unpublished dissertation: Pennsylvania State University, 2004), 308–309.
[75] Ibid., 308–309.

increasingly marginalised in the colonial administrative system by the last decades of the nineteenth century, the domestic space symbolised by women came to be deemed as autonomous and completely distinct from the public sphere,[76] Partha Chatterjee has problematised the notion of the public and the private spheres. He argues that in colonial India, the formation of the public and private spheres did not occur in the same way as in Europe.[77] Rather, the colonised constructed the domains of the 'material' and the 'spiritual' as a way to mark themselves out from the colonisers. The world or the material domain where the colonised was humiliated only reflected the outer self of the colonised. In this domain, nationalists had no qualms in imitating the coloniser in order to retrieve their freedom. However, what was more important for the nationalists was the spiritual domain of family, which epitomised the spirituality of the East.[78] Chatterjee matches this new meaning of the home and the world dichotomy with the identification of social roles by gender. Women became the markers of this inner domain of the 'spiritual'.[79] Thus whatever changes had to be accepted and appropriated were restricted to the material domain. In the spiritual domain the middle-class created new norms of refinement that aimed to construct middle-class women.[80]

Both Sarkar's and Chatterjee's theorisation of the 'public'/ 'private' and the 'material'/ 'spiritual' has been drawn upon in this book. However, these spatial distinctions need to be juxtaposed and read together. While the formulation of the material and the spiritual, as made by Chatterjee, is immensely valuable, the ideas of public/private can also not be obliterated altogether. Without taking into account the notions of the public and the private, the gendering of cooking cannot be explained any further. While the rhetorical politics of colonial middle-class revolved around the discursive formulations of the material and the spiritual, the very materiality of food demanded the imagination of public and private spaces when it came to the matter of setting up a distinction between that which was 'in good taste' and that which was not. The question of 'who' cooks 'where' addressed this distinction. Public cooking was a profession and was taken up by the male cooks, whereas in the private, cooking as a labour

---

[76] Tanika Sarkar, *Hindu Wife, Hindu Nation: Community, Religion, and Cultural Nationalism* (Bloomington, Indianapolis: Indiana University Press, 2001).

[77] Partha Chatterjee, *The Nation and its Fragments: Colonial and Postcolonial Histories* (Princeton, NJ: Princeton University Press, 1993).

[78] Ibid., 120–121.

[79] Ibid.

[80] Ibid.

of love was definitely women's work. Even within the domestic space itself, this distinction was perceptible. For example, in her autobiography, Sarala Devi Chaudhurani (1872–1945), a political activist, makes an interesting distinction between what she calls the public kitchen and the private kitchen.[81] The public kitchen was supervised by hired cooks who cooked for the entire household, whereas the private kitchen was the place where women cooked for their husbands the few items that they most liked.[82] The latter involved wifely affection and care, whereas the former was chiefly professional.

Apparently, the employment of servants in a Bengali middle-class household or in an Anglo-Indian household had many features in common. In both the households, domestic servants were made the 'other' through class, caste or racial segregations. Their so-called dirty and unhygienic habits seem to have worried both the British officials residing in India as well as the Bengali literati. In her recent work on the culture of food in colonial Asia, Cecilia Leong-Salobir has argued that the cooks working in British households in colonial Asia did much more than just menial work. These cooks were actually responsible for the purchase of food for the Anglo-Indians and thus contributed hugely to the emergence of colonial cuisine by bringing in changes in the diet of the British.[83] However, in a middle-class Bengali household a cook did not wield any such power even unwittingly. Middle-class Bengali women had to be more active in her kitchen.

The male cooks were mostly Brahmins. One reason behind the hiring of Brahmin cooks has been cited by Swapna Banerjee in *Men, Women, and Domestics: Articulating Middle-Class Identity in Colonial Bengal*. Banerjee argues that the most significant distinction in the caste status of servants in colonial Bengal was in terms of *jalchal* and *ajalchal*: upper caste Hindus could accept water from a *jalchal* and not from an *ajalchal*.[84] Whereas a servant belonging to an *ajalchal* caste would not have entry into the kitchen, Brahmins, who were *jalchal*, were in high demand as cooks and kitchen staff (*jogare*).[85] The demand for Brahmin cooks increased to such an extent that sometimes other cooks faked their caste identity to get a job as a Brahmin cook. Male workers

---

[81] Sarala Devi Chaudhurani, *Jibaner jharapata* (Calcutta: Rupa, 1975), 9–12.
[82] Ibid.
[83] Cecilia Leong-Salobir, *Food Culture in Colonial Asia: A Taste of Empire* (London and New York: Routledge, 2011).
[84] Swapna M. Banerjee, *Men, Women, and Domestics: Articulating Middle-Class Identity in Colonial Bengal* (Oxford University Press, 2004), 67.
[85] Ibid.

coming to eastern Bengal from Orissa called themselves Brahmins and hired themselves out as cooks.[86] A man named Jagadanda, who was the leader of Oriya palanquin bearers in Dhaka in eastern Bengal, ran a cook-manufacturing factory with the help of a real Oriya Brahmin. In this factory non-Brahmin Oriyas were turned into Brahmin cooks. On an average, around a hundred fake *thakurs* (Brahmin cooks) were manufactured every year in this factory.[87] In his memoir, Pabitra Mohan Pradhan discusses his job in the household of Amar Bijoy Rai in Calcutta where he did most of the household chores and later on took up a job as a cook at another household. Pradhan played a significant role in the 1942 movement in the princely state of Talcher in Orissa. In Calcutta he carried on his political endeavours in his disguise as a cook.[88] Oriya cooks thronged the households of the middle-class and this enabled Pradhan, who actually belonged to agriculturalist caste, to remain in Calcutta as a Brahmin cook.[89]

In fact, one often finds scorn for Brahmin cooks in the popular literature of the period. In his reminiscences, Panchkari Bandopadhyay writes that a middle-class householder never hired a cook for his family kitchen. It was women who cooked and not the Brahmin cook.[90] Giribala Devi mentions in her memoir that *Varendra* Brahmins in northern parts of Bengal like Rajshahi or Pabna never took up the profession of a cook.[91] In fact, higher castes in villages, Giribala Devi observes, refused to eat food cooked by unknown Brahmins. However, Giribala admits that Brahmin cooks from Orissa were

---

[86] Ibid.

[87] Muhammad Waliullah, *Jug bichitra*, cited in Banerjee, *Men, Women, and Domestics*, 70–71.

[88] Pabitra Mohan Pradhan, *Mukti pathe sainika* (Nabajiban Press:Cuttack, 1949 - Second Edn. 1979), 178–194. I came to know of this book from my personal correspondence with Professor Biswamoy Pati, who made me aware of such subversions by the Oriya cooks. Also see Pabitra Mohan Pradhan, "As a Domestic Help in Calcutta," in, *A World Elsewhere: Images of Kolkata in Oriya Autobiographies* ed. Jatindra Kumar Nayek (Postgraduate Department of English(DRS I), Utkal University, in association with Grassroots; Bhubaneswar, 2010), 51–67, translated by Priyamvada Pal from Pabitra Mohan Pradhan, *Mukti pathe sainika (Dhenkanal:Self-Published, Second Edition, 1979).*

[89] Ibid.

[90] Panchkari Bandopadhyay, *Panchkari Bandopadhyayer rachanabali*, vol. 2, ed. Brajendranath Bandopadhyay and Sajanikanta Das (Kolikata, Bangiya Sahitya Parishat, 1951 [1358 BS]), 307–308.

[91] Giribala Debi, "Raybari,"*Giribala Debir rachanabali* ,[Kolkata: Ramayani Prakash Bhavan, 1977 [1384 BS]), 139.

allowed to cook for religious feasts.[92] Mahendranath Datta, the brother of the famous religious preacher Vivekananda, in his reminiscences pointed out how Brahmins never took up cooking at other people's houses in what he considered the 'bygone days'.[93] It was disrespectful for a Brahmin, who belonged to a priestly caste, to take up cooking at another's home. He argued that in earlier period there would be cooks belonging to other castes who would cook just as well as the Brahmins and that even women would cook for the feasts.[94] Brahmins could make *luchis*, but they were never called for cooking in a feast where rice was the chief staple. Women always took the front seat in feasts of the latter kind.[95] Datta narrates a popular account of how the Brahmin cook emerged. He talks of how a specific group of people emerged just to spoil the feasts. These were a random group of people who, as Datta said, took delight in criticising the food cooked in social feasts. Earlier, women cooked for these feasts. They were more demure and could not deal with these feast spoilers. Hence a stronger response to these feast spoilers was needed. This was how the Brahmin cooks emerged, who could yell back at the feast spoilers, although the fact remains that in most cases, they really did not cook well at all.[96]

Datta's account pushes the reader further to think about what was happening in relation to the question of gender and the question of caste in colonial Bengal. If one has to believe Datta, then it appears that having an upper caste cook was not an absolute requirement in Bengal at the time of his childhood. Why then do we see this sudden preponderance of Brahmin cooks? A probable explanation of this would be a consciousness about their caste status among the Bengali middle-class. Formation of a colonial middle-class in Bengal cannot be fully grasped without a reference to the question of caste.[97]

It has been argued by scholars like S.N. Mukherjee that although *bhadralok* (the respectable society, chiefly the Bengali Hindu middle-class) as a category was exclusively a Hindu group, caste did not play a role in the selection of this

---

[92] Ibid.

[93] Mahendranath Datta, *Kolikatar puratan kahini o pratha* (Kolkata, Mahendra Publishing Committee, 1973), 102,

[94] Ibid., 102.

[95] Jogendrakumar Chattopadhyay, "Sekaler bhoj," *Smritite Sekal*, ed. Prabir Mukhopadhyay (Kolkata: Charchapad, 2009),617–628, first published in *Bangashree* (May/June, 1934 [Jaisthya 1341 BS]).

[96] Ibid., 12.

[97] The *bhadralok* would consist of both the aristocratic, landed elites as well as the middle-income intermediate strata.

group.[98] Men who held similar economic positions enjoyed a similar style of living, and received a similar education would be considered a *bhadralok*.[99] While it is true that it was possible for men belonging to the lower castes to climb up the social hierarchy on the basis of the characteristics mentioned by Mukherjee, it does not undermine the fact that the significance of caste never really died down even for the *bhadralok*. It may not have played a role in the formation of the middle-class as a class, but it was ensconced in the everyday practices of the middle-class. Having a Brahmin cook became a marker of the middle-class status in several senses. First, caste became a mode of distancing the middle-class from its 'other.' Second, having a Brahmin cook implied an effort to climb up the ladder of caste hierarchy for some lower caste groups who had become *bhadralok*. And then employing a Brahmin, a priestly caste, by a lower caste, middle-class man could also be represented as a symbol of power for the colonial middle-class. Nonetheless, it needs to be acknowledged that alongside this consciousness of caste, there was also a perceptible change in the way caste hierarchy was viewed by at least a section of the middle-class. The Brahmin cooks remained only a marker of status and for some households like the upper class Tagore family, Brahmin cooks were employed for cooking quotidian dishes like rice and pulses. Tasks of meat preparation were given to lower caste cooks.[100] Blind subscription to the food made by the Brahmin cook had the possibility of overshadowing the discourse of refinement and taste that was being constructed by the Bengali middle-class. As part of this discourse of 'taste,' the food cooked by the Brahmin cook was deemed to be of a much inferior quality when it was compared to the food cooked by the women of the house. What is more interesting is the way the definition of caste was reformulated in relation to the Brahmin cook. Prasannamayi Devi affirms in her autobiography that in the bygone days one would lose their caste status even if they ate food cooked by a high-caste male cook like the Brahmin cooks.[101] No matter how rich a woman was, she cooked for her entire family.[102]

By 1910, the number of Oriya labourers in Calcutta had gone up to more than a hundred thousand. These men were constantly ridiculed by the natives

---

[98] S.N. Mukherjee, *Calcutta: Myths and History* (Calcutta: Subarnarekha, 1977).
[99] Ibid.
[100] Prajnasundari Debi, *Amish o niramish ahar*, vol 1 (1907; repr., Kolkata: Ananda Publishers, 2000), 58.
[101] Prasannamayi Devi, 'Purba-katha,' in *Phire dekha*, vol. 1 (Kolkata: Subarnarekha, 2011), 55, first published in 2010.
[102] Ibid., 103.

of Calcutta, although in almost all the Bengali households, there were Oriya cooks and Oriya domestic helps.[103] Referring to the proliferation of Brahmin cooks from Orissa in the Bengali household, Dinesh Chandra Sen expresses his utter disgust, indicating that the tendency of these cooks to pour excessive salt into food made the food thoroughly unpalatable.[104] Sen's overt generalisation of Oriya Brahmin cooks is accompanied by his insistence that the women of the house should be the ones to cook, and he makes it very clear why women's cooking is so significant:

> *Grihini* (mistress) –is in fact the mistress of the kitchen. She would supervise the cook, as she is acquainted with the likes and dislikes of each of her family members. Food constitutes the essence of one's life. Hence, its charge cannot be left to a paid cook. When *grihini* herself takes charge of the kitchen, she resembles none other than the goddess *Annapurna* (*anna* meaning rice). She is affection personified, which makes the food she prepares, taste like nectar.[105]

Evidently, it was love and affection that set apart women's cooking from those of the hired male cooks. The lady of the house was different from the hired cooks because she did not cook for wages. She was the giver of food– the agent for imbuing culinary practice with the façade of affect and value. The names of *Annapurna* and *Lakshmi*–the rice-giving deities–are repeatedly mentioned in this context. Bipradas Mukhopadhyay, for instance, looked up to the spirituality he said could be found only in women.[106] According to Mukhopadhyay, after a hard day in the outside world, a householder could find solace in what his wife cooked. This satisfaction was unavailable in the food produced by a paid cook.[107]

This abomination for Oriya cooks spilled into post-colonial Bengal as well. *Pakshalar panchali*, written around 1977, is a case in point. The idea of this book was conceived by one Sudakshina Bhattacharya, born sometime in the late 1870s. She asked Nripendrakumar Basu to compose recipes given by her

---

[103] Godabarish Mishra, "House No. 9," in *A World Elsewhere: Images of Kolkata in Oriya Autobiographies* ed. Jatindra Kumar Nayek (Postgraduate Department of English (DRS I), Utkal University in association with Grassroots; Bhubaneswar, 2010), 17–26, 21, translated by Snehaprava Das from *Ardhashatabdira Orissa O tahinre mo sthana* (Cuttack: Granthamandir, 1996).

[104] Dinesh Chandra Sen, *Grihasree*, 84–85.

[105] Ibid.,4.

[106] Bipradas Mukhopadhyay, Pak-pranali, 2–3.

[107] Ibid.

in the form of verses and bring it out as a book.[108] This book traverses a long span of time covering a period that stretches almost from the early twentieth century to post-independent India. Sudakshina Bhattacharya begins with expressing her utter distrust for fake Brahmin cooks who intruded Bengali middle-class kitchens from other provinces of India. The result, according to Bhattacharya, was terrible diseases, and a decadent lifestyle.[109]

> A maid who has eczema in her hands and mucous is cooking
> While stirring with a ladle, she is wiping her nose with her *saree*
> She also wipes her wet hands with the saree, which is also used for wiping dishes.
> She uses the same cloth to wipe the table, sweat and passes oozing from her wounds.
> Her spit gets into the fish curry.[110]

All this was made possible by the lackadaisical nature of the mistress of the house. Thus, Bhattacharya's advice to women was to establish their rightful position back in the kitchen.[111]

THE POLITICS OF AESTHETICIZING WOMEN'S COOKING

The aestheticisation of women's cooking involved the constant valorisation of an act of physical labour, by both men and women. In her work, Dolores Hayden refers to the non-recognition of women's skills in the private sphere.[112] According to Hayden, while women may have gourmet kitchens, sewing rooms and so-called master bedrooms, her role is one of service and not autonomy.[113] While Hayden is right about the non-recognition of women's labour, what she misses out is that it is actually the act of making women autonomous in the kitchen that leads to a non-recognition of her skills. In colonial Bengal, it was the constant aestheticisation of women's labour that made them the mistress of

---

[108] Nripendrakumar Bose, *Pakshalar panchali*. With an introduction by Sudakshini Debi. Kolikata: Nath Brothers, 1977[1384 BS].
[109] Ibid., 2–3.
[110] Ibid., 5.
[111] Ibid.
[112] Dolores Hayden, *Redesigning the American Dream: The Future of Housing, Work, and Family Life* (New York, London: W.W. Norton & Company, 1984).
[113] Ibid., 65–66.

the kitchen and not merely cooks in the middle-class discourse. Thus, while one compared the vegetables chopped by her mother to a heap of jasmine flowers[114], another celebrated the kitchen as a temple.[115] A single vegetable had to be chopped in various manners for different items. Potatoes cut lengthwise went into fish curry with light gravy, rounded potatoes were added to richer dishes and small pieces were added to other vegetable preparations.[116] A popular rhyme in circulation among the middle-class went like this:

> Where the housewife is an able cook
> And can finely pare her vegetables,
> It has been heard spoken,
> That home is never broken.[117]

Hemantabala Debi (b.1894) once lamented that her ground bay leaf did not resemble sandalwood paste, while on the other hand, her mother could grind any spices like she would grind sandalwood.[118] These spices, when put into vegetables, produced different smells and taste. Hemantabala Devi argues that her mother perfected the art of grinding spices since she was a devout *satwik* woman, who did not step into the kitchen because fish was cooked there.[119] Here, Hemantabala not for once blames her mother for not entering the kitchen, since she defines cooking from the angle of purity and religiosity, which made her mother's culinary performance almost divine. This discourse presented women as loving cooks, and obscured the fact that these women were largely overburdened with fulfilling the constant needs of the family.

Here, one needs to make a careful observation about the definition of cooking. Are we supposed to look at cooking as merely a form of labour or is there something more to it as well? Toiling in a dark and dingy kitchen is obviously not a pleasurable task. Even the most passionate of the gourmet would not disagree. But when this act travels to the wider world, or when cooking becomes a profession, much can be said about the crafting of the culinary art.

---

[114] Rani Chanda, *Amar ma'r baper bari* (1977; Repr., Kolikata: Biswabharati, 1986), 6–7.
[115] Sarala Debi Chaudhurani, *Jibaner jharapata*, 9–12
[116] Sudha Mazumdar, *Memoirs of an Indian Woman*, edited with an introduction by Geraldine Forbes (Armonk, New York, London, *England: An East Gate Book* M.E. Sharpe, Inc., 1989), 33–34.
[117] Ibid.
[118] Hemantabala Debi, *Rachanasankalan*, 51–52.
[119] Ibid.

In fact, in eighteenth century France, great chefs like Escoffier took delight in the manner that the food they presented reached that level of refinement and aesthetics, which was very different from domestic culinary skills of women. Artistry became a gendered category for chefs involved in producing French *haute* cuisine.[120] Escoffier specifically states that

> cooking is undoubtedly a fine art, and an accomplished chef is as much of an artist in his particular branch of a work as a painter or a sculptor. There is as much difference as between good cooking and bad as between a symphony performed by a great master on a first-rate instrument and a so-called melody played by some out-of-tune barrel organ. In the ordinary domestic duties it is very hard to find a many equaling, much less excelling, a woman, it is her sphere in life; but cooking rises far above a mere domestic duty; it is, as I have said before, a fine art. --- It is simply that man is more thorough in his work, and thoroughness is at the root of all good, as of everything else. ---
>
> ---One of the chief faults in a woman is her want of accuracy over the smaller items- the exact amount of flavoring, the right condiments to each dish; and that is one of the chief reasons why here cooking pales before that of a man, who makes his dishes preferable on all occasions to hers.[121]

A Bengali middle-class like Bipradas Mukhopadhyay would agree to Escoffier's basic tenet that cooking is undoubtedly a fine art. However, the Bengali middle-class actually constructed a discursive space wherein the finest nuances of cuisine flourished in the domestic space of the kitchen. Women became agents who could imbue ordinary dishes with such subtle flavour that would otherwise never find a place in the new public eateries. This was a middle-class discourse that was not bothered about dining in big and fancy restaurants where chefs conjured complex cuisine. In colonial Bengal, the number of such restaurants was not that high and in whatever existed, there were hardly any such well-known chefs who had such well thought-out ideas on gourmet food, like Auguste Escoffier. A colonial pattern of administration was structured in a manner that hardly offered the middle-class any chances of big investment. Even when some of the upper-middle-class did start investing in hotels and restaurants from the early twentieth century onwards, taking up a culinary profession was unimaginable. The colonial middle-class considered

---

[120] Amy B. Trubek, *The Empire of the Senses*, 244–245.

[121] Auguste Escoffier, "Why Men Make the Best Cooks," *The Epicure* 13, no. 2 (Boston), 9, cited in Trubek, *The Empire of the Senses: French Haute Cuisine and the Rise of the Modern Culinary Profession* (PhD diss., University of Pennsylvania, 1995), 243–144.

public cooking as well as cooking done by the male cook within the home as forms of standardised cuisine, something they never cherished. On the other hand, women through their love and affection brought novelty to the food they cooked. Therefore, she excelled in the domestic sphere. A man who cooked in the hotels or a servant who cooked in the middle-class homes could never match up to her standards, because her affect and love for her family infused her cooking with a supreme sense of accuracy, which no man could ever achieve. Saradasundari Devi(1819–1907), mother of the famous Brahmo reformist Keshab Chandra Sen, gave a slightly different account in her memoir when she wrote that she and her widowed sister-in-law sent their servant to a sweetmeat maker in order to observe how good food was made. This servant would then teach these two women how to prepare good food. Saradasundari Devi and her sister-in-law cooked this food taught by the sweetmeat maker and served it on a silver platter to her father-in-law.[122] Apparently, in this instance, the lesson for what was a fine art and pinnacle of middle-class women's aesthetic creations came not only from men, but in fact, lower class men, who would otherwise be considered inferior in every sense in Bengali middle-class households.

That cuisine is a fine art was an established fact amongst the middle-class. However, in colonial Bengal and even thereafter the middle-class believed that men by nature were haphazard and disorganised. Men could never attain the finesse and care that was needed for cooking, albeit they excelled in supervision.[123] The general view about cooks was summed up by Lutfur Rahman in an imaginary conversation in which a woman advises her sister-in-law (who was soon to be married) on how to organise her household:

> The mistress of the household should never sit idle leaving all the responsibilities of her household with the servants. Those who are mean can never pay heed to cleanliness and hygiene. Servants are mean and uneducated- they are unclean. If the responsibility of cooking is given to them, you will be eating unhealthy food. You should neither trust mean female aides, nor male *Khansamas*. One should only consume food cooked by educated, intelligent women.[124]

---

[122] Saradasundari Debi, *Phire dekha-2*(1913; Repr., Kolkata:Subarnarekha, 2010), 3.
[123] Indumati Sengupta and Satyendranath Sengupta, *Adhunik randhan-bijnan* (Kolikata, 1951 [1357 BS]), 10.
[124] Lutfur Rahman, "Preeti upahar," 165–168.

Education then was supposed to be the parameter by which a class divide was drawn between the middle-class and the lower classes. Education made middle-class women intelligent, but for middle-class Bengalis, women's aspirations had to be confined within the domestic sphere.

Aestheticising cooking enabled the middle-class Bengalis to present domestic labour in a much more palatable mold. Thus even Tagore, who categorically stated in his poem, *'Narir kartabya'* (Duty of Women), that man's pride in his faculty of reason, led him to overlook the extreme monotony of cooking for women[125], took delight in recalling women's assemblies on the family terrace in the afternoon, where food preparation was one of the activities.[126] In these reminiscences, the making of mango pickle became an artistic act.[127] These acts, which were described by Tagore as feminine were also romanticised as being the last of those traits that connected the urban middle-class to its rural origins.[128] This kind of aestheticisation of women's cooking is also visible in his poem *'Nimantran'* (Invitation), where he says that a graceful hand (by which he implies a feminine touch) always made food a delightful affair.[129]

In another memoir, Amritalal Basu(1853–1929), the dramatist and theatre activist, mentions that women made temples of butter, shaped betel nuts in the form of flowers, and made garlands of chick peas.[130] His contemporary Mahendranath Datta wrote about the artistic clay molds that women made in order to give floral shapes to *sandesh*.[131] Rani Chanda gives a detailed account of such molds in her memoir on her maternal grandparents' home:

> When molds are made, it is the season of molds. *Kheer takti, sandesh, gangajoli–* different molds for different sweets. Molds for sweets were curved out (by women) from either stone or clay. Clay molds needed to be burnt later. But molds *for amsattva* (dried mango) were made from stone. There were several

---

[125] Rabindranath Tagore, "Narir kartabya" (1939[1346 BS]), Tagore, *Ravindra Rachanabali*, vol. 23 (Kolikata: Viswabharati, 1979 [1386BS] 54–55.

[126] Tagore, Chhelebela (1940[1347 BS]), in *Ravindra Rachanabali*, vol. 26 (Kolikata: Viswabharati, 1977 [1384B.S]), 583–631.

[127] Ibid., 610–611.

[128] Ibid.

[129] Tagore, "Nimantran" (Chandannagar, 1935), in *Ravindra Rachanabali*, vol. 19 (Kolikata: Viswabharati, 1976), 25–29.

[130] Amritalal Basu, *Amritalal Bosur atmasmriti*, ed. Arunkumar Mitra (Kolkata: Sahityalok, 1982), 169.

[131] Datta, *"Kolikatar puratan kahini O pratha"*, 52.

shapes given to molds like those of birds, lotus, trees, fish. --- Molds for *amsattv*a had to be curved in a different manner. A lotus needed to be curved in the centre of each petal and leaf. --- This was not needed in case of the molds for sweets.[132]

The colonial middle-class' sense of aesthetics, artistry, and refinement was tied to the notion of devotion. Rani Chanda, for instance, draws an image of her maternal aunt walking towards the kitchen from the courtyard, carrying a big utensil filled with chopped gourd and holding it high on her left palm. For Chanda this imagery of her maternal aunt resembles the gait of a worshipper walking towards the temple with flowers.[133] This form of devotion cannot be defined strictly in terms of religiosity. It was something that went beyond religion. This devotion was an integral part of the village life that was lost, a life devoid of all hazards of modernity. Thus, we frequently find mentions of village festivals and *vratas* in several memoirs of our time. In Rani Chanda's memoir there is a detailed list of such *vratas*. Food was a pivotal element in these rituals and the narrator's depiction of food presented gastronomy in its most aesthetic appearance.[134] Descriptions of *Natai Mangalchandi* and its association with sweet pancakes or the making of mustard sauce reach another level in Chanda's memoir:

> Akshay Tritiya day---- it is also the day for preparing *kasundi* (mustard sauce). --- Making *kasundi* is an auspicious job. Not everyone can do it.--- Those who clean mustard, husk it and prepares *kasundi* cannot consume bitter or sour food today. They have to do it in a pure manner with a pure mind.[135]

Cooking was thus an art, the responsibility for which cannot be bestowed on a paid cook. The skills for this art had to be learnt and cultivated over years. Unless a woman cooked everyday, she could never hone the skills needed for appropriate usage of ingredients like salt or oil in food.[136]

This aestheticisation not only made domestic labour more presentable to the women who were supposed to exercise it (indeed women also participated in the discourse); it also carried an element of validation so far as the male

---

[132] Rani Chanda, *Amar ma'r baper bari* [Kolikata: Biswabharati Granthan Bibhag, 1986 [1393 BS], 97.
[133] Ibid., 7.
[134] Ibid.
[135] Ibid., 56–57, 66–70.
[136] Gyanendrakumar Raychaudhuri, *Meenntatwa* (Kolikata, 1882 [1289 BS]), 100–101.

enunciators of this discourse were concerned. It aided the middle-class Bengali men's construction of themselves in relation to their other, the labouring classes. The aestheticisation of women's labour in the kitchen–the most conspicuous form of physical work done in middle-class homes–had the impact of distancing physical labour in respectable society from the laborious toil of the rest of the population.

To buttress the projected element of affect in women's labour, the middle-class Bengalis commented on the inability of a hired cook to cook food to perfection:

> Tremendous problem is created when cooking is done by hired cooks. A cook earns salary for cooking, hence he/she is more careful about the salary and not cooking per se. They cook primarily to be paid. Cooks do not cook well. --- Once a poor woman begged for a handful of rice for her daughter at a middle-class household. When the mistress of the house started calling out to the cook, the cook answered her. The mistress said 'give a little rice to the little girl.' The cook said, 'Where will I get rice now, there is rice enough for just one person. Therefore, I cannot give rice now.' The mistress kept mum, I asked her 'If there is rice enough for one person, why can't you give a handful to that little girl? The cook could have simply cooked some more rice if it seemed less later on for one person.' Mistress answered 'I am scared to say that to the cook, whenever asked to cook for relatives or guests the cook gets angry and retorts that it is difficult for him to cook for so many people at four rupee salary, if he had to cook for more people he would leave the job.' If the mistress herself knew how to cook and cooked herself then her husband, son, in-laws and other family members would not have to consume such bad food. The poor little girl would also not have to go back from her door. ---Nowadays even a clerk's wife needs a cook, but Draupadi, the great Hindu lady was a skilled cook and took delight in culinary art.[137]

Women were dissociated from any association of cooking for profit. The hiring of cooks was also an indication of the growing professionalisation of an elemental aspect of everyday life–the preparation of food and the feeding of the family. Perhaps, these male cooks symbolised those acts of labour which middle-class men abhorred, and brought to fore their own labour in the outside world. Sumit Sarkar elaborates this concern for professionalisation in his writings.

---

[137] Kumudini Ray, "Hindu narir garhyasta dharma," 177–179.

According to Sarkar, the middle-class Bengali Hindus, especially the middle and lower levels of the middle-class, were subject to a new discipline of work regulated by time, which they were not used to in precolonial India.[138] Calcutta, which became the principal site for British Indian bureaucracy, mercantile enterprise and education in the late nineteenth century, Sarkar argues, also nurtured this new discipline of work. To the middle-class, regular hours of work all through the year seemed a departure from their laid-back tempo of work in the villages. Thus the Bengali middle-class abhorred a person who worked for money in what was considered the most sacred space of middle-class life.[139] The aestheticisation of the kitchen was thus an important part of the colonial middle-class efforts to escape the tribulations of the outside world–into a happy, imaginary world, and an imagined past, whereby the more agreeable aspects of life could be placed alongside the losses they had been suffering under the colonial rule.[140]

In her recent work, Swapna Banerjee argues that the formation of the colonial middle-class in Bengal cannot be grasped without analysing the relationship of the middle-class with the domestic servants.[141] Banerjee's work expands to include all categories of domestic servants ranging from gardeners, doorkeepers, and sweepers to cooks and wet-nurses. However, she does not delve into analysing the labour content of these domestic workers. It was the hired cooks whose work was exactly the same as that of women. It is in this context that aestheticisation becomes so essential. Not only was the practice of hiring cooks, who were mostly male, an intrusion into the domestic space of the middle-class Bengalis, it was also an indication of the growing professionalisation of something considered 'natural,' cooking. Hence association of cooking with aesthetics became so visible. Unlike each household, which had its own novelty in cuisine, the hired cooks implied a standardisation of cooking. Mahendranth Datta and Jogendrakumar Chattopadhyay lamented

---

[138] Sumit Sarkar, *Writing Social History* (Delhi, Kolkata, Chennai, Mumbai: Oxford University Press, 1997).

[139] Ibid., 309.

[140] One might compare this aestheticisation of labour by the Bengali middle-class Hindus with Malthus's depiction of the English bourgeois home, where the domesticated housewife sublimated sexual instincts in order to create a cozy home for the male breadwinner who had to struggle for money in a hostile world outside, as cited in Maria Mies, *Patriarchy and Accumulation on a World Scale: Women in the International Division of Labour* (London, Atlantic Highlands, N.J. USA: Zed Books Limited, 1986).

[141] Swapna M. Banerjee, *Men, Women and Domestics*.

that with the coming of the Brahmin cooks the uniqueness of food cooked by each woman disappeared for ever.[142] Basantakumar Chaudhuri writes,

> These days no one's mouth is watered by the mention of the vegetables cooked by the *Ganguly* (a Brahminical last name) women, fish curry cooked by the women of *Mukherjee* (another Brahminical last name) household or the rice pudding made by the women of *Chakrabartys* (Brahminical last name). Earlier elderly women cooked with a sacred attitude after taking a bath and being clad in a fresh *saree*. The food they served reminded one of *Annapurna* (deity giving rice). And now fake Brahmins cook for the feasts. Women of these days cannot stand the smoke exhausting from the kitchen. Thus culinary art which is the novelty of Bengal is fast disappearing.[143]

This emphasis on novelty is inextricably linked with the question of authenticity. As Susan Terrio argues in the context of chocolate manufacturing in France, craft commodities that bear the social identity of their makers are generally produced in limited quantities. Traditional method is used in crafting of these commodities, and hence they call for continuity with the past. These commodities are different from those produced for the mass market. Terrio aptly says that the historicity of these goods give them special value.[144] Similarly, in case of women's cooking in colonial Bengal, what made it special was this imagined continuation of their cooking, which was different from what male cooks made. The latter's food, as already stated, smacked of standardised cooking made in return for money.

It is important to note here that the aestheticisation of women's cooking denuded women's work of any substantial value, and robbed it of its economic potential. As Maria Mies propounds in her classic work, with capitalism the family came to be considered an arena of consumption and love, excluded from production.[145] The rhetoric of the colonial middle-class revolved around a cultural discourse about women's role in the domestic space vis-à-vis the male cooks. This rhetoric, however, is silent about the role of lower class

---

[142] Datta, Op. cit, 12; Jogendrakumar Chattopadhay, "Sekaler bhoj," in *Smritite Sekal*, 99–109, 106, first published in *Bangasri* (Kolikata, May 1934 [Jaistha 1341 BS]).

[143] Basantakumar Chaudhuri, "Baje kharach," *Grihasthamangal*, 5th year, nos. 2 & 3 (Kolikata, May/June–June/July, 1931 [Jaisthya- Asharh 1338 BS]), 30–35.

[144] Susan J. Terrio, "Crafting Chocolates in France," in *The Cultural Politics of Food and Eating: A Reader* ed. James L. Watson and Melissal L. Caldwell (Caldwell: Blackwell, 2005).

[145] Mies, *Patriarchy and Accumulation*.

women who took an equal part in the production process like their male counterparts.

It has long been argued by Marxist feminist scholars that capitalism posited a sharp distinction between paid work and unpaid work by taking work out of the family. The precapitalist family functioned as an integrated economic unit where there was not a sharp division between women's productive and reproductive labour. Women never stopped working, but with industrial capitalism their contribution to family lost its earlier economic significance. Their labour within the domestic sphere could not be counted as real work as it was not paid work.[146] Undoubtedly, women's labour in precapitalist economy was a back breaking one since it combined both public and private work. However, in the precapitalist economy women did have an opportunity to get remuneration from the kind of work that they did.

To understand the nature of women's work an analysis of domesticity or domestic work and understanding its distinction from so-called productive labour is needed. Idealisation of family and domesticity was perhaps most visible in Victorian England. This domesticity was a celebration of the bourgeois ideals of family wherein the middle-class housewife came to be located within the family. In a sharp contrast to earlier families where women were involved in the process of production for the family, the chief role of women in Victorian England became providing emotional support for men who toiled in the new industrial public sphere.[147] However, even in Victorian England the division between the public and the private often became blurred. Leonore Davidoff and Catherine Hall have convincingly argued that networks of familial and female support underpinned the rise of middle-class men to public prominence. The middle-class homes were built on the expropriation of working men and women's labour, whether in the public world of the workplace or the private workplace of the home, which employed majority of the female workforce as servants well into the twentieth century.[148] Most of the early industrial

---

[146] Heidi Hartmann, "The Unhappy Marriage of Marxism and Feminism: Towards a More Progressive Union," in *Women and Revolution: A Discussion of the Unhappy Marriage of Marxism and Feminism*, ed. Lydia Sargent (Boston, MA: South End Press, 1981); Margaret Benston, "The Political Economy of Women's Liberation" (1969), in *The Politics of Housework*, ed. Ellen Malos (London, New York: Allison & Busby, 1980); Peggy Morton, "Women's Work is Never Done," in *The Politics*, ed. Ellen Malos.

[147] Catherine Hall, "The History of Housewife" (1973), in *The Politics*, ed. Ellen Malos.

[148] Leonore Davidoff and Catherine Hall, *Family Fortunes: Men and Women of the English Middle-Class, 1750–1850* (London, Melbourne, Sydney, Auckland, Johannesburg: Hutchinson, 1987).

business firms grew directly from the family household, where all work, be it commercial, manufacturing or professional, was done by the entire family. However, Davidoff and Hall emphasise that even when women actually invested in the business they were never considered an active partner.[149]

Many feminist scholars have addressed this gap between the ideology of domesticity and practice. Vast majority of working class women were engaged in work either inside or outside home. However, the middle-class defined the ideology of domesticity as a universal ideology and tried to impose this ideology on the working class as well.[150] Hall delves into the reason behind the emergence of this new domesticity. The attempt to locate women in the home could act as a justification for defining her work outside home as secondary and more significantly low-paid and unskilled.[151]

The bourgeois ideology of Victorian England thus also became prevalent in middle-class homes in colonial Bengal, and defined the new domestic ideal of the housewife. In her work on women and labour in late colonial India, Samita Sen demonstrates that the idealisation of domestic tasks stripped them off their labour content and subsequently robbed them off their economic value.[152] Sen concentrates on the historical context of late colonial India to understand how women's work came to be viewed in this manner. She argues that this idealisation of domesticity only defined the middle-class woman as the housewife. Poor women always kept working in the production for the household, more so as men increasingly migrated from the villages to the cities. The vacant agricultural jobs thus had to be taken over by rural women. It was chiefly middle-class women who migrated to the cities with their men folk who became the housewives. The housewives in the city was disengaged from a range of activities integrally associated with domesticity in the village, such as food processing, market gardening, livestock tending and spinning. Instead, she became principally responsible for the supervision of a range of tasks related to immediate consumption within the bourgeois household.[153]

An understanding of domestic work, however, cannot be complete without going a little deeper into analysing who the housewife was or what sort of home she was dwelling in. The concept of an ideal housewife had to be constructed,

---

[149] Ibid.,200–201.
[150] Hall, 'History', 66–67. Morton, 'Women's Work', 139–141.
[151] Hall, 'History'. 69.
[152] Samita Sen, *Women and Labour in Late Colonial India: The Bengal Jute Industry* (Cambridge: Cambridge University Press, 1999).
[153] Ibid.

which entailed more than defining domesticity as a universalist ideology. It could not be denied that working class women were engaged in physical labour, a labour that made their work visible and public. Domesticity had to be separated from this publicness. The mark of separation worked towards separating the housewife from the working class woman. This separation between the middle-class and the working class women has been theorised by scholars like Kumkum Sangari and Sudesh Vaid, who argue that this separation is also responsible for the gendering of space. For working class women, their subsistence labour could be carried out in the private sphere of home but in that case home could not be qualified as a private sphere. The paradox is that the definition of their labour as household work could make the public nature of their work invisible and therefore unpaid.[154] The need of the day was to create a 'proper' woman who would be different from the ungentle women of the newly emerging jute-mills[155] as also from the lower class women performing what the middle-class Bengalis considered to be an indiscreet popular culture.[156]

A look at the productive role of the lower class female population, especially in the context of colonial Bengal, is necessary to understand this constructed notion of aesthetic cuisine that went into the making of the Bengali middle-class.Very often, rice-husking, mainly performed by rural women, was a means of supplementing a family's income from cultivation. In the Narra village of Sudder subdivision in the Bankoora district, a report stated that the female members of the house husked rice for the upper classes and were paid for in grain. Women also assisted men in the work of thrashing rice.[157] In Dinajpore also, the income of an average cultivating family was supplemented by women who husked paddy. Apart from rice husking, women also wove gunny bags and weeded crops. Amongst the agricultural laborers in Dinajpore, women earned two to eight rupees per month by husking grains for others, or by purchasing

---

[154] Kumkum Sangari and Sudesh Vaid, "Recasting Women: An Introduction," in *Recasting Women: Essays in Colonial History* ed. Sangari and Vaid (New Delhi: Kali for Women, 1989).

[155] Sen, *Women and Labour*.

[156] Sumanta Banerjee,"Marginalization of Women's Popular Culture in Nineteenth Century Bengal," in *Recasting Women* ed. Sangari and Vaid.

[157] Letter from N.S. Alexander, Esq., Commissioner of the Burdwan Division, to the Secretary to the Government of Bengal, Revenue Department. 16th April 1888, Burdwan, Proceeding No. 7 RG, *Report on the Condition of the Lower Classes of Population in Bengal*, 6–9.

unhusked grains, and selling cleaned rice in the market, the earnings from which supplemented the earnings of the male members and enabled the family to live comfortably.[158] The same situation could also be seen in the Presidency Division.[159] By the early twentieth century, one can see a perceptible decline in lower class women's participation in the process of production. In her classic work on the impact of modernisation on women's labour, Mukul Mukherjee demonstrates that the introduction of rice-mills led to a decline in rural women's rice-husking jobs in early twentieth century Bengal.[160] Mukherjee's work documents how traditionally women have always participated and contributed to subsistence food production of the family. Their skills in husking rice offered them a command over what is considered the staple food of Bengal, rice.[161] Nirmala Banerjee also documents the visibility of women's work prior to rationalisation of production in the latter half of the nineteenth century. She argues that women not only performed for their own families but also sold their products in the markets. Their functions included making dairy products, preservation and processing of grain and pulses, making puffed and flattened rice, rice pounding, flour grinding and the like.[162] Mukherjee's and Banerjee's works on colonial Bengal have documented the harsh effects of capitalist economy on women's labour.[163]

---

[158] Letter from E.E. Lowis, Esq., C.S., Commissioner of the Rajshahye Division, to the Secretary to the Government of Bengal, Revenue (Agriculture) Department, Rampore Beauleah, the 30 April,1888, Proceeding No. 109 M. in *Report on the Condition of the Lower Classes of Population in Bengal*, 41–46.

[159] Letter From A. Smith, Esq., Commissioner of the Presidency Division, to the Secretary to the Government of Bengal, Revenue Department, Calcutta, 17 May 1888, Proceeding No.1 MA, in *Report on the Condition of the Lower Classes of Population in Bengal*, 1–30.

[160] Mukul Mukherjee, "Impact of Modernization on Women's Occupations: A Case Study of the Rice-husking Industry of Bengal," in *Women in Colonial India: Essays on Survival, Work and the State*, ed. J. Krishnamurty(Delhi: Oxford University Press, 1989).

[161] Ibid.

[162] Nirmala Banerjee,"Working Women in Colonial Bengal," in *Recasting Women: Essays in Colonial History* ed. Kumkum Sangari and Sudesh Vaid (New Delhi: *Kali for Women*, 1989), 284.

[163] In case of Sardinia, Carole Counihan has shown how in subsistence wheat and bread production, men and women depended on each other for assistance in exchange of labour. This social interdependence declined with the concentration of wheat production on capital intensive farms and of bread production in a few bakeries. Carole M. Counihan, *The Anthropology of Food and Body: Gender, Meaning, and Power* (New York & London: Routledge, 1999), 25–42.

Within the middle-class home, therefore, women redefined an act of labour and turned it into the labour of love. Thus, even when women's role in subsistence production was referred to, it was cast in romantic terms. Women of the bygone days were praised because they grew their own vegetables for their families.[164] But any sense of the market value of their productive role was completely disregarded in the contemporary discourse. Nurturing a kitchen garden was praised on account of its fresh produce. A kitchen garden was also supposed to make a house look beautiful and thus pure.[165] In an essay in *Bamabodhini*, a women's journal, one woman stated the example of an 'ideal Bengali woman' who saved her husband the cost of a sweetmeat maker by cooking everything herself.[166] Chunilal Basu, the noted chemist compared cooking to fine art and explained emphatically how a woman's cooking could help her husband financially.[167] Although not spelt out clearly, this economic association of women with cooking placed them ultimately in the same position as of a labourer. Just as a professional cook cooked for money, women's cooking was supposed to save her husband and her family from expending on a cook. The motive that lay behind affection thus often had a material basis– of economic convenience.

PLEASURES OF CAPITALISM: RETHINKING FEMINIST HISTORIOGRAPHY

While the capitalist modernity ushered in by colonialism often denuded women's work of its economic content, in many ways capitalism created a new space for middle-class women. This space was created by the Bengali middle-class women themselves who began writing about food. Print-capitalism made possible publication of cookbooks often written by women who took a serious and academic interest in cookery.

---

[164] Hemantabala Debi, *Hemantabala Debir Rachana-Sankalan*, ed. Jasodhara Bagchi, and Abhijit Sen (Kolkata: Dey's, 1992), 235; Subodhkinkar Nanda Majumdar, "Krishi o Sar, Kopir Chash,"*Grihasthamangal*, 3rd year, no. 9 (Kolikata, December 1930 [Poush 1336 BS]), 290–294; Matilal Sengupta, "Palli Jibaner Ekta Abhigyata,"*Grihasthamangal*,3rd year, no10.(Kolikata, December 1930 [Poush 1336 BS]), 316–318.

[165] "Grihasree sampadan," 91.

[166] Mankumari Bose, "Adarsha bangaramani: Banga mahilar patra," *Bamabodhini* (October/November 1888 [Kartik 1295 BS]), republished in *Nari o paribar: Bamabodhini Patrika (1270-1329 Bangabda)*ed. Bharati Ray (Kolkata: Ananda Publishers, 2002), 121-124.

[167] Chunilal Bose, Op cit., 6th ed., 32.

In the very important works of both Tanika Sarkar and Partha Chatterjee, women's role in the public sphere especially in the late nineteenth and early twentieth century Bengal remains considerably under-played. Sarkar admits that in the late 1920s and the early 1930s colonial Bengal saw women getting actively involved in mainstream nationalist movement.[168] In Calcutta, women participated actively in Gandhian nationalist movements organised by the Indian National Congress; they courted arrests, occupied government buildings, and organised demonstrations. Sarkar has argued that deployment of women in certain types of agitation was a deliberate strategy of the Congress. This strategy was expected to reduce the intensity of police repression, especially when it concerned respectable middle-class urban women.[169] Sarkar has argued that these public roles assumed by women were sanctioned only because the Gandhian movement was non-violent and participation in the Congress meant obedience to a particular authority similar to the one in the family. Even if the movements were militant, women's politicisation was interpreted as a sacrifice. Thus Sarkar concludes that participation of women could only come from such traditional moorings.[170]

Partha Chatterjee on the other hand acknowledges women's efforts in the construction of an independent identity, but maintains that women's voice could only be heard in the intimate domain of the nationalist middle-class, the 'spiritual.' Following this argument, the act of autobiography writing and reminiscing about the past gave women autonomy, but of a limited nature. Dipesh Chakrabarty's and Mary Elizabeth Hancock's arguments are more convincing in this respect. Chakrabarty explains how writing in many cases gave women a chance to express their individuality, albeit couched in terms of new patriarchy. Chakrabarty cites the example of a booklet named *Patibrata Dharma* (A Treatise on Female Chastity) written around 1870 by Dayamayi Dasi.[171] While written in a language that may resemble patriarchy, this text as Chakrabarty has shown, could bring women out into the public sphere. In expressing her own personal desire and at the same time recording her joy in the acquisition of literacy, Dayamayi participates in the public sphere.

---

[168] Tanika Sarkar, "Politics and Women in Bengal: The Conditions and Meanings of Participation," *The Indian Economic and Social History Review*, 21:1(1984): 91–101.
[169] Ibid., 97.
[170] Ibid.
[171] Dipesh Chakrabarty, *Provincializing Europe: Postcolonial Though and Historical Difference* (Princeton and Oxford: Princeton University Press, 2000).

Mary Hancock has also argued that domesticity itself could make the home visible in public life.[172] In her work on *Smarta*, a middle-class community in Southern India, Hancock has convincingly shown how modernity is indigenised at the local level. She has adumbrated how nationalist organisations controlled by elite *Smarta* women emphasised the political importance and visibility of the home in order to argue for women's right to education and suffrage. Nationalist women's espousal of home science gave credence to domesticity as a mode of 'indigenising' modernity by transforming activities like consumption, cooking, dress, and grooming.[173]

Writing cookbooks adds a different dimension to this much checkered historiography on the construction of space in colonial India. I argue that recipes were written from within a public/professional domain instead of a private/domestic one. This act of writing demonstrates a more dramatic act of women's agency that is neither reflected through the early twentieth century women's participation in nationalist struggles, nor through simply expressing their desires through autobiographies. The innumerable recipes that women produced cannot be explained away as being engendered by the hand of patriarchy. Writing as a mode of self-expression could take several forms. It is in this context that we need to reconceptualise the 'public' and the 'private.' Through the production of recipes, cooking as a domestic act crossed the boundaries of house and home. Through the writing of recipes, women created new identities for themselves, which were not much different from men who also wrote recipes.

The number of discussion of recipes by women proliferated from the end of the nineteenth century. *Bamabodhini*, a periodical written exclusively for women, published recipes in some of its issues from the year 1884. *Mahila*, another women's journal, which began to be published from 1895, also took initiative in publishing varieties of recipes. Scion of the Tagore family, and wife of Lakshminath Bezbaruah, the famous Assamese litterateur, Prajnasundari Devi edited a journal called *Punya* from 1897, which also had a significant section on recipes. Some other women's periodicals, where such recipes were published, are *Paricharika* and *Antahpur*.[174] Most of these periodicals were monthly periodicals, some edited by middle-class Hindu women, for instance

---

[172] Mary Elizabeth Hancock, *Womanhood in the Making: Domestic Ritual and Public Culture in Urban South India* (Boulder, Colorado, Oxford, UK: Westview Press, 1999).

[173] Ibid., 61.

[174] Sripantha, "*Introduction to Pakrajeswar o byanjan- ratnakar,*"(Kolkata, Subarnarekha, 2004), 9–79.

Prajnasundari Devi. Within this production of recipes, lay the pleasures of gastronomy. Women like Prajnasundari Devi engaged in writing about cooking almost as if it were a form of art. In that sense, her notions of gastronomic pleasure was no different from Brillat-Savarin, the famous French connoisseur of culinary art. Like her contemporary male recipe writers, Prajnasundari took a professional interest in writing recipes. Introductions to her books did not remain confined to instructions for keeping a well-maintained household. In other words, she was not merely interested in elements and processes that go into the making of a particular recipe. Prajnasundari also took an academic interest in the history of gastronomy. One cannot just explain away these cookbooks and columns as a mode of education for 'new' women. Culinary education was definitely deemed necessary for a modern woman, allegedly not adept in cooking skills. However, this body of writing also became infused with an almost academic dimension as vigorous debates on recipes and the like ensued in the pages of the journals mentioned above. A debate between two women's journals about how to make guava jelly gave almost an academic dimension to cooking.[175]

The debate on guava jelly was concerned with issues of authenticity and technicalities involved in making it. This debate took place between two periodicals *Punya* and *Antahpur* in the early twentieth century. A bitter dispute erupted on whose recipe was more authentic. *Antahpur* first published a recipe for making guava jelly in January 1901. According to this recipe, the guavas first needed to be skinned and boiled for a while, then strained to get rid of the seeds. The guava pulp was then to be mixed with sugar, constantly being stirred in the process. When the mixture thickened and had come to a room temperature it could be bottled as guava jelly.[176] This recipe was criticised by *Punya* in its issue of the same month. The main critique was that the recipe given in *Antahpur* was picked up from some other recipe book and not self-tried.[177] *Punya* came up with its own version of guava jelly, which read as follows:

> First put the saucepan on fire with 5 quarters of water. Heat it for about seven minutes and put the guavas in it. After three quarters (*Punya* actually uses the term 'quarter'rather than the Bengali version of it) of the guava becomes

---

[175] Hemantakumati Chaudhuri ed., *Antahpur*, vol. iv, no. 1 (Kolikata, January 1901), 15, Prajnasundari Devi ed. *Punya*, 3rd year, vol. 5 (Kolikata, January 1901), 232, *Punya*, 3rd year, vol. 7 (Kolikata, March 1901), 312–313, 321-325.

[176] Hemantakumati Chaudhuri ed., *Antahpur*, vol. 4, no. 1 (Kolikata, January 1901), 15.

[177] Prajnasundari Devi ed., *Punya*, 3rd year, vol. 5 (Kolikata, January 1901), 232.

boiled, take down the saucepan from stove. Cover it tightly with a cotton cloth. When the entire water is strained, separate the pulp. The pulp can be used for guava cheese. Mix sugar in the liquid and put it on the fire. Stir in lemon juice when it starts to boil. Mix in colour after ten minutes. Take it off the fire after another ten minutes.[178]

Given a sharp response by *Antahpur* in March 1901, *Punya* came up with an even sharper critique. In this critique, *Punya* directly took up the question of authenticity. For *Punya*, *Antahpur*'s recipe was a new one. There was no role of innovation in this recipe. The only authentic guava jelly was the one that was sold in foreign labeled bottles in the shops, and *Punya* had followed that recipe. Hence the recipe for guava jelly in *Punya* was authentic.[179] According to *Punya*, there would have been no problem if *Antahpur* had used another term for its own recipe. Authentic guava jelly had a transparent red glass-like look. If the jelly was mixed with pulp, like it was suggested in *Antahpu*r, it would not look so clear.[180]

The debate on guava jelly that erupted on the pages of *Antahpur* and *Punya* was rather significant. The concern articulated in this debate about issues of authenticity and naming soon formed crucial component of the new rhetoric of gastronomy. It was an important indicator of how the discourse on cooking and good taste in food, originally enunciated by middle-class men, had been appropriated by women– who made a mark in the public domain in terms of their dedicated approach to culinary art. These women, who took an active interest in the art of food preparation, lead us to rethink the feminist understanding of the position of women under the new patriarchy. Prajnasundari, for instance, took delight not only in cooking but also in innovating and improvising new dishes. She wrote down each recipe that she made and later compiled them into cookbooks. The first volume of her *Amish o Niramish Ahar*(Vegetarian and Non-vegetarian food) came out in 1900. Although labeled non-vegetarian, this volume as well as the second volume contained vegetarian recipes only. In 1908, a third volume was published which had non-vegetarian recipes. All these volumes had several reprints. In 1914, she published an abridged version of the same work.[181] Prajnasundari had a personal interest in the art

---

[178] *Punya*, 3rd year, vol. 7 (Kolikata, March 1901), 312–313.

[179] Ibid., 321–325.

[180] Ibid.

[181] Ira Ghosh, "Introduction', in Pragyasundari Devi. *Amish o niramish ahar,* vol. 1 (Kolkata: Ananda Publishers, 1995), 9–11.

of cuisine rather than an imposed one. She was encouraged by her father to learn cooking from the cooks in her childhood, but so were her brothers. Her father himself took an active interest in culinary art. There are few other references to middle-class men who could cook well.[182] Food of course never merely remained an object of consumption. It was something more that went beyond the physicality of sensory pleasures. It ultimately became that high point of aesthetics that defined the colonial middle-class.

In another aspect, these cookbooks written by Prajnasundari and many of her contemporaries epitomised the publicness of cooking. All these cookbooks were results of print capitalism. That these books were often reprinted and even reedited like Prajnasundari's book evince that apart from having an epicurean angle they also brought some remunerative benefits at least for the middle and upper-middle-class women. Most of these periodicals began to be published around the late nineteenth century and continued to be in print for a long period of time; it seems that they had substantial subscription. Thus subscription for domestic manuals or journals such as *Punya* or *Antahpur*, which contained innumerable recipes, brought remuneration as well. But then of course these pleasures of capitalist modernity remained confined to the upper echelons of society. For the vast majority of the population, these pleasures remained distant. Middle-class rhetoric about a constructed 'Golden Age' could not contain it.

---

[182] In Premankur Atarthi's Mahasthabir jatak, one finds Atarthi's father cutting onions and grinding spices for a fish curry he is about to make. In another instance one sees him cutting Hilsa fish sitting on the boat. See Mahasthabir (Premankur Atarthi), *Mahasthabir jatak*, vol. 1 (Kolkata: Dey's, 1981), 49–50, first published in 1945 [1351BS]; The poet Kalidas Ray also reminisced how his father took delight in cooking. See Kabisekhar Kalidas Ray *Smritikatha* (Kolikata, Ray Publications, 1996), 271.

4

Constructing 'Bengali' Cuisine
Caste, Class and Communal Negotiations

Self-fashioning of the middle-class was a project involving constant negotiations. Taste was one of the most significant markers that enabled the middle-class to define themselves. However, this taste did not exist *sui generis*. Constructing a middle-class taste was a process fraught with tensions. While the middle-class endeavoured to claim this taste as having a certain regional tenor, they were not averse to incorporating and internalising other influences in the process. This trait of cosmopolitanism, however, was replete with distaste for 'other' cuisines. Who were to be 'Bengali'? Whose cuisine was a middle-class cuisine? While this abomination for other tastes could be so subtle as to be articulated through the rhetoric of a modern science of nutrition, it also could take forms of a virulent critique of the other food, for instance in the critique of eating beef.

The self-fashioning of the colonial middle-class was of course relational. But scholars have debated the degree to which the middle-class has maintained distance with the 'other.' While some scholars have harped on the fact that middle-class prioritization of education and subsequent emphases on respectability intended to keep the middle-class away from both the peasants and the working class as well as maintain caste status and privileges of rank,[1] others have urged us to look at the complexities involved in the marking of such boundaries.[2] In her recent work, Swarupa Gupta has argued that although the attempts by the middle-class to include the 'lower orders' were always

---

[1] Tithi Bhattacharya, *The Sentinels of Culture: Class, education, and the Colonial Intellectual in Bengal (1848–85)* (New Delhi: Oxford University Press, 2005).

[2] Swarupa Gupta, *Notions of Nationhood in Bengal: Perspectives on Samaj, c.1867–1905* (Leiden: Brill, 2009).

made within mainstream Hinduism and at an inferior level it would be wrong to assume this inclusion simply as paternalistic. At least some of the literati did try to be attentive to the heritage of the lower orders and critical of caste divisions.³ It is undoubtedly true that the way the middle-class maintained its distance with the lower orders was multilayered. However, the politics of otherisation was much more visceral than has been explained by Gupta. While the self-fashioning of the colonial middle-class often verged on romanticisation of 'other' tastes, it never failed to demarcate the middle-class body from 'other' not-so-refined and not-so-pure multitude.

FOOD: A MARKER OF THE 'OTHER'

In the second chapter we have seen how the middle-class often romanticised the diet of a villager on account of its simplicity and nutrition. Scholars who have written on the eating practices of the middle-class highlight the reformist middle-class agenda through food. They argue that the middle-class Hindu Bengalis were interested in creating restraint through food by adopting milder flavours and by eating moderately.⁴ One of the virtues of such modest eating implied building a strong middle-class body. This body, as the medical discourse specified, was a Bengali body different from 'other' bodies. Consider this argument of Chunilal Bose, a professor of chemistry in Calcutta Medical College, who took an active interest in scientific research. In his introductory remarks to one of his essays, he says, 'The present Indian diet is defective and ill-balanced, and is directly responsible for the progressive deterioration of the physical health of the people, particularly of Bengal, and is directly affecting their moral and economic well-being.'⁵ To illustrate his arguments further, Bose cites the example of Col. McCurrison's work. McCurrison, who was the Director of Nutritional Research, Pasteur Institute, had argued that the food taken by the people of Bengal compared most unfavourably in its nutritive value with that of other provinces of India.⁶

---

³ Ibid.

⁴ Srirupa Prasad, "Crisis, Identity, and Social Distinction: Cultural Politics of Food, Taste, and Consumption in Late Colonial Bengal," *Journal of Historical Sociology 19*, no. 3 (September, 2006), 245–265; Bhaskar Mukhopadhyay, "Between Elite Hysteria and Subaltern Carnivalesque: Street-Food and Globalization in Calcutta,", in Bhaskar Mukhopadhyay, *The Rumor of Globalization: Desecrating the Global from Vernacular Margins* (London: Hurst & Company, 2012), 87–104.

⁵ Chunilal Bose, *Food* (Calcutta, 1930), 93–94.

⁶ Ibid.

The Punjabi diet of whole-meal atta (wheat flour), pulses, vegetables and milk, with the addition of meat twice a week, constituted the best of all Indian diets. The Bengali diet, consisting chiefly of rice and nominally of pulses and other protein-containing elements was the worst so far as their nourishing value and vitamin contents were concerned, and it was not surprising that the people of Bengal should stand so low in the matter of their physical qualities, when compared with the other vigorous races of India.[7]

Bose agrees with McCurrison, but he looks back to a 'golden age' in Bengal, to argue that there was a time when the people of Bengal were not unaccustomed to military life, and they formed regiments that fought against the disciplined army of the Mughal Empire. This military prowess was made possible by an abundance of nourishing food in Bengal, which was unavailable in colonial Bengal.[8] Thus Bose contends that the problem lay not with the diet of the Bengalis. In other words, he urges the colonial medical practitioners to look into the reason behind the scarcity of nutritious food in Bengal, especially rice.

In the context of Bengal, rice, which was often the staple food, carried a huge cultural significance. The significance of rice increased in case of scarcities or famines. Srirupa Prasad rightly argues that rice became a symbol of indigenous taste as well as resistance to the colonisation of taste.[9] In this context, rice became even more significant since it became the symbol of emasculated Bengalis as opposed to the 'manly' wheat-eating races of northern India. Wheat was the staple food of a number of non-Bengali communities pejoratively labeled as Hindustanis, who supposedly ate wheat bread and lentils.

Thus, a long debate ensued that primarily concerned the question of whether rice made Bengalis weak as compared to the other races or not. Jogendrakumar Chattopadhyay explained that the view that the Bengalis constituted a weak race because they ate rice was an idea that the Bengali youth had inculcated with the gradual spread of English education.[10] Chattopadhyay argues that most of South-East as well as East Asia considered rice to be a staple food. He takes further recourse to an apocryphal history that was not uncommon

---

[7] Ibid.

[8] Ibid.

[9] Prasad, Op cit., 257.

[10] Jogendrakumar Chattopadhyay, "Amader khadya o swasthya", in *Smritite Sekal*, ed. Prabir Mukhopadhyay (Kolkata: Charchapad, 2009), 237–245, 239–240, first published in *Prabasi* (Kolikata, September/October 1955[Aswin 1361]).

in nationalist historiography– 'rice eating' Bengalis, according to him, once ruled from Kashmir to Simhala (modern Sri Lanka) because of their physical prowess. However, the British needed the Bengalis to serve their administrative purposes. Hence they managed to convince them through English education that they were sharp and intelligent, unlike the martial races such as the Sikhs, the Marathas, the Punjabis or the Gurkhas. The latter, so this apocryphal account went, were much inferior when compared to the former in terms of intelligence.[11] Chattopadhyay was able to keep his finger on the pulse that throbbed with the sense of a loss. His text also alludes to the cultural making of emasculation rather than an actual one.

Many contested the argument that wheat-eating made the people of north India strong as opposed to the rice-eating Bengalis. In 1925, people like Gyanendranath Saha, argued that it was the climate that decided what one should eat:

> Pulses and wheat bread suited those of northern and north-western India, but it could not be a staple in Bengal; this is because pulses and wheat bread can be digested easily in the climate of northern and north-western India. But one cannot digest these in our land. Paddy is grown in large quantity in Bengal, and rice suits the climate of Bengal. Other food items like pulses, vegetables, fish, and milk can be nutritive only when they are taken with rice. There are many such food, much more nutritious and stronger than rice, but there is nothing which qualifies as mild, gentle, and nutritious at the same time.[12]

Saha was however, of the opinion that the mode of cooking rice in present times had lowered the nutritive quality of rice. He argued that taking starch out of rice made it less nutritive.[13] Otherwise, rice was the perfect staple for Bengalis.

While rice was becoming the marker of a 'tradition,' this tradition was not always held in awe, as argued by Prasad. While arguing that the Bengalis constituted a weak race in colonial Bengal, at least some advocated a change in diet. In order to construct an ideal middle-class body, the new Bengali cuisine was not opposed to inculcate other cuisines in its fold. Thus wheat, which was

---

[11] Ibid., 237–238.

[12] Gyanendranath Saha, *Bhater phen gala akartabya, tajjanya edeshbasigan hinabal o nirdhhan hoitechhe*. (Sripur, 1925 [1301 BS]), 3.

[13] Ibid.

considered to be the staple of non-Bengali population, was not always looked down upon. It had started being cultivated in Bengal and was often welcomed as an addition of nutrient to the Bengali diet.

Taranath Chaudhuri, a man affiliated with a Jain association, compared the Bengali Hindus with the Bihari Hindus and wrote in 1912 that the latter was stronger than the former because of their diet. Indubhushan Sen, a *kaviraj* (indigenous medical practitioner) writing in 1928, criticised the Bengalis for having parboiled rice. He argued that having wheat bread and lentils made upcountry men much stronger than the emasculated and feeble Bengalis.[14] Some argued that wheat contained better nutrients, like protein, when compared to rice. This was the reason why Hindustani men were stronger than the rice-eating Bengalis.[15] In *Bangamahila*, a domestic manual, there was a detailed analysis of why rice did not fare well as a food.[16] The author argues that rice was the most inferior of all crops. It was not just less nutritious, it tasted bland too. Therefore rice had to be accompanied by fish, meat, milk, curd, or lentils. Without these additional nutrients rice was hardly sufficient for physical well-being. The ritual of rice harvest also came under attack. The Bengalis observed rice harvest festivals after the harvesting of new rice. The author writes that the celebration of new rice was unnecessary since new rice was even worse than old rice in terms of health. Wheat was projected as the best crop. The north Indians were healthier than the Bengalis as they consumed wheat.[17] Similar opinions were expressed in the health manual *Swasthya*.[18]

Along with the championing of a diet based on wheat, this discourse of nutrition praised the non-Bengalis for their vegetarian diet. The latter diet was labeled a *satwik* or pure diet. In her recent work *Freedom and Beef Steaks: Colonial Calcutta Culture*, Rosinka Chaudhuri has argued that it was only after Gandhi advocated vegetarianism and gathered a nationalist consensus around him that the liberal view that meat-eating was essential for reform in India

---

[14] Kaviraj Indubhushan Sen, *Bangalir khadya: A Handbook on the Principles of Bengali Dietetics* (Arogya Niketan: Kolikata, 7th ed. 1961 [1369 BS].

[15] Nibaranchandra Chaudhuri, *Khadya tattva- A Treatise on Food* (Kolkata: The Indian Gardening Association, 1913), 10.

[16] Anon., "Swasthya raksha," *Bangamahila*, vol. 2, no. 3 (Kolikata, June/July 1876 [Asharh 1283BS]), 62–63.

[17] Ibid., 62–63.

[18] Anon., "Bhat o ruti," *Swasthya, vol. 3, no. 7* (Kolikata, November/December 1899 [Kartik 1306BS], 195–96.

took a backseat.[19] Undoubtedly, some liberals did consider meat-eating as a mode of celebration of freedom. However, even before Gandhi, the middle-class opinion on meat-eating was not unequivocal. Vegetarianism became an extremely complex symbol of contesting colonial ideas about emasculation in colonial Bengal. It became a mode of constructing a tradition, tracing the past back to the Aryans. The Bengali branch of the Christian Vernacular Education Society brought out a text of satirical poems in the late nineteenth century. Conversion to Christianity on a large scale, a modern phenomenon, comfortably co-existed with a mythical Hindu tradition. In one of the satirical poems in this book, a Bengali young man who has returned from England requests his wife to become more Westernized. His wife retorts:

> You fancy that non-vegetarian races are strong.
> The Aryans who once ruled the world,
> Never had fowl curry.[20]

A number of texts made a sharp critique of meat-eating on the ground that it was not a Hindu custom, and it did not exist in the traditions of India. There was less concern with an actual past rather than with an imagined tradition. In fact, in ancient medical treatises like *Susrutasamhita* (written around 3rd or 4th century AD) and *Charakasamhita* (written in 3rd century BC) meat was the first-named in a series of nourishing agents and endowed with pharmaceutical properties.[21] Science in the Christian Vernacular Education text was then being used to make up a tradition whereby meat-eating was being equated with the colonial modern and a source of several ailments.

The tradition constructed was often vaguely defined, but generally alluded to precolonial Bengal and sometimes traced back even to the Vedic period. Meat was defined as not being a staple of the country since beginning with the Aryans, 'Indians' commonly had fruits and vegetables. While there is substantial evidence of consumption of meat in the Vedic period, medieval Bengal too never abstained from eating meat. We get such evidence of meat

---

[19] Rosinka Chaudhuri, *Freedom and Beef Steaks: Colonial Calcutta Culture* (New Delhi: Orient Blackswan, 2012), 25–26.

[20] "Ami to hobo na bibi e pran thakite," in *Abakashranjan* ed. Suryakumar Ghosh (Kolikata, 1878), 118–120.

[21] Cited in Francis Zimmerman, *The Jungle and the Aroma of Meats:An Ecological Theme in Hindu Medicine* (Berkeley, Los Angeles, London: University of California Press, 1987), 213–214, first published in 1982.

consumption from *Chandimangal* (written between 1594 and 1606), and *Annadamangal* (1752),[22] two late medieval and early modern *mangalkavyas*. *Annadamangal* even referred to venison meat, tortoise egg, and dried fish, which were considered almost sacrilegious to the middle-class Bengalis in the nineteenth century.[23] Although it was considered a Hindu text, *Annadamangal* showed considerable Mughal influence on food. It had instances of Hindus having *samosa* (a fried patty like food), and *seekh* kebab (grilled kebab).[24] Panchkari Bandopadyay, a journalist, also argued that the consumption of goat meat and tortoise meat was quite common in the past. According to Bandopadhyay, caste taboos on food were much more flexible and it was with the advent of *Vaishnavism* that non-vegetarianism took a backseat in Bengal.[25] It was only in a romanticised tradition that purely vegetarian Indians existed.

Vegetarianism became a marker of distinction that separated the Bengalis (read Hindus) from the 'other'. On this issue, Bhudeb Mukhopadhyay (1827–1894), who was an educationist as well as a journalist, refuted the view that the Indians became weak because they were vegetarians. However, in order to prove his point, he looked toward Europe rather than looking back to an imagined tradition for the Bengalis. He argued that the Spartans who did not consume meat fared best among the Greeks.[26] Nor did all Europeans consume flesh as much as the British did. To prove his thesis, Mukhopadhyay argued that the French and the Germans constituted two very courageous races. Mukhopadhyay further referred to the newly emerging vegetarianism amongst the British.[27] Thus Mukhopadhyay actually tried to champion vegetarianism from an angle of modernity. His argument was that the simple reason why most of the Indians were vegetarians was because India grew vegetables on a

---

[22] Kabikankan Mukumdaram Chakrabarti, *Chandimangal*, ed. Bijanbihari Bhattacharya (Kolikata, 1966); Bharatchandra Ray, *Annadamangal*, in *Bharatchandra Granthabali* ed. Brajendranath Bandopadhyay and Sajanikanta Das (1943 [1350 BS]); Repr., Kolikata, 1950 [1357 BS]).

[23] *Annadamangal*, 388–389.

[24] Ibid.

[25] Panchkari Bandopadhyay,"SeKal aarEkal,"*Prabahini* (June 1925 [27 *Asharh*, 1322 BS]), republished in *Panchkari Bandopadhyayer Rachanabali*, ed. Brajendranath Bandopadhyay and Sajanikanta Das, *vol. 2* (Kolikata, 1951 [1358 BS]), 314–315.

[26] Bhudeb Mukhopadhyay, *Samajik prabandha*, with an introduction and exegesis by Jahnavikumar Chakrabarty (ed.) (Kolikata: Paschimbanga Rajya Pustak Parshad, 1981), 43–45.

[27] Ibid.

large scale. However, the general opinion was that it was the tropical climate of the country that necessitated a vegetarian diet in India. In *Binapani*, another journal, an author gives an extensive opinion on this matter in 1894/95:

> Both European and Indian physicians hold the climate responsible for their difference in food habits. Food that was appropriate for people living in a cold climate was not conducive for those living in a warm climate. --- Our scriptures have proved that vegetables and fruits are much more beneficial than the consumption of flesh in our country. There is hardly any individual who follow their own diet in this country and still be healthy.[28]

The term climate again was culturally loaded. Climate was more akin to the soil to which the middle-class belonged. These climate theories that supported vegetarianism for Indians were presented in a sort of indigenous/foreign dichotomy. Although men like Bhudeb Mukhopadhyay tried to offer a somewhat sophisticated argument endorsing vegetarianism, there were much more virulent ones that thrashed the English and their meat eating as uncivilised and barbaric. An unnamed author roared against the meat eating practices of the English in an article published in the journal *Mahila*. 'It is clearly evident that consuming meat has made the English aggressive, they become easily cross and with their cruel kicks send innocent and miserable Indian to hell.'[29] Vegetarianism, on the other hand, had a calming effect on the mind.

The politics of vegetarianism was clearly evident. Refraining from meat-eating was labeled pure and indigenous whereas consuming meat became associated with the foreign rulers who had pervaded Indian society with their vulgar customs. This politics was also heavily gendered. Even if Indian men could be forgiven for eating meat, women who indulged in eating chicken were an object of complete abomination.[30] The disgust was even more because very often Muslim chefs cooked meat, and it was served by the *khansama*(a Muslim Steward), who were also Muslim. The gendering of food was clearly

---

[28] Benodebihari Chattopadhyay, "Bangalir durbbalatar karon ki?" *Binapani* vol. 1, no. 7 (May/June 1894 [*Jaisthya* 1301BS]): 147–153.

[29] "Mangsha randhan o bhakshan,"*Mahila* vol. 3, no. 5 (November, 1897 [Agrahayan 1304 BS]): 100–110.

[30] Ibid; "Bangamahilader swadeshi priyoya,"*Mahila* vol. 12, no. 12 (May 1907 [Jaisthya 1314 BS]): 280–282.

perceptible. Sarat Kumari Chaudhurani writes that women were not served meat at the feasts[31], and even in the house there would often be a clear cut rule for who ate what. In her autobiography, Sudha Mazumdar notes that her father and her mother lived in two separate worlds within the same house. Not only did Sudha's father have an English dining room, even his diet consisted of English cuisine, follwing an English diet book. Mazumdar's mother, on the other hand, had her own kitchen presided over by a Brahmin cook. She also had what Mazumdar called a private kitchen where she cooked for her children.[32] The author writing in *Mahila* ridiculed new Hinduism saying that even after having chicken cooked by a *bawarchi* and served by a *khansama* a modern Hindu could still remain a Hindu. S/he narrates an incident where even some of the really reputed Brahmos, known for their vegetarianism, took delight in mutton curry and *korma*. In the author's opinion, Brahmos had begun indulging in vegetarianism only after the death of Keshav Chandra Sen.[33]

The colonial middle-class perception of taste vis-à-vis its other can partly be explained by their socio-economic condition in colonial Bengal following the advent of British rule. Mrinalini Sinha has argued that often colonial state designated the newly Western educated politically self-conscious Indians mostly represented by the middle-class Hindus as the 'effeminate *babus*.' This designation was tied up with political, economic, and administrative imperatives of the colonial rule in the late nineteenth century. Thus, while effeminacy denoted all inhabitants of Bengal in the past, by the second half of the nineteenth century, only the Bengali middle-class was described as 'effeminate.'[34] The Muslims (vast majority of whom belonged to the labouring classes and were underrepresented in the Western-educated community), the

---

[31] Saratkumari Chaudhurani, "Meye joggi," First pub. *Bharati* (August 1908 [Bhadra, 1315 BS], Reprinted in *Saratkumari Chaudhuranir Rachanabali*, ed. Brajendranath Bandopadhyay & Sajanikanta Das(Kolikata, 1950 [1357 BS]), 210–214.

[32] Sudha Mazumdar, *Memoirs of an Indian Woman*, ed. with an introduction by Geraldine Forbes (New York, London: An East Gate Book, H.E. Sharpe, Inc. Armonk, 1989), 3–11.

[33] "Mangsha randhan o bhakshan." Keshab Chandra Sen (1838–1884), was a Brahmo reformer who founded his own Bharatbarshiya Brahmo Samaj in 1866. Later in his life he established nababidhan, which was influenced by Vaishnavism.(Vaishnavism was often equated with vegetarianism in Bengal).

[34] Mrinalini Sinha, *Colonial Masculinity: The "Manly Englishman" and the "Effeminate Bengali" in Late 19th Century (Manchester: Manchester University Press, 1995).*

lower classes and some of the lower castes were absolved from the charge of effeminacy. Effeminacy was applied to the middle-class Bengali Hindus, a majority among the Western-educated community, whose expectations from colonial education remained unfulfilled. According to Sinha, indigenous elite's self-perception of effeminacy arose partly from their economic decline in the second half of the nineteenth century. Unable to control the economy, the professional class defined itself against the traditional Indian elites as well as the vast majority of the population.[35] However, indigenous elites accepted the label given by the colonial state but tweaked it to their own advantage. The middle-class Bengali Hindus held the colonial state responsible for emasculating the Bengalis. Sinha maintains that the middle-class identified their own emasculation with national emasculation.[36] This strategy served to mark their own hegemony over other social groups. Thus, the new rhetoric of taste that was created and the new cuisine that emerged therein often bore the mark of a middle-class Hindu Bengali cuisine, which appropriated other cuisines in its fold.

While Bengali cuisine involved appropriation and internalisation of other cuisines, it nonetheless made a virulent critique of other cuisines as well. While the Bengali middle-class had adopted wheat into their diet or even praised vegetarianism, they often lashed out against the non-Bengalis, pejoratively labeled as 'Hindustanis.' This critique was often made because the middle-class clearly felt that the non-Bengali population in one way or other had dealt a blow to the living conditions of the Bengalis. Food and the practices surrounding consumption were vital to this politics of taste for the colonial middle-class and hence practices of food acquired a central place in their debates on the non-Bengali population of Bengal. These debates become most apparent in the debates on the adulteration of food products.

Anne Hardgrove has argued that the adulteration of food products took on a new cultural status under the British.[37] This was especially so in the case of *ghee* or clarified butter, since *ghee* had a ritual purity for the Indians. Scientific tests made visible the intrinsic qualities of *ghee* and exposed any adulterants. This modern method introduced a new rhetoric of purity and impurity in commodities.[38] A better way to search for techniques to detect adulteration of

---

[35] Ibid.
[36] Ibid.
[37] Anne Hardgrove, *Community and Public Culture: The Marwaris in Calcutta* (New Delhi, New York: Oxford University Press, 2004), 127–180.
[38] Ibid., 168.

ghee became the concern of the day after the Calcutta Municipal Act forbade the adulteration of edibles in the early twentieth century. The Bengali middle-class blamed the Marwari merchants (who migrated from Rajasthan to Bengal even before the coming of the British to Bengal) for evading the technicalities of anti-adulteration law and selling substandard grades of *ghee*.[39] For the Bengali middle-class Hindus, Marwaris were deemed as the outsiders who had captured local trade and business. The main point of concern for the upper caste Hindu Bengalis was around the ritual purity of *ghee*.[40] Babu Surendra Nath Ray, for example, said that *ghee* was being adulterated with animal fat thus making it unfit for use in Hindu religious ceremonies.[41]

Hardgrove provides us with a very significant insight on the concept of pure and impure. In the new rhetoric of nutrition, pure and impure had significant religious connotations. Hardgrove argues that regional boundaries were also drawn along the lines of purity and impurity. However, since Hardgrove's work is on the Marwari community in Calcutta, she does not explore other aspects of this debate on adulteration. The definition of adulteration itself became problematic. What constituted pure and adulterated became a matter of debate. From primarily scientific and economic definitions, the debate took a cultural turn. The end result was a class/caste angle added to the concept of hygiene, albeit couched in the modern language of science.

'OTHER' TASTES

When it came to a critique of non-Bengalis taking over trade of colonial Bengalis, critique of the Marwaris remained virulent, often verging on the caricature of the latter's girth. For the Bengali middle-class, the Marwari merchants became fat sucking the source of life from the Bengalis. Prafulla

---

[39] Ibid., 170.

[40] Jogendrakumar Chattopadhay also wrote at length on adulteration of *ghee* by the non-Bengali traders who were becoming rich everyday by selling this adulterated ghee as pure. See Chattopadhay, Op cit., 243–244.

[41] Ibid., 168. *Ghee*, however, was not necessarily involved with Hindu notions of 'purity.' In the context of the Urdu middle-class milieu in mid-twentietieth century north India, Markus Daechsel has shown how *ghee* was championed as a 'traditional' food, which could make the middle-class body strong as opposed to the modern *vanaspati*, an industrial product. See Markus Daechsel, *The Politics of Self-Expression: The Urdu middle-class milieu in mid-twentieth century India and Pakistan* (London & New York: Routledge, 2006), 101–103.

Chandra Ray, the noted chemist and nationalist entrepreneur was emphatic in his critique against the non-Bengalis. In an essay he laments that the Marwaris excelled in importing rice from Burma into Bengal thus driving out the Bengalis from the business of import and export of rice. Ray mourns how the money that belonged to the *Desh* (In this context *desh* implied the region of Bengal) was drained out of the region by the British as well as the Marwaris.[42]

Ray felt really sad that instead of producing food in the soils of Bengal, Bengali population had to depend on importing items like sugar from Bihar and north-western India.[43] However, what he really mourned was the decline in Bengali entrepreneurship. This decline hit him really hard when it affected everyday life. In his essay, he writes that the Bhatia merchants specialised in manufacturing aluminum utensils for cooking in Bengali kitchens and the kitchens themselves were presided over by Hindustani and Oriya servants. To prove his point he quotes from an article published in a periodical by Jogeshchandra Mukhopadhyay named 'The position of the Bengalis in the internal trade of Bengal':

> 35 years ago trade in *ghee* and sugar was manned by the Bengalis. Now the Marwaris have completely displaced them. Bengalis have lost their place even in the trade in onion. Non-Bengalis dominate the trade in onion that comes from Bombay, Madras and Bihar; whatever little onion Bengal produces is also dominated by the non-Bengalis. Even eight or ten years ago there used to be 15/16 onion store houses in Beleghata (Kolikata) which has dwindled to a number of 7/8. Wheat is now included in the diet of the Bengalis. At least well-to-do Bengalis consume wheat. Marwaris dominate the trade in wheat. There are many electric flour mills in Calcutta.--- Only one such mill is owned by a Bengali. Flour trade is also controlled by the non-Bengali traders.--- Trade in pulses brought in from Bihar and United Provinces is controlled by the non-Bengalis. Hindustanis even dominate big stores for pulses in the Ahiritola locality of Kolikata.--- Mustard oil is an important source of cooking medium for the Bengalis.--- Such oil mills were owned by the Bengalis even three years ago. Now these oil mills have been taken over by the non Bengalis.---[44]

---

[42] Prafulla Chandra Ray, *Anna samasyay Bangalir parajoy o tahar pratikar* (Kolikata, 1936), 139.

[43] Prafulla Chandra Ray, *Atmacharit* (1937; repr., Kolikata: Orient Book Company, 1953 [1360 BS]), 266–269.

[44] Ibid., 331–332.

Gastronomic practices were fundamental to the construction of middle-class taste. Any disruption in these practices made a disruption in the organic unity of the body. This body, as we have seen, was sculpted very carefully. It was certainly a 'Bengali' body but it kept at bay all other bodies in the process. Thus, after making a survey of several markets in Calcutta, Ray laments that only twenty percent of the potato sellers were Bengali. Catfish was sold chiefly by the Oriyas and the rice and pulses were the monopoly of the Marwaris.[45] Fashioning of any taste implies distaste and this disgust for the other tastes is seen in the self-fashioning of the Bengali middle-class as well. Since food was the kernel of this taste, any element that could have the potential of disturbing any process associated with eating practices deeply stirred the colonial middle-class.

Issues of pure and impure were played out in this discourse of taste. Pure food had a double meaning. On the one hand, purity represented a critique of the colonial administration and forced the latter to impose stricter policies in relation to the adulteration of food. On the other hand, pure also signified untouched, which could imply the British as well as those unnamed people ranging from cultivators to cooks and sweetmeatmakers whose food the middle-class was obliged to consume in the colonial present. These two meanings were interwoven and the rhetoric of science could very well coexist with an overt cultural rhetoric about purity.

A particular branch of the municipal administration became exclusively concerned with the inspection of food and restaurants. A yearly statistics of pure and adulterated food was made available to the public. Special care was taken to see that food stuffs or vegetables that came to the Calcutta market from the surrounding areas were unadulterated. Arrangements were made, for example, with the Howrah Municipality for the employment of a special inspector. This inspector inspected all the main trains at Howrah and examined the articles brought back for sale. A large quantity of food stuffs found to be adulterated were destroyed then and there before they could reach the markets of Calcutta.[46] In the year 1919, a total of 3551 samples of foodstuffs were examined altogether. These included 1401 samples of *ghee* (clarified butter), 661 samples of milk, and 454 samples of mustard oil. Out of these, 129 samples

---

[45] Prafulla Chandra Ray, "Cha-er prabhab o desher sarbanash," *Anna samasyay Bangalir parajoy o tahar pratikar* (Kolikata, 1936), 224.

[46] *Report of the Municipal Administration of Calcutta*, vol. 1, 1918–19 (Calcutta, 1919), 22–23.

of *ghee*, 232 samples of milk, and 106 samples of mustard oil were found to be adulterated. 1892 *maunds* of foodstuffs, 1365 bottles of aerated water, 5251 eggs, 40,640 tins of tinned provisions and 100 cases of tea were also destroyed during the same year for being adulterated.[47]

As the government started dealing with the problem of adulteration in a firm manner, food inspection of hotels and restaurants strengthened the middle-class Bengali Hindu's concern about the purity of food from a different angle. A large number of this middle-class was employed in the Municipal administration itself and became quite vocal in their critique of hotels and restaurants. In this discourse both scientific and cultural explanations of pure and impure were associated with the question of class.

Generally speaking, all dairy products that were adulterated became a reason for the middle-class to blame the lower classes. Tracts written on this subject suggested pure milk for the Bengali Hindus. Aswini Biswas asserts emphatically: 'Cow's milk is the purest diet for the Hindus.'[48] Dairy became a concern for its association with the cow, which was considered to be sacred by the Hindus. But of course, the defense of milk was made on the ground of nutrition. According to Kularanjan Mukhopadhyay, milk constituted the best form of protein.[49] Mukhopadhyay analysed the protein elements in milk to give what he considered was a scientific explanation of a proper diet. However, his comparison of milk with meat and the championing of the former was an allusion to his celebration of vegetarianism.[50] The chemical analysis of food was a new phenomenon that was getting intertwined with cultural explanations. Tracts on clean milk became a regular feature in the health supplements of *The Calcutta Municipal Gazette*. P.C. Ray blamed the rentier classes for being apathetic to animal husbandry. He compared the Bengali rentiers with the English rentiers. The latter was praised for taking an active interest in the improvement of cattle.[51]

In this middle-class discourse of nutrition, the culprit who was held for the deteriorating quality of milk, was the lower class milkman or the *goala* as the milkmen were commonly known in Bengal. Dr. Sundari Mohan Das, who became the chairman of Calcutta Corporation's Health Committeee

---

[47] *Report of the Municipal Administration of Calcutta*, vol. 1, 1919–20 (Calcutta, 1920), 25–26.
[48] Biswas, *Ahare arogya*, 37.
[49] Kularanjan Mukhopadhyay, *Khadyer nababidhan* (n.d.), 14–16.
[50] Ibid.
[51] Sir P.C. Ray, "Milk for Calcutta: A Scheme for a Model Dairy Farm," *The Calcutta Municpal Gazette*, 6th Anniversary (Calcutta, 1930): 22–24, 28.

in 1924, narrated a story, which in his opinion made the *goalas* responsible for adulterating milk.[52] Das narrates that he was once traveling in a third class compartment of a train where he heard a conversation between a few milkmen. He was appalled to learn that these men had bribed the railway men to get into the train. More than the conversation, however, Das was aghast at the appearance of the *goalas*. He describes the scene as 'nauseating' and the milkmen as 'dirty' and 'reeking' with their 'dirtiest possible cans emitting odor of decomposed milk.'[53] Thus in the new rhetoric of nutrition it was not just that the milk was unclean and impure. Milkmen also became enmeshed in this discourse of commodity. Unhygienic, dirty and impure became inextricably intertwined.

According to Das, these *goalas* were extremely unscrupulous, besides being dirty. They squeezed as much milk as possible from the cow-keeper. The cow-keepers did not know how to feed their cows properly so as to get an increased supply of milk. As a result, calves starved and died. Das recommended setting up cooperative milk societies that would end the reign of the *goalas*.[54] He, in fact, started a scheme of cooperative milk supply himself. P.C. Ray went a step further and argued that it was the up-country milkmen who migrated to Calcutta from places like United Province and Bihar, who were responsible for adulterating milk. Bengali milkmen were much better when compared to the former.[55] While describing the milk purchased from the milkmen, Chunilal Basu, the chemist, clearly stated that mixing water in milk was typical of the *goala* caste.[56] This new rhetoric continued even after independence when Asoke K. Dutt asked for punishment to be inflicted on milkmen in 1949.[57]

Sweetmeat makers were another source of wrath for the Bengali middle-class Hindus. *The Report of the Municipal Administration of Calcutta* stated that after the Calcutta Municipal Act of 1917 forbade adulteration of edibles, there was a general improvement in the quality of *ghee* sold for public consumption, especially in the wholesale and big retail shops. However the *ghee* used in the

---

[52] Dr. Sundari Mohan Das, "More Milk and Cleaner Milk for Calcutta, What the New Corporation has Done," *The Calcutta Municipal Gazette*, vol. v, no. 1 (Calcutta, November 20, 1926–May 14,1927): 29–35

[53] Ibid., 29–35.

[54] Ibid., 29–35.

[55] Ray, "Milk for Calcutta," 22–24, 28.

[56] Chunilal Basu, *Khadya* (1910; repr., Kolikata, 1924), 255.

[57] Ashoke K. Dutt, "Milk," *The Calcutta Municipal Gazette*, vol. xlix, no. 9 (Calcutta, January 1949): 217.

sweetmeat shops was still of an inferior variety.[58] *Mairas* or the confectioners who generally belonged to the lower castes thus became an object of disgust for the middle-class. Even in the 1860s, several complaints were made to the government against the *mairas*. The class agenda of the middle-class becomes clear from the vitriolic accusations made by Tran nath Chatterjee in 1863: 'Our confectioners being chiefly men from the lower grades of our community and devoid of all education have hardly consciences in them, and so look more to their own interests than the health and lives of their buyers.'[59] Ramesh Chandra Ray, a doctor writing in 1929 accused the *mairas* of being dirty and unhygienic. He almost linked this accusation with the blame that the *mairas* were responsible for adulteration.[60] People like Dr S.N. De, the chief analyst of the Calcutta Corporation and Dr J.P. Chaudhuri, district health officer of the Calcutta Corporation also made similar observations, writing in 1930 and as late as in 1941.[61]

The question of contamination and adulteration was clearly associated with the lower castes. The middle-class was undoubtedly the product of colonial modernity and their discourse of nutrition, as that of taste, bore the marks of this peculiar modernity. Even while expounding so-called 'rational' theories of science, their self-fashioning certainly contained vestiges of caste and communal negotiations. However, the rational invariably co-exists with the irrational. One has to remember that the universality of scientific facts or even logical reasoning associated with science is often socially constructed.[62]

---

[58] *Report of the Municipal Administration of Calcutta, vol. 1 of 1919–20* (Calcutta, 1920), 25–26.

[59] Letter from Baboo Tran nath Chatterjee to the hon'ble A. Eden, Secretary to the Government of Bengal, 4th June 1863, Proceeding No. 328, Proceedings of Lt. Governor of Bengal. Judicial Department, June 1863, 211.

[60] Dr. Ramesh Chandra Ray, "Khabarer janmakatha," *Grihasthamangal* 3rd Year, no. 1. (April/May 1929 [Baisakh 1336BS]): 192–195.

[61] Dr. S.N. De, "Eating Houses in Calcutta," *The Calcutta Municipal Gazette,* 8th Anniversary Number (Calcutta, November 26, 1930): 31–33; Dr. J.P. Chaudhuri, "Eating Houses in Calcutta," *Calcutta Municipal Gazette,* 12th Health Number (Calcutta, 26 April, 1941): 145, 162.

[62] Gyan Prakash has insistently argued how modern imperialism raised its head along with the formation of Western scientific disciplines. These disciplines developed as the West encountered its colonies, which in their turns, served as laboratories for such experiments. For a further discussion on Western scientific disciplines and imperialism, see Gyan Prakash, *Another Reason: Science and the Imagination of Modern India* (New Delhi: Oxford University Press, 2000).

As Bruno Latour astutely observed, scientific facts do not exist on their own. They are rather the consequence of scientific work.[63]

This critique of the confection shops as well as the confectioners was expanded to include within its fold the critique of the restaurants too. The same Ramesh Chandra Ray who wrote on the unsanitary habits of the *goalas* wrote another tract on the restaurants that were gradually emerging in Calcutta. By the 1920s these restaurants had become a ubiquitous sign in Calcutta. Ray was concerned about the unhygienic surroundings and the unhealthy food of the restaurants. However, he made a cultural analysis in the process, bringing in class into the folds of nutrition.[64] It seems from his tract, that for Ray, restaurants implied small and low-classed eateries and not the British-established new and extremely sophisticated large restaurants. The latter was hardly frequented by the Bengali Hindu middle-class. Upperclass Bengali Hindus sometimes visited these clubs and restaurants, but not the middle or the lower-middle-classes. This is the reason why Ray considered students to be the most important patrons of the restaurants. These restaurants, according to Ray, were made dirty and unhygienic by their staff who in Ray's own words 'are recruited from a class in which venereal is almost universal.'[65] There could be a 'gentleman proprietor,' but in Ray's opinion, he was deceived by his personnel who cooked and served at the restaurants.[66]

Ray made a lengthy analysis of the adulteration of food by the lower class staff in the restaurants. He points out that curry was made from stale meat and the left-over cutlets were converted into potato chops. Veal was passed off as lean mutton and lard was used in several restaurants in place of *ghee*. There was an even more detailed description of the adulteration of sweetmeats. Ray claimed that the Co-operative Milk Union sold tons of skimmed milk at cheap rate in the afternoon and this went to sweetmeat shops for the manufacture of cottage cheese and curd. Tons of thickened milk was thus imported daily into Calcutta for the manufacture of rice pudding. He says that thickened milk was made from skimmed milk and represented unwanted protein. They deteriorated during storage and transit. As a result, the sweetmeats that were

---

[63] Bruno Latour, Steve Woolgar, *Laboratory Life: The Construction of Scientific Facts* (Princeton, New Jersey: Princeton University Press, 1986).
[64] Ramesh Chandra Ray, "Restaurants: Mend or End them!"*The Calcutta Municipal Gazette. no. 1, Health Supplement* (29th March 1930): 18–19.
[65] Ibid.
[66] Ibid.

166   *Culinary Culture in Colonial India*

made from the thickened milk were also spoilt.[67] Such views on sweetmeat makers could also be made in the case of milkmen, like P.C. Ray did. He insists in his writing that Bengali confectioners were at least better than their non- Bengali counterparts because the latter used vegetable products like *Vanaspati*, which was mixed with lard.[68]

IMAGE 4: Advertisement of 'Dalda' vegetable oil during its launching period. Advertisement in *Jugantar* (Kolkata, 08.07.1939)

Notes: Image 4 shows a male figure advising women on the advantages of *Vanaspa*ti. Two points need to be noted in this image. First, this advertisement states that *Vanaspati* was free of lard and not touched by hand. Second, it also states in the advertisement that anyone who could find any kind of adulterants in the *Vanaspati* would be rewarded 100 rupees. Thus the concern about "purity," even in advertisements, becomes evident. A product to be sold in India needed to be unadulterated.
(*Courtesy*: Subodh Bose and the Visual Archive of the CSSSC)

Impure was potentially laden with sweat, grime and ills of physical labour of the lower classes. Just as we have seen in case of women's cooking vis-à-vis a male servant's cooking, in this context too, the very physicality of the labour

---

[67] Ibid.
[68] Ray,"Khabarer janmakatha," 192–195.

of the milkmen or sweetmeat makers appalled the middle-class. Food was definitely a part of everyday life, but it had to be aestheticised and sanitised in every respect so that could it could become a nucleus of the middle-class discourse of taste. That the cosmopolitanism of the middle-class was fraught with tension is evident. However, the middle-class often couched its displeasure in ambiguous terms. Thus, the diet of the lower classes was often romanticised. Since the middle-class Bengali Hindu men were constantly ridiculed for their debilitated constitution, a different masculine figure had to be found in order to counteract these allegations. This masculine figure emerged in that of the poorer men, especially the figure of the villager. The general argument was that poorer men had more nutritious meals than the middle-class for the simple fact that they were poor.

Certain commodities became central to defining what would be a proper middle-class Hindu taste. In this respect, rice followed dairy products as another commodity of great significance. For the colonial middle-class, impure rice was a product of modern machines introduced in colonial Bengal. Santoshnath Seth, the author of *Bange Chalttatva* made a critical analysis of machine-husked rice in 1926.[69] He said that most of the markets in Bengal were flooded with rice-husking mills.[70] The question naturally arises as to why people took recourse to this rice if according to Seth it had less nutritive qualities than hand pound rice. Seth answered that it was because of its glossy quality that the machine-husked rice became so popular. Machines husked and cleaned rice better and thus made it look whiter than the rice husked by hand or *dhenkis*. Thus refined rice attracted more buyers.[71] Another doctor, who was also a member of the Nutrition Board in Bengal writes much later in 1941, that since polished rice seemed 'more pleasing to the eye,' the middle-class preferred white rice to coarse and nutritious varieties of rice.[72]

Seth's opinion resonated in Gandhian activist Satishchandra Dasgupta's (b. 1881) voice. His endorsement of the traditional *dhenki* (an indigenous rice husking machine chiefly used in village homes) was steeped in the modern language of nutrition.[73] Dasgupta argued that *dhenki*-husked rice contained

---

[69] Mahajan Shree Santoshnath Seth "Sahityaratna," *Bange chaltattva* (Kolkata, 1926 [1332 BS]).
[70] Ibid., 375–77.
[71] Ibid.
[72] Dr. B. Ganguly, "Rice as a Food: Its Defects and How to Improve Them,"*Calcutta Municipal Gazette*, Twelfth Health No. (26 April, 1941): 99–101.
[73] Satishchandra Dasgupta, *Chauler katha*, introduction by P.C. Ray (Calcutta, 1936).

vitamin 'B', while this was absent in modern machine-husked rice.[74] It was a critique of modernity in a very modern language. Thus it was the rhetoric which was modern in its essence. Aswinikumar Biswas, who wrote a couple of prescriptive tracts on physical well-being in 1935 used the terms 'table rice' and 'coolie rice' to signify machine-milled rice and *dhenki*-husked rice respectively.[75] This terminology was often used by the British to connote what they themselves or the indigenous elites ate and the rice that the lower classes had. Biswas argues that the middle-class was drawn to the sparkling white rice. This 'table rice,' according to Biswas, was responsible for all their ailments. The coarse, red rice that the lower classes ate was called the 'cooly rice.' This was the unhusked rice made from *dhenki*. This rice was much more nutritive than the machine-husked rice, in Biswas' opinion.[76] Biswas appropriates this terminology from the British, but one could not miss a sense of ridicule in his tone. He treats this marker of difference between the two rice as superficial. He tries to cross the class boundaries when he spoke for the 'cooly rice,' and it was obvious that even though he used the new terminology, he was superseding it. However, when it concerned touch, it became essential to keep the middle-class body at a safe distance from the lower classes. Thus what the lower classes ate could be consumed at home. But when there was a bodily contact of the lower classes or the lower castes with food, it became impure.

'OLD' AND 'NEW' FOOD: REFORMULATING THE RHETORIC OF CASTE

At one level, there was this perceptible change in everyday practice of eating. At another level, the abstract category of tradition was constructed in order to make a critique of these eating practices. Issues of caste constituted the core of this debate on tradition versus modernity. In a satirical essay, Bholanath Mukhopadhyay ridicules the new middle-class gentlemen who ate with various castes in the new restaurants.[77] Similar was the surprise of Durgacharan Ray who wrote a fictional travelogue.[78] Ray describes in his travelogue how the

---

[74] Ibid., 9.
[75] Aswinikumar Biswas, *Ahare arogya* (Kolikata, 1935 [1341 BS]).
[76] Ibid., 10–13.
[77] Bholanath Mukhopadhyay, *Apnar mukh apuni dekho* (Kolkata: Pragyabharati, 1982 [1389 BS].
[78] Durgacharan Ray, *Debganer martye agaman*, (Kolkata: Deys Publishing, 1984).

gods who had come down from heaven to take a tour of the world were aghast at the way Hindu Bengali men were consuming food prepared by the Muslims, a practice that amounted to a threat to the caste status of the upper caste Hindus.[79] Both Mukhopadhyay and Ray resents the idea of eating with other castes, which was a characteristic feature of the public eateries as opposed to communal eating of earlier times when men only ate with their caste brethren.

The caste question was being reformulated and intrinsically related to the issue of food as pure and impure. Certain types of food such as rice came to be imagined as pure or impure. The sharing of cooked food, basically implying sharing of rice, symbolised the unity of the family. Family in this context implied one's clan. Thus, if a person partook of rice cooked by another it meant that the latter's clan was accepted by the former's clan.[80] This association of cooked food with rice is best exemplified in Bipinchandra Pal's memoir. Pal narrates an incident in his hostel in Calcutta where an inmate refused to have rice cooked by his friends since he was a Brahmin and his friends were not. However, this person did not mind taking curries or *dal* (lentils) made by the non-Brahmins. He told his friends that no one would ever ask him if he had taken curries or *dal* cooked by non-Brahmins.[81] As Pal said, 'The Bengali idiom never used curries or *dal* as the name for cooked food, *bhat* or cooked rice was the only term used in this context.'[82] Jogendrakumar Chattopadhyay, in an essay on traditional feasts, explains in detail that rice was served only in the houses of the Brahmins. No one partook of rice in the house of a person ranking lower in the caste hierarchy. In fact, as Chattopadhyay claimed, Sudras considered rice served at a Brahmin's place as *prasad* (sacred food that is offered to the Gods) and not merely food.[83] Chattopadhay, however, wrote that men even refused to take *dal* when that was served by a person who belonged to a different caste or even subcaste.[84]

---

[79] Ibid., 258.
[80] Ronald B. Inden and Ralph W. Nicholas, *Kinship in Bengali Culture* (Chicago: University of Chicago Press, 1977).
[81] Bipin Chandra Pal, *Memories of My Life and Times. In the Days of My Youth (1857–84)* (Calcutta: Modern Book Agency 1932), 180–225.
[82] Ibid.
[83] Chattopdhyay, "Sekaler Bhoj," in *Smritite sekal*, ed. Prabir Mukhopadhyay (Kolkata: Charchapad,2009), 99–109, 104–106, first published in *Bangasri* (May 1934 [Jaistha 1341 BS]).
[84] Ibid., 100.

Although rice was the most significant food in the context of commensality, whatever was new came to be considered a caste taboo. Mahendranath Datta, brother of the famous religious preacher Vivekananda, narrates, for instance:

> My youngest uncle used to buy ice and brought it home covered with a blanket. This ice needed to be preserved with sawdust. That was a strange thing. Orthodox Hindus never consumed it. In our house, widows also abstained from it. We tried it out but in a sneaking manner. Maybe that's why we did not lose our caste so soon.[85]

In the satire *Debganer Martye Agaman*, gods who had come to travel the earth note with astonishment that while the Brahmins still held on to their sacred thread, they had no qualms regarding having bread and biscuits prepared by Muslims. The implication was that this sacred threat was the façade that still held the order of society; otherwise the middle-class had completely degenerated.[86] Thus, whatever food was coming in from outside was considered a suspect. This list also included vegetables like cauliflower, cabbage, potato, and pea.[87] Alluding to the new feasts, Jogendrakumar Chattopadhyay sneers and writes that soon cakes, biscuits and goose eggs would be served along with *luchi*.[88]

These issues regarding the relationship between food taboos and caste can be understood most clearly in the case of new social feasts that became a major irritant for those imagining this tradition. New forms of caste rigidities emerged, which were clearly visible in the critique of new feasts. Interestingly, Kedarnath Majumdar, who wrote a regional history of Maymansingha, notes with ridicule that there was a reverse casteism by the lower castes, in this case the untouchables, who refused to take rice served by the Vaidyas and theKayasthas (who ranked lower than the Brahmins in caste hierarchy but were much higher than the untouchables). Muslims too refused to eat at the house of the Kayasthas, unlike what they always did in the past.[89]

We have already seen in the second chapter how the middle-class often compared the feasts in the village with the new urban social feasts and praised

---

[85] Shree Mahendranath Datta, *Kolikatar puratan kahini o pratha* (Kolkata: Mahendra Publishing Committee, 1973), 31.
[86] Durgacharan Ray, *Debganer martye agaman*, Op cit., 258.
[87] Chattopadhyay, "Sekaler bhoj," 100; Datta. *Kolikatar puratan kahini*.
[88] Chattopadhyay, "Sekaler bhoj," 107.
[89] Kedarnath Majumdar, *Maymansingher itihas* (Kolikata, 1906), 197–199.

the former on account of their simplicity and restraint. The middle-class also felt that the new feasts often flouted caste rules, which were strictly observed in the traditional feasts in the villages. Jogendrakumar Chattopadhyay was all praises for the feasts of the bygone days in his memoirs. His description of a traditional feast makes us understand the general contempt for new feasts:

> One of the customs that prevailed in the feasts of the bygone days was communal dining. When all those invited to a feast gathered together they dined with one another. Brahmins would eat first. *Shudras* ate only after the Brahmins were done. No matter how rich or powerful a *Shudra* was, s/he never raised an objection to this practice.
>
> ---Rice was served only at a Brahmin's house because everyone could consume rice at a Brahmin's place, but one could not eat rice at the house of someone belonging to a lower rank in the caste hierarchy unless the organizer of the feast was a caste brethren. If it was an invitation where rice was cooked at the household of a Brahmin, one would say, "There is an invitation for lunch", and if it was an invitation where *luchi* was served, one would say, "It is an invitation for *Prasad* (food cooked for a deity)". A Shudra could invite a Brahmin for a feast at his place only through another Brahmin. Inviting a Brahmin by a Shudra was equivalent to insulting the Brahmin.[90]

Chattopadhyay's account of the feasts in village is replete with such reverence for caste hierarchy. Chattopadhyay, who was a Brahmin himself, had no qualms admitting that this taboo on interdining actually held the society together and had some sort of aesthetic appeal. In fact, these markers of difference actually contributed to the self-fashioning of middle-class men such as Chattopadhyay and many others like him. In another instance, Kalidas Ray (b.1888), the litterateur's relatives refrained from eating at his *bou-bhat* (when the bride first cooks and serves rice to her husband's clan) because many from the bride's family had gone to England and thus allegedly polluted themselves. However, they did not hesitate to eat *luchi* at Ray's wedding.[91] The cosmopolitanism of the middle-class was mired in many such murky terrains that could be explained only by the typical habitus of the middle-class. For instance, the suspicion of the Bengali upper caste middle-class for the use of salt in an intercommunal dining remains a conundrum. We get to know from the middle-class literati like Chattopadhyay, Mahendranath Datta as well as Amritalal Basu that in

---

[90] Chattopadhyay, Op cit., 104–105.
[91] Kabishekhar Kalidas Ray, *Smritikatha* (Kolikata: Ray Publications, 1996), 133, 279.

earlier social feasts salt was not mixed in food.[92] Use of salt had the potential of making a food *shakri*, making it unpalatable for anyone outside of one's own caste.[93] Datta argues that it was the modern English education that made men forego these earlier pleasures of life.[94] That salt was also a marker of caste was quite apparent in a text written by Datta on Ramakrishna, the Bengali religious preacher. By then, Datta had come out of many of his earlier romanticisms about caste. He narrates that in the presence of Ramakrishna, all castes ate together food that had salt in them.[95]

While several middle-class Bengali writings bore evidence of this obsession with a romantic past, their definition of this past were varied. For some, therefore, the past carried an aura of the Vedic four-fold system of caste. At the same time, many claimed that the caste structure in the past was less rigid than in modern times. Panchkari Bandopadhyay ridicules too much obsession with caste and states that it was a new phenomenon in Bengal.[96] Prasannamayi Devi narrates in her memoir that various people, from Brahmins to peasants, did not mind partaking of food from their master, no matter what caste the latter belonged to.[97] Bipin Pal's observation in this regard is perhaps the most illuminating. Pal writes:

> And looking back upon the social life of our village, as it was 60 years ago, it is borne in upon me that in spite of our caste exclusiveness and the restrictions

---

[92] Jogendrakumar Chattopadhay, "Sekaler bibaha," in *Smritite*, 142–153, 151, first published in *Prabasi* (1938 [1345BS]); Datta, *Kolikatar Puratan Kahini*, 70–72; Amritalal Basu, *Amritalal Basur smriti o atmasmriti*, ed. Dr. Arunkumar Mitra (Kolkata, 1982), 162, first published in *Mashik Basumati* (1923/24 [1330/31 BS]).

[93] Chattopadhyay, "Sekaler bibaha," 151. This concept of '*shakri*' does not have an English equivalence and is integrally associated with a Bengali understanding of purity and pollution. Bijanbehari Bhattacharya has argued that '*shakri*' originally implied something associated with rice but then expanded to include other foodstuff in its fold. If one dunks a ladle in a vessel in which rice is being cooked, one needs to rinse hands, otherwise the hand becomes '*shakri*'. Flattened rice or puffed rice is generally not considered to be '*shakri*' until it is wet. If flattened rice or puffed rice is soaked in water or milk, one cannot consume it while sitting on the bed. For an elaborate discussion on '*shakri*', please see Bijanbehari Bhattacharya, "Shakri: Entho," in *Bangabhasha o bangasanskriti* (1985; repr., Kolikata: Ananda Publishers, 1994), 106–111.

[94] Datta, "*Kolikatar purotan Kahini o pratha*".

[95] Mahendranath Datta, *ShreeShree Ramakrishner anudhyan*, ed. Dhirendranath Basu(1943 [1350 BS]; repr., Kolikata, 1979 [1386 BS]), 66–67.

[96] Panchkari Bandopadhyay, "Sekal aar ekal,"314–315.

[97] Prasannamayi Devi, "Sekaler katha," *Antahpur*, vol. iv, no. 5 (1901): 107–110.

that obtained in the matter of eating and drinking between the touchables and the so-called untouchables, and the honour that used to be paid to so-called lower or common people, there was a far more real and powerful spirit of democracy of a kind in our rural life than what strikes the eye today. There was a clear distinction between the obligations of caste and the obligations of social life. For instance, no one in the village, however low his place in the scale of caste, would come and take his food in the house of the highest caste people, Brahmin or Kayestha or Vaidya, unless he was properly invited and properly received and served. He did not want to dine under the same roof or in the same line with the so-called caste people, but he claimed in other respects the same honour which was due from a host to his guest. --- In the house of a Bhadralok, no untouchable Mali would accept food served by another Mali or by a servant of the host, but it had to be served by a Bhadralok. This was a point of honour with them.[98]

To argue that caste was hardly a factor in pre-colonial India would be too simplistic an argument. Pal certainly was not writing about pre-colonial India. His narrative is more about early colonial period when he believed that caste system had not become so structured. Here caste rituals were so much interwoven into the intricacies of daily life that precisely when caste rules predominated rather than a sense of self-respect, is hard to determine. What can be argued with certainty is that with colonial modernity, caste was being redefined. In other regions of India too, this indictment on intercommunal dining was evident. Shibnath Sastri, a noted Brahmo reformer, laments in his autobiography that even among the Brahmos (who apparently believed in monotheism and often made a strong critique of the caste system)in Southern India a Shudra was not allowed to see a Brahmin eat.[99] Sekhar Bandopadhyay argues that the colonial ethnographers ignored the functional and normative aspects of caste and overstressed only its structural implications. To them caste appeared to be a distinct structural entity, concrete and measurable, with definable characteristics.[100] According to Bandopadhay, they overlooked the fact that these units were once tied to each other through an interdependent

---

[98] Bipin Chandra Pal, *Memories of My Life And Times*, vol. 1 (Calcutta: Modern Book Agency, 1932), 105–106.
[99] Shibnath Shastri, "Atmacharit," in *Shibnath Rachanasangraha*, vol. 2 ed. Gopal Haldar and Baridbaran Ghosh (1918; repr., Kolkata: Saksharata Prakashan, 1976), 143.
[100] Sekhar Bandopadhay, *Caste, Poltics, and the Raj: Bengal 1872–1937* (Calcutta: K.P. Bagchi & Co., 1990), 23.

relationship. Of course, texts were redefining caste rules about eating, but only because these rules were falling apart in practice and at least some amongst the middle-class did try to overrule these caste rituals.

Jogeshchandra Ray Bidyanidhi(b.1859), the reputed lexicographer, narrates an incident in his village around 1880, when he decided to eat from the hands of a lower caste woman. After joining college in the town, Ray Bidyanidhi made an attempt to erase rigidities of caste hierarchies in his village. He insisted on having food cooked by a lower caste woman, better known as Rasik's mother, though Rasik's mother shuddered at the thought of cooking for an upper caste. Then it was decided that Ray's grandmother would cook outside the house and Ray would eat there with Rasik and his mother. However, Chattopadhyay found out that Rasik was served on a leaf, much away from Ray Bidyanidhi's plate. When Ray Bidyanidhi sat next to Rasik, his mother begged him to maintain some distance. Ray Bidyanidhi agreed to do that.[101] This incident, Bidyanidhi writes, was quite radical for a village and the news spread like wild fire. He narrates a conversation between two men:

1st: 'What's wrong in it? Touched (Bidyanidhi touched Rasik) while eating, this much?'
2nd: 'It is not a touch by an accident! This is intentional! This cannot be corrected by a simple bath?'
1st: 'God resides in all vessels. He nurtures this attitude at such a young age. He will grow up to be a genuine human being.'
2nd: 'Vessels are different after all. Otherwise why did Rasik take birth at a Bagdi's (one of the lower castes in Bengal) house?'[102]

It may very well be that Ray Bidyanidhi was an exception. However, the conversation that he narrates between two men at least point to the fact that some of the middle-class were ready to concede that the rigidities of caste rituals were not always worthy of clinging to. The bluntness of these rigidities thus became more subtle and camouflaged with other discourses when it came to the self-fashioning of the colonial middle-class. These tensions in the self-fashioning of the Hindu middle-class become most apparent in their relations with the Muslim 'other'.

---

[101] Jogeshchandra Ray Bidyanidhi, *Atmacharit*, ed. Munindrakumar Ray (Bankura, 2002 [1409 BS]), 59–60.
[102] Ibid.

MUSLIM 'OTHER'

The Hindu middle-class rejected several food as 'foreign.' However, this notion of foreign was left vague and ambiguous. Foreign definitely implied food brought from outside India, but even when it was prepared within the country, food could be rejected on its account of being prepared by someone outside the comfort or acceptance zone of the colonial middle-class. The middle-class looked at bread with suspicion because of the popular assumption that Muslim bakers make the bread. Bipin Chandra Pal wrote in his memoir that in the Cachhar district of eastern Bengal, there was a huge uproar among the Hindus regarding the consumption of biscuits. Pal writes, 'When the new English educated middle-class consumed biscuits with tea in their drawing room, the news spread to Sylhet from Cachhar.--- It was only after a rigorous expiation that the rebels could save themselves from being outcastes.'[103]

IMAGE 5: 'For vitality, Energy, and Health Bengal Milk Bread Machine Made untouched by Hand'.

Notes: Image 5 shows that advertisers had to be really careful when advertising bread. Thus the advertisers of "Bengali Milk Bread" had to ensure consumers that this bread was not hand made (by Muslims), but machine made and hence completely 'safe' for consumption and for health.
(*Courtesy*: Parimal Ray and the Visual Archive of the CSSSC)

---

[103] Bipinchandra Pal, *Sattar batsar: Atmajibani* (Kolkata: Kalpan, 2005), 57–59, first published in *Prabasi* from January/February 1926– April/May 1928 [Magh1333 BS– Baisakh 1335 BS].

Pal noted subtle changes in the society within a few years. In the year 1866 Pal moved to Srihatta, where children were already enjoying lemonade from a newly installed soda fountain. Pal noted with his usual sarcasm that no one remembered that consuming water touched by a Muslim had the potential of polluting one's caste. But people were so immersed in this pleasure that they totally chose to ignore the Muslim factor. Even the parents did not bother to investigate this new craze for lemonade amongst the young ones. Pal's father, who was a staunch Hindu, was furious when he learnt about this lemonade-drinking and prohibited Pal from going to school.[104] However, this same man also made Pal drink lemonade when the latter had diarrhea. When asked, Pal's father said that medicine was like food that had been blessed by God.[105] This growing belief that many of the new food had medicinal qualities led even the most orthodox people to gradually accept them. Many of the new pleasures indeed cut across class and caste and gave a new identity to the middle-class. When it came to eating beef, however, cosmopolitanism of the middle-class taste was a much complex affair.

Beef of course was treated as a food that had come from outside India. In that sense, beef was a foreign food and was clubbed together with pork and ham. While pork was also a taboo food for the upper caste Hindus, the resentment for beef was more visceral. The cow became a trope for marking the bodies of the Hindus and the Muslims. In his discussion of the Urdu middle-class milieu in mid-twentieth century India and Pakistan, Markus Daechesel has convincingly shown how the middle-class body is constructed through all kinds of tensions and negotiations.[106] Daechesel has pointed out the differences between a Muslim perception of what a healthy body would be and a Hindu perception of a healthy body. Bengali Hindu's attitude towards beef also revolves around a similar tension about the body.

Constant ridicule as 'effeminate *babus*' led many middle-class Bengalis to question the validity of such jeering. As we have already seen, the middle-class often critiqued the assumption that certain diet necessarily created a debilitating condition for the Bengali body. The middle-class literati noted that beef was the staple of the English as well as the Muslims, but refused to believe that beef made them robust.[107] A small text called *Bharater Godhan Raksha* (*Protection*

---

[104] Ibid.

[105] Bipinchandra Pal, *Sattar batsar: Atmajibani*.

[106] Markus Daechsel, *The Politics of Self-Expression: The Urdu middle-class milieu in mid-twentieth century India and Pakistan* (London & New York: Routledge, 2006).

[107] However, consumption of beef was often blamed for what the Hindu middle-class labeled as 'aggressive' nature of the Muslims.

of cows in India) published by an agricultural organisation of Tahirpur in Rajshahi district in 1887 quoted scriptures to argue against consuming beef. However, the text also provided a presumably scientific explanation against beef-eating. The text quoted a British doctor thus: 'Beef is perhaps the most nutritious of butcher's meat, mutton claiming equality with it in this respect; but it certainly is not the most digestible, and must therefore be partaken of with considerable caution.'[108] But the main purpose of this text was to create a 'difference' of the Hindus not just with the British but with the Muslims as well. Hindus became the generic name for all Indians who had from ancient days never consumed beef. The text further explains:

> Cow is known for its milk and its flesh is not beneficial for health. Hence it is shameful to have beef instead of cow's milk. A couple of children are so monstrous that they take pleasure in biting off their mother's breast while being breast fed. There is no difference between such children and beef eating youth.[109]

Incidentally, Shashisekhar Ray, an influential landlord of Tahirpur argued in favour of banning the practice of cow slaughter in the annual convention of Indian National Congress in Madras in 1887.[110] Several other landlords also took an active part in banning cow slaughter. Mohammad Reyazuddin Ahmad noted in his autobiography that the officials of a Hindu landlord in villages like Gobindapur, Sanatani, Gopinagar, Amla and Gosain pukur tortured Muslim subjects who slaughtered cow for consumption.[111]

Beef has never remained a simple food to be eaten. Its association with cow made beef a constant suspect. Although the general argument was that cow is beneficial for dairy products and consumption of beef had the potential of bringing down the number of cows, actually the fear of beef-eaters remained stark. Critique of the consumption of beef could easily be translated into an abomination for the beef-eater. Rajnarayan Bose writes, 'The British and the Muslims are the chief consumers of beef in our country. Their consumption

---

[108] *Bharater Godhan raksha* (Tahirpur, 1887 [1294 BS]), 29.

[109] Ibid., 36–37.

[110] Wakil Ahmad, *Unish shatake Bangali Musalmaner chinta o chetanar dhara* (1983; repr., Dhaka: Bangla Academy, 1997), 427.

[111] Mohammad Reyazuddin Ahmad, "Amar sangsar jiban," *Islam-Pracharak*, year 8, no. 7 (1907 [1314 BS]), 275, cited in Wakil Ahmad, *Unish shatake Bangali Musalman er chinta o chetanar dhara*, 428.

of beef has led to a drastic decline in the number of cows. This is the reason why milk has become so scarce.'[112] Unlike many others, Bose was wise enough to admit that the Hindus did eat beef in ancient times. However, he asserts that the Hindus in the medieval ages noted the benefits of cow and the health hazards that may spring from eating beef. Thus, the Hindus in the medieval ages forbade the consumption of beef in the scriptures. Bose was convinced that scarcity of milk contributed to the debilitating constitution of the Bengali middle-class.[113] Baneswar Singha, who wrote a number of tracts on agriculture and prevention of scarcity, was also of the same opinion as Rajnarayan Bose.[114]

Beef-eating in particular and consumption of meat in general became the line of separation between the foreign and the indigenous. If Bose was ready to concede that ancient Indians did consume beef, others totally chose to turn a blind eye to this historically verifiable fact from their discourse of taste. Being true to one's *dharma* (innate nature) also implied refraining from certain consumptions considered to be 'foreign'. One Bijyan Chandra Ghosh, associated with the Railways observes,

> Many of us have started consuming indigestible English food such as *Pulao* (type of rice prepared with whole spices and clarified butter), Mutton curry, *korma*(generally a mutton or chicken dish made with yogurt), kebab and chop(a distortion of English lamb chop), cutlet and omelets since the Muslim rule.[115]

Technically speaking, most of the food items that he listed as English food can hardly be described such. However, 'new' when associated with the 'other' became a strong object for suspicion. Nirad Chandra Chaudhuri narrates how the distrust for the Muslims reached its peak especially in the 1920s and 30s. The general assumption was that an upper caste Hindu would lose his *jati* as well as *dharma* (both caste and religious identity) if they took water from the lower castes or from anyone outside their community. This taboo assumed such ridiculous proportions that once when Chaudhuri had an orange in the presence of two Muslim gentlemen in a train compartment that he was traveling in, a Hindu co-passenger exclaimed his utter disgust stating that even an orange

---

[112] Rajnarayan Bose, *Se kal aar ekal* (Kolikata: Bangiya Sahitya Parishat, 1951 [1358 BS]), 42–48, first published in 1874.
[113] Ibid.
[114] Baneswar Singha, "Godhan raksha," in *Durbhiksha nibaraner upay* (Srihatta, 1919 [1326 BS]), 1–2.
[115] Ray Saheb Bijnan Chandra Ghosh, *Aahar* (Kolikata, 1942), 386.

contains water.[116] This incident occurred in the year 1927. This distrust for the 'other' received an equally strong response from the Muslim literati.

'OTHER' RETURNS THE GAZE

Mrinal Sen, the noted Bengali film maker narrated how Jasimuddin, the famous Bengali poet and a friend of Sen's eldest brother, was not served food inside the house but outside, even though Sen's mother claimed to have loved him like a son. Jasimuddin once asked Sen's mother why this differential treatment was meted out to him. Sen's mother explained that the servants would not take it lightly.[117] Dipesh Chakrabarty makes a brilliant observation when he argues that this inability to understand the grief of the Muslim was prejudicial of the Hindu Bengali mindset, which ultimately also made the latter turn a deaf ear to the former's call for a separate home that is Pakistan.[118] Such treatments often made even liberal Muslims be preoccupied about their identity.

In many of the texts written by the Muslim literati in early twentieth century, one can actually see frequent mention of meat dishes in a middle-class Muslim household. Nurunnechha Khatun (b.1892), a litterateur and active in many Muslim women's organisations, described in a novel a Muslim lawyer's household thus: 'Every day at least eight to ten dishes of *korma*, *kalia*(curry), chops and kebabs are cooked.'[119] In an imaginary conversation between Halima, a young girl soon to be married and her sister-in-law Kulsum, the latter makes a case for eating in moderation and strongly reprimands the glutton. However, the simple meal that Kulsum suggests was very different from what a Hindu upper caste Bengali perceived it to be. Kulsum suggests that an ordinary meal should consist of rice, vegetables, and fish. Thus far, Kulsum's list was hardly any different from an average Hindu middle-class diet. But Kulsum

---

[116] Nirad Chandra Chaudhuri, *Amar debottar sampatti* (Kolkata: Ananda Publishers, 1994), 136.

[117] Mrinal Sen, "Chhabi karar ager dinguli," in *Mrinal Sen*, ed. Pralay Sur (Calcutta: Banishilpa, 1987),11, cited in Dipesh Chakrabarty, "The In-Human and the Ethical in Communal Violence," in Dipesh Chakrabarty, *Habitations of Modernity: Essays in the Wake of Subaltern Studies* with a foreword by Homi K. Bhabha (New Delhi: Permanent Black, 2002), 145–146.

[118] Chakrabarty, "The In-Human and the Ethical,"146–147.

[119] Nurunnechha Khatun, "Swapnadrishta," in *Nurnnechha Granthabali* (1923; repr., Dhaka: Bangla Academy, 1970), 45–46.

also adds meat to her list of daily meals, thus marking the difference in what was perceived as a simple meal by each of the two communities[120] Meat was thus increasingly becoming a staple for many Muslim Bengali middle-class.

The need for writing a separate cookbook exclusively devoted to Muslim cuisine prompted Sayeeda Hafeza Khatun to write *Moslem Pak-Pranali* (Muslim cooking). Apparently, Mohammad Reyazuddin Ahmad, Khatun's husband, took an active interest in this cookbook. He collected Urdu recipe books from Hindustan and Punjab and these books acted as guiding sources for *Moslem Pak-Pranali*. Reyazuddin Ahmad wrote a long and elaborate preface to his wife's cookbook. Although not explicitly, he was trying to claim a different identity for the Bengali Muslims, which might be able to prevail over the 'Bengaliness' of the latter's identity. He writes:

> Culinary art reached its peak with the Mughals- several new and delicious food were discovered during this time. Empress Nurjehan also discovered a number of new recipes.---Absence of the printing press prevented the archiving of these recipes. Some of these recipes were conserved in the libraries of Muslim aristocrats. However, cookbooks written in Persian were lost along with other rare manuscripts with the destruction of such libraries in Delhi, Agra, Lahore, Lucknow and Murshidabad. A few have been preserved in Punjab, Hindustan and Bihar after being translated into Urdu. Bengal unfortunately does not house any such cookbooks.[121]

Reyazuddin Ahmad's chief concern was to carry forward the lineage of Mughal cooking for the Bengali Muslims. Sayeeda Katun also informs us that she wrote the book after consulting cookbooks from Hindustan (Lucknow and Kanpur), Delhi, Agra and Punjab.[122] Khatun also specifically mentions that her cookbook could actually teach Muslim recipes to Hindu, Brahmo and Indian Christian women.[123] In her description of recipes for pulao we find Khatun mentioning *Murg Pulao, Nargesi Pulao, Narangi Pulao, Qabuli Pulao, Korma-Pulao, Shajahani Pulao and Habshi Pulao*, all consisting meat.[124]

---

[120] Lutfar Rehman, "Preeti upahar," in *Lutfar Rehman rachanabali*, ed. Ashraf Siddiki, vol. 2(1927; repr., Dhaka: Ahmad Publishing House, 1987), 165–168.

[121] Mohammad Reyazuddin Ahmad, "Preface"(1926 [1333 BS]), in Sayyeda Hafeza Khatun, *Moslem pak-pranali*, vol. 1 (1333 BS [1926]; repr., Kolikata, 930 [1337 BS]), i-v.

[122] Sayyeda Hafeza Khatun, "Introduction", *Moslem pak-pranali*, vol. 1 (Kolikata, 1337 BS[c.1930], ix, first published in 1333 BS (c.1926).

[123] Ibid, vi.

[124] Ibid., 1–135.

This obsession with meat dishes in Muslim cuisine was often a reaction of the Bengali Muslims to the new vegetarian traits of the Bengali Hindu middle-class. The critique of meat eating by the Hindu middle-class provoked the Muslim middle-class to forcefully integrate meat into their cuisine. Muslim feasts almost always involved a great deal of meat preparation. Ibne Majuddin Ahmad, a Muslim preacher, described a feast that he organised in the honour of his fellow preachers who had just returned from a pilgrimage to Mecca. A big fat cow, four castrated goats and thirty chickens were brought for the purpose of this feast. In fact, one of the fellow preachers himself prepared kebab and also taught the village cooks to prepare *korma* and *kalia*. *Kalia* or curry was made from beef and goat.[125] One cow could feed up to five hundred people and a castrated goat had the capacity of feeding hundred people in religious feasts.[126] In the Muslim wedding feasts too, meat was the centre of attraction.[127]

The Muslim middle-class was not only reacting to the aversion for consumption of meat among the Hindus, they were also constructing their own culture of food to what they considered Hindu disgust for their way of life. Abul Mansur Ahmad (1898–1979)[128] talked about the ill-treatment of Muslim subjects by the Hindu *zamindars* in his village in Mymensingh district.[129] He describes how Muslims were prevented from entering into the sweetmeat shops owned by the Hindus in the Mymensingh town. This practice was also prevalent in Calcutta. Ahmad laments:

> One who is born in Calcutta cherishes the memory of *Rasgolla* from Bagbazar, *Methai* from the shop Puntiram in the College Street area and *sandesh* from Bheem Nag in the Boubazaar area.[130] However, I stopped myself from the consumption of such tempting delicacies because all these shops barred bearded and *lungi*(a type of sarong)-clad Muslims from entering their premises.[131]

---

[125] Ibne Majuddin Ahmad, *Amar sangsar-jiban* (Kolikata, 1914 [1321 BS]), 229–237.

[126] Abul Mansur Ahmad, *Atmakatha* (Dhaka, 1978), 52.

[127] Majuddin Ahmad, *Amar sangsar*, 369–370.

[128] Abul Mansur Ahmad was a noted journalist who had joined the Congress party during Khilafat and Non-Cooperation movement. Later he joined the Muslim League and subsequently the health minister in the United Front Cabinet in 1954. He had also served as a temporary prime minister of Pakistan.

[129] Abul Mansur Ahmad, *Amar dekha rajnitir panchash bachhar*, in *Abul Mansur Ahmad rachanabali*, ed. Rafikul Islam, vol. 3 (1968; repr., Dhaka: Bangla Academy, 2001), 6-8.

[130] Rasgolla, methai and sandesh are different types of sweetmeat.

[131] Abul Mansur Ahmad, *Atmakatha* (Dhaka, 1978), 211–213.

Ahmad's account is an evidence of the increasing identity consciousness amongst the Bengali Muslim middle-class. Ahmad tells us that he spent a considerable amount of time with his Hindu colleagues and friends when he was an active member of the Indian National Congress. He had no qualms in eating food cooked by Hindu women. However, in a rather stark note he asserts that he ate *gosht* (Arabic term for meat) at their places and not *mangsho* (Hindu Bengali term for meat).[132] In a rather poignant account, Khanbahadur Ahchhanulla, a prominent advocate of educational reforms for Muslims, narrates how once Hindu youths prevented him from eating bread for *iftar* (an evening meal that Muslims have after fasting throughout the day in the month of *Ramzan* before the festival of *Eid-ul fitr*). It is in this context of everyday modes of avoidance and protests that we have to situate the Muslim middle-class discourse on the consumption of beef.

Pradip Datta has argued how the Muslim middle-class reacted to socially discriminating practices of the Hindu upper caste middle-class, often leading to conflicts between the two communities.[133] A number of Islamic texts devoted to the improvement of material culture of the Muslims made the quotidian life of the Muslims their point of focus. Insisting on purifying Islam of all the vile practices of 'other' religions, these texts also instruct on how to construct an exclusivist Muslim identity.[134] Eating beef became one of the major tenets of such improvement texts.[135]

Many among the Muslim middle-class now started debating on the discourse of beef consumption as Islamic orthopraxis. People like Tamizuddin Khan (1889–1963), who later became the president of the Constituent Assembly of Pakistan failed to understand the Hindu insistence on banning cow killing. He ruefully stated beef was not only a staple but also central to the religious duties of a Muslim. In fact, stopping cow sacrifice was economically unfeasible also, because in substitution for one cow, seven or eight sheep or goats were needed.[136] Others like Maulavi Azhar Ali Bakhtiari, who was sympathetic to Muslim reformist movements like the Tariqa-i- Muhammadiya, was fearful that Muslims might have to forego consumption of beef under immense pressure from the Hindus. He took it upon himself on raising Islamic

---

[132] Ibid.

[133] Pradip Kumar Datta, *Carving Blocs: Communal Ideology in Early Twentieth-century Bengal* (New Delhi: Oxford University Press, 1999).

[134] Ibid., 64–108.

[135] Ibid., 97.

[136] Tamizuddin Khan, *The Test of Time: My Life and Days* (Dhaka, 1989), 38–39.

consciousness among the Muslims and went on citing from *Hadis* (traditions of Prophet Muhammad) to argue for beef eating.[137] Beef became a symbol that divided the Hindus from the Muslims. Other gastronomic practices too came to be marked by this sign. Muslims were also returning the gaze through their culture of food. Abul Fazl (b.1903), the noted journalist, describes prejudices arising from gastronomic practices in his memoir. He writes:

> I once suffered from stomach trouble after eating chicken at a Hindu friend's house. However, it is difficult to ascertain whether my illness was caused by bad cooking or the fact that the chicken was not a sacrificial meat. I came from a family of Maulavis (Islamic religious preachers). Hence this prejudice was not abnormal.[138]

The religio-legal permissibility (*halal*) of a particular item of consumption or of a certain culinary practice was a matter of utmost importance to the Muslim scholars of religion (*ulama*).[139] In this context, eating beef not only

---

[137] Maulavi Azhar Ali Bakhtiyari, *Majmuye Waz Sharif o Hedayeter Saral Path*, vol. 2 (1927; repr., Kolkata: Gaosia Library, 2003 [1410BS]).

[138] Abul Fazl, *Rekha chitra* (Chattagram, 1965), 188.

[139] Throughout the nineteenth and twentieth century, the *ulama* deliberated and issued rulings (*fatawa*) on the religio-legal permissibility of the consumption of particular items of food, explicating their *haram* (permissible) or *halal* (impermissible) status. For example, in northern India Shah Abd al-Aziz Dihlawi (1746–1824), the most influential Sunni Muslim scholar of religion in early nineteenth century Delhi ruled on the status of the rhinoceros, Sayyid Nazir Husain Dihlawi (1805–1902), a colossus of the Ahl-i hadith movement on the owl, Rashid Ahmad Gangohi (1829–1905), a founder of the Deoband movement on the betel (*paan*), Abd al-Hayy Lakhnawi (d.1886–7), a doyen of the Firangi Mahall school on the nutmeg, and Sir Syed Ahmed Khan (1817–1898), the architect of Aligarh movement on the mango. In nineteenth century Bengal, the most celebrated case was undoubtedly that of the Faraizi Muslim's active campaign to make the grasshopper a part of the idealised Muslim diet. Again, Mawlana Karamat Ali Jaunpuri (1800–73), an adherent of the Tariqah-i Muhammadiyah movement and arguably the most influential Muslim scholar of religion in late nineteenth century Bengal, unequivocally recommended the prawn as a permissible (*halal*) item for the Sunni Muslim diet. For the ruling on the consumption of rhinoceros see, Shah Abd al-Aziz, *Surur 'Azizi al-ma'ruf Fatawa-ye 'Azizi*, vol. 1 (Kanpur, Calcutta: Haji Muhammad Said and Sons, n.d.), 200–201; for deliberations on the owl by Nazir Husain Dihlawi, see, Hakim Fazal Husain, *Sawani humri Mawlana Sayyid Muhammad Nazir Husain Muhaddis Dihlawi al-maruf Al-hayat ba'd almamat* (Agra: Matba Akbari, 1908), 74–75; for a ruling on the consumption of betel, see Rashid Ahmad Gangohi,

aided in the construction of a separate Islamic identity, it prepared the ground for larger politics as well. Muslim middle-class gradually realised that even after living together for so many years Hindus had no idea of Islamic practices or beliefs. Abul Fazl rather sarcastically narrates how the wife of his Hindu friend cooked an immensely spicy chicken for him. He writes, 'Probably the Brahmin woman had heard somewhere that the Muslims liked all spices. It seems she demonstrated her skills in Muslim culinary art by using whatever pepper, cloves and cinnamon were available in the market.'[140]

Sarcasm actually became one of the principal modes of critiquing the Hindu abomination for the consumption of beef in most texts written by the Muslim middle-class in early twentieth century. At this point, satire seemed like a weapon that would help the Muslim middle-class vent their wrath against the discriminatory cultural practices of the Hindu middle-class without indulging in actual physical violence. Ibne Majuddin Ahmad, who took an active interest in cattle rearing and dairy farming ridiculed the Hindu middle-class in his village stating that the Hindus were so obsessed with their respectability that they considered cattle rearing to be a menial job. Ahmad quipped that it was after all the 'beef-eaters' shunned by the Hindu middle-class who took an active interest in rearing cows.[141] Perhaps the most significant tract that critiqued the Hindu disgust for the consumption of beef was Reyaz-al-din-Mashadi's *Agnikukkut*.

Mashadi's *Agnikukkut* was written in response to another tract on beef eating by Mir Mosharraf Hussain. Hussain was pained by the increasing communal conflict between the Hindus and the Muslims in India and was convinced that

---

Fatawa Rashidiyah Kamil (New Delhi:Farid Book Depot Private Ltd., n.d.), 190; for a ruling on the nutmeg see, Muhammad Abd al- Hayy Lakhnawi, *Mu'allim al-fiqh tarjumah urdu Majmu'at al-fatawa*, trans. from Farsi to Urdu by Barkatallah Sahib Raza Lakhnawi Firangi Mahalli, vol. 2(Kanpur, Calcutta: Haji Muhammad Said and Sons, n.d.), 355; for the ruling on mangoes by Sir Syed Ahmed Khan see, Christian W.Troll, *Sayyid Ahmad Khan: a Reinterpretation of Muslim Theology* (New Delhi:Vikas Publishing House, 1978), 41; For the debates on the grasshoppersee, Muin-ud-din Ahmad Khan, *History of the Fara'idi Movement* (Dhaka, 1984), 260, 264–5, first published in Karachi, 1965 and for the ruling on the prawn by Karamat Ali Jaunpuri, see, Rajarshi Ghose, *Politics for Faith: Karamat Ali Jaunpuri and Islamic revivalist movements in British India circa 1800–73*, Unpublished PhD Dissertation (University of Chicago, 2012), 164–5. I am thankful to Rajarshi Ghose for locating and translating these references.

[140] Abul Fazl, Op cit., 329–330.

[141] Ibne Majuddin Ahmad, *Amar sangsar-jiban* (Kolikata, 1914[1321 BS]), 40–41.

the Muslims should refrain from eating beef if they wanted this communal violence to stop. Hussain referred to the intimacy between the Hindus and the Muslims who constituted the two main communities in Bengal. He was of the opinion that since the Hindus have stood by the Muslims from time immemorial, the latter should not hurt the sentiments of the former.[142]

Mosharraf Hussain's concerns were sincere. He was arguing from a regional perspective. He made the argument that 'Bengali' taste was indeed unique and should not be conflated with any other taste. These specificities warranted a specific diet for the Bengalis, which would also be suitable for the climate in Bengal. Since Bengal had an abundant supply of fish, Mir Mosharraf Hussain saw no reason to not substitute that for beef. Beef, he argued, was not an integral part of the quotidian life of Bengali Muslims.[143]

> We are Bengali. What is our staple diet? What we occasionally eat cannot be labeled our normal food.--- The food that we have every day, for instance, rice, pulses, vegetables, milk, and fish etcetera is worth having.--- If beef was a food or a means for survival of the Bengalis, then we would have seen it every day in the kitchen. It would then be eaten along with rice every day with every morsel of food.--- He (God) has allotted specific diet to specific countries.--- If consuming beef is our duty, then why does Bengal have an abundance of fruits and vegetables? Why is there an abundance of fish in the rivers? Almighty has given each country whatever it needs. Should we follow the European diet while living in Bengal, or should we eat like the Arabs do?[144]

In this passage, Mir Mosharraf Hussain sends out a clear message to the Muslims. He asks them to choose one identity over another. His text is a clear indication that he was condemning an exclusivist Islamic identity among the Muslims and reminding them that they were exclusively Bengali. In a way, like the Hindu Bengali middle-class, Mir Mosharraf Hussain too was defining what a 'Bengali' taste was. After *Go-jeeban* was published in the newspaper *Ahmadi*, there were massive protests from the Muslim middle-class. Hussain was termed a *kafer*(infidel) and became embroiled in legal disputes as well. Mohammad Naimuddin of *Akhbare Islamiya* published from Tangail, and Shaikh Abdul Rahim and Mohammad Reyazuddin Ahmad associated with the weekly journal *Sudhakar* published from Calcutta lashed out at Mir

---

[142] Mir-Mosharraf Hussain, *Go-jeeban* (1888).
[143] Ibid., 330–333.
[144] Ibid.

Mosharraf Hussain.[145] Amidst this controversy Reyaz-al-din- Mashshadi under the pseudonym Fakir Abdullah-bin-Ismail Al-Koreshi Al-Hindi, wrote his *Agnikukkut* as a response to *Go-Jeeban*.[146]

Reyaz-al-din-Mashshadi was not merely an ordinary religious preacher. He was in fact, a learned professor of Sanskrit and Bangla in Calcutta. One of the central arguments of Mashshadi's text was refutation of many Hindu middle-class and Mir Mosharraf Hussain's assumptions that cows were becoming scarce because of the consumption of beef. He also ridiculed *Go-Rakshini Sabha* (Organization for protection of cows) of Kashi and 'Cow Memorial Fund' for actively participating in saving cows. Mashshadi's text is written in the form of a debate between a Hindu and a Muslim in which the Muslim tries to refute each point raised by the Hindu on the problems of eating beef.[147]

Mashshadi begins by ridiculing the assumption that dairy was becoming scarce and expensive because of a rise in consumption of beef. Mashshadi asks if that was indeed the case then how does one explain a rise in prices for fish, eggplant, *patol*, sugar, jaggery, honey, and gold?[148] When the Hindu man brings up the issue of non violence, Mashshadi actually tears apart the very crux of the discourse on which the Hindu middle-class arguments were based. The Muslim protagonist tells the Hindu man:

> If killing animals is a sin, why does that apply only for the Muslims? ---One cow is enough for the consumption of hundred Muslims, but you (Hindus) consume hundreds of fish every day.--- When one puts a knife to cut the cow's throat, it screams which implies its grief. A fish cannot scream. Does it imply that a fish does not have any grief? A cow is sacrificed within five minutes but when you skin a live cat fish and it writhes in pain, is that a pretty sight? --- Therefore a cat fish' pain is a hundred times more than a cow's pain. Hence killing a cat fish should be stopped before banning the sacrifice of cow.[149]

Mashshadi was attacking the obsession with vegetarianism of the new Hindu middle-class by pointing out the latter's hypocrisy. He also blew away

---

[145] Ahmad, *Unish shatake Bangali Musalmaner chinta*, 429–432.
[146] Anisuzzaman, *Muslim manas o Bangla sahitya (1757–1918)* (Dhaka: Lekhak Sangha Prakashani, Dhaka Biswabidyalay,1968), 228–230.
[147] Fakir Abdullah-bin-Ismail Al-Koreshi Al-Hindi, "Agnikukkut," in Reyaz-al-din Ahmad Mashshadi Al- Koreshi Al- Hindi, *Mashshadi Rachanabali*, vol. 1, ed. Abdul Qadir (Dhaka: Kendriya Bangla Unnayan Board, 1970), 239–302.
[148] Ibid, 242.
[149] Ibid, 248–249.

the argument that beef was not suitable for a tropical climate stating that since the Muslims had originally come from Arabia or Egypt, which were even hotter, there was no reason why consuming it should be a problem in the much cooler climate of India.[150]

In *Agnikukkut* Mashshadi also draws a distinction between the political life and the social life of the Hindus and the Muslims of India. He was willing to cooperate with the Hindus in the political realm. However, when it came to the practice of his innate nature, Mashshadi clearly states that the Muslims and Hindus did not need to coexist. He writes that a Muslim would not invite a Hindu to his house and thus Muslims need not think about the latter's likes and dislikes.[151] There was a thus a clear division between the political realm and the social realm as far as Mashshadi was concerned. Two points can be noted from Mashshadi's arguments. First, Mashshadi claimed through endorsing separate diet for the Muslims that the Hindus were indeed the 'other.' At the same time, he was tolerant enough to admit that despite these differences in the religious and the social realms, there was no reason why the Hindus and the Muslims could not unite under the same banner in the political realm.

This separation between the political realm and the social realm that Mashshadi drew was not uncommon in most discourses on cuisine. We have seen how the middle-class Hindu's perceptions of a cuisine were laid out differently in the public and the private sphere. The table has been used as a discourse of resistance as well as distrust for the 'other' in all parts of the world. The Jews in colonial North Africa were ready to consume French dishes outside their homes. This distinction was maintained because the colonial became the world of the impure whereas Jewish self was represented as pure and the ultimate sacred register.[152] While it is true that the colonial often became marked as the site of the impure, this stigmatisation as we have seen was extended to any category that did not conform to the self. Thus, while the project of self-fashioning of the Hindu middle-class was predicated on communal, gendered and casteist negotiations, the Muslim middle-class too returned the gaze by claiming an exclusivist gastronomic identity. However, neither the former, nor the latter took into account what the majority of the population was actually consuming.

---

[150] Ibid.,257.

[151] Ibid., 269–270.

[152] Joelle Bahloul, 'On "cabbages and Kings": The Politics of Jewish Identity in Post-Colonial French Society and Cuisine', in *Food in Global History*, ed. Raymond Grew (Boulder, Colorado: Westview Press, 1999), 92–108.

MYTH OF THE SELF-SUSTAINING VILLAGE COMMUNITY

We have noted how in the middle-class discourse of taste there was a subtle critique of colonial economy in the romanticisation of villages and subsistence economy. In his writings, Panchkari Bandopadhyay notes with some nostalgia that no one ever bought rice from the market in the past. Villagers had their own paddy fields that would supply them with whatever they needed. If anyone bought food from the market he would pejoratively be called a *lakshmichhara* (one deserted by *Lakshmi* i.e. prosperity).[153] This glorification of a subsistence economy was in a sense a critique of capitalist modernity, the increasing circulation of money and a growing market economy, which encouraged consumerism and new pleasures in turn. Thus whatever could be bought came to be an object of annoyance for many.

What seemed like a self-sustaining village community was often an exaggeration. The tradition was insularly defined. The food of the past that the texts mentioned was an extremely upper caste Hindu food. The majority of the villagers were Muslims and lower castes like Haris, Bhowries, Dhangars, and Domes. Often, especially in times of scarcity, the lower castes survived on the consumption of snails, frogs, crabs, shrimps and even snakes.[154] Only a few villagers could afford to have plenty of vegetables, milk, fish, and rice. These groups might have had a few fields of their own where they grew produce. Thus when they moved to the city, it seemed like a great loss of a lifeworld. However, for the majority, that is the lower classes, whether living in the village or in the city had never been so easy. They benefited neither from the pure, uncorrupted food imagined by people like Jogendrakumar Chattopadhyay, Panchkari Bandopadhyay, and Hemantabala Debi, nor from the new pleasures of gastronomy.

It was revealed in a survey on the Bengal famine of 1943 that the day-labourers, petty agriculturalists, artisans, and traders who formed more than

---

[153] Panchkari Bandopadhyay, Op cit., 308. Paul Greenough demonstrates that *Lakshmi* was portrayed as a compassionate mother who took pity upon the poor and suffering by giving them subsistence in the mythology of Bengal. See Paul R. Greenough, *Prosperity and Misery in Modern Bengal: The Famine of 1943–44* (New York: Oxford University Press, 1982), 23.

[154] Letter from R.D. Hume, Esq., Offg. Collecor of Beerbhoom, to The Commissioner of Revenue, Burdwan Division, Soory, 29th June 1874, File no. 13–708–711, in Proceedings of the Hon'ble Lieutenant-Governor of Bengal, Scarcity & Relief, General Department. (Calcutta, WBSA, July 1874).

65 percent of the population of Bengal, could not afford to pay for milk, meat, eggs, vegetables, and sweets. In many cases they produced these articles, but even under normal conditions their low average income forced them to sell these products in order to purchase rice, the staple.[155] An average diet of a lower class villager remained almost unchanged throughout the period. This diet consisted of very coarse rice and *dal* (lentils). Vegetables were consumed but only occasionally.[156] In a survey of a village in the Midnapore district of Bengal, *Baboo* Bisweshar Banerjee, the deputy collector, found out that the ordinary villager could hardly afford two full meals of coarse rice. Peasants in Midnapore could not afford to have pulses and vegetables every day. Vegetables for them consisted simply of boiled eggplant. They chiefly ate tank plants for their subsistence.[157] Even if the cultivator or the artisan did not suffer from insufficiency of food, they never tasted the 'new' pleasures that had started dominating the pages of new cookbooks. For them, vegetables basically consisted of edible leaves, eggplants, pumpkins, and wild potatoes. The condition of the lower classes varied from one district to another. Irrespective of regional differences, one can argue that a twice-a-day meal was something that the lower classes could afford only in ordinary times. But the situation was different in the times of scarcity.

During the times of scarcity, the decline in the standard of living was steep. Satishchandra Dasgupta, the Gandhian nationalist, led a relief camp during the scarcity of 1931 in Bengal. He reported that in Camp Roumari, in the Rangpur district of eastern Bengal, children ate arum stalks without salt. In another place called Kathgirai, a man named Bastulla ate the dirt that came out after husking rice and which was generally given to the cow. Observers noticed that people would often starve for three consecutive days. The situation came to such a state that Khsitishchandra Dasgupta, an observer, reported that Zaher Sheikh, who used to be the secretary of a local co-operative bank and therefore can be assumed to have been a man of some means, had to survive on arum leaves.[158]

---

[155] Tarakchandra Das, *Bengal Famine (1943)* (Calcutta, 1949), 2.
[156] Letter from N.S. Alexander, Esq., Commisioner of the Burdwan Division, to- the Secretary to the Government of Bengal, Revenue Department, Burdwan, 16th April, 1888, Proceeding No. 7RG, in *Report on the Condition of the Lower Classes of Population in Bengal* (Calcutta, National Library, 1888), 9–18.
[157] Ibid.
[158] Report by Khsitishchandra Dasgupta, in Satishchandra Dasgupta, *Sankat tran-samiti* (Kolikata, 1931), 13–17.

This description of the condition of the people in the villages dealt a rude blow to the romanticisation of the village where a so-called 'traditional' world might have existed. The dark and macabre side of colonial modernity reached its height with the Bengal famine of 1943. In a survey on the destitutes in Calcutta, Tarakchandra Das, a lecturer in anthropology, described in detail the condition of those who had fallen victims to the famine. Das lashed out virulently at the Government relief centres in Calcutta. According to Das, the food distributed at many of these centres lacked in both quality and quantity. The government's insistence on the use of *bajra*(millet) in these relief centres wreaked havoc on the digestive system of the people. Already their digestive system, the author suggested, was weakened by the consumption of unwholesome food, which was worsened by the consumption of *bajra*.[159] A passage from the survey reveals the horrors of colonial modernity.

> In Calcutta they took to cast-off skins of vegetables and to rotten fruits. They collected the former from the streets and the latter from near about the fruit-stalls in the markets. The receptacles of street-garbage were regularly hunted, morning and afternoon for the crumbs of food which were thrown into them.--- Even the carcasses of dogs, rats, cats, etc. were welcome-food to these miserable remnants of humanity.[160]

New pleasures had broken down many caste taboos. The pain of the famine had similar effects as well. This situation brought the very materiality of colonial modernity out into open. The 'purity' of food or caste remained in

---

[159] Das, *Bengal Famine*, 6–7. A similar situation could be seen during the scarcity of 1873 when the government of Bengal, instead of paying more attention to the production of more food-crops, almost forced people to consume rice imported from Burma. Although people complained against the consumption of the Burma rice on the ground that it was unwholesome, the government dismissed it as unfounded. The colonial state stated that the people of Orissa, who died in 1866, after eating Burma rice were so reduced by starvation that they could not digest any food. However, the government admitted that the Burma rice actually harmed their digestive system more than ordinary Bengal rice could have done. Letter from C. Bernard, Esq., Offg. Secretary to the Government of Bengal, Statistical Department, To- The Commissioners of Patna, Bhaugulpore, Rajshahye and the Superintending Engineers of the Soane Canal and the Northern Bengal Railway, 18th December, 1873, File no. 14–5, Pro. No. 4031, in Proceedings of the Hon'ble Lieutenant-Governor of Bengal. General Department, Scarcity & Relief. General Department (Calcutta, WBSA, December 1873), 590.

[160] Das, *Bengal Famine*, 8.

texts, but the materiality of the situation made the fluidity of caste much more palpable. Jogeshchandra Raybidyanidi (b.1859) also noted this absence of caste consciousness among the Brahmins during times of scarcity in his village.[161] The famine almost did away with caste rules regarding interdining.[162] In Calcutta, Hindus received cooked food from the Muslims and vice versa.[163] In Bibhutibhshan Bandopadhyay's novel *Ashanisanket* (Sign of Thunder), also about the Bengal's famine of 1943, even the priestly class was ready to eat snails (eaten by the lower castes) when struck by the famine.[164]

---

[161] Jogeshchandra Ray Bidyanidhi, *Atmacharit*, ed. Munindra Kumar Ray (Bankura, 2002 [1409 BS]), 13.
[162] Das, *Bengal Famine*, 9.
[163] Ibid.
[164] Bibhutibhshan Bandopadhyay, "Ashani sanket," in Bibhutibhshan Bandopadhyay, *Upanayas Samagra*, vol. 1 (1959; repr., Kolkata: Mitra o Ghosh, 2005).

5

Fashioning the 'Bengali' Middle-Class
Dilemma of the Regional and the Subregional

Within the idea of Bengal, there was a subregional consciousness of history. There was not necessarily a contradiction between the exploration of the history of a smaller region within Bengal and the exploration of a broader history of Bengal. This subregional consciousness could take several forms. It definitely flourished through the writing of history of a particular region in Bengal. This history-writing as a middle-class project aimed at infusing a sense of belonging in the region. However, there were other traits of everyday politics that defined this subregional consciousness. Often found references on *bangal* (residents of eastern parts of Bengal) and *ghoti* (residents of western parts of Bengal) crowded the pages of innumerable memoirs and autobiographies. While these distinctions never took an academic tenor, they made an impact on the conversations among the middle-class on the culinary skills of different parts of Bengal. Whether a *bangal* cuisine fared better than a *ghoti* cuisine animated everyday politics of the middle-class.

In her book, Swarupa Gupta has argued that subregional consciousness of the colonial middle-class emerged from an aspiration to understand the whole through its parts.[1] In her opinion, micro histories, familial narratives and genealogical accounts that distinctively marked subregional particularisms actually added up to writing the history of a region. An individual like Nagendranath Basu, who wrote a subregional history of *Uttarrarh*, could at the same time also narrate the history of Bengal as a whole.[2] Through her exploration of subregional histories Gupta concludes that these micro-histories

---

[1] Swarupa Gupta, *Notions of Nationhood in Bengal: Perspectives on Samaj, c.1867–1905* (Leiden: Brill, 2009).
[2] Ibid., 273.

of localities, villages, dynastic accounts and societies were contextualised within the framework of a discourse on continuous Bengal, which connected local histories towards the formation of a pan-regional identity.[3]

While not disputing Gupta's claim, I read these subregional histories in a different manner. Undoubtedly, these histories were written keeping in mind the construction of a 'Bengali' self. However, what also needs to be noted is that these histories narrate in minute details the everyday life of different regions of Bengal. Sudhir Kumar Mitra's *Hooghly jelar itihas o bangasamaj* or Satish Chandra Mitra's *Jashohar-Khulnar itihas* exemplify how a region's history was imagined to have existed in everyday life.[4] Indeed in other parts of India, for instance in contemporary Maharashtra, there was a keen interest in subregional specialisations.[5] In this context one might refer to Niharranjan Ray's conceptualisation of regional memories and regional consciousness in his *Bangalir itihas*.[6]

In his classic work on the history of the Bengali people in ancient Bengal, Niharranjan Ray explains the lack of a national consciousness amongst the ancient people of Bengal. Even when the rulers tried to claim sovereignty for an entire region, ordinary men and women associated more with the memory and consciousness of a subregion like *Rarh, Pundra, Varendra, Banga, Harikel and Samatat*.[7] There was hardly an amalgamation of the subregional with a

---

[3] Ibid.

[4] Satish Chandra Mitra, *Jashohar-Khulnar itihas*, vol. 1, 2nd edition (1914/15[1321 BS]; repr., Kolikata,1928/29 [1335 BS]); Sudhir Kumar Mitra, *Huglijelar itihas o bangasamaj*, vol. 1, 2nd Edition (1948; repr., Kolikata, 1962).

[5] For a discussion on how Maratha regional consciousness and its relationship to a broader concept of nationalism was reflected in history-writing from late nineteenth century see Prachi Deshpande, *Creative Pasts: Historical Memory and Identity in Western India, 1700–1960* (New York: Columbia University Press, 2007).

[6] Niharranjan Ray, *Bangalir itihas: Adi parba* (1949; repr., Kolkata: Dey's Publishing, 1993 [1400 BS]), 696–697.

[7] Barrie M. Morrison also found the existence of four sub-regions in the Bengal delta through his detailed analysis of property-transfer inscriptions dated between A.D. C.433 and A.D.C.1283. Morrison concluded from his study of the inscriptions that there were four significant political and cultural centers in the Bengal Delta. These were the Bhagirathi–Hooghly area namely the western part or what was also known as *Rarh, Varendra* or the northern part of the Delta, the central part of the Delta on either side of the river Padma in the modern Dhaka and Faridpur districts and *Samatata* lying on the eastern side of the Meghna river. For further reference see Barrie M. Morrison, *Political Centers and Cultural Regions in Early Bengal* (Jaipur-Delhi: Rawat Publications, 1980), 151–155.

national consciousness or even with the consciousness of a greater boundary.[8] Inhabitants of each region again felt an affinity for their community. Ray found the reason behind this community consciousness and subregional consciousness in the reliance on agriculture in Bengal. As Ray argues, the mainstay of ancient Bengal has always been land and agriculture (except for the period between third century BCE and sixth and seventh century when trade occupied a large source of social capital).[9] Trade makes the trader move and this mobility in its turn loosens his ties with his community, village and the region. However, a rural life that revolved around land also wove its imagination around this land. A family or a community grew around these lands. Even when the traders came back to their villages they invested their capital in this land. Ray argues that the many dimensions of trade and industry connect it to a much stronger and deep relation with other humans at large and ultimately prepares the path for a national consciousness. However, a land-based rural life was one of happiness and containment with communal and local memories, which made it difficult for them to be able to resist when a catastrophe struck, as it did in the thirteenth century. Ray concludes that even after the Muslim rulers took over after thirteenth century they did not bring about any significant change in the structure of agriculture-based rural life and thus could hardly make the Bengalis confident.[10]

Although I have drawn on Ray's conceptualisation of the subregional consciousness here, I aim to demonstrate that this subregional consciousness, which was always present in the history of Bengal, actually prevented the formation of an all-encompassing, homogenising 'Bengali' self by constantly making evident the fissures in it. Local imaginings and subregional memories kept alive small traditions of everyday life and subverted any efforts to delineate a discourse of a cosmopolitan Bengali who was hierarchical to its core. There was a definite attempt at homogeneity that is the making of a pan-Bengali cuisine, but distinctive marks of culinary skills of each region of Bengal were also narrated in minute details. This heterogeneity of Bengali cuisine fractures the concept of any one particular Bengali middle-class. While scholars have dealt explicitly with subregional history writing, I explore memoirs, cookbooks, and autobiographies in order to understand this subregional consciousness. In the first section I look at certain late medieval and early modern texts called the *Mangalkabyas* as well as ballads to understand the variations in Bengali cuisine.

---

[8] Ray, Op cit.
[9] Ibid., 697.
[10] Ibid., 697–711.

BENGALI CUISINE: SUBREGIONAL VARIATIONS

As Kumkum Chatterjee describes, the *Mangalkabyas* refer to a large corpus of narrative poetry that was produced in Bengal during the fifteenth to eighteenth centuries and beyond it as well. The theme of a *Mangalkabya* focused on how the worship of a particular deity was established on earth. *Mangalkabyas* written in honour of the deities *Manasa* (the snake goddesses) and *Chandi* (originally the patron deity of forests and animals, later metamorphosed into the Brahmanical *Durga*, the consort of Shiva) were composed through the latter part of the fifteenth century until the end of the eighteenth century and into the nineteenth century as well. These texts consisted of stories that were set to music and were sung. As Chatterjee has argued, these *kabyas* represent a later-written form of an earlier oral tradition which was circulated among ordinary people in Bengal.[11]

It is in this context of ordinary life, therefore, that we have to situate the *Mangalkabyas*. Although these texts purported to be primarily stories about deities, they were more about the everyday life of the ordinary people. The lives of the deities were very much akin to the lives of the ordinary people and the power struggles through which the deities like *Manasa, Chandi, Annada* or *Dharma Thakur* gained a foothold on earth also symbolized the struggle for existence of the people. These texts bore the traces of local histories, memories, and accounts of everyday life in Bengal. Thus, it is not enough to analyse a single text of *Chandimangal* or *Dharmamangal*. People who wrote these texts were conscious of where they belonged and this consciousness is evident in these texts. While singing the paean of deities, the author carefully narrates the everyday life of the people of the region he belonged to. This subregional consciousness of the authors became evident when they described culinary practices of a region. Thus, what was being cooked in a *Dharmamangal* written in northern Bengal could be very different from what was being consumed in a *Dharmamangal* of western Bengal.

Before delving into the *Mangalkabyas* it is pertinent to have at least a rough idea about the different subregions of Bengal. Niharranjan Ray demonstrated that the subregions in ancient Bengal were named after the tribes inhabiting them. For instance, *Rarh* was named after the *Rarhah* tribe, so was *Vanga*.[12] Roughly speaking, these regions could be categorised as *Harikel* (close to

---

[11] Kumkum Chatterjee, *The Cultures of History in Early Modern India: Persianization and Mughal Culture in Bengal* (New Delhi: Oxford University Press, 2009), 90–94.

[12] Ray, Bangalir itihas, 108.

modern Srihatta in the east), *Samatat* (modern Tripura), *Bangal* (eastern Bengal and the coastal parts of southern Bengal), *Pundra* (east of modern Munger), *Varendra* (northern Bengal), *Rarh* (western Bengal) and other divisions.[13] These regional divisions continued to change till much later when they became classified as districts in the colonial archives. Durgachandra Sanyal, an advocate (b. 1847 [1254 BS]), who wrote a social history of Bengal, classified territories of ancient Bengal as *Varendrabhumi, Banga, Mithila, Rarh* and *Bakdwip*. *Mithila* was bordered with *Varendrabhumi* in the east, river Ganges in the south, river Narayani in the west, and Nepal in the north; *Varendrabhumi* was bordered with Kartoya river and Chalanbil in the east, Mithila in the west, river Padma in the south and Cooch Behar in the north; To the east of *Bangadesh* lay river Brahmaputra, to its south flowed river Padma, *Varendrabhumi* lay in its west and it was bordered by forests in the north. *Rarh* was bordered with river Bhagirathi in the east, Orissa in the south, *Magadh* in the west and Ganges in the north and finally, *Bakdwip* was bordered with River Padma in the east, Ganges in the north, Bhagirathi in the west and the sea in the south.[14] The dialect, according to Sanyal, could be classified into *Gauriya* Bangla spoken in *Rarh* and *Varendra*, *Bangabhasha* spoken in eastern Bengal and the people in Calcutta simply spoke a dialect which was unique to Calcutta.[15] The cuisine described in the *Mangalkabyas* can also be broadly described to inculcate the taste of *Rarh* or western Bengal, *Varendra* or northern Bengal and eastern parts of Bengal.

Addressed to the goddess *Chandi*, the *Chandimangal*, written by *Mukundaram Chakrabarty*, is one of the most popular versions of the *Chandimangalkabya*.[16] Mukundaram was an inhabitant of *Rarh* and lived in a village called Daminya in Bardhaman. However, he composed Chandimangal in late sixteenth century under the patronage of Ragunath Ray, the king of Bankura.[17] Let us first look at the culinary delights Mukumdaram mentions in his text. For each social occasion, Mukundaram points out, there would be an elaborate menu. Here of course, we need to make a distinction between what lower classes or castes

---

[13] Ibid., 112–124.
[14] Durgachandra Sanyal, *Bangalar samajik itihas*, ed. Fakirchandra, rev. ed. (1906[1313 BS]; repr. Kolikata: Lokenath and Company, 1910 [1317 BS]), 1–10.
[15] Ibid., 5.
[16] Mukundaram Chakrabarty, *Chandimangal*, ed. with an introduction by Panchanan Mandal (Kolkata: Bharbi, 1992).
[17] Sukhamay Mukhopadhyay, *Madhyajuger Bangla sahityer tathya o kalakram* (1974; repr., Kolkata: Bharati Book Stall, 2011), 97–98.

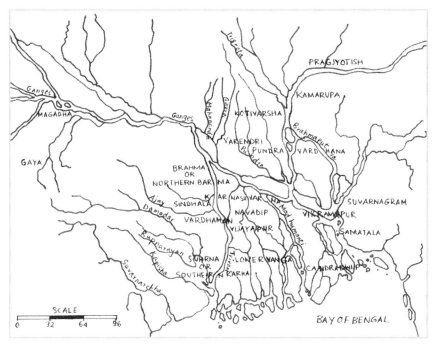

MAP 1: Early Medieval Eastern India

were eating in western Bengal, and the upper classes. Nidaya's(who is the wife of a hunter-gatherer) baby shower included *bathua* leaves (goosefoot), leaves of bottle gourd, fish *chochchori*[18] with *kumro bori* (small sundried cones of lentil paste mixed with wax gourd, a little spicy and hard) thrown into it, fried *sarpunti* (Puntius sarana*),* yogurt mixed with sugar, popped rice, and banana, stale rice with radish and eggplant, hilsa, *pithe* (sweet and savory cakes made with rice flour or cream of wheat) made with thickened milk, coconut and sesame, a preparation of bottle gourd made with milk, sesame and jaggery, porridge mixed with yogurt, cream and banana, *kolmi* (water spinach), *pui shak* (Indian spinach), *helencha* (marsh herb or Enhydra fluctuans*),* *gima shak* (kangkong or Ipomoea reptans), *polta* leaves (a type of bitter leaves), fried balls of duck eggs, fried balls of shrimp, barbecued rabbit, margosa leaves cooked with radish, eggplant and flatbeans/broadbeans.[19] This sumptuous feast was perhaps partially imagined by Mukundaram for it seems a little improbable that

---

[18] *Chochchori* is generally a dish made of vegetables cut in longish strips. When made with skins and bones of fish, it becomes a fish *chochchori*.
[19] Chakrabarty, *Chandimangal*, 46.

a poor hunter-gatherer family to which Nidaya belonged could afford this meal. However, this feast is significant because it characterises the cuisine of *Rarh* and its people. Mukundaram's *Chandimangal* also has elaborate lists of what was being cooked in the families of the trading castes, who were definitely among the most affluent ones. For instance, Lahana, the first wife of Dhanapati, a trader, cooks leaves of jute fried in clarified butter, green gram, bengal gram made with ginger, *shol* (sole or Channa striatus), fried *sarpunti*, fried balls of shrimp, fried *chitol* (clown knifefish or Notopterus chitala*)*, rohu fish curry with *kumro bori*, small fried pumpkins and feeds Khullana, the second wife of Dhanapati.[20] In another instance, Khullana cooks for husband a *shukto* (a bitter vegetable dish with a light broth) of eggplant, pumpkin, green banana and banana blossom spiced with asaphoetida, cumin and fenugreek, *notey shak* (leaf amaranth) cooked with *phulbori* (a very light sundried cake made from moth bean), shrimp and dried seeds of jackfruit, jute leaves, bottle gourd made with milk, lentil cooked with sugar cane juice, *koi* (climbing perch or Anabas testudineus) cooked with ginger and pepper, fried *chitol*, rohu fish curry, *helencha* leaves, fried shrimp balls, *shol* fish with mango, *pithe* such as *mug-samli* or *kheer-puli*. Generally, the spices used for cooking fish and mutton were asaphoetida and cumin.[21] For a much bigger feast that Khullana cooks for her clan, we see different leafy vegetables, *koi* made with ginger, green gram, fried *chitol*, rohu cooked with pumpkin, *shol*, *sarpunti*, shrimp, fried pumpkin, mutton, rice pudding and *pithe* among other delicacies.[22]

Now, let us look at *Chandimangal* written in other regions of Bengal, specifically the eastern and the northern regions. Neither Dwija Madhab or Dwija Ramdev nor Manikdatta describe such an elaborate spread of food like Mukundaram does. However, a close look at these three texts brings out the essence of the region they belong to. Dwija Madhab wrote his *Chandimangal* around the latter half of sixteenth century. Although he himself was a resident of western Bengal, his text gained much popularity in eastern Bengal, especially Chattagram. Thus it is tad difficult to ascertain which regional influence played out in the culinary culture described in Dwija Madhav's *Chandimangal*. Here Lahana's cooking is a much simple fare of leafy vegetables, green gram, rohu fish curry, an acidic preparation of olives cooked with mustard, fried *shol*.[23]

---

[20] Ibid., 152.
[21] Ibid., 161.
[22] Ibid., 188.
[23] Dwija Madhab, *Mangalchandir geet*, ed. Sudhibhushan Bhattacharya (Kolikata: Kolikata Biswabidyalay, 1965), 170.

The leaves that Dwija Madhab says are cooked for Khullana's baby shower are *bathua, notey*, spinach, *basak* leaves, *nata chandiya* and *amritalata* (indigenous greens).[24] While Manikdatta does mention the presence of spinach, other leaves are not mentioned. Instead we find *helencha, gima, pui, kalambu* and *tit porla* in Manikdatta's *Chandimangal* written in the fifteenth century.[25] Manikdatta was a resident of modern Malda or *Varendrabhumi* where perhaps some of the greens commonly found in either western or eastern parts were absent. Dwija Ramdev's version of *Chandimangal* or the *Kalikamangal* written in 1649 introduces us to a fish named *boal* (wallago catfish or wallago attu), immensely popular in eastern Bengal, but not so common in *Rarh* or western Bengal. Ramdev's (a resident of Chittagong) *Kalikamangal* mentions an acidic preparation of *boal* made with tamarind as well as fried hilsa with ground pepper.[26] Although hilsa is also mentioned in Mukumdaram's *Chandimangal*, it was definitely much popular in eastern Bengal. Other recipes mentioned are *bathua*, fried rohu fish, rohu fish head cooked with green banana, *katla* (carp or catla catla) spiced with pepper, venison meat cooked with clove and asaphoetida. Another vegetable preparation called *pachan* (a recipe with five different vegetables) is mentioned, which is also unique to eastern parts of Bengal.[27]

While we do get a sense of subregional influences on Bengali cuisine in the *Chandimangals*, it is perhaps not that atypical given that Chandi ultimately became the pantheon of a much wider world reaching across to the middle and the upper classes. However, *Mangalkabyas* were not a homogenising discourse about upper class/caste deities. From the eighteenth century, *Mangalkabyas* about deities like *Dharma Thakur, Dakshin Ray* (tigergod), *Banbibi* (the Goddess of the forest), the goddess *Shitala* were gaining popularity. However, the growing popularity of these deities does not necessarily imply their acceptance by the upperclass/castes. These deities were part of local memories and myths and hence these texts had more currency among the lower class people. *Dharmamangal*, for instance, captured the essence of *Rarh* or western parts of Bengal. It could be written in Hoogly, Bardhaman or Birbhum, that is, it could be widely read from southern *Rarh* to northern *Rarh*, but its kernel was the everyday life of *Rarh*. How ordinary men and women resisted the

---

[24] Ibid., 232.
[25] Manikdatta, *Chandimangal*, ed. Sunilkumar Ojha (Shiliguri: Uttarbanga Biswabidyalay, 1977 [1384 BS]), 283.
[26] Dwija Ramdeb, *Kalikamangal*, ed. Ashutosh das (Kolkata: Kolikata Biswabidyalay, 1957), 187, 197.
[27] Ibid., 197.

hostile environment and topography of *Rarh* became central to the narrative of *Dharmamangal*. *Manasamangal*, devoted to *Manasa*, the snake goddess can be found in *Rarh, Varendrabhumi* as well as in eastern Bengal. Its popularity was widespread. Wherever there was a fear of snake, *Manasa* worship gained popularity. *Manasamangal*, in fact, gives us perhaps the clearest picture on variations in subregional cuisine.

The preponderance of dishes made of fish is much more evident in the *Manasamangals* written in eastern Bengal and even northern Bengal than those written in western parts. While texts in western Bengal do list some fish in them, they are not as detailed as those in eastern Bengal. Bipradas Pippilai, an inhabitant of the present-day 24 Parganas or southern Bengal, writing in the fifteenth century, does not specify which fish is cooked for the baby shower of Sanaka, the wife of trader Chand Sadagar, but concentrates on sweet and savory cakes known as *pithe*, which are made of milk, jaggery, coconut, white sugar, and candied sugar. These were *ashke pithe* (steamed rice flour cakes), *kheer-puli* (has a lot of *kheer* or thickened milk and is soft and creamy), *dugdha-chushi*(made with semolina and coconut and dunked in milk), *mug samli* (a sweet pancake made of green gram, rice flour, sugar and coconut), *saruchakli* (a thin pancake made with rice and black gram).[28]

Two other *Manasamangals*, written in *Rarh* and the westernmost parts of Bengal, however, do mention fish preparations in a more detailed manner. Ketakadas Khemananda, who was an inhabitant of the modern Hooghly region around the seventeenth or eighteenth centuries, does mention fried *sarpunti, boal* cooked with *helencha* and burnt fish along with rice pudding and *pithe*. [29] A late eighteenth century text written by Nityananda of eastern Medinipur also concentrates on fruits and sweets like thickened milk, cottage cheese, watermelon, rice pudding, *ashke pithe, gur pithe*(savory cakes made with jaggery), berries, plums, banana and puffed rice with coconut and radish. However, Nityananda also mentions *shol* cooked with mango, which we found in Mukundaram's *Chandimangal*, rohu fishhead, *magur*(catfish), a *chochchori* made with *punti* (swamp barb or Puntius sophora) and *phulbori*, and

---

[28] Bipradas Pippilai, *Manasa-Vijaya*, ed. Sukumar Sen (Calcutta: Asiatic Society, 1953), 150.

[29] Ketakadas Khemananda, *Manasamangal*, ed. Tanmay Mitra, Rezaul Karim, Subodh kumar Jash (Kolkata: Bangiya Sahitya Samsad, 2010), 29; Ketakadas Khemananda, *Manasamangal*, ed. Jatindramohan Bhattacharya ed. vol. 1 (1943; repr., Kolikata: Kolikata Biswabidyala, 1949), 211.

koi fried in mustard oil.[30] *Dharmamangals* too do not go into baffling details about fish preparations. At least fifty varieties of *pithe* become essential to the feasts mentioned in Narasingha Basu's *Dharmamangal*. Written around the first half of eighteenth century in Bardhaman (part of *Rarh*), Narasingha Basu's *Dharmamangal* mentions spinach prepared with ginger, asaphoetida, and coconut; green gram made with allspice; margosa leaves mixed with broad bean and eggplant; a vegetable made from bottle gourd; *phulbori* with jaggery; fried pumpkin, and fried water chestnut.[31] Manikram Ganguly, who was an inhabitant of Hooghly, (also a part of *Rarh*) mentions a few fish preparations that can be found in other texts written in the Rarh such as *notey* leaves with dried seeds of jackfruit and shrimps; *koi* with *phulbori;* and burnt *punti*, apart from vegetables like *sushni* leaves thickened with a ground rice batter and mustard paste.[32] Manikram also mentions fried water chestnut like Narasingha Basu does, and his mention of fried pointed gourd and *thor* (white pith of banana plant stem)[33] are also included in the feast described by Ghanaram Chakrabarty (who belonged to *Rarh* as well). Ghanaram is also particularly focused on *pithe*, thickened milk, cottage cheese, sugar and butter, which alludes to the preference of sweeter varieties of food in the western parts of Bengal.[34] A *Dharmamangal* written in northern Rarh by Shyam Pandit and Dharmadas Banik mentions a more or less simple fare of *notey* leaves, pumpkin curry, a spicy preparation of eggplant, taro and string beans with sundried cakes, margosa leaves with radish, eggplant and broad bean, *gima* leaves, Bengal gram, acidic preparation of berries, olives, and gram flour fritters.[35]

Mansamangals written in eastern parts of Bengal are a complete contrast to those written in the western parts, especially when we compare the fare described in these texts. Perhaps Mukumdaram's *Chandimangal* is close to these texts as far as the elaboration of the menu is concerned. But the skills

---

[30] Nityananda, *Manasamangal*, compiled and edited by Shyamal Bera, *Kabi Nityanander Manasamangal* (Mecheda o Kolkata: Sahajiya o Manfakira, 2006), 28.

[31] Narasingha Basu, *Dharmamangal*, ed. Sukumar Maiti, *Narasingha Basur Dharmamangal* (Bidyasagarpur: Bijan-Panchanan Sangrahashala o Gabeshana Kendra, 2001), 153–154.

[32] Manikram Ganguly, *Dharmamangal*, eds. Bijitkumar Datta, Sunanda Datta (Kolikata: Kolikata Biswabidyalay, 2009), 100–101.

[33] Ibid., 267; Ghanaram Chakrabarty Kabiratna, *Dharmamangal* (Kolikata 1883 [1290 BS]), 388–389.

[34] Chakrabarty, *Dharmamangal*, 388–389.

[35] Shyam Pandit and Dharmadas Banik, *Dharmamangal* (*Niranjan mangal*), ed. Sumitra Kundu (Shantiniketan: Rarh-Gabeshana-Parishad), 99.

and flair present in descriptions of cooking in the texts of eastern Bengal go beyond imagination. In these texts, the women said to be cooking not only create magic with fish, but the panache with which they cook vegetables is also unimaginable. Bijaygupta's *Manasamangal* written in Barishal/Bakharganj in the fifteenth century describes what Sanaka cooked for her six sons: red gram with grated coconut; *palta* (a type of bitter leaves) with coriander and eggplant; *pachan* with green banana; fried *gima* leaves; *bathua* leaves; fried pumpkin; pumpkin leaves cooked with coconut; *chhenchki* (tiny pieces of vegetables) made with ridge gourd; charred eggplant; *thor;* water taro prepared with mustard paste; string beans spiced with pepper; green gram; bottle gourd mixed with milk; pumpkin with coconut; black gram; an acidic preparation of lime; rohu made with *kalta* (indigenous leaves); *magur* with *gima* leaves; shrimp head stuffed with pepper and tied with a thread; fried rohu and *chitol;* *koi* spiced with pepper; *choi* (a type of local herb); eel; *shol* head cooked with eggplant; an acidic preparation of *shol* made with raw mango; raw jackfruit cooked together; with *thor;* green leaves with radish. Generally, the spices used were cumin and pepper, which were also found in western or southern parts of Bengal. However, in eastern Bengal *radhuni* (wild celery seeds) is a common spice used in cooking. What Sanaka does with meat is also considerably elaborate. She cooks goat with coconut and makes a preparation with diced up sheep skin.[36] While we do get descriptions of *shol* and *koi* preparations in the texts of western parts of Bengal, we hardly find any variation or diversity in cooking them. However, within a single text like Bijaygupta's *Manasamangal*, we get three varieties of preparations of shol and two kinds of preparations for magur. Sanaka's baby shower included one *shol* preparation with banana stem and another cooked with giant taro and yam. *Magur* was cooked with ginger. There were also other preparations of fish like an acidic preparation of *cheng* (very small indigenous fish) made with green mango and an intricate preparation of *utpal* (another indigenous fish), deboned and spiced with pepper.[37] Another edition of the same text includes the name of another fish, *dhain*, (Pangasius pangasius) cooked for Sanaka's baby shower.[38] This same edition also mentions *koi* cooked with taro, mashed nail fish (small indigenous fish) and fried *shol*.[39] Narayan Deb's *Padmapuran* written in Mymensingh

---

[36] Bijaygupta, *Manasamangal*, ed. Achintya Biswas (Kolkata: Anjali Publishers, 2009), 177.
[37] Ibid., 230–231.
[38] Bijaygupta, *Padmapuran*, ed. Jayantakumar Dasgupta, *Kabi Bijaygupter Padmapuran* (Kolikata: Kolikata Biswabidyalay, 2009), 228–230.
[39] Ibid.

around fifteenth or sixteenth century also has a long and elaborate list of food cooked by Taraka, Behula's (the protagonist in *Manasamangal*) sister-in-law for the latter's wedding. Taraka cooked jute leaves, *helencha* leaves, bottle gourd, green gram, sundried cakes made from green gram, sesame balls, pumpkin cooked with sesame, an acidic preparation of ripe banana, fried *chitol, magur* curry spiced with pepper, *koi*, lentil cooked with rohu fish head, *katla* cooked with mango, baby *shol* cooked with ground powder of dried mango, *boal*, an acidic preparation of *khalisa*(Colisa fasciata) made with tamarind, *paba* (Indian butter fish or Ompok pabda), castrated goat fried in clarified butter, an acidic preparation of venison, pigeon, leg of baby tortoise, and different savory cakes.[40] Narayan Deb's *Padmapuran* also mentions acidic preparation of a fish called *mahashol*, which is not found in any other region other than Mymensingh.[41] Nirmal kumar Bose, the noted Gandhian anthropologist has also noticed in his survey of the districts of Bengal in the 1940s that *mahashol* could not be found in Padma, the most significant river of eastern Bengal.[42]

Food mentioned in the texts written in northern Bengal or *Varendrabhumi* was similar to those mentioned in the texts of Mymensingh or Barishal. Jagajjiban Ghoshal, who was a resident of Dinajpur in northern Bengal mentions in his *Manasamangal* written in the late seventeenth century, fried banana stem marinated in turmeric, charred *cheng* cooked with lime, fried *chitol* and *boal*, fried castrated goat and castrated goat curry, *chuchura* (another local fish) cooked with bamboo shoots, fried pumpkin, leafy vegetables cooked with broad bean, margosa leaves cooked with eggplant, dried fish cooked with bottle gourd, fried *koi* and pigeon, gravy made from rohu, fish head, and *katla* cooked with mango.[43]

A comparative analysis of all the texts clearly shows the difference in culinary culture between different regions of Bengal. The common fish preparations mentioned in the texts in the western parts of Bengal are of rohu, *koi*, shrimps, and *chitol*. *Magur* and *boal* are rarely found whereas *dhain, eel* and *cheng* are totally absent. *Koi* was mostly cooked with pepper or cumin. The diversities of eastern or northern Bengal are absent in the fish preparations of *Rarh*.

---

[40] Narayan Deb, *Padmapuran*, ed. Tamonash Chandra Dasgupta (1942; Kolikata: Kolikata Biswabidyalay, 1947), 47–49.

[41] Ibid.

[42] Nirmalkumar Basu, *Biallisher Bangla (Rajshahi bibhag [division] and Kuchbihar Rajya [district]*) (Kolikata: Saraswat Library, 1969 [1376 BS]), 21.

[43] Jagajjiban Ghoshal, *Manasamangal*, ed. Achintya Biswas (Kolkata: Ratnabali, 2010),122.

Even the vegetable dishes remain the same except for the leafy vegetables. In most cases, it is either margosa leaves cooked with eggplant and broad beans or a preparation of bottle gourd. Here too, eastern Bengal surpasses *Rarh*. Although one might expect the western parts to be skilled in making *pithes*, ballads sung in the eastern parts of Mymensingh mention the making of a wide variety of *pithe*, like *chitoi* (made with rice flour), *chandrapuli* (a half-moon shaped sweet made of coconut and solidified milk) and *malpoa* (a fried pancake made from a batter of semolina and dunked in sugar syrup), hence asserting its claim of better culinary skills.[44] What is also worthy of mention is the prevalence of onion seeds in the culinary culture of eastern Mymensingh, as evident in the ballads.[45] Western parts of Bengal do not mention venison meat or consumption of pigeons, unlike in northern Bengal or Mymansingh. Bharatchandra's *Anndamangal* written in the eighteenth century is definitely an exception here. Bharatchandra does mention the cooking of venison in Bhabananda, a wealthy man's house.[46] Although Bharatchandra was born in Bardhaman, *Annadamangal* was staged for the first time at the court of Maharaja *Krishnachandra* Roy of Nadia. Here the audience included associates, dependents/protégées and employees of the high rank of the king.[47] Hence, it is hardly surprising that the menu we find in Bharatchandra's *Annadamangal* bear traces of upper class prosperity. Thus we have a long list of names of fish cooked in Bhabananda's house like *rohu*, *katla*, *bekti*, *chitol*, *ba*cha (Clupisoma murius), *shol*, and *khoira* (chakunda gizzard shad or Badis badis). The preparations, like those in other texts of western Bengal, do not indicate a wide range.[48]

It is not my intention to argue here that there was a stark difference between the culinary cultures of different parts of Bengal. However, even subtle differences as can be ascertained from these texts need to be taken into account, for these differences are not only the repositories of the nitty-gritty of everyday life, they also suggest the possibility that the middle-class discourse of taste and Bengali cuisine is fractured and at best, discursive. These early modern texts do not necessarily contain a very sharp regional consciousness as the idea of a greater Bengal was pretty much absent to which the authors

---

[44] "Malua," *Maimansingha geetika* [*Purbbanga geetika*] in Dineshchandra Sen ed. vol. 1, no. 2 (Kolikata: Kolikata Biswabidyalay, 1958), 60–61; "Kajalrekha," *Maimansingha geetika*, 330–331.

[45] "Mahua," *Maimansingha Geetika*, 10–11; "Malua," *Maimansinghar Geetika*, 60–61.

[46] Raygunakar Bharatchandra, *Annadamangal* (Kolkata: Sahityalok, 2002), 180–181.

[47] Chatterjee, "Persianization of Itihasa," 20.

[48] Bharatchandra, *Annadamangal*, 180–181.

of *Mangalkabyas* could contrast the memory of the regions they wrote about. However, the culture of food of different regions of Bengal is a constant reminder that diversity has always been the mainstay of the everyday life of ordinary people. Hence, Bharatchandra proudly recalls at least fifty varieties of rice grown in *Rarh* and not found anywhere else: *Ashu, boro, aman, dalkachu, orkachu, ghikala, patra, meghhasa, kalamona, ray, panitara, kalindi, kanakchur, chayachur, pudi, shuashali, harilebu, guyathubi, sundi, ghishali, poalabira, kalamocha, kaijuri, khajurchhari, china, dhalbar, dadushahi, banshphul, chilat, karuchi, kelejira, padmaraj, dudsar(dudhraj), luchi, kantarangi, konchai, kapilabhog, dhule, banshgajal, bajal, marichshali, bhura beneaphul, kajla, shankarchina, maku, mete, mashilot, shibjata, dudhpana, gangajal, sudha, dudhkalam, gandheswari, payraras, banshmati, kadma, kusumshali, gandhamalati, and latamou.* This regional consciousness will become more poignant from the nineteenth century onwards.[49]

SUBREGIONAL HISTORIES

The colonial period saw the beginnings of a new consciousness in the history of a region. Everyday life of the people of the region became a kernel of this history-writing. Kiranlekha Ray's *Varendra-randhan* is a major example of regional negotiations within Bengali cuisine.[50] Kiranlekha Ray came from what one might call an upperclass Hindu Bengali background. Her husband Sharatkumar Ray was a landlord of Dighapatia in northern Bengal. He was a member of the *Varendra* cultural society and took an active interest in promoting the regional history of *Varendrabhumi* (Northern Bengal). He also encouraged Kiranlekha, his wife, to write *Varendra Randhan*, a food history of this region. Writing a history of a region was definitely an integral part of self-fashioning because this history explored the lifeworld of the people of the region. This was a time when Bengal as a cultural entity became an object of academic and antiquarian inquiry.

Varendra Randhan, which was initially conceptualised as a compilation of local sayings, *vratas*, folklores, recipes, and local customs could not be completed because of Kiranlekha's untimely demise. However, her husband

---

[49] Raygunakar Bharatchandra, "Annadamangal," in *Bharatchandra-Granthabali* ed. Brajendranath Bandopadhay and Sajanikanta Das (1943 [1350 BS]; repr., Kolikata: Bangiya Sahitya Parishat, 1997 [1404 BS]), 432.

[50] Kiranlekha Ray, *Varendra-randhan* (Kolkata:Subarnarekha, 1999[1406BS]).

MAP 2: Early twentieth century Eastern India.

took it upon himself to publish the recipes as *Varendra Randhan*.[51] Ray dedicated this book to his daughters and wrote: 'I bequeath to you all your mother's compilation of the cookery of your "*janak-bhu*"(fatherland).'[52] Ray's use of the term '*janak-bhu*' is significant because the recipes used in the book somehow tries to explain to the reader why a recipe is unique to *Varendrabhumi* or the soil of *Varendra* region. For instance, one recipe is named reddish potato of *Varendra*. For this recipe, Ray suggests the use of only a specific variety of

---

[51] Sharatkumar Ray, Introduction to *Varendra-randhan* by Kiranlekha Ray, 5–6.
[52] Sharatkumar Ray, Dedication to *Varendra-randhan* by Kiranlekha Ray, 3.

potato found in *Varendra*. These were small potatoes containing more gluten and less starch. Hence they had a reddish tinge.⁵³

The spices that were used in *Varendra* were also different from other parts of Bengal. *Panchphoron* (a mixture of five spices, which is a combination of cumin, coriander, fennel, fenugreek, and onion seeds) is a popular spice used in Bengali cooking. However, Kiranlekha Ray tells us that this much popular spice was absent in *Varendra* cooking. Instead, fenugreek and cumin prevailed in most of the cookery of this region.⁵⁴ Although these two were the spices most used, they were never used together in a particular cooking.⁵⁵ Use of spices brings out the distinctive character of a particular region's cooking. The use of spices in *shukto* can illustrate this point further. Although cumin and *panchphoron* are widely used in *shukto*, the *shukto* that one finds in *Varendra* uses fenugreek and mustard or onion seeds and *randhuni* (wild celery).⁵⁶ Ray herself was aware of the particularities of different cuisines when she wrote how mustard paste was more prevalent in southern parts of Bengal than in *Varendra* (northern parts).⁵⁷

It was not really in the foodstuff consumed, but in the patterns of cooking that a distinctiveness of a region lay. While the middle-class discourse certainly talked about one 'Bengali' self and a refined taste that aided in the construction of that self, the material culture of each region of Bengal constantly reminded one of the peculiarities of this middle-class self. Thus, a particular food item became the distinctive marker of one region. Whoever talked of the vegetarian dishes of the *Varendra* region never failed to mention *chapor ghanto*.⁵⁸ *Chapor ghanto* was a hodge podge of finely chopped vegetables cooked with *chapor* (a flat and round cake made from ground and fried pulses).⁵⁹ Such minuscule differences constantly made the cracks visible in the construction of a regional middle-class. Apparently, residents in Mymensingh preferred goat to fish, whereas those in Rajshahi liked fish more.⁶⁰ Even within the *Varendra* region

---

⁵³ Kiranlekha Ray, *Varendra-randhan*, 29.
⁵⁴ Ibid., 55.
⁵⁵ Ibid.
⁵⁶ Ibid., 67.
⁵⁷ Ibid.
⁵⁸ Ray, *Varendra-randhan*, 74–75; Giribala Debi, *Giribala Debir rachanabali*, vol. 2 (Kolkata: Ramayani Prakash Bhaban, 1977 [1384 BS]), 173.
⁵⁹ Ray, *Varendra-randhan*, 74–75.
⁶⁰ Hemantabala Debi, *Hemantabala Debir rachana sankalan*, ed. Jasodhara Bagchi and Abhijit Sen (Kolkata: Dey's Publishing, 1992), 68.

there were differences in food preferences in villages as compared to cities. While village homes in the *Varendra* were not much appreciative of batter made from Bengal gram, city dwellers quite relished it.[61]

Writing the history of a region not only had the potential of excavating and glorifying the culture of a particular region, it could also provide a critique of the present. Kumudnath Mullick (1880–1938) was full of praises for the art of sweetmeat-making in the district of Nadia. Mallick writes that since most of the sweets in Bengal were made from dairy, ingredients like milk, cream, thickened milk, sugar, and jaggery were absolute essentials for the craft of sweetmeat making. Since these ingredients were easily available in Nadia, it became the birth place of a distinctive sweetmeat industry.[62] Within Nadia again each town had its own specialties. While Krishnanagar was famous for its *sarpuria*, *sarbhaja* and *sartakti*, Shantipur was known for its *nikhuti*. Mullick described these sweetmeats in precise details to define their uniqueness. *Sarpuria* was a soft sweet that was made from applying cream on ground cottage cheese and thickened milk, whereas thick and square cream was soaked in sugar syrup to make *Sarbhaja* or dried to make *sartakti*.[63]

Mullick laid out a long list of specialties of each town of Nadia. Thus, Ranaghat was praised for its *pantua* fried in *ghee*, while Muragachha excelled in *jilapi* made from cottage cheese. Nabadwip's yougurt and *rajbhog* made Mullick nostalgic as he does not fail to mention *raskadamba* of Debgram. Mullick laments that the unique flavour, smell, and color of these sweetmeats of Nadia were becoming increasingly scarce because of adulteration. In place of skilled craftsmen, Nadia's confections were fast becoming *kritrim*(fake).[64] Claiming history for a particular region also becomes noticeable in such history writing. It is generally believed that Navin Das of Bagbazar in Calcutta introduced *Rasogolla* (a type of cottage cheese ball soaked in sugar syrup).[65] Thus, citing Indranath Bandopadhyay, Mullick claims *Rasogolla* for Nadia.[66]

---

[61] Ray, *Varendra-randhan*, 35.
[62] Kumudnath Mullick, *Nadia kahini*, ed. Mohit Ray (1910 [1317 BS]; repr., Kolkata; Pustak Bipani, 1986), 379–380.
[63] Ibid.
[64] Ibid.
[65] Jatindramohan Datta, "Sandesher katha," in *Jamdatter diary o anyanya rachana*, compiled and edited by Krishanu Bhattacharya (Kolikata: Rita Prakashani, 2006), 105–105, first published in *Jashtimadhu*, January/February 1966 [Magh 1373 BS]; Pranab Ray, *Banglar khabar* (Kolkata: Sahityalok, 1987), 50.
[66] Mullick, *Nadiakahini*, 379–380.

Let me write down the archeology of *Rasogolla*. It is not more than 59/60 year old. The village of Phulia which gave birth to Krittibas happens to be the birthplace of *Rasogolla*. Haradhan, the sweetmeat maker who resided in Phulia made sweetmeat for the Palchaudhuris of Ranaghat. His little daughter was crying. In order to pacify her he (Haradhan) dropped some cottage cheese in the sugar syrup that was boiling on the stove top. The result was a fine product. Palchaudhuris who were the landlords named this product *Rasogolla*.[67]

Claiming a sweet for a region had its significance since sweets became the marker of identity of a subregion. Maniklal Singha, the noted historian of *Rarh*, associated the origins of sweets made of cottage cheese with the spread of *Vaishnavism* in Bishnupur. According to Singha, Srinivas Acharya, the renowned *Vaishnava* preacher, brought along with him ornate verses written by the *Vaishnava* poets, and music like *Dhrupad* (classical music) from Vrindavan(in modern Uttar Pradesh) to Bishnupur. The practice of offering sweets made of cottage cheese to the deities of Radha and Krishna followed the other common *Vaishnava* practices.[68] After the Malla kings of Bishnupur converted to *Vaishnava* faith, they popularised the worship of Radha Krishna in Bishnupur and in order to do so ordered the building of several temples. Families of milkmen and sweetmeat makers were asked to settle next to the temples so that they could ensure a steady supply of sweets made of cottage cheese for Radha and Krishna. Thus the expansion of Gaudiya Vaishnavism also increased the consumption of sweets made of cottage cheese at least among the upper classes of *Rarh*.[69] Maniklal Singha here makes a significant argument by saying that there was a fundamental transformation in the taste of at least the upper classes of Bishnupur with the expansion of Vaishnava faith. Having sweets made of cottage cheese definitely became one of the markers of their identity as they distinguished themselves from those who had not adopted Vaishnavism or have not refrained from having meat or alcohol, unlike the former.[70]

While there is no doubt that specialties of each region were ultimately counted as something belonging to the entire region of Bengal, the history of each region unfolds along with the history of these sweets. The literati and the connoisseur of food cannot erase the stories that surround the sweets of

---

[67] Indranath Bandopadhyay, *Indranath granthabali*, 1925 [1332 BS]), cited in Mullick, *Nadiakahini*, 379–380.
[68] Maniklal Singha, *Rarher jati o krishti*, vol. 3 (Bishnupur, 1982), 88–89.
[69] Ibid.
[70] Ibid.

a particular region. Bipradas Mukhopadhyay, who was known for his recipe columns as well as cookbooks, also wrote extensively on sweetmeat making. While he provides detailed instructions for making *khaichur*, he never forgets to mention *khaichur*'s connections with Dhanekhali, the region where it is made.[71] Pranab Ray, a much later writer on food habits of Bengal puts his entire focus on the sweetmeat of particular sub-regions in Bengal. Apart from dealing with minute details of how a sweet is made, Ray's purpose is also to make his reader aware of the history of a particular sweet.[72] Ray tells us that certain sweets are popular in certain regions only. For instance, *jeelapi* made from green gram is found only in the Narajol region in Nadia district.[73] The craft of sweetmeat making was associated with the history of a land. Thus when a sweetmeat maker from Bishnupur invented a type of *motichur* from gram flour made from a particular seed, he was given the title of 'mandal' by the king of Bishnupur.[74] Apparently *sitabhog* and *mihidana* of Bardhaman also received considerable patronage from the king of Bardhaman.[75] Such crafting genius had the potential of enhancing the status of a particular region.

Certain regions became particularly known for their sweetmeat making. Names of some sweetmeats became interlinked with the name of particular regions to the extent that the two could not be dissociated. Remembrance of the history of a particular region also brought to mind names of sweetmeats associated to that region. The middle-class literati never failed to draw up a list of particular sweetmeats. Jatindramohan Datta was all praises for *gunpo* of Panihati, *ramchaki* of Sodepur, and *kanchagolla* of Ranaghat-Shantipur.[76] Bijnan Chandra Ghosh had his own list of particular favorites- *kanchagolla* from Bangaon and Gopalnagar, *pantua* from Ranaghat, *patksheer* from Dhaka and Bikrampur and sweet yogurt from Mograhat.[77] While there is a slight difference among the literati about the list given above, they all identified Janai with *manohara*, Chandananagar with *talsansh* and Dhanekhali with *khaichur*. The stories that come up with the mention of these sweets tell us the nuances of a subregional consciousness.

---

[71] Bipradas Mukhopadhyay, *Mishtanna-pak*, vols. 1 & 2, revised ed. (1898 [1305BS]; repr., Kolikata, 1904 [1311 BS]), 60–61.

[72] Pranab Ray, *Banglar khabar* (Kolkata: Sahityalok,1987).

[73] Ibid., 41.

[74] Ibid., 43.

[75] Ibid., 107.

[76] Datta, "Sandesher katha," 105.

[77] Ray Saheb Bijnan Chandra Ghosh, *Ahaar* (Kolkata,1942), 66.

Manohara, Datta tells us, was made in order to hone the pride of a particular region. When Manohar, who was a resident of Janai and a sweetmeat maker himself, visited his in-laws in Bardhaman, he was ridiculed by his brothers-in-law and sisters-in-law. They claimed that Bardhaman was famous for its sweets like *sitabhog, mihidana, langcha* from Shaktigarh or *nabat* from Ghorungi, while the region that Manohar came from had nothing to take pride in. To refute their claim, Manohar made a particular sweet and popularised it on coming back to Janai. This sweet was named *manohara* in his honour.[78] While peculiarities of a particular region were implicit in its sweets, those from other regions had no qualms in appreciating their worth. The literati, who were also connoisseurs, took delight in the uniqueness of a region's specialty. These sweets could become a part of the diet of the Bengali middle-class while still retaining their uniqueness.

History, myth-making and culinary skills of a particular region also became entangled with the narratives of a lost world. Thus Pranab Ray recapitulates the history of Khirpai through a genealogy of *babarshah*. Ray writes that unless we get to know the ancient history of Khirpai, it is not possible to delineate the history of *babarshah*, a sweet made from flour.[79] He explains,

> Khirpai and its neighboring Kashiganj were known for its handloom and silk industry.---The British and the French established their trade bases here in mid eighteenth century.---Local well off weavers became immensely rich doing trade with the foreign traders. It was then that Khirpai became a large town. It was first included in the district of Bardhaman, but later came under the jurisdiction of Hooghly. In 1872 it came to Medinipur. There was a cultural efflorescence here along with the increase in prosperity that came with the rise in handloom and silk industry.
>
> ---*Rasogolla* or *sandesh* was not available in this region at that time. Sweetmeat makers generally made sweets with whatever was available locally such as paddy, wheat, jaggery, sugar and clarified butter. ---The British and the French traders residing here ate whatever was prepared locally. A British trader named Edward Babar asked local sweetmeat makers for something new. What Paran Ata, a sweetmeat maker made for him with flour, clarified butter and sugar syrup came to be known as '*babarshah*'.---
>
> *Babarshah* constitutes the link between the past and present history of Khirpai. The glorious temples, handloom and silk of this region have eclipsed. ---Khirpai's history is left with *babarshah*.[80]

---

[78] Datta, "Sandesher katha," 106.
[79] Ray, *Banglarkhabar*, 110.
[80] Ibid., 110–113.

Identity of a region became integrally associated with the history of a particular food the region has been known for. These markers of identity could often traverse the boundaries of caste and community. However, often a community's history also became connected to the taste of a particular region. Thus, a Muslim middle-class discourse of taste could often be different from that of a Hindu Bengali middle-class. Many of the Muslims in pre-partition Bengal were actually Urdu speaking. Their memoirs actually reveal another aspect of regional history to us, which is significantly different from the world of the Hindu middle-class Bengali.

Hakim Habibur Rahman Akhundzada (1881–1947) was trained in *unani* medicine in Agra and practiced in Dhaka as a *hakim* from 1904. He played a significant role in popularising Urdu in Dhaka and edited *Al Mashriq*, the first Urdu monthly newspaper in Dhaka in 1906.[81] In 1945, Habibur Rahman narrated his memories of Dhaka of fifty years before (that is around late nineteenth century), which was broadcast from the All India Radio in Dhaka. This series of narration in Urdu named 'Dhaka aaj se pachas baras pahle', (Dhaka 50 years ago) was later published as *Dhaka pachas baras pahle* from Lahore in 1949. This text contains the history of Dhaka, and its material culture.[82]

Dhaka pachas baras pahle has several chapters on the history of Dhaka, the old industry of Dhaka, the celebration of the Islamic festivals of Ramzan, sports, music, and festivals in Dhaka. However, Rahman seems most engrossed with narrating the culture of food in Dhaka, to which he devotes at least four chapters. Rahman's text recounts the history of the Mughal influence on the material culture of Dhaka. This history often remains absent in the history of the region by the Hindu Bengali middle-class.[83]

Hakim Habibur Rahman specifies that he is reminiscing about the cuisine of the Muslims living in Dhaka. He says that there has been a Mughal influence on this cuisine as well as that of the Armenians, who inhabited Dhaka in the Mughal period. However, certain traits of cuisine were unique to Dhaka.

---

[81] Mohammad Rezaul Karim, "Lekhak marhum Hakim Habibur Rahman prasange," Hakim Habibur Rahman, *Dhaka: Panchash bachhar age (Dhaka pachas baras pahle)*, translated from Urdu to Bengali by Mohammad Rezaul Karim (Dhaka: Papyrus, 2005), 12–14.

[82] Mohammad Rezaul Karim, introduction to *Dhaka: Panchas bochor age*, by Rahman, 7–11.

[83] For a discussion of culinary history of Dhaka from the precolonial times to contemporary period, see *Dhakai khabar*, ed. Habiba Khatun and Hafeeza Khatun (Dhaka: Bangladesh Asiatic Society, 2010).

While *pulao* or pilaf was central to Islamic cuisine, the way it was cooked by the Muslims in Dhaka was very different. In other regions, rice was semi cooked and then mixed with other spices and cooked with the mouth of the vessel sealed with dough. But in Dhaka rice was never cooked beforehand and chicken pieces were not kept whole like in other places. This *pulao* known as the *morag pulao* (chicken pilaf) was unique to Dhaka.[84] The prevalence of *rui pulao* (rohu pilaf) or *ilish pulao* (hilsa pilaf) of Dhaka was unheard of in the greater Islamic world.[85]

Some of the culinary habits of the Muslim upper and upper-middle-classes of Dhaka were not much different from their Hindu counterparts. The appreciation of *khichuri* (a mixture of rice and lentil) was popular all over India. However, introducing *paneer* (cottage cheese) into it was again unique to Dhaka, so was putting boiled egg sautéed in clarified butter in *khichuri* made of dry roasted green gram.[86] The local influence on the culinary habits of the Muslims in Dhaka cannot be ignored, in Hakim Habibur Rahman's opinion. The practice of making *khatta* (a sour preparation made with tamarind and jaggery) with bottle gourd or eggplant was a culinary habit that the Muslims, albeit not the upper classes, learnt from the local Hindu population.[87]

The pride of place, however, went to *Bakarkhani* bread, which, like the *babarshah* of Khirpai, became conjoined with the memory of the gastronomic culture of Dhaka. The popular saying was that Mirza Aga Bakar, who was a landlord of greater Barishal, introduced *Bakarkhani* in Dhaka.[88] *Bakarkhani* is made from flour, which is mixed with cottage cheese and made into fine dough. This dough is then flattened with hand and coated with clarified butter. After brushing the dough with ghee or clarified butter, it is folded several times and each fold is brushed with ghee. Then again it is kneaded back into dough. After the dough is rolled, sesame seeds are sprinkled on the bread and the bread is put into oven with a sprinkling of milk on it.[89] *Bakarkhani*, Rahman reminds us, cannot be found in any other region. In fact, although Hindus did not sell bread anywhere else, in Dhaka they had no qualms in selling *bakarkhani*. *Bakarkhani* was the pride of Dhaka and this pride inspired the Hindus to take up this job of selling *bakarkhani*.[90]

---

[84] Hakim Habibur Rahman, *Dhaka: Panchas bachchar age*, 61.
[85] Ibid.
[86] Ibid.
[87] Ibid., 68.
[88] Ibid., fn, 48.
[89] Ibid., 46.
[90] Ibid., 47.

Food was an organic part of the quotidian life of ordinary men and women. The significance of food was almost visceral as it came to define the identity of a region. This region was definitely a part of greater Bengal, but many liked to remember it as having a life of its own. Apart from the topography and economy, gastronomic practices were the core of a region's identity. Thus when Hariananda Barari (b.1929) recalls his childhood days in Bikrampur in eastern Bengal, he does not forget to mention that fish and rice were integrally connected with the life and culture of the inhabitants of Bikrampur.[91]

THE SUBREGIONAL 'OTHER'

There is no denying the fact that there was definitely a difference in the gastronomic practices between regions. Even within a particular region, there could be subtle variations. These differences in culinary patterns often sprang from the supply factor. For instance, the prevalence of dried fish or *shuntki* in Sylhet can be explained by the scarcity of fresh fish in the area. Although *shuntki* is attributed to the diet of Muslims and the lower classes, many Hindu middle-class Bengali in Sylhet consumed *shuntki*. There were two types of *shuntki*. One kind was dried in the sun and it was comparatively easier to digest. The other kind was made to rot under wet soil. The latter version was definitely tastier but had a more pungent smell than the former and was quite heavy.[92] Although in some places like Maymansingh or Bagura district *shuntki* was indeed consumed, it was more popular among the lower caste men and women. In Hill Tippera, however, the middle-class Hindus did consume *shuntki*. Here again, low availability of fresh fish explains the consumption of *shuntki* among the middle-class. But the middle-class preferred the dried version of bigger fish like *pabda* (Indian butter fish or Ompok pabda) and *aar* (*Mystus aor*)whereas the lower castes like the kaibartas made a *shuntki* out of *punti* (swamp barb). The latter was more moist than the former and was known as *shijal shuntki*.[93] One man's pleasure invoked another's disgust and

---

[91] Hariananda Barari, *Amar Bikrampur*, translated from English H.A. Barari, *In Sun and Shower*, by Nandita Mukhopadhyay (Kolkata: Ananda Publishers,2006), 195.

[92] Brajendra Narayan Chaudhuri, *Smriti o pratiti* (Kolikata: Oriental Book Company, 1982), 198–199.

[93] Nirmalkumar Basu, *Biallisher Bangla: Dhaka bibhag*, (Kolikata: Saraswat Library, 1969 [1376 BS]), 25–26; Basu, *BiallisherBangla: Rajshahi bibhag o Kuchbihar rajya*,34; Basu, *Biallisher Bangla:Chattagram bibhag o parbatya Tripura* (Chattagram Division and Hill Tippera), 24–25.

while many scowled upon the consumption of *shuntki*, many others actually championed the cause of *shuntki*. Maulavi Hamidullah Khan Bahadur, who wrote a history of the Chittagong region in 1855, narrates in his book that the Bengali literati of this region relished *shuntki* made from dried fish and such *shuntki* was also exported to the markets of Calcutta for the consumption of the British residents there. He reprimands those who ridiculed *shuntki*. In Khan Bahadur's opinion, those who lived far from coastal areas were not accustomed to consuming *shuntki* and even spread rumors about the ill effects of the consumption of *shuntki*. Khan Bahadur lashes out against these people accusing them of being orthodox and unwise. In support of his defense of *shuntki*, he also alludes to the existence of an international market for *shuntki*.[94]

A dislike for *shuntki* often arose from a distrust of the 'other.' *Shuntki* did have strong subregional connotations and Hamidullah Khan Bahadur's championing of *shuntki* had much to do with his 'belonging' to the region. This belonging was also intertwined with his Islamic belief when he asserted that since the Prophet Muhammad himself had liked *shuntki* it was un-Islamic to not like *shuntki*. Khan Bahadur was essentially emphatic that where there was enough supply of fish like in the coastal regions, consumption of *shuntki* was natural.[95] Supply of course raised demand in many regions. Supply of enough milk in Faridpur district ensured manufacturing of plenty of thickened milk, *rasagolla*, (cottage cheese balls dunk in sugar syrup) and *sandesh* (another sweet made from cottage cheese).[96] However, in local memory hard facts like supply and demand took a backseat. What remained ensconced in the memory of ordinary men and women were the associations and the nostalgia that it tagged along. Faridpur's *ghee* (clarified butter) thus became a clue in identifying a person in a short detective fiction written by Sambuddha or Amulyakumar Dasgupta (1911–1973).[97]

We certainly find the construction of a 'Bengali' taste at the level of the discursive and even the material. But this taste was constantly punctuated

---

[94] Maulavi Hamidullah Khan Bahadur, *Ahadisul Khaoanin: Chattagramer prachin itihas*, translated from Farsi by Khaled Masuke Rasul (Dhaka: Anupam Prakashani, 2013), 61–62.
[95] Ibid., 63–64.
[96] Basu, *Biallisher Bangla: Dhaka bibhag*, 17.
[97] Sambuddha, "Chheledhara Jayanta," in Amulyakumar Dasgupta, *Sambuddha rachanabali*, ed. Prabir Mukhopadhyay with a preface by Gautam Bhadra, vol. 1(Kolkata: Ababhas, 2007), 257–297, first published in *Galpabharati* (October/November-November/December 1951 [Kartik/Agrhayan 1357 BS]).

with regional preferences. Pride in one region necessitated an 'other' region. While someone from Bankura district would certainly bear the attributes of a 'modern' Bengali middle-class, in the gaze of the inhabitants of other regions they would always retain the traces of Bankura. Jatindramohan Datta (b.1894 [1301 BS]), better known as Jamdatta, who wrote a number of essays on the urban and rural life of nineteenth century Bengal as well as regional or local histories, narrates an incident where this point becomes clear. Jamdatta writes about the preferences of the inhabitants of *Rarh* (westerns parts of Bengal) for poppy seeds and black gram. On the occasion of a visit from his brother-in-law, poppy seed curry, fried balls made from ground poppy seeds, fried poppy seeds and black gram were cooked, since the brother-in-law was from Bardhaman, a part of *Rarh*. Jamdatta and others constantly mock the brother-in-law as '*rerho*' (one from *Rarh*) and recites limericks aimed at regional idiosyncrasies.

> Uncivilized inhabitants of Bankura consume plenty of puffed rice; ---
> One, whose abode is Ulo, loves to eat *mulo* (radishes);
> One, who lives in Hooghly, likes to eat *googly* (snail).[98]

In response to this mockery of the inhabitants of *Rarh*, Kunja, a servant who came with Datta's brother-in-law retorts back with a song praising black gram.

> Shiva himself wrote in the *Tantrasar*.
> Split Black gram has the nutritive qualities of meat.
> Whoever blames such a legume,
> Has to be tied up and sent into exile.
> Inhabitants of Bankura Bardhaman Hooghly,
> Are strong because of black gram.[99]

The association of black gram with *Rarh* was wide spread. Nilmani Chakrabarty, a Brahmo preacher, remembers that while preaching in Tarakeswar in Hooghly, they stayed at the place of a man called Umapada Ray. Ray's family consumed black gram almost every day. Adinath Chattopadhyay, another preacher hailing from eastern Bengal, shrieked in disgust one day: 'Bringing me to *Rarh*, these people plan to kill me by feeding black gram'.[100]

---

[98] Jatindramohan Datta, "Karaier daler geet" Jatindramohan Datta, *Jamdatter diary*, 91-93, first published in *Jashtimadhu*, March/April 1961 [Chaitra, 1368 BS].
[99] Ibid.
[100] Nilmani Chakrabarty, *Atmajibansmriti* (1920(?); repr., Kolikata: Sadharan Brahmosamaj, 1975 [1382 BS]), 73.

In a response to this, Chakrabarty asked Brajalal Ganguly, a noted singer associated with the Brahmo Samaj, to sing a song: 'His *bangalness* (*bangal* was the pejorative term for those residing in eastern parts of Bengal) cannot be erased even if he eats black gram a hundred times.'[101] Chakrabarty, who was himself an inhabitant of western parts of Bengal, was mocking another region in the defense of his region. Such mockery was a part and parcel of everyday life in Bengal, which is also evident in the proverbs and popular sayings in Bengali. The residents of Bankura came to be known for their enormous consumption of puffed rice[102], whereas those living in Birbhum were identified with poppy seeds, acidic preparation of vegetables, fruits or fish, and black gram.[103]

While each region had its attributes and could be mocked by another region for its idiosyncrasies, there was a broad divide between the gastronomic culture of east Bengal and that of west Bengal. In the middle-class discourse of taste this divide can be widely located. Thus while someone could take pride in the culinary culture of Sylhet, for that person Sylhet also came to symbolise eastern Bengal. They could be equally boisterous about the culture of food in Dhaka. The absence of sweets made of cottage cheese in the district of Sylhet actually made its inhabitants proud.[104] Sweets made from cottage cheese thus became affixed to western Bengal whereas eastern Bengal was lauded for its aesthetic presentation of sweets like *narikeler chinra* (juliennes of coconut that looked like flattened rice) or *gangajali* (another intricately done sweet).[105] This aestheticisation was significant because it aimed at valorising the cooking of women of eastern Bengal as a form of art.[106] Sweets made from cottage cheese like *sandesh*, *rasagolla* or *luchi* somehow were linked up with an urban culture and this urban culture revolved around Calcutta. It will not be an exaggeration to argue that Calcutta largely became the epicenter of a specifically 'Bengali' taste. It became an abode of pleasure for many and at the same time these pleasures were looked down upon. Vivekananda often lashed out at the urban culture and the 'modern civilisation' of Calcutta.

---

[101] Ibid.
[102] Sushilkumar De, ed., *Bangla prabad chhora o chalti katha* (1945 [1352 BS]; repr., Kolikata: A Mukherjee & Co., 1952 [1359 BS]), 84.
[103] Ibid., 84, 527.
[104] Bipinchandra Pal, *Sattar batsar: Atmajibani* (Kolkata: Kalpan, 1955 [1362 BS]), 64, first published in *Prabasi* (January/February 1926-April/May1928 [Magh 1333- Baishakh 1335BS]); Brajendra Narayan Chaudhuri, *Smriti o pratiti* (Kolikata: Oriental Book Company, 1982), 211.
[105] Ibid.
[106] Pal, *Sattar batsar: Atmajibani*, 64.

Vivekananda offered a critique of 'modern' eating habits. However, in doing so, he draws the regional boundaries quite sharply and compliments eastern Bengal on its food habits, although he himself hailed from the western parts. His critique itself is full of prejudices against what he calls *'adha saontali* Birbhum and Bankro' (semi-tribal [*saontal*: a tribe living in western parts of Bengal and Bihar] Birbhum and Bankura) and in defense of the upper caste cuisine of Dhaka and Bikrampur in eastern Bengal.

> Proper nutritious and cheap Bengali cuisine can be found only in eastern Bengal, so try to imitate them as much as you can. Do not lean towards the west (here by west he means western parts of Bengal). Ultimately we will be left with black gram and sour preparation of fish made in the semi-Santhal Birbhum and Bankura! You are the inhabitants of Calcutta, entrapped and seduced by the shops of the *mairas* or sweetmeat makers Birbhum and Bankura have thrown away all their puffed rice into Damodar (a river flowing through these regions), black gram has been thrown into streams and even Dhaka and Bikrampur have floated away *Dhain*,(Pangasius pangasius*)* and tortoise into water and becoming civilized!! Is this what your urban culture is all about, you have corrupted yourselves and now are bent upon corrupting the entire region? Shame on you! They are also so stupid that even after they suffer from dyspepsia caused by eating those garbage produced in Calcutta they will never say that they cannot digest it. They want to be urban by hook or crook.[107]

If we carefully follow this passage, at the first glance we can see some inconsistencies in what Vivekananda is arguing. Although at first he mocks the inhabitants of Bankura and Birbhum for their black gram, they are again blamed for discarding the black gram for the taste of Calcutta. Black gram certainly becomes the marker of identity of Bankura and Birbhum and when compared to the culinary culture of eastern Bengal, the former has no significance for Vivekananda. However, for him black gram also signifies a rural culture and when compared to the food consumed in the public eateries of Calcutta, it becomes associated with a 'tradition' that is fast eroding under the waves of urbanity and colonial modernity, which is epitomised by the gastronomic culture of Calcutta. Thus, the regions find its 'other' in Calcutta. Regions contain 'tradition' while Calcutta becomes synonymous with the 'modern.' A deep nostalgia for the rural past makes the middle-class often crave for their regional identity even when they became a part of a larger 'Bengali' self.

---

[107] Swami Vivekananda, *Prachya o paschatya* (Kolikata: Udbodhan Karjalay, 1954[1361 BS]), 39–64.

For many, Calcutta became a sign of decay and adulteration that could never be an ideal place for refined taste. Brajendra Narayan Chaudhuri comments:

> The taste and nutritive qualities of hilsa curry cooked and served in a hotel in Calcutta for Rs. 5 cannot be compared to the hilsa gravy and rice served for 10 paise (100 paise=1 INR) or 3 annas (1 anna=1/16th of 1 INR) at Narayanganj Goaland hotel. A modern man will never understand that the food served in a Narayanganj hotel is superior in quality.--- Frozen hilsa found in Calcutta does not have the smell and flavor of the hilsa caught in Padma.[108]

A modern middle-class man, according to Chaudhuri, was incapable of comprehending and appreciating the flavour of hilsa found in Padma because he was a product of colonial modernity. He was the product of an education system and a cultural background that was archetypal of Calcutta. Hence he had nothing to ruminate on, whereas one who had migrated from eastern Bengal to Calcutta in search of livelihood or other options carried the burden of nostalgia and a deep pain for the past. And thus, Padma does not simply remain a river; it becomes poetry for the inhabitants of Dhaka.[109] Even the caste rituals around food practices in Calcutta became a matter of confusion for nationalists like Bipin Pal, who came from Sylhet to Calcutta in late nineteenth century. He observes,

> We never knew that a Brahmin ceased to be a Brahmin if he had rice at a *Shudra's* place. We used to offer rice to deities on occasions such as Durgapuja.[110] Brahmins used to cook and the priests ate at our place on those occasions without any hesitation. In Calcutta, however, I have heard rice could be offered to the Gods only at a Brahmin's house. *Kayastha* or other castes that ranked lower than the Brahmins in the caste hierarchy do not have this right. They could only offer something which was uncooked to the Gods. We never heard of such peculiar customs. Our district never had this sort of Brahminical dominance.[111]

Pal's memoir reveals an interesting fact about the gastronomic culture of Calcutta. While Calcutta did become the epicenter of whatever was 'new' in

---

[108] Brajendra Narayan Chaudhuri, *Smriti o pratiti* (Kolikata: Oriental Book Company, 1982), 211.
[109] Ibid.
[110] Largest Bengali Hindu religious festival for the worship of Goddess Durga.
[111] Pal, *Sattar Batsar: Atmajibani*, 67–68.

colonial Bengal, if Pal is to be believed it still held onto certain rigid practices. We have already seen in chapters two and four how several changes had seeped into the new social feasts, especially in cities like Calcutta and its urban environs. But at the same time, some middle-class men and women still clung to what they considered their 'traditions.' These traditions of caste rigidities, however, were no less modern than the new social feasts of Calcutta. Had there been any one tradition of such rules regarding interdining among the Bengali middle-class, it would be the same across regions. Interestingly, men like Iswarchandra Gupta (1811–1858 [1218 BS-1265BS]), the satirist from western Bengal, who was also known for his periodical *Sambad Prabhakar*, expressed his utter dismay when on a visit to eastern Bengal in 1854 (1261 BS) he saw that Brahmins in large parts of east Bengal like Bikrampur, Barishal, Srihatta, Chattagram, Kumilla, and Bhulua had no qualms in eating at the houses of Vaidyas and Kayasthas. In fact, Gupta was surprised that they even consumed mutton and tortoise meat.[112] Gupta was also shocked to find out that in places like Barishal, even respectable Bengali men consumed yogurt made by the Muslims.[113] Dietary restrictions imposed by the Hindu scriptures on the widows also seemed quite flexible to Gupta in places like Dhaka, Bikrampur, Barishal, Tripura, Kumilla, Bhulua, Sudharam, Chattagram and Noakhali.[114] While in other regions in Bengal, widows did not even drink a drop of water on days like *ekadashi* (fasting without water), in these regions of eastern Bengal, widows from respectable families had fruits, flattened rice, and popped rice on *ekadashi*.[115]

Apart from such sharp distinctions between the caste rituals in Calcutta and norms of interdining in eastern Bengal, autobiographies and even cookbooks were replete with instances of differences in patterns of cooking in the two regions. For many, eastern Bengal became typecast as consumer of spicy food. Even those from Pabna in northern Bengal could be aghast by the use of monstrous amounts of chilies and pepper in the cuisine of Dhaka, Bikrampur, and Maymansingha.[116] This mockery of spicy food in Bengal

---

[112] Ishwarchandra Gupta, "Bhramankari bandhur patra," in *Ishwar Gupta rachanabali*, ed. Shantikumar Dasgupta and Haribandhu Mukhoti, vol. 1, (Kolikata: Dattachaudhuri & Sons, 1974 [1381 BS]), 240–241, first published in *Sambad Prabhakar* on 5th January, 1854 [5 Magh, 1261 BS].
[113] Ibid., 277, first published in *Sambad Prabhakar* on 21st April, 1854 [21 Chaitra 1261 BS].
[114] Ibid., 278, first published in *Sambad Prabhakar* on 25th April, 1854 [25 Chaitra 1261 BS].
[115] Ibid.
[116] Prasannamayi Debi (1857–1939), "Purbbakatha," in *Phire dekha-1: A Collection of Late 19th Century Autobiographies* (Kolkata: Subarnarekha, 2011), 61.

was turned on its head by those who claimed that use of chilies in cooking in eastern Bengal actually made their food far superior than the food in central or western parts of Bengal.[117] Sayeeda Hafeza Khatun, a writer of what she called Islamic cooking, stated in her cookbook that the way chicken *korma* (generally consumed by the Muslims) was prepared in Dhaka, Faridpur, Barishal, or Tripura was far more skilful and fine than the cooking pattern found in western parts or even northern parts of Bengal.[118] Although Ishwar Gupta did acknowledge the availability of fresh fish and vegetables in certain parts of east Bengal, he sneered at the culinary habits of Barishal. He writes, 'Cooking and eating is disgusting (in Barishal). They cook everything with fish and mash it up.'[119] However, Gupta did like *hattal mula*, which was cooked with adding radish to *shol* fish and mashing it up. Gupta expressed surprise at the way fish curry was cooked without oil. He was also quite amazed at how the inhabitants of Barishal relished goat and tortoise meat cooked with grated coconut and yogurt mixed with sugar.[120]

Although inhabitants of one particular region were generally critical to the gastronomic and culinary practices of another region, there were exceptions as well. The famous litterateur Bankimchandra Chattopadhyay, who was from west Bengal, was apprehensive about Nabinchandra Sen, the poet, being able to consume meat by the former's wife. Chattopadhyay says, 'I have had food cooked by women of eastern Bengal. Women in this region (west Bengal) cannot cook fish or meat properly.'[121] Jogeshchandra Raybidyanidhi, who himself was from southern *Rarh*, amply praised women of eastern Bengal for their culinary skills and aesthetic presentation of food.

> Women from eastern Bengal know how to cook; women from western Bengal do not even come close to that. One reason for this is the availability of milk, fish and vegetables in east Bengal. This was when Narayan Ganesh Chandravarkar, the famous Brahmo preacher from Bombay came to Calcutta. He wanted to have Bengali food. Umapada took its responsibility. Chandravarkar was a vegetarian. Wife of Mitra (who was from Dhaka) and two or three other women from east Bengal went to the kitchen and prepared

---

[117] Sayeeda Hafeza Khatun, *Moslem pak pranali*, vol. 1 (1926 [1333 BS]; repr., Kolikata, 1930 [Agrhayan 1337 BS]), vii–ix.
[118] Ibid., 177–178.
[119] Gupta, *Iswar Gupta rachanabali*, 278.
[120] Ibid.
[121] Nabinchandra Sen, *Amar jiban*, ed. Sajanikanta Das, vol. 2 (Kolikata: Bangiya Sahitya Parishat, 1955 [1366 BS]), 458.

twenty five to thirty vegetarian dishes. --- If I had not eaten it, I would never know that so many flavors could come out of banana, eggplant, potato, bottle gourd and pumpkin. Eastern Bengal is known for its coconut, that coconut was made into really fine pieces and put into rice pudding.[122]

These distinctions between eastern Bengal and western Bengal have much older roots and the word *bangal* (a derogatory label used by the natives of western parts of Bengal for the inhabitants of eastern Bengal) can be found as early as in a thirteenth century text, *Sadukti karnamrita*.[123] The accounts of Chaitanya, the leader of the Vaishnava faith in Bengal, in which he makes caricatures of the manners of residents of east Bengal of late fifteenth to early sixteenth centuries are also well-known.[124] As more and more people move from the eastern parts to the expanding city of Calcutta from late nineteenth century onward, *bangal* becomes a standard term for ridicule in literature like in Bhabanicharan Bandopadhyay's *Kalikatakamalalaya* (1823) or Dinabandhu Mitra's *Sadhabar ekadashi* written in 1866.[125] However, the exact origins of the word *ghoti* (the term used by the *bangals* for labeling the inhabitants of western Bengal, after a distinctively shaped vessel used in west Bengal) cannot be found until after 1947, the partition of India.[126]

The violence of partition resulting in the displacement of millions of Hindus from east Bengal is central to understanding *bangal/ghoti* politics in post partition Bengal. Forced to settle down often in the squalors of the newly emerging suburbs of Calcutta, the *udvastus* (refugees)[127] on the one hand were torn by the memories of their homeland in the villages of eastern Bengal where they could never return, and on the other had to deal on a day-to-day

---

[122] Jogeshchandra Ray Bidyanidhi, *Atmacharit*, ed. Munindrakumar Ray (Bankura, 2002 [1409BS]), 102.

[123] Cited in Boria Majumdar and Kausik Bandopadhyay, *A Social History of Indian Football: Striving to Score* (Oxon: Routledge, 2006), 94.

[124] Girijasankar Raychaudhiri, *Bangla Charit Granthe Sri Chaitanya* (Calcutta: Kolikata Biswabidyalay, 1949), 89, cited in Dipesh Chakrabarty, "Memories of Displacement: The Poetry and Prejudice of Dwelling," in Dipesh Chakrabarty, *Habitations of Modernity: Essays in the Wake of Subaltern Studies* with a foreword by Homi K. Bhabha (New Delhi: Permanent Black,2002), 127.

[125] For exact reference, see Chakrabarty, "Memories of Displacement," 127.

[126] Gautam Bhadra, "Ghoti Bangal Kulaji Katha,"*Rabibaroari*, Sunday, 9th December, 2012, 76–77.

[127] For a critical analysis of the term *udvastu*, see Chakrabarty, *Habitations of Modernity*, 120–121.

basis with the Hindu settlers of Calcutta who dominated the political, socio-economic, and cultural life in Calcutta. The memories of eastern Bengal that are sketched in the memoirs of *bangals* depict a portrait of an eastern Bengal central to the imagination of a Hindu nationalist, where the notions of the sacred and the beautiful are tied to whatever is Hindu. While the Muslim had a place in it, the image of the home constructed was certainly a Hindu home and with the migration of Hindus from eastern Bengal to western parts after 1947, east Bengal was supposedly a dead land.[128]

The emotions that the *bangals* shared with the *ghotis* were of a different tenor. Dipesh Chakrabarty has astutely observed that these emotions of the former towards the latter can be explained by what he calls 'proximity.' These two, Chakrabarty asserts, lived in proximity to each other.[129] Chakrabarty distinguishes proximity from identity, by which he implies that the mode of relating to the politics of difference is either frozen, or completely erased. Proximity is a mode by which difference is neither reified nor erased, but negotiated. These negotiations were actually played out through the culture industry in post-partition Calcutta as a result of the influx of the refugees from east Bengal. Radio and films played a significant part in these cultural negotiations.[130] But the fields of football and cuisine were the most significant tools through which the *bangals* tried to construct an identity for themselves in Calcutta.

Maidan, the enormous field in Calcutta where many sporting events took place became a cultural space where the opposed identities of the *ghotis* and *bangals* came to be produced through a bitter rivalry between the clubs Mohun Bagan (chiefly constituted of the supporters of west Bengal) and East Bengal (constituted of the supporters of east Bengal).[131] Boria Majumdar and Kausik Bandopadhyay have tried to explain these rivalries as a way of assimilating the migrants into the culture of the settler community and an opportunity for establishing their social identity in the land where they had been forced to migrate.[132] The link between food and club rivalries was distinct. If the East Bengal club won, the price of Hilsa, which came to be a symbol of the identity

---

[128] Chakrabarty, "Memories of Displacement," 133–137.

[129] Dipesh Chakrabarty, "The In-Human and the Ethical in Communal Violence," *Habitations of Modernity: Essays in the Wake of Subaltern Studies* with a foreword by Homi K. Bhabha(New Delhi: Permanent Black, 2002), 140.

[130] Ibid.

[131] Boria Majumdar and Kausik Bandopadhyay, *A Social History of Indian Football*, 93–94.

[132] Ibid.

of the *bangals*, went up; whereas the *ghotis* celebrated with buying prawns and thus pushing up the price of prawns when Mohun Bagan won a match.[133] Although with time this fluid subregional culture of football gave way to much virulent club rivalry,[134] what remained was the pride in the culinary skills of the respective communities.

Till almost the beginning of the twenty-first century (sometimes even now), *bangals* kept complaining about the tendency of the *ghotis* to put too much sweet in their food whereas the *ghotis* detest what they call the overt use of chilies in *bangal* cuisine. The subtle regional differences between Sylhet and Dhaka or Medinipur and Bardhaman are erased here and a loosely defined *bangal* or *ghoti* cuisine takes its place. A conversation between Radhaprasad Gupta, an aficionado of art and cultural life of Calcutta, and Kamalkumar Majumdar the noted litterateur, is a case in point. Both Majumdar and Gupta were shocked to see that the *bangals* settled in west Bengal had the audacity to claim Hilsa caught in Padma to be superior to the Hilsa caught in the Ganges.[135] Ridiculing the *bangal*'s love for Hilsa, Gupta narrates an incident where, he claims, a *bangal* family went to the extent of breaking parts of their windows in absence of wood to cook Hilsa in the middle of the night.[136] In a rather heartless manner, Majumdar scorns the *bangals*' inability to go back to their home stating that the 'bangals might have history, but no geography.'[137]

The *bangals*, of course, always retorted back. In an issue on *bangal/ghoti* in *Rabibaroari*, a Calcutta weekly, Amitabha Malakar, a food columnist constantly ridicules the *ghotis* for their lack of innovation in culinary skills. He says that a *ghoti* can be identified by what is cooking in his/her kitchen— a light broth of katla fish and their tendency to put loads of sugar in lentil, potato fries, as well as mutton curry.[138] Malakar also makes fun of the way a *ghoti* speaks. *Luchi* becomes *nuchi* in a *ghoti* dialect and *lebu* (lime) is pronounced as *nebu*. It is only after the migrants settled down in Calcutta after 1947 that the original settlers of Calcutta have realised what good food means. However, Malakar

---

[133] Chakrabarty, "The In-Human and the Ethical," 139; Moti Nandy, "Football and Nationalism," trans. from Bengali by Shampa Banerjee, in *The Calcutta Psyche* ed, Geeti Sen (New Delhi: India International Centre, 1990–91), 241–254, 249.

[134] Majumdar and Bandopadhyay, *A Social History of Indian Football*, 93–94.

[135] Kumarprasad Mukhopadhyay, "Kichhu khuchro adda,"*Desh*, Year 62, no.5 (Kolkata, 31 December, 1994), 31–40, 40.

[136] Ibid.

[137] Ibid.

[138] Amitabha Malakar, "Ki misti byabahar,"*Rabibaroari*, Sunday 9th December, 2012, 86.

is all praises for the sweets made in west Bengal, which he suggests are much superior to the sweets made in entire Bangladesh.[139]

This championing of regional flavour remained a constant in the fashioning of the middle-class discourse on taste. *Bangal/ghoti* dichotomy, which became a significant part of identity politics in postcolonial Bengal never had the violent tenor of Hindu/Muslim identity politics perceived most virulently in the discourse on beef eating. At the most, Bangal/ghoti distinctions in food remained immured within the bounds of neighbourly gossips or friendly chitchats ridiculing the other for their culinary skills. These regional variations in culinary skills of the 'other' could however be appreciated on rare occasions by the 'self.' What is noteworthy is how a culinary skill unique to only one region could become an integral part of universal aesthetic.

GAHANA BORI OF MEDINIPUR: A CASE OF UNIVERSAL AESTHETIC

Gahana boris are extremely decorative and ornamented sundried cones of lentil paste. The chief ingredient for *gahana bori* is moth bean. Moth bean is primarily used because of its viscosity. Moth bean is soaked in water a night before making the *boris* so that its skin can come off easily the next morning. This soaked bean, when ground, forms a sticky texture, which is required for making *gahana bori*. The batter for *bori* usually has a creamy consistency.[140] It needs to be constantly stirred so that the batter is fluffy and the resultant *bori* is light in weight and looks white. At first, poppy seeds are spread out on a large plate. Then the batter is tied up in a cloth with holes in the bottom. A cone is then tied to this cloth and moved clockwise on the poppy seeds to create motifs.[141] *Gahana bori* is then sun-dried thoroughly. These are made

---

[139] Ibid.
[140] Mira Maiti, *Manomugdhakar Shilpa Naipunye Bhara Gahanabori o Nakshabori Tairir Padhdhati, Rakshanabekshan o Sangrakshan* (Medinipur, n.d.), 1–2; Mananjali Bandopadhyay and Kalyan Chakrabarty, "Grihinir barai gahana bori,"*Sahitya-Parishat-Patrika*, Year 111, nos. 3-4 (2005 [Kartick-Chaitra 1411BS]): 153–169, 157–159.
[141] Maiti, Op cit.; Bandopadhyay & Chakarabarty, Op cit; Nirmalendu Bhowmick, "Medinipurer gaynabori," Lokayat, Year 6 (Medinipur, 2000 [1407 BS]), 3–6,5–6;Kamalkumar Kundu, "Gahanaborir Angane," *Desh*, Year 59, no. 13 (January 25, 1992): 49–54, 53–54; Amiyakumar Bandopadhyay, "Gayna Bori," in Amiyakumar Bandopadhyay, *Dekha Hoy Nai* (1973 [1380 BS]; repr., Kolikata: Ananda Publishers, 1976 [1383 BS]), 217–221, 219–220.

in winter to avoid moist weather, which is not conducive to making *gahana boris*.[142]

The fine motifs of *gahana bori* have led scholars of folk art like Nirmalendu Bhowmick, to assert that the origin of *gahana bori* lies in the *alpana* given in the *vratas*. *Vratas* are often integrally associated with the quotidian life of women, who bring out the essence of that life in these motifs. Drawing ornaments or food is an essential element of *alpana* and it certainly had an impact on *gahana bori* motifs.[143] Mostly, *gahana boris* are designed in the form of paisley, lotus, or ornaments like necklace, tiara, earrings, and bracelets.[144] Abanindranath Tagore, the famous litterateur and artist from the Bengal School of Art took a deep interest in folk art and inspired many to introduce animal motifs like elephant, butterfly, deer, peacock, fish or parrot into the designs for *gahana bori*.[145] This delicate intricacy involved in the making of *gahana bori,* which made it a visual delight for those dealing in the fine arts, also led it from being a specialty of eastern Medinipur to an art to be preserved.

Gahana bori was, and still is, specifically made in eastern Medinipur. Women of *mahishya* caste in Tamluk, Mahishadal, Sutahata, Nandigram, and Mayna are adept in making these sun-dried cones.[146] *Gahana bori*, which was at first specific to just three families, soon acquired wide-spread popularity. Of course, its popularity had much to do with its eye-catching designs as well as crisp taste. However, the way *gahana bori* was praised by Rabindranath Tagore, his nephew Abanindranath Tagore, and Abanindranath's disciple Nandalal Bose, one of the finest artists of Bengal School of Art, speaks much about its transformation into a fine art. This fine art originated in Medinipur but it became a pride of entire Bengal.

Seba Maity of Mahishadal in Medinipur, a student in Shantiniketan in the 1930s, gifted Rabindranath Tagore *gahana bori* made by her mother Hiranmayi Devi and her grandmother Sharatkumari Devi. The fineries and delicate skills that went into the making of *gahana bori* immediately captured Tagore's

---

[142] Maiti, "Manohar Shilpa Naipunye Bhara Gahana Bari,"3–4; Bandopadhyay, "Grihinir barai gahana bori", 220.

[143] Bhowmick, "Medinipurer Gaynabori," 3.

[144] Bandopadhyay & Chakarabarty, Op cit., 156–157; Shankar Mahapatra, "Gahana Bori o Rabindranath,"*Lokayat*, Year 3 (December/January 1997 [Poush 1404 BS]), 21–24,21; Bandopadhyay, op cit, 219.

[145] Mahapatra, "Gahana Bori o Rabindranath," 21.

[146] Kundu, "Gahanbarir angane."

IMAGE 6: A paisely motif of *gahana bori*. (*Photo courtesy*: Shyamal Bera) IMAGE 7: A tiara motif of *gahana bori*. (*Photo courtesy*: Shyamal Bera)

attention, who wrote a letter to Hiranmayi and Sharatkumari, expressing his interest in preserving photographs of *gahana bori* in Kala Bhavan (Fine Arts department in Viswa Bharati University, established by Tagore).[147] An item of food, which was the staple of a particular caste, suddenly was affixed the glorified label of a fine art.

Once *gahana bori* earned this title of being a fine art, it could no longer remain confined to the platter of ordinary men and women of eastern Medinipur. The *bori* was no longer a simple delectable to be devoured. It was a product that yielded aesthetic pleasure. Abanindranath Tagore thus wrote in an undated letter: 'These *'nakashi' boris* from the Lakhsa village of Medinipur are not only a visual delight but also whet one's appetite. However, grinding this bori with one's teeth or cooking it in the form of curry is equivalent to frying and eating a fine piece of art.'[148] Rabindranath Tagore too exclaimed that 'these were to be seen and not for consumption'.[149] He even claimed to find fundamental similarities between the artistic endeavours of *gahana bori* and archaeological finds of Khotan in Central Asia and ensured that *gahana bori* was properly exhibited as a work of art.[150] Both the Tagores' penchant for folk art is widely known. It is thus not surprising that they wanted to preserve

---

[147] Kundu, "Gahanbarir angane,"49–50; Bhaskarbrata Pati, "Gaynaborir nei ko juri," in *Medinipurer lokoshilpa* (Medinipur: Upatyaka, 2009), 9–13, 9; Mahapatra, "Gahana bori o Rabindranath," 23.

[148] Kundu, "Gahana borir angane," 51.

[149] Salilkumar Bandopadhyay, *Rabindranath o loksanskriti* (1983; repr., Kolkata: Dey's Publishing, 1994), 237; Mahapatra, "Gahana bori o Rabindranath," 24.

[150] Ibid.

what they perceived as a fine sample of folk art, as a part of the tradition of Bengal. Nandalal Bose wanted to bring out a book on *gahana bori* since he was amazed to see what he considered 'a jewel found in the broken box of mother Bengal'.[151] In February 1954, thirty *gahana boris* of thirty-two diameters were displayed at the 59th 'Kalyani Convention' of the Indian National Congress.[152]

On the one hand, we do see this appreciation of *gahanabori* as part of a larger history of Bengal although the presence of *gahanabori* before late nineteenth century is not warranted by any historical evidence. On the other hand, *gahana bori* is still celebrated as the part and parcel of everyday life of a very specific region of Bengal. At that level, the making of *gahana bori* is as much about the nitty-gritty of domesticity as it is about a sense of pride in this local art of Medinipur. To describe this phenomenon of ornamented *bori* as a form of subregional consciousness would be an overstatement. However, there is no doubt that alongside the claim of a universal aesthetic, local appreciations and regional pride never ceased to be associated with *gahana bori*.

---

[151] Kundu, "Gahana borir angane," 51; Bandopadhyay, "Gayna-bori," 221.
[152] Pati, *Medinipurer lokshilpa*, 11.

Conclusion

> Bengali food, long confined to grandmother's kitchen, is breaking out of the home-food mould in cities across India. New Bengali restaurants are opening their doors to patrons in all the metros, be it Delhi, Mumbai or Bangalore. Even Calcutta, which has long been firmly in the grip of Chinese and Continental fare, is taking to it like never before. No less than four new Bengali restaurants have opened in Calcutta in the last year and some are expanding to the other metros.[1]

The passage above, which appeared in the Calcutta daily *Telegraph*, indicates how Bengali cuisine is increasingly spreading its wings from the domestic kitchen to the tables laid in the newly emerging restaurants. The general view is that as the nuclear families increase in number and women cease to be homemakers, so-called traditional and intricate Bengali culinary delights are no longer cooked and consumed within one's home. Here, the new restaurants step in and claim to provide one with the pleasures of authentic home-cooked Bengali cuisine.

This new trend of accessing and enjoying what earlier would be considered a home-cooked meal in a public place might at first appear to revert one of the major arguments of this book– that for the colonial Bengali middle-class the superiority of Bengali cuisine existed in its domesticity. However, a closer scrutiny of this trend reveals that even these newfangled Bengali restaurants in no way attempt to overturn the domesticity of Bengali cuisine. These places act more like a quasi-home reflecting a familial environment rather than

---

[1] Shrabonti Bagchi, "Bengal on the menu," *The Telegraph*, 8th October, 2005, Calcutta edition.

the exotic.[2] Strong claims regarding the authenticity of the food they serve define these restaurants. Even now, there is hardly an attempt made by these restaurants to present Bengali cuisine as pan-Indian cuisine. The essence of Bengali cuisine still seems to lie in its being 'Bengali'. However, sometimes basic elements of cooking Bengali food are reversed or rendered more complex by adding other ingredients that still retain the flavour of cosmopolitanism in this cuisine.

This openness to new taste coexisting with a desire to create a sense of belonging through food is often considered to be a contemporary phenomenon. Tension between creating such memory through food and the attempts to escape its confinements are inevitably seen in the lives of immigrants.[3] However, as suggested in this book, such tensions are atypical to the self-fashioning of any middle-class and not just the immigrants. In fact, one of the chief arguments of this book, has been the suggestion that the roots of this regionalism juxtaposed with some kind of cosmopolitanism go back to a much longer period. While the desire to let in a waft of new pleasures prodded some of the colonial middle-class, it also irked many amongst them. A sense of region, at least in the gastronomic culture, continued from early modern times.

The final part of the book will try to bring together some of the major arguments and implications of this study for a better understanding of the self-fashioning of the middle-class through a discourse of taste. The concluding section presents a brief epilogue of the role of political economy in the middle-class discourse of taste.

IMPLICATIONS OF THE STUDY

This book has examined the connection between taste and class formation in colonial Bengal. Specifically, it has explored the realm of culinary taste and a culture that was growing around food among the middle-class, especially in urban Bengal, from the latter half of nineteenth century. My understanding of cuisine is drawn from Sidney Mintz, who argues that cuisine helps us analyse an entire community and is not just an allusion to culinary culture. In addition, the argument here asserts that cuisine needs to be analysed in its entirety. This

---

[2] For a detailed discussion of how contemporary Bengali restaurants try to uphold a lost world of traditional Bengali cuisine, see Manpreet K. Janeja, *Transactions in Taste: The Collaborative Lives of Everyday Bengali Food* (New Delhi: Routledge, 2010).

[3] Krishnendu Ray, *The Migrant's Table: Meals and Memories in Bengali-American Households* (Philadelphia: Temple University Press, 2004).

book has thus critically examined the new experimentations in production of rice, especially the colonial experiments with Carolina rice in colonial Bengal in the 1860s, with the deliberate intention of making a connection between these experiments and the changes in the material culture of the Bengali middle-class. There was a sea change in the material culture of the colonial Bengali middle-class from mid-nineteenth century onwards, which defined their habitus. Development of new restaurants enabled the middle-class to experience 'new' food in a new environ while increase in the production of cookbooks fuelled by print medium ensured that 'exotic' cuisine also became possible at home. This book has suggested that the claim for a refined Bengali cuisine needs to be contextualized within this material culture of colonial Bengal because a discourse on 'Bengali' cuisine sprouted from within this material culture.

This book has first and foremost argued that despite its constricted approach to many issues, the colonial Bengali middle-class can be labeled as cosmopolitan. There was certainly a desire on the part of the middle-class to embrace many of the new changes that were seeping into the colonial society. Their approach to the changes in gastronomic culture and the new pleasure emanating from 'new' food demonstrates the liberal traits inherent in the self-fashioning of the colonial middle-class. A constant process of experimentations with new crops and incorporation of new ingredients is perceptible in the colonial middle-class' culture of food. In contemporary world, experience shows that contrary to what has been described as a complete 'McDonaldisation' or what is loosely defined as 'glocalisation,' there is always an attempt to make the 'foreign' or the 'new' familiar through creative responses.[4] While these experiments with globalisation are often perceived as contemporary phenomenon, such creativity was not altogether absent in colonial societies. In fact, capitalist modernity made available a situationthat provided the colonial society umpteen choices to rediscover itself. The colony thus came up with creative and imaginative responses that would also eventually have tremendous impact on the metropole. Ultimately, the end product was a hybrid cuisine, which however, was cast

---

[4] James L. Watson, "China's Big Mac Attack," in *The Cultural Politics of Food and Eating: A Reader*, ed. James L. Watson & Melissa L. Caldwell (Malden, MA: Blackwell Publishing, 2005), 70–79; Yunxiang Yan, "Of Hamburger and Social Space: Consuming Mcdonald's in Beijing," in *The Cultural Politics*, ed. Watson & Caldwell, 80–103; Eriberto P. Lozada, Jr., "Globalized Childhood? Kentucky Fried Chicken in Beijing," in *The Cultural Politics*, ed. Watson & Caldwell, 163–179; Melissa L. Caldwell, "Domesticating the French Fry: McDonald's and Consumerism in Moscow," in *The Cultural Politics of Food*, ed. Watson & Caldwell, 180–196.

in an idiom of authenticity and a specifically modern understanding of the 'traditional.' The contestation of hybridity and authenticity is not surprising, given the contradictions inherent in modernity itself. The cuisine produced from it reflected the pleasures as well as the pains that the colonial middle-class experienced under colonial modernity as well as the hegemonic discourse they formulated around it. Thus the cosmopolitanism of the middle-class was complex. While Bengali cuisine, as it developed from late nineteenth century, certainly had its public face, it was far from being a *haute* cuisine. Rather, new gastronomic pleasures were appropriated within the folds of domestic cuisine.

Drawing from the first suggestion of the cosmopolitan traits of colonial middle-class taste, this study has also made the observation that this cosmopolitamism can at best be called a 'hierarchical cosmopolitanism.' The middle-class discourse of taste of course celebrated the universalism of its cosmopolitanism. But this claim was a fantastic claim and like all cosmopolitanisms, this universalism that the colonial middle-class claimed for its discourse of taste was incomplete and marred by several particularisms. As the chapters in this book show, the cosmopolitanism of the colonial middle-class was marked by hierarchy.[5] The self-fashioning of the colonial middle-class was made possible through the construction of various 'other' of the middle-class. Thus, the discourse of taste and the project of self-fashioning of the middle-class entailed constant negotiations with categories like class, caste, community, and gender. Such hierarchy in taste is inevitable and within a developing social formation, modes of individual behavior, cultural tastes, intellectual ideas, social stratification, political power, and economic organisations become closely related to each other in complex ways that change over time. The use of a monolithic structure to emphasise the homogeneity of the groups the structuralists[6] study have long been critiqued by Norbert Elias

---

[5] It has long been argued by Arjun Appadurai that food can create social relations characterised by equality, but it can also create segmentations by augmenting conflicts over food transaction. See Arjun Appadurai, "Gastro-Politics in Hindu South Asia," *American Ethnologist*, vol. 8, no. 3, Symbolism and Cognition (Aug., 1981), 494–511.

[6] The major influence in structuralist thought was that of Claude Levi-Strauss, for whom cooking constitutes a crucial cultural code. See, Claude Levi-Strauss, *The Raw and the Cooked: Introduction to a Science of Mythology* 1 (London: Jonathan Cape, 1970). While Mary Douglas disagreed with Levi-Strauss's notion of a universal gustatory code, she still treated food categories as an essentially static code containing meaning. See, Mary Douglas, "Deciphering a Meal," in *Food and Culture: A Reader*, ed. Carole Counihan and Penny Van Esterik (1972; repr. New York: Routledge, 1997), 36–54.

and following him Stephen Mennel, who suggest that such uniformities are exaggerated and it is necessary to look at the evolving conflicts and competitions among social groups to understand the development of taste and cuisine.[7]

This book has suggested that the way the colonial middle-class drew boundaries between them and the other classes, including lower castes or other communities, was tied to their endeavours to create a refined taste. This discourse of a refined taste, which defined the 'habitus' of the colonial middle-class, has also been an integral part of the 'civilizing process' that aided the self-fashioning of the bourgeoisie in the West.[8] These civilizing tendencies have also been noted by the Bengali literati like Bankimchandra Chattopadhyay and Bhudeb Mukhopadhyay at the turn of the nineteenth century. It has recently been argued by Bhaskar Mukhopadhyay, that the Bengali literati, much like their European counterparts, were trying to discipline taste and bring in restraint and moderation in gastronomic culture in order to discipline the incipient nation.[9] Such disciplining of palate involved abandonment of subaltern food like the sour tamarind and the hot and spicy chili.[10] While it is partly true that the colonial middle-class did urge for refinement of taste, this disciplining was often subverted. As discussions provided in this book shows, many actually relished spicy food. In fact, such subversions crawled through the veins and arteries of this discourse of refined taste. We have seen how the gendered experience of the colonial middle-class entailed an aestheticisation of women's cooking to differentiate it from the labour of the hired cooks. But women actually added another angle to such aestheticisations. Their cooking did not remain confined to the domestic realm as was expected of them. Many

---

[7] Norbert Elias, *The Civilizing Process: Sociogenetic and Psychogenetic Investigations*, rev. ed. (Oxford: Blackwell, 2000); Stephen Mennell, *All Manners of Food: Eating and Taste in England and France from the Middle Ages to the Present* (Oxford, UK, New York, USA: Basil Blackwell, 1985). In the context of South Asia, such competitions and gastronomic practices have been commented on most vividly by Arjun Appadurai. Appadurai has argued that these conflicting encounters decide the relationship between self and other, high and low and inside and outside. See, Arjun Appadurai, "Gastro-Politics in Hindu South Asia," *American Ethnologist*, vol. 8, no. 3, Symbolism and Cognition (Aug., 1981), 494–511.

[8] Elias, *The Civilizing Process*.

[9] Bhaskar Mukhopadhyay, "Between Elite Hysteria and Subaltern Carnivalesque: Street-Food and Globalization in Calcutta," in Bhaskar Mukhopadhyay, *The Rumor of Globalization: Desecrating the Global from Vernacular Margins* (London: Hurst & Company, 2012), 87–104.

[10] Ibid.

middle-class women easily straddled the private and the public through the medium of print and taking a serious interest in writing about cooking. The middle-class Hindu overtone of the gastronomic culture was regularly mocked by their Muslim counter parts and the obsession with aesthetic presentation of food received sharp jolts when the poor cutting across caste and communities had to rummage for crumbs from the streets during famines.

An image of an ideal Bengali prototype cuisine that was central to the middle-class discourse of taste and ultimately to the self-fashioning of the colonial Bengali middle-class was thus always marred by these tensions arising from categories like class, caste, gender, and community. As this study has conclusively shown, there was no one Bengali middle-class. All we get is an image of a fractured consciousness and a desire to claim something as unique to Bengal. However, the discourse of taste was multilayered with different categories pulling the notion of a 'Bengali' self to several concerns. Even the concept of Bengal as a region, which apparently seems so significant to the self-fashioning of the colonial middle-class in Bengal, was left considerably ambiguous since many of the middle-class often took pleasures in reminiscing about or championing cuisine of specific subregions within Bengal. Of course, this is not to suggest that this subregional consciousness marked a sharp departure from a regional consciousness; that the former existed is a proof enough that self-fashioning of the 'Bengali' middle-class was left incomplete.

In her recent work on the Bengali middle-class in contemporary West Bengal and Bangladesh, Manpreet Janeja has projected the view expounded by this study, that the colonial middle-class in Bengal was formed through its constant and various negotiations with different categories.[11] Despite several egregious errors in her book,[12] Janeja is right in suggesting that everyday food practices tend to create normality for the Bengali middle-class, which often gets shaken by various boundaries. Janeja asserts that for the middle-class Bengalis in contemporary West Bengal and Bangladesh, normal Bengali food signifies fluid and contested networks of identities like east/west Bengalis, Hindu/Muslim, and middle-class/poor.[13] Despite her attempts to understand how food tends to create normality through demarcating boundaries, Janeja fails to problematise the notions of Bengaliness fully. Her explanations of

---

[11] Manpreet Janeja, Transactions in Taste: The collaborative Lives of Everyday Bengali Food (Routlage India, 2009)

[12] Janeja seems confused about the meanings of even simple everyday food like *begun basanti*.

[13] Janeja, *Transaction in Taste*.

how everyday food practices create 'Bengaliness' for the Bengali middle-class never ascertains that 'Bengali' as a project is fractured, incomplete, and subject to contestations. Because of her total lack of comprehension about what constituted the emergence of this Bengali middle-class, she leaves us wondering with the image of a middle-class that is ahistorical. Her vague references to colonialism and partition of Bengal do not explain the particular situatedness of the contemporary Bengali middle-class. The multilayered discourse of taste that aided the self-fashioning of the colonial middle-class, this study has shown, was a combination of cosmopolitanism as well as regionalism. The contradictoriness of this discourse is what makes this middle-class a fascinating object of study. This middle-class was as comfortable gorging on chicken cutlets as it was critiquing new food and ways through a cultural discourse of refined and restrained taste and creating its 'other' through a visceral gastro-politics. This middle-class could also become virulent and critique food policies of the colonial state through a well-formulated political economy.

EPILOGUE

Political Economy of Gastronomic Culture

We have seen in this book how in the middle-class discourse of taste a rhetoric of political economy was often intertwined with another narrative of cultural imagination. It was required by capitalist modernity to imagine a precolonial past in order to make a critique of the colonial economy. At the same time, the middle-class also found a way to indigenise new realities of the colonial capital and the new enchantments that came along with modernity. But as mainstream nationalism reached its peak and the nation was just a few years away from achieving independence, one could see a perceptible change even in the critique of the middle-class. The harshness of colonial economic policies, the rise in prices, the famine of 1943–44, all made the middle-class aware of the futility of a solely cultural critique. They were no longer merely satisfied with imagining a past of abundance.

While the colonial administration desperately struggled to keep its policies under control, occasional voices of dissent brought them out in the open. One such voice of dissent came from Syed Mohammad Afzal, a member of the Paddy and Rice Enquiry Committee, and Amulya Dhan Addy. Both of them were extremely sympathetic to the cause of the cultivator. Mohammad Afzal chastised the colonial state for importing the Burma rice into Bengal. This import of the Burma rice into Bengal made the supply of rice greater than the demand of the province, which resulted in an inevitable fall in the price of rice.[14] Afzal argued for a duty of import on paddy from Burma, which would consequently raise the price of the paddy produced by cultivators in Bengal and improve their economic condition. Afzal was definitely arguing for a focus more on the production of rice and less on the cultivation of jute. However, Afzal here was not romanticising any perceived notion of a tradition of abundance. He instead tried to find economic solutions for the cultivators and made a critique of the capitalist modernity that had impoverished the peasants of Bengal.

Like Afzal, Amulya Dhan Addy, another government official, also criticised the government for its decision to fix a minimum price for rice and paddy. He argued that fixing a price for rice would have serious pitfalls for the export of rice from India to foreign countries. Addy endorsed Afzal's view that the price of rice cultivated by peasants should be increased. He further maintained that although an increase in the price of rice would adversely affect the middle-class Bengali population, it would benefit the majority of the population that survived on agricultural production.[15]

Addy's and Afzal's points were soon being endorsed by several people who lashed out at the government for being insensitive to the economic conditions of the ordinary cultivators. They were not merely satisfied with a cultural self-fashioning. They were in fact keeping their fingers on the pulse of the colonial state in order to find out the root cause of the scarcity of food. The Bengal famine of 1943 brought out the organic reality of the colonial state. Hemendra Prasad Ghose, who was the editor of the newspaper *Dainik Basumati*, identifies three reasons behind the famine. He argues that there was a gross failure on the part of the colonial administration in bringing about positive changes in agriculture.[16] First of all, the British colonial state totally neglected irrigation. Second, no steps were taken to restore the fertility of the soil, and third, serious encroachments were made by the colonial state on the land in which rice used to be grown.[17] Apart from this, Ghose pointed out

---

[14] Minute of Dissent by Khan Sahib Syed Mohammed Afzal. M.L.A. & member, Paddy & Rice Committee of the Government of Bengal, *Paddy & Rice Enquiry Report* (Bengal, 1940), 101–102.

[15] Replies from Mr. Amulya Dhan Addy to questionnaire on paddy, *Paddy & Rice Enquiry Report*, vol II (Bengal, 1940), 149–157.

[16] Hemendra Prasad Ghose, "The Bengal Famine," *Calcutta Review* 93 (Calcutta, November 1944), 42–47.

[17] Ibid.

that the Secretary of State submitted unreliable reports on the famine to the House of Commons in Britain.[18]

These authors made clear that the British government could no longer boast of a rational mode of agriculture. Its visions of progress and modernity, if they ever existed at all, were merely empty words. The colonial state had finally lost its moral authority to rule. It was no longer the flag-bearer of 'civilisation,' but represented the ugly face of capitalism. Although even in earlier periods, people had made indirect critiques of colonial policies, now they made a much stronger critique of colonial political economy. While new food crops were already internalised into the diet of the Bengali middle-class, this class also came to realise that the seduction of 'modernity' did not necessarily benefit the cultivators.

---

[18] Ibid.

Select Bibliography

GOVERNMENT DOCUMENTS

(A) Archival Materials

India Office Library (London)

Bengal Revenue Proceedings, Miscellaneous (Calcutta, 1884).
Report on the Progress of the Recommendation of the Food Grains Policy Committee (Delhi, 1944).
Council of State Debates, vol. II, no. 1 (Delhi, 1944).

West Bengal State Archives (Calcutta)

Agricultural & Industries Department Proceedings, Branch Agriculture, Local Self-Government, File: P.A. 13-28 (Calcutta, 1930).
Financial Department Proceedings, Branch II, Agriculture, File 6-14, (3540) (Calcutta, 1874); (63), (146), File 17-1-2, File 6-12 (162, 132, 249) (Calcutta, 1875).
General Department Proceedings, General Branch, (1602c) (Calcutta, 1869); (1109) (Calcutta, 1874).
General Department Proceedings, Scarcity & Relief, File 15-1, 15-2, 15-4/5 (Calcutta, 1873); File 13-708-711, File 14-5(4031) (Calcutta, 1874).
Judicial Department Proceedings (328) (Calcutta, 1863).
Municipal Department Proceedings, Municipal Branch, (91, 99, 4681) (Calcutta, 1890); File 477-78B (Calcutta, 1902), (96) (Burdwan, 1907), File M/3-M/6 (Calcutta, 1908).
Revenue Department Proceedings, Land Revenue Branch, (1, 23) (Calcutta, 1870).

(B) Published Materials

A Report on the Indian Industrial and Agricultural Exhibition. Calcutta, 1906–07.
First Annual Report of the Director of the Agricultural Department of Bengal. Calcutta, 1886.

Report of the Bengal Paddy & Rice Enquiry Committee, vols. 1 & 2. Bengal, 1940.
Report of the Municipal Administration of Calcutta, vol. 1, 1918–19.Calcutta, 1919.
Report of the Municipal Administration of Calcutta, vol. 1, 1919–20. Calcutta, 1920.
Report on the Condition of the Lower Classes of Population in Bengal. Calcutta, 1888.

Primary Sources (Bangla and Urdu)

Ahmad, Abul Mansur. "Amar dekha rajnitir panchash bachhar." In vol. 3 of *Abul Mansur Ahmad Rachanabali*, edited by Rafikul Islam, ... Dhaka: Bangla Academy, 2001. First published in 1968.

———, *Atmakatha* (Dhaka, 1978). In vol. 3 of *Abul Mansur Ahmad Rachanabali*, edited by Rafikul Islam, Dhaka: Bangla Academy, 2001.

Ahmad, Ibne Majuddin. *Amar sangsar-jiban.* Kolikata: 1914 [1321 BS].

Al-Koreshi Al-Hindi, Fakir Abdullah-bin-Ismail. "Agnikukkut." In vol. 1 of *Mashshadi rachanabali.* edited by Abdul Qadir. Dhaka: Kendriya Bangla Unnayan Board, 1970, 235–302.

Anon. "Ami to hobo na bibi e pran thakite." In *Abakashranjan*, edited by Suryakumar Ghosh. Kolikata, 1878, 118–120.

Anon. "Bangamahilader swadeshi priyoya." *Mahila* 12, no. 12 (May 1907 [Jaisthya 1314 BS]): 280–282.

Anon. "Banganaridiger abastha." *Mahila* 12, no. 4 (November 1906): 88–93.

Anon. "Banglar aharjya samasya." *Grihasthamangal* 3rd year, no. 6 (September/October 1930 [Aswin 1336 BS]).

Anon. *Bharater godhan raksha.* (Tahirpur, 1887 [1294 BS]).

Anon. "Bhat o ruti." *Swasthya* 3, no. 7 (October/November 1899 [Kartik 1306 BS]): 195–196.

Anon."Byanjan-ratnakar."In *Pakrajeswar o Byanjan-ratnakar,* edited by Sripantha. Kolkata: 2004, 1–86.

Anon. "Grihasree sampadan." *Bamabodhini* (September/October 1883 [Aswin, 1290 BS]). Republished in *Nari o paribar: Bamabodhini Patrika(1270–1329 Bangabda). Compiled and edited by Bharati Ray,* 89–93.

Anon. *Hindusthaner khetra.* Sreerampore: 1822.

Anon. "Mangsha randhan o bhakshan." *Mahila*3, no. 5 (December 1897): 100–110.

Anon. "Ramanir kartabya." *Bamabodhini* (January/February 1886 [Magh1293BS]). Republished in *Nari o paribar: Bamabodhini Patrika (1270–1329 Bangabda).* Compiled and edited by Bharati Ray, 112–115.

Anon."Ramanir kartabya." *Bamabodhini* (February/March c. 1886 [Phalgun 1293BS]. Republished in *Nari o Paribar:Bamabodhini Patrika (1270–1329 Bangabda).* Compiled and edited by Bharati Ray, 115–116.

Anon. "Ramanir kartabya," *Bamabodhini* (March/April 1886 [Chaitra 1293BS]). Republished in *Nari o Paribar: Bamabodhini Patrika (1270–1329 Bangabda)*. Compiled and edited by Bharati Ray, 117–119.
Anon. "Swasthya raksha," *Bangamahila* 2, no. 3 (June/July 1876 [Asharh 1283 BS]): 62–63.
Bandopadhyay, Amiyakumar. "Gayna bori." In *Dekha hoy nai*, 217–221. Kolikata: Ananda Publishers Ltd., 1976 [1383 BS].
Bandopadhyay, Bibhutibhushan. "Adarsha Hindu Hotel." In *Upanyas Samagra*, vol. 1. Kolkata: Mitra o Ghosh, 2005, 292–408.
———. "Ashani sanket." In *Upanyas Samagra*, vol. 1. Kolkata: Mitra o Ghosh, 2005, 861–938.
Bandopadhyay, Mananjali, and Kalyan Chakrabarty. "Grihinir barai gahana bori." *Sahitya-Parishat-Patrika*, Year 111, nos. 3–4 (2005 [Kartick-Chaitra 1411BS]): 153–169.
Bandopadhyay, Panchkari. *Panchkari Bandopadhyayer rachanabali*, vol.2. Edited by Brajendranath Bandopadhyay and Sajaniknata Das, Kolikata: Bangiya Sahitya Parishat, 1951 [1358 BS].
Bandopadhyay, Panchkari. "Sekal aar ekal." *Prabahini* (June 1925 [27 *Asharh*, 1322 BS]).Republished in *Panchkari Bandopadhyayer rachanabali*, vol. 2. Edited by Brajendranath Bandopadhyay and Sajanikanta Das, Kolikata: Bangiya Sahitya Parishat, 1951 [1358 BS]. 307–317.
Bandopadhyay, Radhikanath. *Durbhikkha o daridrata. karon anusandhan ebong nibaranerupay*. Kolkata, 1896/97.
Bandopadhyay, Salilkumar. *Rabindranath o loksanskriti*. Kolkata: Dey's Publishing, 1994.
Barari, Hariananda. *Amar Bikrampur*. Translated by Nandita Mukhopadhyay. Kolkata: Ananda Publishers, 2006.
Basak, Baishnabcharan. *Soukhin pak-pranali* (Kolikata, 1916).
Bhowmick, Nirmalendu. "Medinipurer gaynabori." *Lokayat*, Year 6 (2000 [1407 BS]): 3–6.
Bijaygupta. *Manasamangal*. Edited by Achintya Biswas. Kolkata: Anjali Publishers, 2009.
———. "Padmapuran." In *Kabi Bijaygupter padmapuran*. Edited by Jayantakumar Dasgupta, Kolikata: Kolikata Biswabidyalay, 2009.
Biswas, Aswinikumar. *Ahare arogya*. Kolkata, 1935 [1341 BS].
———. *Rogarogyakar*. Kolkata, 1935 [1341 BS].
Bose, Amritalal. *Amritalal Bosur atmasmriti*. Edited by Arunkumar Mitra. Kolkata: Sahityalok, 1987.
———. "Puratan panjika." In *Amritalal Basur smriti o atmasmriti*. Edited by Dr Arunkumar Mitra. Kolkata: Sahityalok, 1982. First published in *Mashik Basumati* between 1923–1924 [1330–31 BS].

Bose, Buddhadeb. *Bhojan shilpi Bangali*. Kolkata: Bikalapa Prakashani, 2004.
Bose, Chandranath. *Garhyasthapath*. 2nd edition. Kolikata, 1887 [1294BS].
Bose, Chunilal. *Khadya*. Kolikata, 1924.
Bose, Mankumari. "Adarsha Bangaramani: Banga mahilar patra." *Bamabodhini* (October/November 1888 [Kartik 1295 BS]). Republished in *Nari o Paribar: Bamabodhini Patrika (1270–1329 Bangabda). Compiled and edited by Bharati Ray, 121–124*. Kolkata: Ananda Publishers, 2002.
Bose, Narasingha. "Dharmamangal." In *Narasingha Basur Dharmamangal*. Edited by Sukumar Maiti. Bidyasagarpur: Bijan-Panchanan Sangrahashala o Gabeshana Kendra, 2001.
Bose, Nirmalkumar. *Biallisher Bangla: Chattagram bibhag o parbatya Tripura* (Chattagram Division and Hill Tippera).
———. *Biallisher Bangla: Dhaka bibhag* (Dhaka Division). Kolikata: Saraswat Library, 1969 [1376 BS].
———, *Biallisher Bangla: Rajshahi bibhag [division] and Kuchbihar rajya* [district]. (Kolikata: Saraswat Library, 1969 [1376 BS]).
Bose, Nripendrakumar. *Pakshalar panchali*. With an introduction by Sudakshina Debi. Kolikata: Nath Brothers, 1977 [1384 BS].
Bose, Priyanath. *Grihadharma*. Kolikata, 1936.
Bose, Rajnarayan. *Se kal aar Ekal*. Edited by Brajendranath Bandopadhyay and Sajanikanta Das. Kolkata: Bangiya Sahitya Parishat, 1951 [1358 BS], first published in 1874.
Butler, Hasan. *Pak pranali siksha*. n.d.
Chakrabarty, Ghanaram Kabiratna. *Dharmamangal*. Kolikata 1883 [1290 BS].
Chakrabarty, Kabikankan Mukundaram. *Chandimangal*. Edited with an introduction by Panchanan Mandal. Kolkata: Bharbi, 1992. .
Chakrabarty, Nilmani. *Atmajibansmriti*. Kolikata: Sadharan Brahmosamaj, 1975 [1382 BS].
Chakrabarty, Shibram. "Pakpranalir bipak." In *Shibram Rachana Samagra*, 208–212. complete edition, vol. 2. Kolikata: Annapurna Prakashani, 1991 [1398 BS].
Chanda, Rani. *Amar ma'r baper bari*. Kolikata: Viswabharati, 1977 reprint 1986.
Chattopadhyay, Bankimchandra. "Prachina o nabina." In Bibidha Prabandha, 2nd part, *Bankim rachanabali*, 249–254. 2nd vol. Kolikata: Sahitya Samsad, 1973 [1380 BS].
Chattopadhyay, Basantakumar. *Jyotirindranather jibansmriti*. Kolkata: Pragyabharati, 1919.
Chattopadhyay, Benodebihari. "Bangalir durbbalatar karon ki." *Binapani*1, no. 7 (May/June 1894 [Jaisthya 1301]): 147–153.
Chattopadhyay, Jogendrakumar. "Amader khadya o swasthya." In *Smritite sekal.*, Edited by Prabir Mukhopadhyay, 237–245. Kolkata: Charchapad, 2009.
———."Sekaler bhoj." In *Smritite sekal*. Edited by Prabir Mukhopadhyay, 99–109. Kolkata: Charchapad, 2009. First published in *Bangasri* (May 1934 [Jaistha 1341 BS]).

———."Sekaler bibaha." In *Smritite sekal*. Edited by Prabir Mukhopadhyay, 142–153. Kolkata: Charchapad, 2009.

Chattopadhyay. Jogendrakumar . "Smritie sekal: Amader lok amader katha." In *Aitihasik*, vols 7 and 8. Compiled and edited by Prabir Kumar Mukhopadhyay. Calcutta, 1998 & 1999.

———. *Smritite Sekal*. Edited by Prabir Mukhopadhyay. Kolkata: Charchapad, 2009.

Chattopadhyay, Ratanmani. "Anna-samasya o Bangalir nischestata." *Mashik Basumati* 2, no.5 (February/March 1922 [Phalgun 1329 BS]): 550–559.

Chattopadhyay, Sunitikumar. "Amader samajik pragati." In *Bharat-Sanskriti*, 204–209. Kolikata: Mitra o Ghosh, 1963 [1370 BS].

Chaturvedi, Banarasidas. "Bordada Srijukta Dwijendranath Thakur."*Biswabharati Patrika* Nabaparjay 8 (July/August 2003 [Sraban 1410 BS]): 66-72. First published *Bharatiya Gyanpith* (Kashi, 1988).

Chaudhurani, Sarala Devi. *Jibaner jharapata*. Kolkata: Rupa, 1975.

Chaudhurani, Saratkumari. "Meye joggi." *Bharati* (August 1908 [Bhadra 1315 BS]). Reprinted in *Saratkumari Chaudhuranir rachanabali*. Edited by Brajeswar Bandopadhyay and Sajanikanta Das.Kolkata, 1950 [1357 BS], 210–214.

Chaudhurani, Saratkumari. "Meye joggir bishreenkhala." *Bharati* (December 1909 [Poush 1316 BS]). Reprinted in *Saratkumari Chaudhuranir rachanabali*. Edited by Brajeswar Bandopadhyay and Sajanikanta Das. Kolkata: Bangiya Sahitya Parishat 1950 [1357 BS].215–222.

Chaudhuri, Basantakumar . "Baje kharach." *Grihasthamangal* Year 5, nos. 2&3 (May/June-June/July 1931 [Jaisthya/Asharh 1338 BS]): 30–35.

Chaudhuri, Brajendra Narayan. *Smriti o pratiti*. Kolikata: Oriental Book Company, 1982.

Chaudhuri, Hemantakumari, ed., *Antahpur 4*, no.1 (January 1901).

Dasgupta, Nagendrachandra. "Bangalir swasthahani o tahar karon." *Mashik Basumati* year 3, vol. 1 (1924 April/May-September/October [1331 BS Baisakh-Aswin]): 550–555.

Chaudhuri, Nibaranchandra. *Khadya tattva: A Treatise on Food*. Kolkata: The Indian Gardening Association, 1913

Chaudhuri, Nirad Chandra.*Amar debottar sampatti*.Kolkata: Ananda Publishers Ltd., 1994.

———. *Atmaghati Bangali: Aji hote shatabarsha age*. Vol.1.Kolkata: Mitra o Ghosh Publishers Ltd., 1991 [1399 BS]. Das, Sarachchandra. "Dine dakati." (Kolkata, 1913 [1338 BS]). Reprinted in *Goenda aar goenda. Edited by Ranjit Chattopadhyay and Siddharth Ghosh*. Kolkata: Ananda Publishers, 1992 [1399 BS], 60–74

Das, Snehalata. *Randhan-siksha*, vol. 3, 3rd ed. Kolikata, 1948.

———. "Sulabh khadya." *Bangalakshmi*, year 6, no. 4 (February/March 1931 [Phalgun 1337 BS]): 326–329.

Dasgupta, Satishchandra. *Chauler katha*. With an introduction by P.C. Ray. Calcutta, 1936.

———. *Sankat tran-samiti.* Kolkata, 1931.

Datta, Nikunjabehari. "Banglay matsyabhab." *Mashik Basumati Sahitya Mandir,* year 3, vol. 1 (April/May– June/July 1925 [Baisakh-Asharh 1331BS]): 660–666.

Datta, Jatindramohan ."Karaier daler geet." In *Jamdatter Diary o anyanya.* Compiled and edited by Krishanu Bhattacharya. Kolkata: Rita Prakashani, 2006, 91–93.

———. "Sandesher katha." In *Jamdatter Diary o anyanya rachana.* Compiled and edited by Krishanu Bhattacharya. Kolkata: Rita Prakashani, 2006.105–108.

Datta, Mahendranath. *Kolikatar puratan kahini o pratha.* Kolkata: Mahendra Publishing Committee, 1973.

———. *Londone Swami Vivekananda.* Vols. 2 & 3. Kolikata: Mahendra Publishing Committee, 1978.

———. *Shree Shree Ramakrishner anudhyan.*Edited by Dhirendranath Basu. Kolikata: 1979 [1386 BS].

De, Sushilkumar, ed., *Bangla prabad chhora o chalti katha.* Kolikata: A Mukherjee & Co., 1952 [1359 BS].

Deb, Narayan. *Padmapuran.* Edited by Tamonash Chandra Dasgupta. Kolikata: Kolikata Biswabidyalay, 1947.

Debi, Giribala. *Raybari.* Kolkata, 1974.

———. "Raybari." *Giribala Debir rachanabali.* Kolkata: Ramayani Prakash Bhavan, 1977 [1384 BS], 17–230.

Debi, Hemantabala. *Hemantabala Debir rachana-sankalan.* Edited by Jasodhara Bagchi, and Abhijit Sen. Kolkata: Dey's Publishing, 1992.

Debi, Jyotirmayi. *Jyotirmayi Devir rachana-sankalan.* Edited by Gourkishor Ghosh. Kolikata, Dey's Publishing, 1994.

Debi, Prajnasundari. *Amish o niramish ahar.* Vols 1 & 2. Kolkata: Ananda Publishers, 2000.First published in 1907.

Debi, Prajnasundari, ed., *Punya,* year 3, vol. 5 (Kolikata, January 1901), 3rd year, vol. 7 (Kolikata, March 1901), 3rd year, vol. 8 (Kolikata, April 1902).

Debi, Prasannamayi. "Purbbakatha." In *Phire dekha-1: A Collection of Late 19th Century Autobiographies.* (Kolkata: Subarnarekha, 2011).

Debi, Prasannamayi. "Sekaler katha." *Antahpur 4,* no. 5 (1901): 107–110.

Debi, Saradasundari. *Phire Dekha-2: A Collection of Late 19th Century Autobiographies.* Kolkata: Subarnarekha, 2010.

Debi, Sucharu, ed. *Paricharika.* Kolkata, April 1905.

Dwija Madhab. *Mangalchandir Geet.* Edited by Sudhibhushan Bhattacharya. Kolikata: Kolikata Biswabidyalay, 1965.

Dwija Ramdeb. *Kalikamangal.* Edited by Ashutosh das. Kolkata: Kolikata Biswabidyalay, 1957.

Fazl, Abul. *Rekhachitra.* Chattagram: 1965.

Gangopadhyay, Mohanlal. *Dakshiner baranda.* Kolkata: Biswabharati, 2007 [1414 BS]), 120-121, first published in 1388 BS(c.1981).

Ganguly, Manikram. *Dharmamangal.* Edited by Bijitkumar Datta, Sunanda Datta. Kolikata: Kolikata Biswabidyalay, 2009.

Ghosh, Pratap Chandra. *Bangalir Europe darshan.* Kolkata, 1888.

Ghosh, Ray Saheb Bijnan Chandra. *Ahaar.* Kolkata, 1942.

Ghoshal, Jagajjiban. *Manasamangal.* Edited by Achintya Biswas. Kolkata: Ratnabali, 2010.

Gilpin, Mrs. John. *Pakwan-ki-Kitab: Memsahib's Guide to Cookery in India.* Bombay: 1914.

Goswami, Srishchandra. "Bangali chhatroder swasthya gelo je." *Grihasthamangal,* year 4, no.1 (April/May 1930 [Baisakh 1337 BS]): 1–5.

Guha, Haladhar. *Krishiniyamabali o jamidari mahajani hisheb.* Dhaka: 1875.

Gupta, Iswar. "Bhramankari bandhur patra." In *Iswar Gupta rachanabali.* Vol. 1. Edited by Shantikumar Dasgupta and Haribandhu Mukhoty. Kolikata, Dattachaudhuri & Sons.1974 [1381 BS].

Gupta, Pratulchandra. *Alekhya darshan.* Kolkata: Ananda Publishers Limited, 1990.

Hakim Fazl Husain. *Sawanih umri Mawlana Sayyid Muhammad Nazir Husain Muhaddis Dihlawial- maruf Al-hayat ba'd almamat.* Agra: Matba Akbari, 1908.

Haldar, Gopal. *Adda.* Kolkata: Punthipatra, 2004.

Hossain, Rokeya Sakhawat."Sugrihini." In *Rokeya Rachana Samgraha.* Edited by Miratun Nahar. Kolkata: Biswakosh Parishad, 2001). First published in 1904.

Hussain, Mir-Mosharraf. *Go-jeeban,* 1888.

Jamdatta. "Kayekti sekele galpa." *Jugantar (Samayiki),* 15 June/July, 1951, 9–11.

———. "Sekele katha." *Jugantar (Samayiki),* 20 May, 1951, 9–10.

Kabibhushan, Pyarimohan, ed., *Pakprabandha.* Kolikata, 1934.

Khatun, Habiba, and Khatun, Hafeeza, eds., *Dhakai khabar.* Dhaka: Bangladesh Asiatic Society, 2010.

Khatun, Nurunnechha. "Swapnadrishta."In *Nurnnechha Granthabali.* Dhaka: Bangla Academy, 1970. First published 1923.

Khatun, Sayeeda Hafeza. *Moslem pak pranali.* Vol. 1. Kolikata, 1930 [1337 BS].

Khemananda, Ketakadas. *Manasamangal.* Edited by Tanmay Mitra, Rezaul Karim, and Subodh kumar Jash. Kolkata: Bangiya Sahitya Samsad, 2010.

———. *Manasamangal.* Vol. 1. Edited by Jatindramohan Bhattacharya. Kolikata: Kolikata Biswabidyala, 1949.

Kundu, Kamalkumar. "Gahanaborir angane."*Desh,* year 59, no. 13 (25 January, 1992): 49–54.

Mahapatra, Shankar. "Gahana bori o Rabindranath."*Lokayat,* year 3(December/January 1997 [Poush1404 BS]): 21–24.

Mahasthabir [Premankur Atarthi]. *Mahasthabir jatak.* Vol. 1. Kolkata: Dey's, 1981.

Maiti, Mira. *Manomugdhakar shilpa naipunye bhara gahanabori o nakshabori tairir padhdhati, rakshanabekshan or sangrakshan.* Medinipur, n.d.

Majumdar, Jaminiranjan. *Alur chash.* Kolikata, 1929 [1335 BS].

Majumdar, Pratapchandra. *Streecharitra*. 3rd ed. Kolikata: 1936.

Majumdar, Subodh Kinkar Nanda. "Krishi o sar: 'Kopir Chash'." *Grihasthamangal,* year 3, no. 9 (December/January 1930 [Poush 1336 BS]): 290– 294.

Manikdatta. *Chandimangal.* Edited by Sunilkumar Ojha. Shiliguri: Uttarbanga Biswabidyalay, 1977 [1384 BS].

Maulavi Azhar Ali Bakhtiyari. *Majmuye Waz Sharif o Hedayeter Saral Path.* Vol. 2, Kolkata: Gaosia Library, 2003 [1410BS]. First published 1927 [1335 BS].

Mitra, Binapani.*Randhan-sanket.* Kolkata, 1953.

Mitra, Nagendrachandra. "Englande niramish bhojan chole kina." *Dasi 4*, no. 8 (August 1895): 460–469.

Mitra, Satish Chandra. *Jashohar-Khulnar itihas.* Vol. 1. 2nd edition (Kolikata, 1928/29 [1335 BS].

Mitra, Sudhir Kumar. *Hugli jelar itihas o Bangasamaj.* Vol. 1. 2nd edition. Kolikata, 1962. Muhammad Abd al- Hayy Lakhnawi. *Muʿallim al-fiqh tarjumah urdu Majmuʿat al-fatawa*. Trans. from Farsi to Urdu by Barkatallah Sahib Raza Lakhnawi Firangi Mahalli. Vol. 2. Kanpur, Calcutta: Haji Muhammad Said and Sons, n.d.

Mukhopadhyay, Bholanath. *Apnar mukh apuni dekho.* Kolkata: Pragyabharati, 1982 [1389 BS]).First edition 1863.

Mukhopadhyay, Bhudeb. *Paribarik prabandha.* Hooghly, 1895 [1302 BS].

———. *Samajik prabandha*. Edited with an introduction and exegesis by Jahnavikumar Chakrabarty. Kolikata: Paschimbanga Rajya Pustak Parishad, 1981.

Mukhopadhay, Bipradas. *Pak-pranali.* Kolkata, 1883.

Mukhopadhyay, Bipradas. *Pak pranali.* Vols. 1–5 Kolkata: 1928 [1335 BS]. First published in 1887 [1304 BS].

———. *Mishtanna-pak.* Vols. 1 & 2, revised ed. Kolikata, 1904 [1311 BS]): 60–61. First published 1898 [1305 BS].

Mukhopadhyay, Jadunath. *Bangalir meyer niti-siksha (putrir prati pitar upadesh).* Ranaghat: 1889 [1296 BS].

Mukhopadhyay, Kularanjan. *Khadyer nababidhan.* Kolkata, n.d.

Mukhopadhyay, Kumarprasad. "Kichhu khuchro adda."*Desh,* year 62, no. 5 (31 December, 1994): 31–40.

Mukhopadhyay, Radhakamal. *Daridrer krandan.* Baharampur, 1915 [1322 BS].

Mullick, Kumudnath. *Nadia kahini.* Edited by Mohit Ray. Kolkata; Pustak Bipani, 1986.

Nityananda."Manasamangal."Kabi Nityanander Manasamangal. Compiled and edited by Shyamal Bera. Mecheda o Kolkata: Sahajiya o Manfakra, 2006.

——— Pal, Bipinchandra. *Sattar batsar: Atmajibani.* Kolikata, 2005. First published in 1926 [1333 BS].

Pandit, Sharatchandra. "Aahar madhuri."In *Dadathakur Rachana Samagra*. Edited with an introduction by Hiren Chattopadhyay. Kolkata: Biswabani Prakashani, 2006 [1403BS], 181. First published in *Jangipur Sangbad*, ye ʾr 16, no. 18 (1929 [1336 BS])

———. "Sabhyer sahadharmini."In *Dada Thakur Rachana Samagra. Kolkata: Biswabani Prakashani,* 2006[1403BS], 181. First published in *Jangipur Sangbad,* Year 16, no. 19, 1336 BS (c.1929).

Pandit, Shyam, and Dharmadas Banik. *Dharmamangal (Niranjan mangal).* Edited by Sumitra Kundu. Shantiniketan: Rarh-Gabeshana-Parshad.

Parashuram. "Ratarati." (1919–20). Reprinted in *Parashuram Galpasamagra.* Edited by Dipankar Basu Kolikata: M.C. Sarkar & Sons Pvt. Ltd., 1992.

Pati, Bhaskarbrata. "Gaynaborir nei ko juri."In *Medinipurer lokoshilpa,* 9–13. Medinipur: Upatyaka, 2009.

Pippilai, Bipradas. *Manasa-Vijaya.* Edited by Sukumar Sen. Calcutta: Asiatic Society, 1953.

Rahman, Hakim Habibur. *Dhaka: Panchash bachhar Age (Dhaka pachas baras pahle).* Translated from Urdu to Bengali by Mohammad Rezaul Karim. Dhaka: Papyrus, 2005.

Rahman, Lutfur. "Preeti upahar." In *Lutfar Rahman rachanabali,* vol. 2. Edited by Ashraf Siddiki. Dhaka: Ahmad Publishing House, 1987.

Rashid Ahmad Gangohi. *Fatawa Rashidiyah Kamil.* New Delhi: Farid Book Depot Private Ltd., n.d.

Ray, Bharatchandra. *Annadamangal.* In *Bharatchandra granthabali.* Edited by Brajendranath Bandopadhyay and Sajanikanta Das. Kolikata, Bangiya Sahitya Parishat, 1950 [1357 BS], 1–443.

Ray, Bharati, ed.,*Nari o paribar: Bamabodhini patrika* (1270–1329 Bangabda). Kolikata: Ananda Publishers, 2002.

Ray, Dinendrakumar. *Pallibaichitra.* Kolikata: Ananda Publishers, 1982 [1389BS]). First published in 1905 [1312 BS].

———. *Pallichitra.* Kolikata: Ananda Publishers, 1983 [1390BS]. First published in 1904 [1311 BS].

Ray, Durgacharan. *Debganer martye agaman.* Kolkata: Dey's Publishing, 1984.

Ray, Hemendrakumar. "Sajahaner mayur." In *Hemendrakumar Ray Rachanabali,* vol. 9. Edited by Geeta Datta and Sukhamay Mukhopadhyay. Kolkata: Asia Publishing Company, 1986.

———. "Sonar paharer jatri." In *Hemendrakumar Ray Rachanabali,* vol. 5. Edited by Geeta Datta and Sukhomoy Mukhopadhyay. Kolkata: Asia Publishing Company, 1983.

Ray Bidyanidhi, Jogeshchandra. *Atmacharit.* Edited by Munindrakumar Ray. Bankura, Kallol, 2002 [1409BS].

Ray, Kabishekhar Kalidas. *Smritikatha.* Kolikata: Ray Publications, 1996.

Ray, Kiranlekha. *Jalkhabar.* Edited by Aruna Chattopadhyay. Kolikata: 2000). First published in 1924 [1331 BS].

———. *Varendra-randhan.* Kolkata: Subarnarekha, 1999 [1406BS]).

Ray, Kumudini."Hindu narir garhyastha dharma: Bamaganer rachana." *Bamabodhini* (October/November, 1894 [Kartik 1301BS]). Republished in *Nari o paribar:*

Bamabodhini patrika (1270-1329 Bangabda), 176– 179. Compiled and edited by Bharati Ray. Kolkata: Ananda Publishers, 2002.

Ray, Prafulla Chandra. *Anna samasyay Bangalir parajoy o tahar pratikar.* Kolikata, 1936.

———. *Atmacharit.* Kolikata: Orient Book Company, 1953 [1360 BS].

Ray, Ramesh Chandra. "Khabarer janmakatha." In *Grihasthamangal.* Edited by Aswinkumar Chattopadhyay. 3rd year, no. 1 Kolikata: April/May 1929 [Baisakh 1336 BS]: 192–195.

Raychaudhuri, Gyanendrakumar. *Meenntatwa.* Kolikata, 1882 [1289 BS].

Raygunakar Bharatchandra. "Annadamangal." In *Bharatchandra-granthabali.* Edited by Brajendranath Bandopadhay and Sajanikanta Das. Kolikata: Bangiya Sahitya Parishat, 1997 [1404 BS]

———. *Annadamangal.* Kolkata: Sahityalok, 2002.

Saha, Gyanendranath. *Bhater phen gala akartabbya tajjanya edeshbasigan hinabal o nirdhhan hoitechhe.* Sreepur, 1925 [1301 BS].

Sambuddha. "Chheledhara Jayanta."In*Sambuddha rachanabali,* 257– 297, vol. 1. Edited by Prabir Mukhopadhyay with a preface by Gautam Bhadra. Kolkata: Ababhas, 2007). First published in *Galpabharati* (October/November - November/December 1951 [Kartik/Agrhayan 1357 BS]).

Sanyal, Durgachandra. *Bangalar samajik itihas.* Edited by Fakirchandra. Rev. ed. Kolkata: Lokenath and Company, 1910 [1317 BS]). First published in 1906 [1313 BS]

Sen, Dineshchandra. *Grihasree.*3rd ed. Kolkata: 1917.

———. *Maimansingha Geetika* [*Purbbanga Geetika*], vol. 1, no. 2. Kolikata: Kolikata Biswabidyalay, 1958.

Sen, Kaviraj Indubhushan. *Bangalir khadya.* Calcutta, 1928.

Sen, Nabinchandra. *Amar jiban,* vols. 1 & 2. Edited by Sajanikanta Das Kolikata: Bangiya Sahitya Parishat, 1959 [1366 BS].

Sen, Umeshchandra. *Krishi-chandrika.* 1st and 2nd part. Serampore, 1875.

Sengupta, Baradakanta. *Bharat bhraman.* Vol. 1. Kolkata, 1877 [1284 BS].

Sengupta, Indumati and Sengupta, Satyendranath. *Adhunik randhan-bijnan.* Kolikata, 1951 [1357 BS].

Sengupta, Matilal. "Palli jibaner ekta abhigyata." In *Grihasthamangal,* year 3rd, no. 10 Kolikata, December/January 1930 [Poush 1336 BS]: 316–318.

Seth, Mahajan Shree Santoshnath. *Bange chaltatwa.* Kolikata, 1925 [1332 BS].

Shah Abd al-Aziz. *Surur-i 'Azizi al-ma'ruf Fatawa-ye 'Azizi,* vol. 1. Kanpur, Calcutta: Haji Muhammad Said and Sons, n.d.

Shastri, Shibnath. "Atmacharit."In *Shibnath Rachanasangraha,* vol. 2. Edited by Gopal Haldar and Baridbaran Ghosh. Kolkata: Saksharata Prakashan, 1976.

Singha, Baneswar. *Durbhikhha nibaraner upay.* Srihatta, 1919 [1326 BS].

———. *Krishi-prabandha.*Srihatta, 1918.

Singha, Maniklal. *Rarher jati o krishti.* Vol. 3.Bishnupur, 1982.

Sripantha, ed., *Pakrajeswar o byanjan-ratnakar.* Kolkata, Subarnarekha, 2004.

Swami Vivekananda. *Prachya o paschatya.* Kolikata: Udbodhan Karjalay, 1954 [1361 BS].

Tagore, Rabindranath. Chhelebela. (1940[1347 BS]). In *Ravindra Rachanabali.* vol. 26 (Kolikata: Viswabharati, 1977 [1384 BS]), 583-631.

———, "Narir kartabya". (1939[1346] BS). In *Ravindra Rachanabali.* Vol. 23(Kolikata: Viswabharati, 1979 [1386 BS]), 54-58.

———, "Nimantran." (Chandannagar, 1935), In *Rabindra Rachanabali.* Vol. 19. (Kolikata: Viswabharati, 1976), 25–29.

Tagore, Rwitendranath. *Mudir dokan.* Kolikata, 1919 [1316 BS].

Tarkalankar, Bisweshar. *Pakrajeswar.* 2nd ed., *Pakrajeswar o byanjan- ratnakar,* edited by Sripantha. Kolkata, 2004. First published in 1831.

Primary Sources (English)

A Lady Resident. *The Englishwoman in India: Containing Information for the Use of Ladies Proceeding to, or Residing in, The East Indies, or the Subjects of Their Outfit, Furniture, Housekeeping, The Rearing of Children, Duties and Wages of Servants, Management of the Stables, And Arrangements for Travelling. To which are added Receipts for Indian Cookery.* 2nd ed. London: Smith, Elder & Co., 1865.

A Thirty-Five Years Resident. *The Indian Cookery Book: A Practical Handbook to the Kitchen in India Containing Original and Approved Recipes in Every Department for Summer Beverages and Home-made Liqueurs: Medicinal and Other Recipes Together With a Variety of Things Worth Knowing.* 1869; repr., Calcutta: Thacker, Spink & Co., Rpt. 1931.

Anon. "Indian Economic Botany and Gardening." *The Calcutta Review* 49 (Calcutta, 1869): 187–205.

Bose, Chunilal. *Food.* Calcutta, 1930.

Burton, David. *The Raj at Table: A Culinary History of the British in India.* London, Boston: Faber and Faber, 1993.

Chaudhuri, J.P. "Eating Houses in Calcutta." *Calcutta Municipal Gazette*, 12th Health Number (26 April, 1941).

Chaudhuri, Nirad C. *The Autobiography of an Unknown Indian.* Mumbai: Jaico Publishing House, 2000.

Das, Sundarimohan. "More Milk and Cleaner Milk for Calcutta. What the New Corporation has Done." *The Calcutta Municipal Gazette* 5, no. 1 (November 20 1926–May 14 1927): 29–35.

Das, Tarakchandra. *Bengal Famine (1943).* Calcutta, 1949.

Day, Rev. Lal Behari. *Bengal Peasant Life.* New ed. London: Macmillan And Co., Ltd, 1928.

De, S.N. "Eating Houses in Calcutta." *The Calcutta Municipal Gazette*, 8th Anniversary Number (26 November, 1930): 31–33.

Dutt, Ashoke K. "Milk." *The Calcutta Municipal Gazette* 49, no. 9 (January 1949).

Ganguly, B. "Rice as a Food: Its Defects and How to Improve Them." *Calcutta Municipal Gazette*, Twelfth Health No. (26 April, 1941):99–101.

Ghose, Hemendra Prasad. "The Big Famine." *Calcutta Review* 193 (November 1944): 42–47.

Grant, Colesworthy. *An Anglo-Indian Domestic Sketch. A letter From an Artist in India to His Mother in England.* Calcutta, 1849.

Hume, A.O. *Agricultural Reform in India.* London, 1879.

Hunter, W.W. *A Statistical Account of Bengal: Districts of the Twenty-Four Parganas and Sunderbans.* Vol. 1. London, 1875.

———. *A Statistical Account of Bengal. Nadiya and Jessor.* Vol. 2. London, 1875.

Khan, Tamizuddin. *The Test of Time: My Life and Days.* Dhaka, University Press, 1989.

Knighton, William. *Tropical Sketches–or Reminiscences of an Indian Journalist.* Vol. 1. London, 1855.

Liotard, L. *Memorandum Regarding Introduction of Carolina Rice into India.* Calcutta, 1880.

Mazumdar, Sudha. *Memoirs of an Indian Woman.* Edited with an introduction by Geraldine Forbes. New York, London: An East Gate Book, H.E. Sharpe, INC., Armonk, 1989.

Mishra, Godabarish. "House No. 9." In *A World Elsewhere: Images of Kolkata in Oriya Autobiographies.* Edited by Jatindra Kumar Nayek. Bhubaneshwar: Postgraduate Department of English (DRS I), Utkal University in association with Grassroots, 2010. Translated by Snehaprava Das from *Ardhashatabdira Orissa O Tahinre Mo Sthana,* Cuttack: Granthamandir, 1996. 17–26.

Mullick, Bulloram. "The Grihini or Materfamilia." In *Essays on the Hindu Family in Bengal.* Calcutta, 1882, 40–44.

Pal, Bipin Chandra. *Memories of My Life and Times. In the Days of My Youth (1857–84).* Calcutta, Modern Book Agency

Sattar Batsar - Kalpan, 1932.

Pradhan, Pabitra Mohan. "As a Domestic Help in Calcutta." In *A World Elsewhere: Images of Kolkata in Oriya Autobiographies,* 51–67. Edited by Jatindra Kumar Nayek. Bhubaneshwar: Postgraduate Department of English (DRS I), Utkal University in association with Grassroots, 2010. Translated by Priyamvada Pal from *Mukti Pathe Sainika,* 2nd ed. Dhenkanal: Self - Published, 1979.

Ray, P.C. "Milk for Calcutta: A Scheme for a Model Dairy Farm." *The Calcutta Municipal Gazette*, 6th Anniversary. (1930): 22–24, 28.

———. "On the Chemical Examination of Certain Indian Food Stuffs, Part I, Fats and Oils." *Journal of the Asiatic Society of Bengal,* 63, part 2, Natural Science, no. 1 (1894): 59–80.

Ray, Ramesh Chandra. "Restaurants: Mend or End Them!" *The Calcutta Municipal Gazette*, 7th Health Supplement (29 March 1930): 18–19.

Roy, B.V. "Calcutta; Old and New: Taverns and Hotels." *The Calcutta Municipal Gazette* 45, no. 3 (14 December 1946): 45–46.

Schrotthy, Eugene S. *The Principles of Rational Agriculture Applied to India and its Staple Products.* Bombay, 1876.

Steel, F.A. and G. Gardiner. *The Complete Indian Housekeeper and Cook: Giving the Duties of Mistress and Servants the General Management of the House and Practical Recipes for Cooking in all its Branches.* London: William Heinemann, 1902. First published in 1898.

Wyvern. *Culinary Jottings for Madras.* Madras, 1879.

Secondary Sources

Articles and Books (English)

Achaya, K.T. *Indian Food: A Historical Companion.* Delhi: Oxford University Press, 1994.

Amin, Sonia Nishat. "The Orthodox Discourse and the Emergence of the Muslim Bhadramohila in Early Twentieth Century Bengal." In *Mind Body and Society: Life and Mentality in Colonial Bengal.* Edited by Rajat Kanta Ray. Calcutta: Oxford University Press, 1995, 391–422.

Appadurai, Arjun. "Gastro-Politics in Hindu South Asia." *American Ethnologist* 8, no. 3, Symbolism and Cognition (Aug., 1981): 494–511.

———. "How to Make a National Cuisine: Cookbooks in Contemporary India." *Comparative Studies in Society and History.* Cambridge: Cambridge University Press, 1988: 3–24.

———. "Introduction: Commodities and the Politics of Value." In *The Social Life of Things: Commodities in Cultural Perspective.* Edited by Arjun Appadurai. Cambridge: Cambridge University Press, 2007, 3–63.

———. *Modernity at Large: Cultural Dimensions of Globalization.* New Delhi: Oxford University Press, 1997.

Aquil, Raziuddin, and Partha Chatterjee, eds. *History in the Vernacular.* Ranikhet: Permanent Black, 2008.

Arnold, David. "The 'Discovery' of Malnutrition and Diet in Colonial India." *The Indian Economic and Social History Review* 31, no. 1 (January–March, 1994): 1–26.

Auslander, Leora. *Taste and Power: Furnishing Modern France.* Berkeley, Los Angeles, London: University of California Press, 1996.

Bahloul, Joelle. 'On "Cabbages and Kings": The Politics of Jewish Identity in Post-Colonial French Society and Cuisine.' In *Food in Global History.* Edited by Raymond Grew. Boulder, Colorado: Westview Press, 1999, 92–108.

Bandopadhyay, Sekhar. *Caste, Politics, and the Raj: Bengal 1872–1937.* Calcutta: K.P. Bagchi & Co., 1990.

Banerjee, Nirmala. "Working Women in Colonial Bengal." In *Recasting Women: Essays in Colonial History.* Edited by Kumkum Sangari and Sudesh Vaid. New Delhi: Kali for Women, 1989.

Banerjee, Sumanta. "Marginalization of Women's Popular Culture in Nineteenth Century Bengal." In *Recasting Women: Essays in Colonial History.* Edited by Kumkum Sangari and Sudesh Vaid. New Delhi: Kali for Women, 1989.

Banerjee, Swapna M. *Men, Women, and Domestics: Articulating Middle-Class Identity in Colonial Bengal.* New Delhi: Oxford University Press, 2004.

Barr-Melej, Patrick. *Reforming Chile: Cultural Politics, Nationalism, and the Rise of the Middle-Class.* Chapel Hill: University of North Carolina Press, 2001.

Barry, Jonathan. "Review: The Making of the Middle-Class?" *Past and Present* 145, no. 1 (1994): 194–208.

Barry, Jonathan, and Christopher Brooks, eds. *The Middling Sort of People: Culture, Society and Politics in England, 1550–1800.* New York: St. Martin's, 1994.

Beardsworth, Alan, and Teresa Keil. *Sociology on the Menu: An Invitation to the Study of Food and Society.* London and New York: Routledge, 1997.

Belasco, Warren, and Philip Scranton, eds., *Food Nations: Selling Taste in Consumer Societies.* New York, London: Routledge, 2002.

Benston, Margaret. "The Political Economy of Women's Liberation." In *The Politics of Housework.* Edited by EllenMallos. London, New York: Allison & Bushby, 1980, 100–109.

Berg, Maxine. *Luxury and Pleasure in Eighteenth-Century Britain.* Oxford: Oxford University Press, 2005.

———. "New Commodities, Luxuries and their Consumers in Eighteenth-Century England." In *Consumers and Luxury: Consumer Culture in Europe 1650–1850.* Edited by Maxine Berg, and Helen Clifford. Manchester and New York: Manchester University Press, 1999, 63–85.

Berger, Rachel. "Between Digestion and Desire: Genealogies of Food in Nationalist North India." *Modern Asian Studies*, First View Article, (May 2013): 1–22.

Bhadra, Gautam. *From an Imperial Product to a National Drink: The Culture of Tea Consumption in Modern India.* Calcutta: Center for Studies in Social Sciences, Calcutta in association with Tea Board India, 2005.

Bhaduri, Amit. "The Evolution of Land Relations in Eastern India under British Rule." *The Indian Economic and Social History Review*, (January–March, 1976): 45–53.

Bhattacharya, Tithi. *The Sentinels of Culture: Class, Education, and the Colonial Intellectual in Bengal (1848–85).* New Delhi: Oxford University Press, 2005.

Borthwick, Meredith. *The Changing Role of Women in Bengal, 1849–1905.* Princeton, NJ: Princeton University Press, 1984.

Bourdieu, Pierre. *Distinction: A Social Critique of the Judgement of Taste*. Cambridge, Massachusetts: Harvard University Press, 1984.

Brennan, Jennifer. *Curries and Bugles: A Memoir and a Cookbook of the British Raj*. New York: Harper Collins Publisher, 1990.

Brillat-Savarin, Jean Anthelme. *Gastronomy as a Fine Art or the Science of Good Living*. Trans. R.E. Anderson. London: Chatto and Winders, 1877.

Broomfield, Andrea. *Food and Cooking in Victorian England: A History*. West Port, Connecticut, London: Praeger Publishers, 2007.

Broomfield, J.H. *Elite Conflict in a Plural Society: Twentieth-Century Bengal*. Berkeley & L.A.: University of California Press, 1968.

Burnham, Douglas. *An Introduction to Kant's Critique of Judgment*. Edinburgh: Edinburgh University Press, 2004.

Caldwell, Melissa L. "Domesticating the French Fry: McDonald's and Consumerism in Moscow." In *The Cultural Politics of Food and Eating: A Reader*. Edited by James L. Watson, and Melissa L. Caldwell. Malden, MA: Blackwell Publishing, 2005, 180–196.

Cariertka, Katarzyna J. "Western Food and the Making of the Japanese Nation-State." In *The Politics of Food*. Edited by Marianne Elisabeth Lien and Brigitte Nerlich. Oxford, New York: Oxford University Press, 2004, 121–139.

Carney, Judith A. *Black Rice: The African Origins of Rice Cultivation in the Americas*. Cambridge, Massachusetts, London, England: Harvard University Press, 2001.

Chakrabarty, Bidyut. "Social Classes and Social Consciousness." In *History of Bangladesh 1704–1971, vol. 3, Social and Cultural History*. Edited by Sirajul Islam. Dhaka: Asiatic Society of Bangladesh, 1992, 164–203.

Chakrabarty, Dipesh. "Postcoloniality and the Artifice of History: Who Speaks for 'Indian' Pasts." *Representations*, no. 37. Special Issue: Imperialist Fantasies and Postcolonial Histories (Winter 1992): 1–26.

———. *Provincializing Europe: Postcolonial Thought and Historical Difference*. Princeton and Oxford: Princeton University Press, 2000.

———. *Habitations of Modernity: Essays in the Wake of Subaltern Studies*. New Delhi: Permanent Black, 2002.

Chakravarti, Uma. "Whatever Happened to the Vedic Dasi: Orientalism, Nationalism, and a Script for the Past." In *Recasting Women: Essays in Colonial History*. Edited by Kumkum Sangari and Sudesh Vaid. New Delhi: Kali for Women, 1989.

Chatterjee, Kumkum. *The Cultures of History in Early Modern India: Persianization and Mughal Culture in Bengal*. New Delhi: Oxford University Press, 2009.

Chatterjee, Partha. "Agrarian Structure in Pre-Partition Bengal." In *Perspectives in Social Sciences 2. Three Studies on the Agrarian Structure in Bengal 1850–1947*. Edited by Ashok Sen, Partha Chatterjee, and Saugata Mukherjee. Calcutta: Oxford University Press, 1982.

Chatterjee, Partha. *Bengal 1920–1947: The Land Question*. Vol. 1. Calcutta: K.P. Bagchi & Comp., 1984.

———. *Nationalist Thought and the Colonial World: A Derivative Discourse?* Delhi: Oxford University Press, 1986.

———. *Nation and its Fragments: Colonial and Postcolonial Histories.* Princeton, NJ: Princeton University Press, 1993.

Chatterjee, Piya. *A Time for Tea: Women, Labor and Post/Colonial Politics on an Indian Plantation.* Durham and London: Duke University Press, 2001.

Chaudhuri, Binay Bhushan. "Commercialization of Agriculture." In *History of Bangladesh 1704–1971.* Vol. 1, *Political History.* Edited by Sirajul Islam. Dhaka: Asiatic Society of Bangladesh, 1992.293–348.

Chaudhuri B.B. "Growth of Commercial Agriculture in Bengal 1859–1885." In *Agricultural Production and South Asian History.* Edited by David Ludden. New Delhi: Oxford University Press, 1994.

Chaudhuri, Nupur. "Shawls, Jewelry, Curry, and Rice in Victorian Britain." In *Western Women and Imperialism.* Edited by Nupur Chaudhuri and Margaret Strobel. Bloomington and Indianapolis: Indiana University Press, 1992.

Chaudhuri, Rosinka. *Freedom and Beef Steaks: Colonial Calcutta Culture.* New Delhi: Orient Blackswan, 2012.

Chowdhury, Indira. *The Frail Hero and Virile History: Gender and the Politics of Culture in Colonial Bengal.* Delhi, New York: Oxford University Press, 1998.

Cocklanis, Peter A. "Distant Thunder: The Creation of a World Market in Rice and the Transformations It brought." *The American Historical Review* 98, no. 4 (October 1993): 1050–1078.

Collingham, E.M. *Imperial Bodies: The Physical Experience of the Raj, c.1800–1947.* London: Polity, 2001.

Collingham, Lizzie. *Curry: A Biography.* London: Chatto and Winders, 2005.

Conlon, Frank F. "Dining out in Bombay." In *Consuming Modernity: Public Culture in a South Asian World.* Edited by Carol A. Breckenridge. Minneapolis/London: Universityof Minnesota press, 1995.

Coveney, John. *Food, Morals, and Meaning: The Pleasure and Anxiety of Eating.* London & New York: Routledge, 2000.

Cowan, Brian. "New World, New Tastes: Food Fashions after the Renaissance." In *Food: The History of Taste.* Edited by Paul Friedman. Berkeley/Los Angeles/London: University of California Press, 2007.

———. *The Social Life of Coffee: The Emergence of the British Coffeehouse.* New Haven, London: Yale University Press, 2005.

Crosby, Alfred W. *The Columbian Exchange: Biological and Cultural Consequences of 1492.* Westport, Connecticut: Greenwood Publishing Comp, 1972.

Counihan, Carole M. *The Anthropology of Food and Body: Gender, Meaning and Power.* New York, London: Routledge, 1999.

Daechsel, Markus. *The Politics of Self-Expression: The Urdu Middle-Class Milieu in Mid-Twentieth Century India and Pakistan.* London and New York: Routledge, 2006.

Datta, Pradip Kumar. *Carving Blocs: Communal Ideology in Early Twentieth-century Bengal.* New Delhi: Oxford University Press, 1999.

Davidoff, Leonore, and Catherine Hall. *Family Fortunes: Men and Women of the English Middle-Class, 1750–1850.* London, Melbourne, Sydney, Auckland, Johannesburg: Hutchinson, 1987.

Davis, Jennifer J. *Defining Culinary Authority: The Transformation of Cooking in France, 1650–1830.* Baton Rouge: Lousiana State University Press, 2013.

Deshpande, Prachi. *Creative Pasts: Historical Memory and Identity in Western India, 1700–1960.* New York: Columbia University Press, 2007.

Douglas, Mary. "Deciphering a Meal." In *Food and Culture: A Reader.* Edited by Carole Counihan, and Penny van Esterik. New York: Routledge, 1997, 36–54.

——— . *Purity and Danger: An Analysis of the Concepts of Pollution and Taboo.* New York: Routledge, 2000.

Donner, Henrike, ed., *Being Middle-Class in India: A Way of Life.* London and New York: Routledge, 2011, 47–72.

Donner, Henrike. "Gendered Bodies, Domestic Work and Perfect Families: New Regimes of Gender and Food in Bengali Middle-Class Lifestyles." In *Being Middle-Class in India.* Edited by Henrike Donner. London and New York: Routledge, 2011.

Dube, Saurabh. "Introduction: Enchantments of Modernity." *The South Atlantic Quarterly* 101, no.4 (Fall 2002): 729–755.

Earle, Peter. *The Making of the English Middle-Class: Business, Society and Family Life in London, 1660–1730.* Berkeley and Los Angeles: University of California Press, 1989.

Elias, Norbert. *The Civilizing Process: Sociogenetic and Psychogenetic Investigations.* Revised edition. Oxford: Blackwell, 2000.

Farb, Peter, and George Armelagos. *Consuming Passions: The Anthropology of Eating.* Boston: Houghton Mifflin Company, 1980.

Fernandes, Leela. *India's New Middle-Class: Democratic Politics in an Era of Economic Reform.* Minneapolis, MN, USA: University of Minnesota Press, 2006.

Fischer, Johan. *Proper Islamic Consumption: Shopping among the Malays in Modern Malaysia.* Copenhagen, Denmark: Nias Press, 2008.

Freedman, Paul, ed. *Food: The History of Taste.* Berkeley: University of California Press, 2007.

Friedberg, Susanne. "French Beans for the Masses: A Modern Historical Geography of Food in Burkina Faso." In *The Cultural Politics of Food and Eating: A Reader.* Edited by James L. Watson and Melissa L. Caldwell. Malden, MA, Oxford, Victoria: Blackwell, 2005, 21–41.

Gallagher, John, Gordon Johnson, and Anil Seal, eds. *Locality, Province and Nation: Essays on Indian Politics 1870 to 1940.* Cambridge: Cambridge University Press, 1973.

Ghosh, Anindita. *Power in Print: Popular Publishing and the Politics of Language and Culture in a Colonial Society, 1778–1905.* New Delhi: Oxford University Press, 2006.

Goody, Jack. *Cooking, Cuisine, and Class: A Study in Comparative Sociology.* Cambridge: Cambridge University Press, 1982.

Greenough, Paul R. *Prosperity and Misery in Modern Bengal: The Famine of 1943–44.* New York: Oxford University Press, 1982.

Grew, Raymond, ed. *Food in Global History.* Boulder, Colorado: Westview Press, 1999.

Guha-Thakurta, Tapati. *The Making of a New 'Indian' Art: Artists, aesthetics and nationalism in Bengal, c.1850–1920.* Cambridge: Cambridge University Press, 1992.

Gunn, Simon. "Between Modernity and Backwardness: The Case of the English Middle-Class." In *The Making of the Middle-Class: Toward a Transnational History.* Edited by Ricardo A. Lopez, and Barbara Weinstein, with an afterword by Mrinalini Sinha. Durham and London: Duke University Press, 2012, 58–74.

Gupta, Swarupa. *Notions of Nationhood in Bengal: Perspectives on Samaj, c.1867–1905.* Leiden: Brill, 2009.

Habib, Irfan. "Mughal India." In *The Cambridge Economic History of India, vol. 1, c.1200–c.1750.* Edited by Tapan Raychaudhuri, and Irfan Habib. Cambridge: Cambridge University Press, 1982.

———. *The Agrarian System of Mughal India 1556–1707.* revised edition. New Delhi: Oxford University Press, 1999.

Hall, Catherine. "The History of Housewife." (1973) In *The Politics of Housework.* Edited by Ellen Malos. London, New York: Allison & Busby, 1980, 34–58.

Hollows, Joane. "Science and Spells: Cooking, Lifestyle and Domestic Femininities in British *Good Housekeeping* in the Inter-War Period." In *Historicizing Lifestyle: Mediating Taste, Consumption and Identity from the 1900s to 1970s.* Edited by David Bell, Joanne Hallows. Hampshire, England, Burlington, VT, USA: Ashgate, 2006, 21–40.

Hancock, Mary Elizabeth. *Womanhood in the Making: Domestic Ritual and Public Culture in Urban South India.* Boulder, Colorado, Oxford, UK: Westview Press, 1999.

Hardgrove, Anne. *Community and Public Culture: The Marwaris in Calcutta.* New Delhi, New York: Oxford University Press, 2004.

Hartmann, Heidi. "The Unhappy Marriage of Marxism and Feminism: Towards a More Progressive Union." In *Women and Revolution: A Discussion of the Unhappy Marriage of Marxism and Feminism.* Edited by Lydia Sargent. Boston, MA: South End Press, 1981, 1–42.

Hayden, Dolores. *Redesigning the American Dream: The Future of Housing, Work, and Family Life.* New York, London: W.W. Norton & Company, 1984.

Haynes, Douglas E., Abigail Mcgowan, Tirthankar Roy, and Haruka Yanagisawa, eds. *Towards a History of Consumption in South Asia.* New Delhi: Oxford University Press, 2010.

Inden, Ronald B., and Ralph W. Nicholas. *Kinship in Bengali Culture.* Chicago: University of Chicago, 1977.

Jaffrelot, Christophe, and Peter Van der Veer, eds. *Patterns of Middle-Class Consumption in India and China.* New Delhi: Sage, 2008.

Jain, Kajri. *Gods In The Bazaar: The Economics of Indian Calendar Art.* Durham and London: Duke University Press, 2007.

Janeja, Manpreet K. *Transactions in Taste: The Collaborative Lives of Everyday Bengali Food.* New Delhi: Routledge, 2010.

Jhala, Angma D. "Cosmopolitan Kitchens: Cooking for Princely Zenanas in Late Colonial India." In *Curried Cultures: Globalization, Food, and South Asia.* Edited by Krishnendu Ray and Tulasi Srinivas. Berkeley/ Los Angeles/ London: University of California Press, 2012, 49–72.

Joshi, Sanjay. *Fractured Modernity: Making of a Middle-Class in Colonial North India.* New Delhi: Oxford University Press, 2001.

Joshi, Sanjay. "Thinking about Modernity from the Margins: The Making of a Middle-Class in Colonial India." In *The Making of the Middle-Class: Toward a Transnational History.* Edited by Ricardo A. Lopez, and Barbara Weinstein. Durham and London: Duke University Press, 2012, 29–44.

Joyce, Patrick, ed. *Class.* Oxford, New York: Oxford University Press, 1995.

Kant, Immanuel. *Critique of Judgment.* Trans. with an introduction by J.H. Bernard. New York: Hafner Press, London: Collier Macmillan Publishers, 1951.

Khare, R.S. *Culture and Reality: Essays on the Hindu System of Managing Foods.* Simla: Indian Institute of Advanced Study, 1976.

———. *The Hindu Hearth and Home.* Durham: Carolina Academic Press, 1976.

Kidd, Alan, and David Nicholls, eds. *Gender, Civic Culture and Consumerism: Middle-Class Identity in Britain 1800–1940.* Manchester, UK: Manchester University Press, 1999.

Korsmeyer, Carolyn. *The Taste Culture Reader: Experiencing Food and Drink.* Oxford, New York: Berg, 2007.

Kraemer, David. *Jewish Eating and Identity through the Ages.* New York, London: Routledge, 2007.

Langland, Elizabeth. *Nobody's Angels: Middle-Class Women and Domestic Ideology in Victorian Culture.* Ithaca: Cornell University Press, 1995.

Latour, Bruno, and Steve Woolgar. *Laboratory Life: The Construction of Scientific Facts.* Princeton, New Jersey: Princeton University Press, 1986.

Levi-Strauss, Claude. *The Raw and the Cooked: Introduction to a Science of Mythology I.* London: Jonathan Cape, 1970.

Leong-Salobir, Cecilia. *Food Culture in Colonial Asia: A Taste of Empire.* London and New York: Routledge, 2011.

Liechty, Mark. *Suitably Modern: Making Middle-Class Culture in a New Consumer Society.* Princeton, New Jersey: Princeton University Press, 2003.

Lopez, A. Ricardo, and Barbara Weinstein, eds. *The Making of the Middle-Class: Toward a Transnational History*. With an afterword by Mrinalini Sinha. Durham and London: Duke University Press, 2012.

Lozada, Eriberto P. Jr., "Globalized Childhood? Kentucky Fried Chicken in Beijing.", In *The Cultural Politics of Food and Eating: A Reader*. Edited by James Watson, and Melissa L. Caldwell.Malden, MA: Blackwell Publishing, 2005.

Majumdar, Boria, and Kaushik Bandopadhyay. *A Social History of Indian Football: Striving to Score*. Oxon: Routledge, 2006.

Majumdar, Rochona. *Marriage and Modernity: Family Values in Colonial Bengal*. Durham: Duke University Press, 2009.

Mani, Lata. *Contentious Traditions: The Debate on Sati in Colonial India*. Berkeley/Los Angeles/ London: University of California Press, 1998.

Marshall, P.J. "General Economic Conditions under the East India Company." In *History of Bangladesh (1704–1971), vol. 2, Economic History*. Edited by Sirajul Islam. Dhaka: Asiatic Society of Bangladesh, 1992, 67–164.

Maza, Sarah. *The Myth of the French Bourgeoisie: An Essay on the Social Imaginary 1750–1850*. Cambridge, Massachusetts, and London, England: Harvard University Press, 2003.

Maza, Sarah C. *Servants and Masters in Eighteenth Century France: The Uses of Loyalty*. Princeton, New Jersey: Princeton University Press, 1982.

McGowan, Abigail. "An All-Consuming Subject? Women and Consumption in Late-Nineteenth and Early Twentieth Century Western India." *Journal of Women's History* 18, no. 4 (2006): 31–54.

McGuire, John. *The Making of a Colonial Mind: A Quantitative Study of the Bhadralok in Calcutta, 1857–1885*. Canberra: Australian National University, 1983.

McMichael, Philip, ed. *Food and Agrarian Orders in the World-Economy*. Westport, Connecticut, London: Greenwood Press, 1995.

Mennell, Stephen. *All Manners of Food: Eating and Taste in England and France from the Middle Ages to the Present*.Oxford, UK, New York, USA: Basil Blackwell, 1985.

Mies, Maria. *Patriarchy and Accumulation on a World Scale: Women in the International Division of Labor*. London, Atlantic Highlands, N.J., USA: Zed Books, 1986.

Mintz, Sidney W. *Sweetness and Power: The Place of Sugar in Modern History*. New York: Viking Penguin Inc., 1985.

———. *Tasting Food, Tasting Freedom*. Boston: Beacon Press, 1996.

Misra, B.B. *The Indian Middle-Classes: Their Growth in Modern Times*. London: Royal Institute of International Affairs, 1961; reprint, Delhi: Oxford University Press, 1983.

Mitchell, Timothy, ed. *Questions of Modernity*. Minneapolis, London: University of Minnesota Press, 2000.

Montanari, Massimo. *Food is Culture*. Translated from the Italian by Albert Sonnefeld. New York: Columbia University Press, 2004.

———. *The Culture of Food*. Oxford, UK, Cambridge, Massachusetts, USA: Blackwell, 1994.

Morrison, Barrie M. *Political Centers and Cultural Regions in Early Bengal*. Jaipur-Delhi: Rawat Publications, 1980.

Morton, Peggy . "Women's Work is Never Done." In *The Politics of Housework*. Edited by Ellen Malos. London, New York: Allison & Busby, 1980, 1110–134.

Muin-ud-din Ahmad Khan. *History of the Fara'idi Movement*. Dhaka, 1984.

Mukherjee, Mukul. "Impact of Modernization on Women's Occupations: A Case Study of the Rice-husking Industry of Bengal." In *Women in Colonial India: Essays on Survival, Work and the State*. Edited by J. Krishnamurty. Delhi: Oxford University Press, 1989, 180–198.

Mukherjee, Saugata. "Some Aspects of Commercialization of Agriculture in Eastern India 1891-1938." In *Perspectives in Social Sciences. Three Studies on the Agrarian Structure in Bengal 1850–1947*. Edited by Ashok Sen, Partha Chatterjee, and Saugata Mukherjee. Calcutta: Oxford University Press, 1982, 225–284.

Mukherjee, S.N.*Calcutta: Myths and History*. Calcutta: Subarnarekha, 1977.

Mukhopadhyay, Bhaskar. "Between Elite Hysteria and Subaltern Carnivalesque: The Politics of Street-Food in the City of Calcutta." *South Asia Research* 24, no. 12004): 37-50.

———. "Between Elite Hysteria and Subaltern Carnivalesque: Street-Food and Globalization in Calcutta." In *The Rumor of Globalization: Desecrating the Global from Vernacular Margins*. Edited by Bhaskar Mukhopadhyay. London: Hurst & Company, 2012 , 87–104.

Murshid, Ghulam. *Reluctant Debutante: Response of Bengali Women to Modernization, 1849–1905*. Rajshahi: Rajshahi University Press, 1983.

Nandy, Moti. "Football and Nationalism." Trans. Shampa Banerjee, in *The Calcutta Psyche*. Edited by Geeti Sen. New Delhi: India International Centre, 1990-91, 241–254.

Narayan, Uma. "Eating Cultures: Incorporation, Identity, and Indian Food." In *Dislocating Cultures/Identities, Traditions, and Third-World Feminism*. New York and London: Routledge, 1997.161–219.

Nash, R.C. "South Carolina and the Atlantic Economy in the Late Seventeenth and Eighteenth Centuries." *Economic History Review*. Vol. 45, no. 4 (1992): 677–702.

O'Dougherty, Maureen. *Consumption Intensified: The Politics of Middle-CLass Daily Life in Brazil*. Durham: Duke University Press, 2002.

Ohnuki-Tierney, Emiko. "We Eat Each Other's Food to Nourish Our Body: The Global and the Local as Mutually Constituent Forces." In *Food in Global History*. Edited by Raymond Grew. Boulder, Colorado: Westview Press, 1999, 240–272.

Owensby, Brian. *Intimate Ironies: Modernity and the Making of Middle-Class Lives in Brazil.* Stanford: Stanford University Press, 1999.

Philip, Kavita. *Civilizing Natures: Race, Resources, and Modernity in Colonial South India.* New Brunswick, New Jersey: Rutgers University Press, 2004.

Pollock, Sheldon. "The Cosmopolitan Vernacular." *The Journal of Asian Studies* 57, no. 1 (February 1998): 6–37.

Pollock, Sheldon, Homi K. Bhabha, Carol A. Breckenridge, and Dipesh Chakrabarty. "Cosmopolitanism." *Public Culture* 12, no. 3 (Fall 2000).

Prakash, Gyan. *Another Reason: Science and the Imagination of Modern India.* New Delhi: Oxford University Press, 2000.

Prasad, Srirupa. "Crisis, Identity, and Social Distinction: Cultural Politics of Food, Taste, and Consumption in Late Colonial Bengal." *Journal of Historical Sociology* 19, no. 3 (September 2006): 246–265.

Ray, Krishnendu. *The Migrant's Table: Meals and Memories in Bengali-American Households.* Philadelphia: Temple University Press, 2004.

Ray, Krishnendu, and Tualsi Srinivas, eds. *Curried Cultures: Globalization, Food, and South Asia.* Berkeley/ Los Angeles/ London: University of California Press, 2012.

Ray, Rajatkanta. *Social Conflict and Political Unrest in Bengal, 1875–1927.* Delhi: Oxford University Press, 1984.

Raychaudhuri, Tapan. *Europe Reconsidered: Perceptions of the West in Nineteenth Century Bengal.* Delhi: Oxford University Press, 1988.

Rosselli, John. "The Self-Image of Effeteness: Physical Education and Nationalism in Nineteenth-Century Bengal." *Past and Present* 86, no. 1 (February 1980): 121–148.

Roy, Parama. "Meat-Eating, Masculinity, and Renunciation in India: A Gandhian Grammar of Diet." *Gender and History* 14, no. 1 (April 2002): 62–91.

———. "Reading Communities and Culinary Communities: The Gastropoetics of the South Asian Diaspora." *Positions: East Asia Cultures Critique* 10, no. 2 (2002): 471–502.

Said, Edward W., *Orientalism.* New York: Pantheon Books, 1978.

Sangari, Kumkum, and Sudesh Vaid. "Recasting Women: An Introduction." In *Recasting Women: Essays in Colonial History.* Edited Kumkum Sangari, and Sudesh Vaid. New Delhi: Kali for Women, 1989, 1–26.

Sanyal, Hiteshranjan. *Social Mobility in Bengal.* Calcutta: Papyrus, 1981.

Sarkar, Sumit. *The Swadeshi Movement in Bengal 1903–1908.* New Delhi: People's Publishing House, 1994.

———. *Writing Social History.* Delhi: Oxford University Press, 1997.

Sarkar, Tanika. "Politics and Women in Bengal: The Conditions and Meanings of Anticipation." *The Indian Economic and Social History Review* 21, no. 1 (1984): 91–101.

———. *Hindu Wife, Hindu Nation: Community, Religion, and Cultural Nationalism.* Bloomingdon, Indianapolis: Indiana University Press, 2001.

Sartori, Andrew. *Bengal in Global Concept History: Culturalism in the Age of Capital.* Chicago: University of Chicago Press, 2008.

Seal, Anil. *The Emergence of Indian Nationalism: Competition and Collaboration in the Later Nineteenth Century.* London: Cambridge University Press, 1968.

Sen, Asok. "Agrarian Structure and Tenancy Laws in Bengal, 1850–1900." In *Perspectives in Social Sciences. Three Studies on the Agrarian Structure in Bengal 1850–1947.* Edited by Asok Sen, Partha Chatterjee, Saugata Mukherjee. Calcutta: Oxford University Press, 1982, 1–112.

Sen, Samita. *Women and Labour in Late Colonial India: The Bengal Jute Industry.* Cambridge: Cambridge University Press, 1999.

Sengupta, Jayanta. "Nation on a Platter: The Culture and Politics of Food and Cuisine in Colonial Bengal." *Modern Asian Studies* 44, no. 1 (2010): 81–98.

Shannon, Brent. *The Cut of His Coat: Men, Dress, and Consumer Culture in Britain, 1860–1914.* Athens: Ohio University Press, 2006.

Sinha, Mrinalini. *Colonial Masculinity: The 'Manly Englishman' and the 'Effeminate Bengali' in the Late Nineteenth Century.* Manchester: Manchester University Press, 1995, 168–186.

———. "Britain and the Empire: Towards a New Agenda for Imperial History." *Radical History Review* 72, no. 1 (1998): 163–174.

———. "How History Matters: Complicating the Categories of 'Western' and 'Non-Western' Feminisms." In *Is Academic Feminism Dead? Theory in Practice.* Edited by The Social Justice Group at the Center for Advanced Feminist Studies University of Minnesota. New York: New York University Press, 2000.

———. *Specters of Mother India: The Global Restructuring of an Empire.* Durham & London: Duke University Press, 2006.

Sinha, Pradip. *Nineteenth Century Bengal: Aspects of Social History.* Calcutta: Firma K.L. Mukhopadhyay, 1965.

Smail, John. *The Origins of Middle-Class Culture: Halifax, Yorkshire 1660–1780.* Ithaca and London: Cornell University press, 1994.

Sokolov, Raymond. *Why We Eat What We Eat: How the Encounter between the New World and the Old Changed the way everyone on the Planet Eats.* New York: Summit Books, 1991.

Solow, Barbara L., and Stanley L. Engerman. *British Capitalism and Caribbean Slavery: The Legacy of Eric Williams.* Cambridge, New York: Cambridge University Press, 1987.

Stoler, Anne Laura, and Frederick Cooper. "Between Metropole and Colony: Rethinking a Research Agenda." In *Tensions of Empire: Colonial Cultures in a Bourgeois World.* Edited by Frederick Cooper, and Anne Laura Stoler. Berkeley/ Los Angeles/ London: University of California Press, 1997, 1–56.

Tarlo, Emma. *Clothing Matters: Dress and Identity in India.* Chicago: The University of Chicago Press, 1996.

Terrio, Susan J. 'Crafting Grand Cra Chocolates in contemporary France', *The Cultural Politics of Food and Eating: A Reader.* Edited by James L. Watson and Melissa L. Caldwell. Caldwell: Blackwell 2005. 144-161.

Trautmann, Thomas R. *Aryans and British India.* Berkeley/ Los Angeles/ London: University of California Press, 1997.

Troll, Christian W. *Sayyid Ahmad Khan: A Reinterpretation of Muslim Theology.* New Delhi: Vikas Publishing House, 1978.

Varma, Pavan K. *The Great Indian Middle-Class.* New Delhi, India: Viking, 1998.

Venkatachalapathy, A.R. *In Those Days there was no Coffee: Writings in Cultural History.* New Delhi: Yoda Press, 2006.

Wahrman, Dror. *Imagining the Middle-Class: The Political Representation of Class in Britain,c.1780– 1840.* Cambridge: Cambridge University Press, 1995.

Walsh, Judith E.*Domesticity in Colonial India: What Women Learned when Men gave them Advice.* Lanham, Boulder, New York: Rowman and Littlefield Publishers, Inc., 2004.

Walton, Whitney. *France at the Crystal Palace: Bourgeois Taste and Artisan Manufacture in the Nineteenth Century.* Berkeley, Los Angeles, London: University of California Press, 1992.

Walvin, James. *Fruits of Empire: Exotic Produce and British Taste, 1660–1800.* New York: New York University Press, 1997.

Watson, James L. "China's Big Mac Attack." In *The Cultural Politics of Food and Eating: A Reader.* Edited by James L. Watson, and Melissa L. Caldwell. Malden, MA: Blackwell Publishing, 2005.

Watson, James L. and Melissa L. Caldwell, eds. *The Cultural Politics of Food and Eating: A Reader.* Malden, MA: Blackwell Publishing, 2005, 70–79.

Williams, Eric.*Capitalism and Slavery.* Introduction by D.W. Brogan, D.W. London: Andre Deutsch, 1964.

Wurst, Karin. *Fabricating Pleasure: Fashion, Entertainment, and Cultural Consumption in Germany, 1780–1830.* Detroit: Wayne State University Press, 2005.

Yan, Yunxiang. "Of Hamburger and Social Space: Consuming Mcdonald's in Beijing." In *The Cultural Politics of Food and Eating: A Reader.* Edited by James L. Watson and Melissa L. Caldwell. Malden, MA: Blackwell Publishing, 2005, 80–103.

Young, Linda. *Middle-Class Culture in the Nineteenth Century: America, Australia and Britain.* Houndmills. Basingstoke, Hampshire: Palgrave Macmillan, 2003.

Zimmerman, Francis. *The Jungle and the Aroma of Meats: An Ecological Theme in Hindu Medicine.* Berkeley/ Los Angeles/ London: University of California Press, 1987.

Zlotnick, Susan. "Domesticating Imperialism: Curry and Cookbooks in Victorian England." *Frontiers: A Journal of Women's Studies* 16, no. 2/3, Gender, Nation, and Nationalisms (1996): 51–68.

Zuckerman, Larry. *The Potato: How the Humble Spud Rescued the Western World.* Boston & London: Faber & Faber, 1998.

Articles and Books (Vernacular)

Ahmad, Wakil. *Unish shatake Bangali Musalmaner chinta o chetanar dhara.* Dhaka: Bangla Academy, 1997.

Anisuzzaman. *Muslim manas o Bangla sahitya (1757–1918).* Dhaka: Lekhak Sangha Prakashani, Dhaka Biswabidyalay, 1968.

Basu, Pradip Kumar. "Adarsha paribare adarsha randhanpranali." *Anushtup* 32, no. 1 (1997): 14–40.

Bhattacharya, Bijanbihari. "Adwaitacharya ebong Sarbabhouma Bhattacharyer grihe Mahaprabhur bhojanbilas." In *Bangabhasha o Bangasanskriti.* Kolikata: Ananda Publishers, 1994.

———. "Shakri: Entho." In *Bangabhasha o Bangasanskriti.* Kolikata: Ananda Publishers, 1994, 106–111.

Mukhopadhyay, Sukhamay. *Madhyajuger Bangla sahityer tathya o kalakram.* Kolkata: Bharati Book Stall, 2011.

Ray, Niharranjan. *Bangalir itihas: Adiparba.* Kolkata: Dey's Publishing, 1993. First published in 1949 [1356 BS].

Ray, Pranab. *Banglar khabar.* Kolkata: Sahityalok, 1987.

Unpublished Dissertations

Davis, Jennifer J. "Men of Taste: Gender and Authority in the French Culinary Trades, 1730–1830." PhD diss., Pennsylvania State University, 2004.

Ghose, Rajarshi. "Politics for Faith: Karamat Ali Jaunpuri and Islamic Revivalist Movements in British India circa 1800–73." PhD diss., University of Chicago, 2012.

Trubek, Amy B. "The Empire of the Senses: French Haute Cuisine and the Rise of the Modern Culinary Profession, 1870–1910." PhD diss., University of Pennsylvania, 1995.

Index

Adarsha Hindu Hotel (Ideal Hindu Hotel), 56
adda (social gathering of friends), 78, 80–81
Adhmoni Kailas, 86
Adhmoni Kailash, 86–87
adulteration of food
　Calcutta Municipal Act, 159
　definition of, 159
　of edibles, 159
　of *ghee*, 158
　policies in relation to, 161
　in restaurants, 165
　techniques to detect, 158–159
aesthetic judgment, Kant concept of, 80
Agnikukkut, 184, 186–187
Agricultural & Horticultural Society, 35
agricultural jobs, 140
agricultural policies of colonial state, 27–33
agriculture, commercialisation of, 121
Agri-Horticultural Society of India, 21, 47
Ahchhanulla, Khanbahadur, 182
Ahmad, Abul Mansur, 181
Ahmadi, 185
Ahmad, Ibne Majuddin, 181, 184
Ahmad, Mohammad Reyazuddin, 177, 180
ajalchal, 125
Akhbare Islamiya, 185
Akhundzada, Hakim Habibur Rahman, 212
Ali, Taleb, 74–75

ambarish (a pan for frying bread), 73
American *bhoota* (corn), 102
American Historical Review, 33
Amish o Niramish Ahar (Vegetarian and Non-vegetarian food), 63, 147
amritee, 104
Anandabazar Patrika, 25
ancient Bengal, 8
Anglo-Indian cooking, 99
Anglo-Mughlai Café, Calcutta, 1
animal bones or skins use in food, 54
animal husbandry, 162
Anjuman-e-Ahbabe-Islamiya, 110
Annadamangal, 155
Annapurna, 51
Annapurna (the bounty deity), 119
Antahpur journal, 21, 145–148
Ashanisanket (Sign of Thunder), 191
authenticity of food, 62, 66, 232
Aztecs, 13

bajra (millet), 190
Bakhtiari, Maulavi Azhar Ali, 182
Bamabodhini, 112–113, 115, 143, 145
Bandopadhyay, Bibhutibhshan, 56, 191
Bandopadhyay, Panchkari, 51, 94, 116–117, 188
Bandopadhyay, Sekhar, 173
Banerjee, Nirmala, 142
Banerjee, Swapna, 125, 137
Bangadarshan, 95

bangal (residents of eastern parts of Bengal), 192
Bangalir Itihas, 193
Bangalir Itihas (History of the Bengali people) Niharranjan Ray, 8
Bangamahila, 153
Bange Chalttatva, 167
Barari, Hariananda, 214
Barendra-randhan (Kiranlekha Ray), 9
Basu, Amritalal, 91, 134
Basu, Chandranath, 113
Basu, Chunilal, 87–88, 115, 143, 163
Basu, Nagendranath, 192
Basu, Nripendrakumar, 129
Basu, Rajnarayan, 86
Basu, Rajshekhar, 1
bawarchis (Indian Muslim cooks), 102–103, 157
beef. *see also* beef-eaters; cow slaughter
    Bengali Hindu's attitude towards, 176–177
    consumption of, 177–178, 182–183
    Hindu abomination for, 184
beef-eaters, 177–178
    shunned by the Hindu middle-class, 184
Bengal famine of 1943, 188, 190–191
Bengali cookbooks and recipe, 15
Bengali cosmopolitan, 74–81
Bengali cuisine, 2, 8–12, 19, 27, 75, 105, 158, 194, 229, 231
    aestheticisation of, 74
    developed from late nineteenth century, 232
    domesticity of, 81–91 (*see also* regional cosmopolitanism)
    hybridity of, 14–15
    making of, 92–98
    as pan-Indian cuisine, 230
    romanticisation of, 76
    subregional variations, 195–205
Bengali culinary, 76, 229
Bengali diet, features of, 151
Bengali domestic manuals on cookery, 118

Bengali entrepreneurs, 9
Bengali food, 9, 21, 74, 77, 229
Bengali gastronomic culture, 97
Bengali Hindu middle-class, 2, 6, 8, 11–12, 20–21, 27, 51, 78, 104, 231, 234
    cultural perception of, 48
    past symbolised, 85
Bengali kitchens, 76, 160
Bengali marriage ceremony, 93, 95
Bengaliness, 8, 13–14, 22, 33, 62, 78, 81, 104, 180, 234–235
Bengali peasants, 52
Bengali prototype cuisine, 234
Bengali recipes, 63–65
Bengali self, 193–194
Bengali sweetmeat makers, 76
Bengali sweets, 119–120
bhadralok, 127–128
Bhagabati Yatra (cow worship), 82
bhaji, 73
Bharater Godhan Raksha, 176–177
Bharati, 95
bhater hotel, 56
Bhattacharya, Sudakshina, 129–130
Bhattacharya, Tithi, 2
Bhim Nager Rasogolla, 25
Bhojan shilpi Bangali (Buddhadeb Bose), 75
bhrastra, 73
Bidyanidhi, Jogeshchandra Ray, 174
Binapani, 156
biscuits, consumption of, 175
Biswas, Aswinikumar, 168
Bnatul, 1
boiled rice, 54
bone-meal, 54
Borthwick, Meredith, 110–111
Bose, Buddhadeb, 79–81
Bose, Chunilal, 103, 150
Botanical Gardens, 43, 48
Bourdieu, Pierre, 15, 17
Brahmin cooks, 75, 138
    demand for, 125–128
    proliferation of, 129
Brennan, Jennifer, 103

Index

British cuisines, 65
British economic interest, 4
British Empire, 108
British Indian bureaucracy, 137
Burma supplied rice during Bengal famines, 30
Butler, Hasan, 117
Byanjan-ratnakar, 63

cabbage, 65
Café-de-Monico, 2
Calcutta, 108–109, 121, 126, 129, 137, 190
Calcutta-curry-powder, 67
Calcutta Municipal Act, 159, 163
Calcutta Municipal Gazette, The, 162
Calcutta Review, 44
Californian rice, 14
capitalist modernity, 80, 188
    for middle-class women, 143
    and rethinking of feminist historiography, 143–148
    women labour, impact on, 142
Carney, Judith, 34
carolina rice experiments in colonial Bengal, 33–38, 231
Chaitanya, 106
Chakrabarty, Dipesh, 5, 80, 144, 223
Chali rice, 48–50
Chanda, Rani, 134–135
Chandimandaps, 24
Chandimangal, 155, 198–199
Charakasamhita, 154
Chatterjee, Partha, 110, 123–124, 144
Chatterjee, Trannath, 164
Chattopadhay, Sunitikumar, 95
Chattopadhyay, Bankimchandra, 113, 233
Chattopadhyay, Jogendrakumar, 95, 97, 137, 151, 169–171, 188
Chattopadhyay, Saratkumari, 97
Chattrejee, Partha, 5
Chaudhuri, Brajendra Narayan, 219
Chaudhurani, Sarala Devi, 125
Chaudhurani, Sarat Kumari, 157
Chaudhuri, Basantakumar, 138

Chaudhuri, Binay Bhushan, 27–28
Chaudhuri, Nibaranchandra, 86
Chaudhuri, Nirad Chandra, 178
Chaudhuri, Rosinka, 153
Chaudhuri, Taranath, 153
Chinese cuisine, 76
chocolate, 47
    manufacturing in France, 138
Christian Vernacular Education Society, 154
class agenda, of the middle-class, 164
Cocklanis, Peter, 33
cocoa, 47
coffee hotels, emergence in Tamilnadu, 18
Collingham, Lizzy, 60, 67, 102
colonial Bengal middle-class, 6, 8, 231
colonial middle-class, politics of, 124
Colonial modernity, 19–20
    complexities of, 11
colonial modernity, horrors of, 190–191
colonial political economy, 48–55
colonial transformation of production relations, 6
Columbian Exchange, 15, 26–27
commercialization of agriculture, 27–28
communal eating, 169
consumption
    of commodities, 7
    scenario in Calcutta, 58
cookbooks, 111, 115, 117, 145–147, 180
    archiving of, 180
    publication of, 143, 148
cooked rice, 51
cooking European food in India, 24
cooking in Colonial Bengal
    aesthetics of, 106–107, 137
    business of, 106
    colonial influence on cuisine, 119
    in educational institutions, 110
    as feminine task, 122
    gender roles in, 106
    and glorification of women's cooking, 119
    in middle-class homes, 107–108

268   Index

by Oriya Brahmins, 108
   pedagogy of, 110–121
   practice of, 120
   professionalisation of, 136–137
   in *Vaishnava* literature, 106
cooks, 161
   hiring of, 121, 136–137
   male *versus* female, 109, 118, 121–130, 166–167
cooperative milk supply, 163
Co-operative Milk Union, 165
cosmopolitanism, 21–22, 62, 98–105, 230, 232
   of Bengali cuisine, 63, 80
   regional (*see* regional cosmopolitanism)
Cow Memorial Fund, 186
cow slaughter
   convention to ban, 177, 182
   halal, 183
Crosby, Alfred, 26–27
cuisine, hierarchisation of, 122
culinary education for women, 114, 146
Culinary Jottings, 99
culinary practices, gendering of, 122
culinary profession, 132
culinary skills, learning of, 110–111, 113
   educational curriculum for, 111, 117, 120
   rational and scientific mode of, 114
   in schools and colleges, 111, 117
cultural capital, Bourdieu concept of, 5
curriculum on cookery, 111, 117, 120
curry, 65, 76. *See also Pak pranali*
   powder, 62, 66–67, 99
   recipes for, 62, 66–67

Dadathakur. see Pandit, Sharatchandra
Daechesel, Markus, 176
Dainty Dishes for Indian Table, 103
dairy, 162
'Dalda' vegetable oil, 166
Dasgupta, Satishchandra, 167
Dasi, Dayamayi, 144
Das, Sarachchandra, 121
Das, Snehalata, 120

Das, Sundari Mohan, 162
Das, Sundarimohan, 89
Datta, Mahendranath, 98, 127, 137
Datta, Nikunjabehari, 86
Davidoff, Leonore, 139
Davis, Jennifer, 123
Day, Lal Behari, 83
Debganer Martye Agaman, 170
Debi, Hemantabala, 131, 188
Devi, Giribala, 126
Devi, Prasannamayi, 119
Devi, Saradasundari, 133
dhenkis, 167–168
diet, political nature of, 19
'Dine Dakati,' 121
domestic cuisine, 61, 232
domesticity and practice, ideology of, 140–141
domesticity, Victorian ideas of, 115
Dum-dum nursery, 53

eating nutritious food, 86
eating patterns change in colonial Bengal, 62
Eid-ul fitr, 182
ekadashi (fasting without water), 220
Elias, Norbert, 232
English cookery, 120
English education, spread of, 151–152
English housekeeping, 115
English recipes, 69
Escoffier, Georges Auguste, 13, 132
Euro-American domestic manuals on cookery, 118
European cuisine, 74, 76
European foods, 73
European gardening system, 39
European modernity, 5
European vegetable gardening, 45
exchange of recipes by middle-class women, 10

Faizunessa Girls High School, Comilla, 109
famines, 151

Fazl, Abul, 183–184
feasts
    in Muslim wedding, 181
    in village, 171
female education, 109–110, 134, 145
First Annual Report of the Agricultural Department of Bengal (1886), 54
fish *chochchori*, 197
fish recipes, 120
food, 104
    adulteration of (*see* adulteration of food)
    chemical analysis of, 162
    in colonial Asia, 125
    definition of, 58
    experiments with, 26–27
    gendering of, 156–157
    inspection of, 161
    insufficiency of, 189
    as marker of the 'other,' 150–159
    and notion of foreign, 175
    nucleus of world, 91
    'old' and 'new' food, 168–174
    preparation, art of, 147
    production of, 142
    purity of, 191
foreign culture, 36
foreign food, 40, 72, 90–91, 176
foreign rice, 14
Freedom and Beef Steaks: Colonial Calcutta Culture, 153
French cuisines, 65, 80, 100

Gahana boris of Medinipur, 225–228
Gandhian nationalist movements, 144
gardeners rewarded for growing exotic crops, 46
gastronomic culture, 10, 234
    cosmopolitan nature of, 103
    of middle-class, 74
    political economy of, 235–237
gastronomic pleasure, notion of, 24, 146–147, 187
genteel taste, 17
ghee (clarified butter), 158–159, 161–163

ghoti (residents of western parts of Bengal), 192, 223
Gilpin, John, 101–102
glocalisation, 231
goalas, 162–163
    unsanitary habits of, 165
goddess Durga festival, 91
Go-jeeban, 185–186
Golap Keno Kalo (Why is the rose black), 77
'Golden Age' of Bengal, 116, 148
Goody, Jack, 122–123
Go-Rakshini Sabha, 186
gosht, 182
Goswami, Srishchandra, 88
Grant, Colesworthy, 44
Greenough, Paul, 48, 51
guava jelly, 146–147
Guha, Haladhar, 54
Gupta, Swarupa, 149–150, 192–193
gustatory pleasure, 19

Habershams, Robert, 36
Habib, Irfan, 54–55
Hadis (traditions of Prophet Muhammad), 183
Hajar Jinish, 75
halal, 183
Haldar, Gopal, 78–81
Haldar, Rangin, 79
Hall, Catherine, 139
Hancock, Mary Elizabeth, 144–145
Hardgrove, Anne, 158–159
haute cuisine, development of, 84, 122–123, 132, 232
haute cuisine, French, 2, 9, 22
Hayden, Dolores, 130
healthy body, perception of
    Hindu, 176
    Muslim, 176
Hemantabala Debi, 90–91
hierarchical cosmopolitanism of middle-class taste, 6, 12–20, 232
hierarchy in taste, 232
higher education in English language, 4

hilsa, 79
Hindu-Aryan identity, 116
Hindu identity, construction of, 116
Hindu middle-class Bengali body, 19
home-cooked
 Bengali cuisine, 229
 food/meal, 103–104
home science, 145
Hooghly jelar itihas o bangasamaj (Sudhir Kumar Mitra), 193
Horticultural Gardens, 47
Horti-Floricultural exhibition (1859), 47
Hossain, Rokeya Sakhawat, 113
housewives, 140. *see also* working class women
 ideal housewife, concept of, 140–141
Howrah Municipality, 161
Humanist cuisine, Italy, 12
Hume, Alan Octavian, 44
Hunter, W.W., 30, 121
husked rice, 30–32
Hussain, Mir Mosharraf, 184–185
hybrid cuisine, 13, 62, 231–232
hybridity of food, 66, 72, 74, 232
hybrid recipe, 62
hygienic trainings, 110

Icmic cooker, 115
iftar, 182
Inden, Ronald, 51
Indian Cookery Book, The, 101, 103
Indian diet
 Bengali, 150
 features of, 150
 Punjabi, 150
Indian Industrial and Agricultural Exhibition, 24
Indian National Congress, 44, 144, 177, 182
Indian Tea Association, The, 60
indigenous food, 72
indigenous taste, symbol of, 151
industrial capitalism, 139
industrial working class, 109

Islamic identity, construction of, 184
Italian cuisines, 65

Jaffrey, Madhur, 66
Jain, Kajri, 6
jalchal, 125
Jalkhabar (Kiranlekha Ray), 68
janak-bhu (fatherland), 206
Janeja, Manpreet, 234
Japanese millet, 55
Jashohar-Khulnar itihas (Satish Chandra Mitra), 193
jogare, 125
Jones, William, 74
Joshi, Sanjay, 5
Jugantar, 86
jute, 28–29, 50, 198, 236

kafer (infidel), 185
Kalikamangal, 199
Kashmiri lentils, 68
Kathasahitya, 86
Khadya, 115
khansamas, 133, 156–157
Khan, Tamizuddin, 182
Khatun, Nurunnechha, 179
Khatun, Sayeeda Hafeza, 180, 221
Khidmatgar, 101
King, G., 43
Kitchen, 10
kitchen
 aestheticisation of women labour in, 136–137
 Bengali, 160
 importance of clean, 113–114
kitchen garden, 143
korma (meat dish made with yogurt), 112, 120

labour, as household work, 141
Lakshmi, 51
lakshmichhara, 188
land-based rural life, 194
Latin America tropical climate, 47

Leong-Salobir, Cecilia, 125
luchi (fried flour bread), 79, 93–94, 96–97, 127, 170, 224
luxury, definition of, 17

McCurrison, Col., 150–151
McDonaldisation, 231
Madhya Bangla Sammilani, 110
madrasa (Islamic educational institution), 53
Mahakali Pathshala, 110
Mahila, 145, 156–157, 157
mairas, 164
Majumdar, Jaminiranjan, 55
Majumdar, Rochona, 93
Majumdar, Subodhkinkar Nanda, 55
Malay consumer, 6
male cooks
    culinary profession, 132
    versus female cooks, 109, 118, 121–130, 166–167
    public cooking, 133
mali (gardner), 45
Mangalkabyas, 194
mangalkavyas, 155
mangsho, 182
market economy, 188
Marwaris, 159–160
masalchis (assistant cooks), 121
Mashik Basumati, 52
mass cooking, 107
mass eating, 107
meat dishes, in Muslim cuisine, 181
meat-eating practices, 153–156, 180. *see also* beef-eaters
    by Hindu middle-class, 181
Mennell, Stephen, 122–123
Mexican food, 13
middle class, Indian, 2, 21
    colonial, 5
    in colonial Bengal, 9, 20
    consumption of, 7
    culture of drinking coffee, 18
    definition of, 4

    discourse of taste, 52, 232
    material practices of, 16
    politics, 4, 11
    self-fashioning of (*see* self-fashioning of middle class)
    as a status group, 5
    taste and consumption role in, 17
    women delight in purchasing new dress fabrics, 23
middle-class romanticisation of rice, 52
Mies, Maria, 138
migratory labour, 11
milk
    adulteration of, 163
    cooperative supply, 163
    quality of, 162
Mintz, Sidney W., 27, 230
mlechcha (foreign and impure), 117
modern agriculture, 34, 37–38, 44
Modern Review, 86
modesty in food preferences, 15
Moslem Pak-Pranali (Muslim cooking), 180
Mudir dokan, 73
Mughal Empire, 151
Mughal-inspired dishes, 14
Mughlai cuisine, 63–64, 105
Mughlai recipes, 68
Mukherjee, Mukul, 142
Mukherjee, Saugata, 29
Mukhopadhyay, Bhaskar, 233
Mukhopadhyay, Bholanath, 58, 168
Mukhopadhyay, Bhudeb, 119, 155–156, 233
Mukhopadhyay, Bipradas, 63–68, 112, 115–116, 129, 132, 210
Mukhopadhyay, Jadunath, 111
Mukhopadhyay, Jogeshchandra, 160
Mukhopadhyay, Kularanjan, 162
Mukhopadhyay, Radhakamal, 50
Mukhopadhyay, Satishchandra, 86
Munke Raghu, 86
Murgir French malpoa (a confection similar to pancake), 1–2
Muslim cuisine, meat dishes in, 181

Muslim 'other,' 175–179
Muslim wedding feasts, 181

Narayan, Uma, 65–66
Narir kartabya (Duty of Women), 134
Natai Mangalchandi, 135
Navanna (rice harvest), 83–84
new Bengali restaurants, 229
new cuisine, 63–74
new eating places, 56–611
new food consumption, 56–61
new food crops introduction by colonial state, 26–27, 38–48, 231
N.G. Chatterjee Pikeparrah Nursery, 53
Nicholas, Ralph, 51
Nilgiri Hills, 42
Nimantran (Invitation), 134
non-vegetarian food/recipes, 63, 76, 93, 95–96
nourishment, 51
nutrition, science of, 149, 162

Oriya cooks, 126
   abomination for, 129

Padmapuran (Narayan Deb), 202–203
paka-dekha (fixing the match), 95
Pakprabandha, 63–64
Pak pranali, 63–66, 115
Pak-Pranali Siksha, 117
Pakrajeswar, 63–64
Pakshalar panchali, 129
Pakwan-ki-kitab: Memsahib's Guide to Cookery in India (John Gilpin), 98
Pal, Bipin, 58–59, 92, 219
Pal, Bipinchandra, 169, 172, 175–176
Pallibaichitra (Wonders of a village), 82
Pallichitra (Images of a village), 82
Pandit, Sharatchandra, 108
Parashuram, 'Ratarati' (1929–1930), 1–2
Paricharika, 21, 72, 145
Patibrata Dharma (A Treatise on Female Chastity), 144
patol (striped gourds), 94

philanthropic interests, 38
Philip, Kavita, 42
pice hotel, 56
pishtak, 14
planting, 40–41
pleasure of eating, notion of, 107
Prabasi, 86, 95
Pradhan, Pabitra Mohan, 126
Prajnasundari Devi, 64–65, 67–69, 73–74
Prasad, Srirupa, 151
print capitalism, publication of cookbooks, 143, 148
printmedia, 12
productive labour, 139
public cooking, profession of, 124, 133
public eateries, 169
'public'/'private,' notion of, 124
pulao (fancy rice dish), 102, 112
   recipes for, 180–181
Punjabi diet, features of, 151
Punya, 21, 145–148
pure food discourse, 19

Rabibaroari, 224
Rahman, Lutfur, 133
Ramanir Kartabbya (Women's Responsibilities), 112
Ramzan, 182
Randhansanket (Binapani Mitra), 69
Randhan-siksha (Learning to Cook), 120
rational agriculture, 21, 37
rationalisation, 26
Raybidyanidi, Jogeshchandra, 191
Ray, Dinendrakumar, 82
Ray, Hemendra Kumar, 105
Ray, Kalidas, 171
Ray, Kiranlekha, 68, 72
Ray, Niharranjan, 193–194
Ray, Prafulla Chandra, 159–160, 163, 166
Ray, Pranab, 210
Ray, Rajat Kanta, 3–4, 109
Ray, Ramesh Chandra, 165
Ray, Saratchandra, 68
Ray, Shashisekhar, 177

Index

recipes, comparison between Indian Englishwoman and Prajnasundari Devi, 70–72
refined Bengali cuisine, 20
refined taste, 17
regional consciousness, 193
regional cosmopolitanism, 19, 21, 81–91, 98–105. *See also* cosmopolitanism
regional memories, 193
regional nationalism, 8
religious conversion, 154
religious identity, 178
Report of the Bengal Paddy & Rice Enquiry Committee (1940), 29–30
Report of the Municipal Administration of Calcutta, The, 163
restaurants, inspection of, 161
Reyaz-al-din-Mashadi, 184, 186–187
rice
    Californian (*see* Californian rice)
    commercialization, 28–29, 52
    cooly, 168
    decline as a subsistence food crop, 50
    -eating Bengalis, 40, 52
    machine-husked, 167–168
    pudding, manufacture of, 165
    'rice eating' Bengalis, 152
    rice harvest, ritual of, 153
    significance of, 151–152, 170
    staple of Bengalie diet, 48
    table rice, 168
romanticisation of rural life, 82
Royal Botanical Garden, 42
Roy, Parama, 66

Saha, Gyanendranath, 152
Sahitya, 95
Sambad Prabhakar, 220
Sankranti, 83, 85
Sanskrit literature, 74
Sanyal, Hirankumar, 79, 81
Sarkar, Sumit, 7, 136–137
Sarkar, Tanika, 123–124, 144
Sastri, Shibnath, 173
Schrotthy, Eugene, 37

seduction of biscuits, 56–611
self-fashioning of middle class, 3–8, 10, 12, 14–17, 232
self-sustaining village community, myth of, 188–191
self-sustaining village life, notion of, 82
Sen, Dinesh Chandra, 114, 129
Sen, Indubhushan, 153
Sen, Keshab Chandra, 133
Sen, Nabindchandra, 78
Sen, Samita, 140
Sen, Umesh Chandra, 53
Seth, Santoshnath, 167
shaker ghonto, 1
Shanibarer Chithi, 86
shukto (a light broth of vegetables), 75, 120
singara, 94
Singha, Baneswar, 52, 54, 178
Singh, Damayanti Basu, 76
Sinha, Mrinalini, 118
Smarta, 145
social honor, 92
soojee, Indian, 15
sora bandha (carrying home left-over food), 96–97
Soukhin khadya-pak, 63–64
Sparkman, James R., 36
spontaneous materialism, 16
Stalkkart, J., 43
standard of living, 189
Statistical Account of Bengal, A, 121
subregional consciousness of colonial middle-class, 192, 194
subregional histories, 205–214
subregional other, 214–225
subsistence agriculture, 48, 50–51, 55, 86
subsistence economy, 42
    glorification of, 188
Susrutasamhita, 154
Swasthya, 153
sweetmeatmakers, 161, 163, 167

table rice, 168
Tagore, Abanindranath, 74
Tagore, Dwijendranath, 104

Tagore, Rabindranath, 104, 134
Tagore, Rwitendranath, 73–74
Tariqa-i-Muhammadiya, 182
taste, 15, 17, 78, 233
    colonial middle-class perception of, 157
    colonisation of, 151
    indigenous, 151
    middle-class discourse of, 108
    'other' tastes, 159–168
    pure and impure, issues of, 161
    refined (*see* refined taste)
Tattvabodhini, 95
tea, 18
Telegraph, 229
Terrio, Susan, 138
Tetka, 48–50
traditional food, 88–89

ulama, 183
unhusked rice, 30–32
upper-middle-class Bengalis, 96
urban professional Bengalis, 4
Uttarrarh, 192
Utterparah Hitakari Sabha, 110

Vaishnavism, advent of, 155
Varendra Brahmins, 126
Varendra-randhan (Kiranlekha Ray), 205
Vedic *pup*, 73
vegetarianism in colonial Bengal, 153–154, 156, 162, 186
Victoria College, 111
Victorian England
    bourgeois ideology of, 140
    role of women in, 139
village festivals, 135

Vivekananda, 88, 94
vratas, 135

Walsh, Judith, 117
Western food and modernisation, 14
westernisation in food buying, 94
Western middle-class, 6
    idealized modernity of, 16
Western modern/modernity, 6, 18
wheat
    diet based on, 153
    significance of, 153
women in Victorian England, role of, 139
women cooking, 106
    aestheticisation of, 108, 114
        labour in the kitchen, 136
        politics of, 130–143
    and culinary education for women, 114, 120
    discourse on, 123
    domestic culinary skills, 132
    economic aspects of, 143
    for love to the family, 133
    versus male servant's cooking, 166–167
    non-recognition in private sphere, 130
    for profit, 136
women labour
    effects of capitalist economy on, 142
    impact of modernisation on, 142
Worcester sauce, 119
working class women, 141

yagna, 119
yellow lentils, 68

zamindars (landlords), 28, 181